Electronic Commerce

Electronic Commerce

A Simplified Approach

Munesh Chandra Trivedi

JAICO PUBLISHING HOUSE
Ahmedabad Bangalore Bhopal Chennai
Delhi Hyderabad Kolkata Lucknow Mumbai

Published by Jaico Publishing House
A-2 Jash Chambers, 7-A Sir Phirozshah Mehta Road
Fort, Mumbai - 400 001
jaicopub@jaicobooks.com
www.jaicobooks.com

ELECTRONIC COMMERCE
ISBN 978-81-8495-117-2

First Jaico Impression: 2010
Second Jaico Impression: 2011

Printed by
Pashupati Printers (P) Ltd., Delhi-95

Dedicated to
my parents
and loving daughter
Soumya

Preface

Electronic commerce is a subject that is an integral component of the ubiquitous soft computing paradigm. An in depth understanding and appreciation of the field requires some background knowledge of accounting, e-learning and computer programming, which is a difficult task. This book aims to give a balanced approach to these areas. Electronic commerce attempts to provide methods to handle these complexities and enable us to produce reliable real time systems with maximum productivity.

This book is for students who have not had any previous training in electronic commerce, and is suitable for a one-semester course. It covers the syllabi of all Indian universities. It will also be useful for a project based introductory course in electronic commerce in which both the students and the instructor can follow the chapters in the order given, in the lectures as well as in the project.

Acknowledgements

During various stages in the writing of this book, a number of people have given invaluable comments on the manuscript. In this regard, we owe a debt of gratitude to Prof B.S. Garg Chancellor J.R.N. Rajasthan Vidyapeeth University, Udaipur and Prof Lokesh Bhatt Vice-Chancellor J.R.N. Rajasthan Vidhyapeeth University, Udaipur.

We are also grateful to Dr. R.K. Bharadwaj, Director I.M.S. Ghaziabad, Dr. Ashok Patel Director M.C.A. Programme North Gujrat University Patan, Dr. Sanjay Sah Director M.C.A. Programme Kadi M.C.A. College, Kadi, Dr. Neeraj Bharadwaj Director M.C.A. Programme M.D.S University Ajmer,Saurabh Choudhary and Sachin Malhotra I.M.S. Ghaziabad, for his encouragement at the very outset of this project. Excellent support in writing this book was received from Dr. S.S. Sarangedevot, Director (Computer Science & IT) J.R.N. Rajasthan Vidhyapeeth University, Udaipur.

Contents

8. ELECTRONIC PAYMENT SYSTEMS 199-224

9. ELECTRONIC DATA INTERCHANGE 225-244

10. E-BUSINESS 245-272

CHAPTER 1

Introduction

Electronic commerce (e-commerce) is a modern business methodology that addresses the needs of organizations, merchants and consumers in cutting costs while improving the quality of goods and services and increasing the speed of service delivery.

The term is also applied to the use of a computer network to search and retrieve information to support human and corporate decision-making. E-commerce is today associated with the buying and selling of information, products and services via computer networks today and in the future this will extend to carrying out transactions via any one of the myriad of networks that make up the information superhighway (I-way).

The effects of e-commerce are already appearing in all areas of business, from customer service to new product design. It facilitates new types of information based business processes for reaching out to and interacting with customers, such as on line advertising and marketing, on line ordering and on line customer services, to name a few. Finally, e-commerce enables the customer to access information on new types of information based products, such as interactive games, electronic books, on demand, which can be very profitable for content providers and useful for consumers. Clearly a key element of e-commerce is information processing.

The information processing activity is usually in the form of business transactions for which several broad categories are observed:

i) Transactions between a company and the consumer over public networks for the purpose of home shopping or home banking using encryption for security and electronic cash, credit or debit tokens for payment.

ii) Transactions with a trading pattern using EDI (Electronic Data Interchange).

iii) Transactions for information gathering such as a market search using bar code scanners, information processing for managerial decision making or organizational problem solving and information manipulation for operations and supply chain management.

iv) Transactions for distribution of information to prospective customers, including interactive advertising sales & marketing.

1.1 ELECTRONIC COMMERCE - TECHNOLOGY AND PROSPECTS

Commerce (the trading of goods) has been a major impetus for human survival since the beginning of recorded history and even prior to it. The mass adoption of the Internet has created a paradigm shift in the way businesses are conducted today. The past decade has seen the emergence of a new kind of commerce, namely e-commerce, i.e., the buying and selling of goods over the Internet. Traditional physical trading of goods and currency is becoming increasingly unpopular and more businesses are jumping on the e-commerce bandwagon. Today, the line between e-commerce and traditional commerce is becoming more blurred as more businesses start and continue to integrate the Internet and e-commerce technologies into their business processes.

1.2 DEFINITION OF E-COMMERCE

E-commerce can be defined as a modern business methodology that addresses the needs of organizations, merchants and consumers in cutting costs while improving the quality of goods and services and increasing the speed of service delivery, by using the Internet. It differs from traditional e-commerce in that it enables the trading of goods, money and information electronically via computers. Business is carried out electronically and there is no need for physical currency or goods to conduct business.

1.3 EVOLUTION OF E-COMMERCE

The evolution of e-commerce can be attributed to a combination of regulatory reform and technological innovation. Though the Internet (which played an important role in evolution) appeared in the late 1960s, e-commerce as it functions today took off with the arrival of the World Wide Web and browsers in the early 1990s. The liberalization of the telecommunications sector and innovations such as optic fibres, DSL (Digital Subscriber Line) etc. (which has helped to expand the volume and capacity of communications) have helped in the process of rapid growth. As a result the barriers to entering and engaging in e-commerce have fallen rapidly. A brief timeline of evolution is as follows:

- 1969 Internet/Arpanet
- 1989 WWW HTML invented at CERN (Conseil Europeen pour la Recherche Nucleaire) – European Organisation for Nuclear Research

- 1991 NSF (National Science Foundation) lifts restrictions on commercial use of the Internet
- 1993 Mosaic browser invented at the University of Illinois, Urbana Champagne, is released to public
- 1994 Netscape releases Navigator browser
- 1995 Dell, Cisco, Amazon etc. began aggressively to use the Internet for commercial transactions

The growth of the Internet has a special significance in the growth of e-commerce. It has the potential to involve lay persons into the process thereby increasing its reach far beyond large companies.

1.4 CONDUCTING BUSINESS ONLINE (E-COMMERCE)

Electronic commerce is carrying out business online. The four main areas in which companies conduct business online today are:

1. Direct marketing, selling and services.
2. Online banking and billing.
3. Secure distribution of information.
4. Value-chain trading and corporate purchasing.

1.4.1 Direct Marketing, Selling and Services

Today, more websites focus on direct marketing, selling and services than on any other type of electronic commerce. Direct selling was the earliest type of electronic commerce, and has proven to be a stepping-stone to more complex commerce operations for many companies. Successes such as *Amazon.com*, *Barnes and Noble*, *Dell Computer* and the introduction of e-tickets by major airlines, have catalyzed the growth of this segment, proving the reach and customer acceptance of the Internet.

1.4.2 Financial and Information Services

A broad range of financial and information services are performed over the Internet today and sites that offer them are enjoying rapid growth. These sites are popular because they help consumers, businesses of all sizes and financial institutions to distribute some of their most important information over the Internet much more conveniently than through other channels. For example:

- Online banking
- Online billing
- Secure information distribution

1.4.2.1 Online Banking

Consumers and small businesses can save time and money by banking over the Internet.

Paying bills, making transfers between accounts, and trading stocks, bonds and mutual funds can all be performed electronically over the Internet, which connects consumers and small businesses with their financial institutions.

1.4.2.2 Online billing

Companies, which need to send bills, can achieve significant cost savings and marketing benefits through the use of Internet-based bill-delivery and receiving systems. Today, consumers receive an average of 23 bills per month by mail from retailers, credit card companies and utilities.

1.4.2.3 Secure distribution of information

To many businesses, information is their most valuable asset. Although the Internet can enable businesses to reach huge new markets regarding their information, businesses must also safeguard that information to protect their assets. Digital rights management provides protection for intellectual and information property rights, and is a key technology to secure information distribution.

1.4.3 Maintenance, Repair and Operations (MRO)

The Internet also offers enormous time and cost savings for corporate purchasing of low-cost, high-volume goods for maintenance, repair and operations (MRO) activities. Typical MRO goods include office supplies (such as pens and paper), office equipment and furniture, computers and replacement parts. The Internet can transform corporate purchasing from a labour and paperwork-intensive process into a self-service application. Company employees can order equipment on websites, company officials can automatically enforce purchase approval and policies through automated business rules, and suppliers can keep their catalogue information centralized and up-to-date. Purchase order applications can then use the Internet to transfer the order to suppliers.

In response, suppliers can ship the requested goods and invoice the company over the Internet. In addition to reduced administrative costs, Internet-based corporate purchasing can improve the accuracy of order-tracking, better enforce purchasing policies, provide better customer and supplier service, reduce inventories, and give companies more power in negotiating exclusive or volume discount contracts. In other words, the Internet and e-business have changed the way enterprises serve customers and compete with each other, and have heightened the awareness for competing supply chains.

1.4.4 Value-Chain Integration

No other business model highlights the need for strict integration across suppliers, manufacturers, and distributors quite like the value chain. Delays in inventory tracking and management can cause ripples from the cash register all the way back to production of raw material, creating inventory shortages at any stage of the value chain. The resulting out-of-stock events can mean lost business. The Internet promises to increase business efficiency by reducing reporting delays and increasing reporting accuracy. Speed is clearly the business imperative for the value chain.

1.5 IMPACT OF E-COMMERCE ON BUSINESS

E-commerce will change the way the businesses are being conducted. It will lead to the emergence of new businesses as well as new business practices and also create a new role for intermediaries. Indeed, all the functional areas of business will undergo change as follows:

- The new technology will transform business processes, the way products and services are created and marketed, dynamics of competitions, the organization structure of the enterprise and the nature of the enterprise itself. This will include marketing, supply management, customer and sales management, product development, etc.
- Local proximity may no longer be a significant factor in retaining customers. Local markets will be replaced by global markets. Indeed it may realize the goal of making the whole world a global family.
- Transparency and openness continue, and will continue, to be effective business strategy. Already many businesses have started recognizing key customers, employees and suppliers as partners in the business. E-commerce will lead to better customer service, more personalized products, reduced costs, supply chain efficiency and faster time to market. The most significant aspect of e-commerce is new market development. Once the e-commerce links and infrastructure are initially set up, they can be successfully used in other sectors.
- The change in business functions will lead to new business models and create new sets of facts and circumstances that can materially change the incidence of taxation.
- The Internet will emerge as a new platform for marketing of products and services that will displace and rebuild the existing economy. It will affect the organizational structure; and requires different skills for negotiation, a new regulatory and legal framework, electronic money, taxation amongst other things. The evolution of e-commerce will have a profound impact on competition, mobility of enterprises, effect on consumer behaviour and the way the work is defined and managed. The net will enable businesses to save time on product design, as they can be designed according to individual customer specifications, order and delivery of components, tracking sales and getting feedback from customers.

The businesses can have a virtual project team and virtual learning space so that employees who are dispersed over various countries can work together as if they are present physically in one room. Business can be connected to the retail points in order to ascertain market trends and product demand, with the suppliers upstream to order the desired requirements. Better demand forecasting and stock replenishment can lead to significant reduction in costs.

Selling through websites is the fastest growing method of trading worldwide. There are two main forms of e-commerce:

- Business to business (B2B) trading where companies trade and exchange information using the World Wide Web.

- Business to consumer (B2C) trading where companies deal directly with customers through web pages, and ordering is carried out online.

There are many different types of products and services that are traded online including books, CDs, cars, holidays and insurance. In response to e-tailing and e-trading, most businesses have now set up their own websites. Trading online enables businesses to reach much wider audiences while cutting the costs of traditional retailing methods. For example, an e-tailer does not have to spend so much on an expensive high street presence. Until recently *The Times 100* was a paper-based resource that was used by every school in the United Kingdom. Now the resource appears in two formats - in a photocopiable folder of material, and online. The online presence has opened up viewing of *The Times 100* to a global market and a large number of hits are recorded from students in almost every country in the world. Existing users are able to benefit from the convenience of quickly accessing case studies online and a range of additional online features have been added such as a theory section, and a range of tests and questions for students.

Although the outlay on developing a good website is substantial, the potential benefits are enormous in providing most types of businesses with a competitive advantage. One group of businesses that have been particularly successful as a result of the development of the web are specialist suppliers of items such as paintings, photographs, confectionery and other items. Individuals working from home can now advertise and sell their produce worldwide. A web page is a single document. A website is a collection of related documents. The World Wide Web consists of graphic and text documents that can be connected together through clickable 'hypertext' links.

1.6 ISSUES IN IMPLEMENTING ELECTRONIC COMMERCE

Although it is simple to describe their benefits, it is not nearly as easy to develop and deploy commerce systems. Companies can face significant implementation issues such as:

- Cost
- Value
- Security
- Leveraging existing systems
- Interoperability

1.6.1 Cost

Electronic commerce requires significant investment in new technologies that can touch many of a companys core business processes. As with all major business systems, electronic commerce systems require significant investments in hardware, software, staffing and training. Businesses need comprehensive solutions with greater ease-of-use to help foster cost-effective deployment.

1.6.2 Value

Businesses want to know that their investments in electronic commerce systems will produce a return. Business objectives such as lead generation, business-process automation, and cost reduction must be met. Systems used to reach these goals need to be flexible enough to change when the business changes.

1.6.3 Security

The Internet provides universal access, but companies must protect their assets against accidental or malicious misuse. System security, however, must not create prohibitive complexity or reduce flexibility. Customer information also needs to be protected from internal and external misuse. Privacy systems should safeguard personal information critical to building sites that satisfy customer and business needs.

1.6.4 Leveraging Existing Systems

Most companies already use information technology (IT) to conduct business in non-Internet environments, such as marketing, order management, billing, inventory, distribution and customer service. The Internet represents an alternative and complementary way to do business, but it is imperative that electronic commerce systems integrate existing systems in a manner that avoids duplicating functionality and maintains usability, performance, and reliability.

1.6.5 Interoperability

When systems from two or more businesses are able to exchange documents without manual intervention, businesses achieve cost reduction, improved performance and more dynamic value chains. Failing to address any of these issues can spell failure for a system s implementation effort. Therefore, a companys commerce strategy should be designed to address all these issues to help customers achieve the benefits of electronic commerce. The companys vision for electronic commerce should also be to help businesses establish stronger relationships with customers and industry partners. For example, a successful strategy for delivering this vision is described by three work-flow elements (platform, portal and industry partners), each backed by comprehensive technology, product, and service offerings. From self-service portals to transaction processing, a successful work-flow strategy could be the underlying engine delivering state-based, processed-focused control services for e-business applications. Human labour is expensive, and work-flow technology allows e-businesses to supplement, and in some cases eliminate, reliance on human supervision and intervention.

1.7 HOW TO WORK WITH E-COMMERCE

E-commerce is about setting a business on the Internet, allowing visitors to access the website, and go through a virtual catalogue of the companys products/services online. When a visitor wants to buy something he/she likes, they merely "add" it to their virtual shopping basket. Items in the virtual shopping basket can be added or deleted, and when they are set to checkout, they go to the virtual checkout counter, which has the total amount payable. It asks for the name, address etc., of the buyer and method of payment (usually via credit card). Once this information is entered (which is transmitted securely) the buyer can just wait for delivery.

1.8 COMPARISON BETWEEN TRADITIONAL COMMERCE AND E-COMMERCE

In many cases business processes use traditional commerce activities very effectively, and these processes cannot be improved upon through technology. Products that buyers prefer to touch, smell or examine closely are difficult to sell using electronic commerce. For example, customers might be reluctant to buy high-fashion clothing and perishable food products, such as meat or produce, if they cannot examine the products closely before agreeing to purchase them. In the case of traditional commerce, retail merchants have years of experience in creating store environments that help to convince a customer to buy. This combination of store design, layout and product display knowledge is called merchandising. Sales people in course of time develop skills that allow them to identify customer needs and find products and services that meet those needs. The arts of merchandising and personal selling can be difficult to practice over an electronic link. However, branded products such as books or CDs can be easily sold through e-commerce. As one copy of a new book is identical to another and because a customer would not be concerned about freshness he would willingly order a title without examining the specific copy he would receive. The advantage of electronic commerce, namely the ability of one site to offer a wider selection of titles than even the largest physical bookstore, can outweigh the advantage of a traditional bookstore, namely the facility to browse. Some examples of business processes that suit either e-commerce or traditional commerce are listed in Table 1.1.

Table 1.1: ***Business processes suited to e-commerce or traditional commerce***

Electronic Commerce	Traditional Commerce
• Sale/purchase of books and CDs • Online delivery of software • Advertising and promotion of travel service • Online tracking of shipments	• Sale/purchase of high-fashion clothing • Sale/purchase of perishable food products • Small denomination transactions • Sale of expensive jewelry and antiques

1.9 E-COMMERCE TECHNOLOGIES

Most of the information technologies and Internet technologies that are discussed throughout the book are involved in e-commerce systems, viz:

- The Internet, intranets and extranets are the network infrastructure or foundation of e-commerce.

- Customers must be provided with a range of secure information, marketing, transactions and processing and payment services.
- Trading and business partners rely on the Internet and extranets to exchange information and accomplish secure transactions; including electronic data interchange (EDI) and other supply chain and financial systems and databases.
- Company employees depend on a variety of Internet and intranet resources to communicate and collaborate in support of their EC work activities.
- Information system professionals and end users can use a variety of software tools to develop and manage the content and operations of the websites and other EC resources of a company.

1.10 ECONOMIC POTENTIAL OF E-COMMERCE

Consumers are pushing retailers to the wall, demanding lower prices, better quality and a large selection of in-season goods. Retailers are scrambling to fill orders. They are slashing back-office costs, reducing profit margins, reducing cycle times, buying more wisely, and making huge investments in technology. They are revamping distribution channels to make sure that warehouse costs are decreased, by reducing their average inventory levels and coordinating the consumer demand and supply patterns. In the drive to reduce prices, more and more retailers are turning to overseas suppliers, partly because of cheaper labour costs. The effect of e-commerce can also be seen in the retail industry and marketing.

1.10.1 E-commerce and the Retail Industry

Retailers are the first to bear the brunt of cost cutting, and they in turn put pressure on the manufacturers and suppliers. At the same time, the quest for efficiency has led to both turmoil and consolidation within the retail industry. The pressure experienced by retailers and suppliers can be seen in the disappearance of jobs, in mergers, and in the increase in the number of business failures in the manufacturing sector. The problems are indeed serious. Electronic markets could provide a partial solution by promising customers more convenience, and merchants greater efficiency and interactivity with suppliers to revitalize the troubled retailing sector.

1.10.2 E-commerce and Marketing

Electronic commerce is forcing companies to rethink the existing ways of target marketing (isolating and focusing on a segment of the population), relationship marketing (building and sustaining a long-term relationship with existing and potential customers), and even event marketing (setting up a virtual booth where interested people can come and visit). Consider the case of conventional direct marketers, who devote some 25 percent of their revenues to such costs as printing and postage for catalogues. Interactive marketing could help cut such expenses and may even deliver better results. Interactive marketing is accomplished in electronic markets via interactive multimedia catalogues that give the same look and feel as a shopping channel. Users find moving images more appealing than still images and listening more appealing than reading text on screen. These are two powerful reasons why every text-based and still-picture-based interactive experimental-based service has never generated anywhere near the volume of retail merchandise orders that televised shopping channels have achieved. Maximum public acceptance will require that interactive catalogue services have a more entertaining visual appearance than traditional text-intensive catalogues have had. Ideally, an interactive shopping program should produce full-motion demonstrations of selected products, but such a practical and economical technology has yet to be developed.

1.11 INCENTIVES FOR ENGAGING IN E-COMMERCE

A basic fact of Internet retailing is that all retail websites are created equal as far as the "location, location, location" imperative of success in retailing is concerned. No site is any closer to its web customers and competitors offering similar goods and services may be only a mouse click away. This makes it vital that businesses find ways to build customer satisfaction, loyalty and relationships, so customers keep coming back to their web stores. Thus, the key to e-commerce success is to optimize several key factors such as selection and value, performance and service efficiency, the look and feel of the site, advertising and incentives to purchase, personal attention, community relationships, and security and reliability. The incentives for engaging in e-commerce are as follows:

1. **Selection and value:** Attractive product selections, competitive prices, satisfaction guarantees, and customer support after the sale.
2. **Performance and service:** Fast, easy navigation, shopping, and purchasing, and prompt shipping and delivery.
3. **Look and feel:** Attractive web storefront, website shopping areas, multimedia product catalogue pages, and shopping features.
4. **Advertising and incentives:** Targeted web-page advertising and e-mail promotions, discounts and special offers, including advertising at affiliate sites.
5. **Personal attention:** Personal web pages, personalized product recommendations, web advertising, and e-mail notices, and interactive support for all customers.
6. **Community relationships:** Virtual communities of customers, suppliers, company representatives, and others via newsgroups, chat rooms, and links to related sites.
7. **Security and reliability:** Security of customer information and website transactions, trustworthy product information, and reliable order fulfillment.

1.12 DRIVING FORCES BEHIND E-COMMERCE

The various driving forces behind e-commerce can be listed as below:

1. **Global customers:** Global customers are individuals who travel to different places or companies with global operations. Global IT can help provide fast, convenient service.
2. **Global products:** Products are the same throughout the world or are assembled by subsidiaries throughout the world. Global IT can help manage worldwide marketing and quality control.

3. **Global operations:** Parts of a production or assembly process are assigned to subsidiaries based on changing economic or other conditions. Only global IT can support such geographic flexibility.
4. **Global resources:** The use and cost of common equipment, facilities and personnel are shared by subsidiaries of a global company. Global IT can keep track of such shared resources.
5. **Global collaborations:** The knowledge and expertise of colleagues in a global company can be quickly accessed, shared, and organized to support individual or group efforts. Only global IT can support such enterprise collaboration.

1.13 ADVANTAGES OF E-COMMERCE

1.13.1 Primary Benefits of E-Commerce

The tremendous potential of information technology for purposes of communication and information storage and retrieval has impacted the commercial world like nothing before. The quality of communication on the web has progressed in quantum leaps and has more effectively bridged the distance between the markets and customers, as compared to traditional methods of commerce.

Firstly, carrying out business online increases its visibility; a vital effect for any business. Secondly, it opens the customer base, as it is easier to carry out business transactions, and thirdly it slashes costs, enhances productivity and stream lines the entire business process.

Global accessibility and sales reach: An e-business can receive orders from any country in the world. The global reach of local companies that have become e-businesses has posed a major threat to many established firms, thus enhancing competition in the market.

Increased profit: With e-business, companies reach more and diverse customers and gain exposure in new markets not covered by existing physical channels, thus increasing the profits.

Improved customer service and loyalty: e-commerce enables a company to be open for business whenever a customer needs it. Up-to-date information about products can be offered on the web, making it easier and more convenient for customers to serve themselves. Combining the interactive nature of the web with a proper understanding of a customers needs helps a merchant to provide products and services built to order for each customer, and thus to build long term relationships, increase loyalty and sustain a competitive edge.

Shorter time-to-market: e-commerce makes for fast and flexible execution and response to market opportunities. The web enables a company to introduce a new product into the market, get immediate customer reaction to it, and refine and perfect it.

Supply chain integration: e-commerce enables the full integration of the business, making the entire supply chain more efficient from the point of customer contact all the way back through physical distribution, ware housing, manufacturing, resource management and purchasing.

Capturing valuable market information from customers: e-commerce enables a company to obtain potential customers details and buying habits, facilitating an easy marketing strategy and building a direct customer relationship.

Release from working hour restrictions: e-commerce removes the restrictions enforced on the operating hours of a business. An online business provides 24 × 7 access to customers. It permits taking orders and selling goods to customers worldwide, without any barriers on time.

E-commerce—the way to do it: If a company wants to get into electronic commerce, it is vital that prior to entering into any sort of business activity, the company must be traceable relatively easily on the Internet. An appropriate and generic domain name would enable a company to conduct on-line transactions with ease and likewise enable customers and suppliers to trace them quickly.

A part of an e-commerce strategy is characterized by the use of a web server. Setting up independent Web server operations may be costly and time consuming and potential customers may rate it as unreliable due to frequent shut downs. With the types of Internet services and technologies becoming more advanced, e-business has become a major source of trading worldwide. In addition with more and more banks and other financial institutions going online, the prospects of electronic trade or web based trading have increased manifold. From the point of view of the service provider e-businesses can be classified mainly as follows:

- ISP (Internet service provider)
- ASP (Application service provider)
- LSP (Logistics service provider)

Internet service providers provide the services for the Internet and net connectivity at various speeds as per the demands of the user and according to their service providing capability. Application service providers are Internet citizens who develop and support applications on the web and provide all kinds of application development and support as per the clients demand; logistics service providers mainly carry out more of consultancy over the web rather than application development and deployment. ASPs and LSPs cannot exist on their own, i.e., they are interdependent, but more importantly, the services provided by the application and logistics providers are mainly dependent on the type of service provided by the ISPs.

1.13.2 Advantages of E-commerce

With the astonishing growth of the Internet, many companies are finding new and exciting ways to expand their business opportunities. There are very few successful companies that do not use computers in their everyday business activities, which also means that there are few companies that do not use e-commerce. The advantages of the Internet and e-commerce in general are:

1. Speed: The Internet and World Wide Web provide businesses opportunities to exchange messages or complete transactions almost instantaneously. Even with the slowest connections, doing business electronically is much faster than using traditional methods. With increased speeds of communication, the delivery time is expedited, making the whole transaction more efficient from start to finish. Even more significant is the fact that information appearing on the Internet can be changed extremely rapidly. This gives business owners the ability to inform customers of any changes in the services offered and allows the company to update marketing and promotional materials as often and as frequently as they like.

2. Cost savings: By using the Internet the costs of marketing, distribution, personnel, phone, postage and printing, among many others, can be reduced. A business in cyberspace can be started for a few thousand rupees. Most businesses will spend more than this but compared to the cost of opening a physical store, the savings are tremendous. These funds can then be diverted to marketing and advertising the company's products and/or services.

3. No boundaries: Cyberspace has no boundaries, this means that business can be carried out all over the world as easily as in the neighbourhood. Since the Internet connects everyone in cyberspace, information is transmitted at the speed of sound or the speed of light, depending on the connection. Either way, distance becomes meaningless, so that any two places on the globe can be linked. This makes doing business on the Internet attractive to customers in any part of the world.

4. Ease of Networking: One advantage of the Internet is that it allows people to easily connect, gather data/information and stay in touch with others at a very low cost. Now almost everyone can automatically put his/her business to the international market. The web enables firms to build on the assets that they already possess, like brand name recognition, operational infrastructure, information, and customer relationships in order to develop new markets and distribution channels. Connecting with new networks, locally and from other countries, can be done anytime and anywhere now.

1.13.2.1 Advantages to customers

1. **Reduced prices:** Costs of products are reduced since stages along the value chain are decreased. For instance, intermediaries can be eliminated by the company directly selling to the consumer instead of distributing through a retail store.
2. **Global marketplace:** Consumers can shop anywhere in the world. Currently, according to the World Trade Organization (WTO) there are no custom duties on products bought and traded globally, electronically. This also provides a wide selection of products and services to consumers.
3. **24-hour access:** Online businesses never close unlike brick and mortar businesses. E-commerce allows people to carry out business without the barriers of time or distance. One can log on to the Internet at any point of time, be it day or night and purchase or sell anything one desires with a single click of the mouse.
4. **More choices:** It provides consumers with more choices. For example, before making any purchase, a customer can study all the major brands and features of any item. It also provides consumers with less expensive products and services by allowing them to shop in many places and make quick comparisons.
5. **Quicker delivery:** Allows quick delivery of products and services (in some cases) especially with digitized products.

6. Consumers can receive relevant and detailed information in seconds, rather than in days or weeks.
7. Makes it possible to participate in virtual auctions.
8. Allows consumers to interact with other consumers and electronic communities and exchange ideas as well as compare experiences.

1.13.2.2 Advantages to business

1. **Increased potential market share:** The Internet enables businesses to have access to international markets thereby increasing their market share. Companies can also achieve greater economies of scale.
2. **Low-cost advertising:** Advertising on the Internet costs less than advertising in print or on television depending on the intricacies and extent of the advertisement. A company can still spend a lot on advertising on the Internet if the company hires an external party to create their advertisements but advertising on the Internet itself is cheaper since there is less cost associated with it in terms of printing and limited television spots.
3. **Low barriers to entries:** Anyone can start a company on the Internet. Start-up costs are a lot lower for companies since there is less capital is required.
4. **Strategic benefit:** The strategic benefit of making a business 'e-commerce enabled is that it helps reduce the delivery time, labour costs and the costs incurred in the following areas:
   - Preparation of documents
   - Detection and correction of errors
   - Reconciliation
   - Correspondence
   - Telephone calls
   - Data entry
   - Overtime
   - Supervision expenses

1.13.2.3 Advantages to society

1. Enables people in third world countries and rural areas to enjoy products and services which would otherwise not be available to them.
2. Facilitates delivery of public services at a reduced cost, increases effectiveness, and/ or improves quality.
3. Enables more individuals to work at home, and travel less for shopping, resulting in less traffic on the roads, and lower air pollution.
4. Allows some merchandise to be sold at lower prices since the organization may not need physical space and a full inventory.

1.13.2.4 Advantages to women

The general concept is that women, unlike men are reluctant to purchase online. On the contrary, NPD (Narcissistic Personality Disorder) research has shown that women tend to shop online more than men in most product categories. The study asserted that women were more likely to shop for toys, clothing, games and make up online. In short all the major advantages of e-commerce can be summarized as follows:

1. Cost reduction due to competitiveness in the procurement of products. Many suppliers of the product compete for customer patronage in open electronic markets. This competition brings down the product price.
2. Cost reduction due to reduction of paper work. The cost effective electronic documents will be delivered almost instantly and safely. This enables both parties to take quick decisions.
3. Information dissemination at a wider level is possible. Information about the product, cost, size, specifications etc. may be made available to the customer located at widely distant geographical locations.
4. Improved customer relationship may be achieved by rapid dissipation of information to the potential customers.
5. Since all orders and inquiries are processed online, the product is directly supplied to the customer. This eliminates the need for wholesalers and retailers and brings down the product prices.
6. Total reduction of time in the order processing, as e-commerce minimizes the time taken from order to delivery.
7. Provides better, faster and effective linkage with the clients. Since all information has to be processed in the electronic medium, that is online, it is possible to identify the customers requirements that lead to quick product design.
8. Opens new vistas for the organization and generates better business avenues because of easy and cheap reach to the potential customer base.
9. Enhances the organizations product and market analysis as the organization gets faster feedback from the customer. These feedbacks may be processed online.

1.14 DISADVANTAGES OF E-COMMERCE

Although the list of the advantages of e-commerce is long, the e-commerce environment is far from perfect. In fact, some of the problems of e-commerce pose considerable problems to both consumers and businesses. Although cost savings is mentioned as one of the main advantages, there are hidden costs that can quickly turn credit into debit. In addition, the technology is not perfect, for example, the unreliability of the network is a continuing concern. Some other concerns involve security, the loss of privacy, low and remote service levels, and complex legal issues. The disadvantages are discussed in the following sections.

1.14.1 Hidden Costs

Although buying on-line is convenient, the cost of this convenience is not always clear at the front end. For example, on-line purchases are often accompanied by high shipping and re-stocking fees, a lack of warranty coverage, and unacceptable delivery times. Online purchases must be shipped and the shipping charges may be considerable. In fact, too many e-commerce companies have developed a reputation of overcharging for shipping and handling.

1.14.2 Network Unreliability

With a user population of well over 100 million in North America alone, the Internet is a very busy information highway. Although the Internet is designed to overcome failure problems, there have been several well-publicized incidents of network failures during the past few years. An e-commerce website that cannot serve its customers loses sales, credibility, and even customers. In effect, a network failure can be compared to having a location at an exclusive mall that is in middle of nowhere and has no access roads that lead to it. Network reliability problems may be caused by factors such as:

- Equipment failure in the network connection provider or ISP.
- Long response time due to increased network traffic or inadequate bandwidth.
- Accidental problems caused by nature, such as lightning, floods, earthquakes that affect communication lines; or by human error, such as a road construction worker severing a network line by accident.

1.14.3 The Cost of Staying in Business

Operational cost savings and lower barriers of entry feature in the list of e-commerce advantages. That is, getting into business is relatively easier in an e-commerce environment. Unfortunately, the flip side of the coin is that staying in business may be more difficult. Easy access means increased competition, thus causing businesses to operate with very low profit margins. To be profitable, an e-business must maintain high sales volumes, which in turn means developing and maintaining a large and loyal customer base. Attracting customers and making them repeat buyers is the key to profitability. To survive and remain competitive, businesses must invest heavily in often costly technology. The introduction of computer technology in a business not only automates the business process but it also changes the way the company does business internally and externally. Such synergy between technology and business operations makes the company more dependent on technology, making it more vulnerable to the pace and network failures.

1.14.4 Lack of Security

One of the main roadblocks to the wide acceptance of e-commerce by businesses and consumers alike is the perceived lack of adequate security for on-line transactions. For example, consumers are growing increasingly wary about providing credit card information over the Internet. During the past few years, the press has been filled with reports about hackers breaking into e-business websites and stealing credit card information. In many cases, the break-ins went on for several months before either the seller or buyer discovered the problem. Securing on-line transaction data during its generation and then safeguarding it after it has been stored in the database are critical issues to be faced. For example, in June of 2001, a small computer retailer exposed credit card information through its website. The problem, caused by a coding error in a web page, allowed unauthorized access to stored order and credit card information of thousands of customers, dating as far back as one year.

1.14.5 Lack of Privacy

Ensuring the security of data is of paramount importance to customers and to the credibility of the business. Customers also worry about the privacy implications of data gathered by organizations of all types and sizes. The incredible data collection process is a mixed blessing to customers. Even at the simplest data level, sales information is stored in databases connected to web servers, thus exposing the information to cyber criminals. Because data gathering on the web is so easy, databases routinely contain information about the purchasing habits of customers, demographic data, credit information, and so on. In many cases, companies sell customer database information to marketing companies.

In turn, the marketing companies engage in massive e-mail campaigns to attract new customers. It does not take long for a customers e-mail box to be filled with unwanted and unsolicited e-mail (also known as "spam"). The growing sales of personal firewalls and the large number of "hits" on websites that deal with privacy issues are testimony to the fact that customers are becoming increasingly worried about their online privacy, and that they are seeking ways to protect themselves from cyber attackers.

1.14.6 Low Service Levels

Another common complaint about doing business online is the low level of customer service that online companies tend to provide. Although technology has automated business transactions to a large extent, there is a real need for the human touch. Therefore, customer service has become a major differentiating factor. Because the web buying experience is much more impersonal than the traditional one, providing good customer service is critical to the survival of any e-business. Therefore, e-commerce websites must provide:

- A pleasant and problem-free pre-ordering and ordering experience. The website design is an important interface.
- Readily available, easily used feedback options. Major customer complaints include the lack of contact information on websites and the difficulty of contacting a customer service representative.
- Quick and courteous resolution of complaints.
- Timely and low-cost shipping and prompt delivery of merchandise to customers.

1.14.7 Legal Issues

Legal problems encountered in the e-commerce environment include:

- **Software and copyright infringements:** The amount of illegal content flowing freely on the Internet is illustrated by the so-called Napster case. Napster, a popular music website, was sued by the Recording Industry Association because it hosted millions of illegal digital copies of copyrighted songs that were freely downloaded by millions of users worldwide. After court action, Napster was forced to change its business model and to eliminate all illegal material from its website.
- **Credit card fraud and stolen identities:** The lack of security mentioned earlier has put credit card fraud on the proverbial front burner. In addition, lack of security makes it relatively easy to assume another person s identity in order to make fraudulent transactions. Loss of confidence in the security of online transactions is a brake on the e-business train.
- **Business fraud:** Online fraud also takes place in the form of companies that fail to deliver products and/or services to the customers who paid for them.

1.15 REASONS FOR E-COMMERCE NOT BEING VERY SUCCESSFUL

Although vast amounts of money have been invested into making e-commerce work, and although it causes vast amounts of money and large numbers of goods to change hands every day, it has so far failed to deliver the goods for a broad audience. The answer to why e-commerce has not been an overwhelming success for the masses can roughly be answered as follows:

1. Not everybody has access to a computer.
2. Buying goods over the internet is not 'natural':
   - One cannot feel or see the products as in real life
   - The interaction is unnatural, there is no salesperson present.
3. People are concerned that it is unsafe to buy over the internet.

1. Limited access to computers: The computer is essential to access e-commerce sites on the Internet. On a computer screen, people have visual access to a large amount of information, i.e., a large number of goods to choose from. They can browse, select, and get in-depth information and overviews and so on, all at the click of a mouse button. But there are still a large number of people who do not have access to computers and therefore they are not able to take the advantage of the era of e-commerce.

2. Lack of natural quality: There are two issues to be addressed with respect to the lack of natural quality in e-commerce. The first pertains to the fact that people are not able to touch and feel products with their own hands before buying something. Buying something just by looking at its picture is essentially different from buying it in a shop. People probably only tend to buy things over the Internet, with which they are familiar and know what the product looks/feels/sounds like, and which have little between-product variation (examples are books, CDs and videotapes) or products that they can assess from behind their computer (an example is software). This seems to be a problem for e-commerce, which can be labelled as the 'seeing is believing' problem.

The second natural quality problem has to do with natural interaction during a purchase. People are used to talking to a salesperson when they purchase something. Asking questions like: "Is this product really waterproof?" or "Do I get a money back guarantee on this item?" help people in purchasing goods. It guarantees that they get what they want.

3. **Unsafe buying:** The third problem of e-commerce is that of unsafe connections to the vendor. When sending credit card information over the internet, hackers could seize this information and use it for illegal transactions.

1.16 FRAMEWORK OF THE ELECTRONIC COMMERCE INDUSTRY

E-commerce applications will be built on the existing technology infrastructure – a myriad of computers, communication networks and communication software forming the nascent information superhighway.

Any successful e-commerce application will require the I-way infrastructure in the same way that regular commerce needs the interstate highway network to carry goods from point to point. One must travel across this highway, whether they are in an organization purchasing supplies or a consumer ordering a movie on demand.

The I-way will be a mesh of inter-connected data highways of many forms, such as:

- Telephone wires
- Cable TV wires
- Radio based wireless
- Cellular and satellite

1. Common business service infrastructure -> To facilitate the buying and selling process.
   - Security
   - Authentication
   - Electronic payment
   - Directories catalogue
2. Messaging and information distribution infrastructure -> As a means of sending and retrieving information.
3. Multimedia content and network publishing infrastructure -> To create a product and a means to communicate about it.
4. The information superhighway infrastructure consists of

- Telecom
- Cable TV
- Wireless
- Internet

For providing the highway system along which all e-commerce must travel

Applications of electronic commerce:

- Supply chain management
- Video on demand
- Remote banking
- Procurement and purchasing
- On line marketing and advertising
- Home shopping.

The two pillars supporting all e-commerce applications and infrastructure are:

i) **Public policy** – to govern universal access, privacy and information pricing.

ii) **Technical standards** – to dictate the nature of information publishing, user interfaces and transport in the interest of compatibility across the entire network.

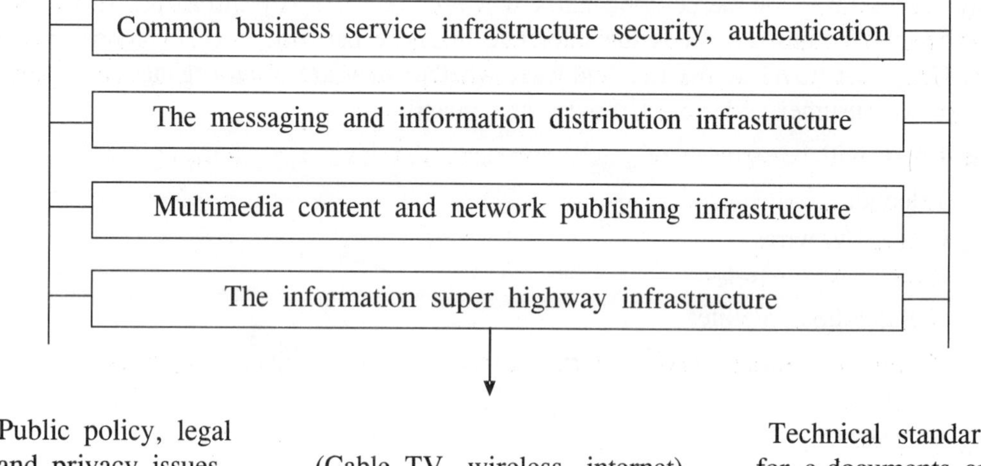

Public policy, legal and privacy issues multimedia

(Cable TV, wireless, internet)

Technical standards for e-documents and network protocols

Fig. 1.1: ***Generic framework for e-commerce***

1.17 ELECTRONIC MARKET

An electronic market is an information system that links together many buyers and sellers, so that they can exchange information on products, services and payments, etc., i.e., a market place that is created by computer and communication technologies linking many buyers and sellers.

E-commerce: Electronic commerce is the process of buying and selling goods and services electronically with computerized business transactions using the internet, networks and other digital technologies. It also encompasses activities supporting those market transactions, such as advertising, marketing, customer support, delivery and payment.

E-business: The term e-business is used to distinguish the use of the Internet and digital technology for the management and coordination of other business processes from electronic commerce.

1.18 TYPES OF E-COMMERCE/E-COMMERCE MARKET MODELS

E-commerce conducted between businesses differs from that carried out between a business and its consumers. There are five generally accepted types of e-commerce:

- Business to Business (B2B)
- Business to Consumer (B2C)
- Consumer to Business (C2B)
- Consumer to Consumer (C2C)
- Business to Government (B2G)

1.18.1 Business to Business (B2B)

Business to Business or B2B refers to e-commerce activities between businesses. An e-commerce company may deal with suppliers or distributors or agents. These transactions are usually carried out through electronic data interchange or EDI. EDI is an automated format of exchanging information between businesses over private networks. This allows more transparency among the businesses involved; therefore a business can run more efficiently, for instance, a supplier can respond faster to diminishing stock of a particular product. EDI comprises standards that enable businesses computers to conduct transactions with each other without human intervention. In general, B2Bs require higher security needs than B2Cs. For example, manufacturers and wholesalers are B2B companies.

With the help of B2B e-commerce, companies are able to improve the efficiency of several common business functions, including supplier management, inventory management and payment management. Using e-commerce enabled business applications, companies are able to better control their supplier costs by reducing purchase order (PO) processing costs and cycle times. This has the added benefit of being able to process more POs at a lesser cost in the same amount of time. E-commerce technology can also serve to shorten the order-ship-bill cycle of inventory management by linking business partners together with the company to provide faster data access. Businesses can improve their inventory auditing capabilities by tracking order shipments electronically, which results in reduced inventory levels and improves upon the ability of the company to provide "just-in-time" service.

This e-commerce technology is also being used to improve the efficiency of managing payments between a business and its partners and distributors. By processing payments electronically, companies are able to lower the number of clerical errors and increase the speed of processing invoices, which results in lowered transaction fees.

1.18.2 Business to Customer (B2C)

Business to customer or B2C refers to e-commerce activities that are focused on consumers rather than on businesses. For instance, a book retailer such as Amazon.com and other companies that follow a merchant model or brokerage business models would be B2C companies. Other examples are purchasing services from an insurance company, conducting online banking and employing travel services.

1.18.3 Customer to Business (C2B)

Customer to business or C2B refers to e-commerce activities, which use reverse pricing models where the customer determines the prices of the product or services. In this case, the focus shifts from selling to buying. There is increased emphasis on customer empowerment. In this type of e-commerce, consumers have a choice of a wide variety of commodities and services, along with the opportunity to specify the range of prices they can afford or are willing to pay for a particular item, service or commodity. As a result, it reduces the bargaining time, increases the flexibility and simplifies procedures at the point of sale for both the merchant and the consumer.

1.18.4 Customer to Customer (C2C)

Customer to customer or C2C refers to e-commerce activities, which use an auction style model. This model consists of a person-to-person transaction that completely excludes businesses from the equation. Customers are also a part of the business and C2C enables customers to directly deal with each other. An example of this is peer auction giant, **Ebay**.

1.18.5 Business to Government (B2G)

This is a new trend in e-commerce. This type of e-commerce is used by government departments to directly reach citizens by setting-up websites. These websites state government policies, rules and regulations related to the respective departments. Any citizen may interact with these websites to know more details. This helps people to know the facts, without physically going to the respective departments. This saves the time of the employees as well as the citizens. The concept of Smart City has been evolved from B2G e-commerce.

1.19 DIFFERENCES BETWEEN B2C AND B2B E-COMMERCE

From all the e-commerce models described above, the two most widely used models are B2C and B2B e-commerce. The major difference between these two models concerns the customer. In the B2B (business to business) model, the customers are other companies while in B2C (business to consumer), the customers are individuals. Overall, B2B transactions are more complex and have higher security needs. Over and above there are two major distinctions:

- **Negotiation:** Selling goods to another business involves bargaining over prices, delivery and product specifications. This is not so with most consumer sales. That makes it easier for retailers to put a catalogue online, and this is why the first B2B applications were for buying finished goods or commodities that are simple to describe and price.
- **Integration:** Retailers do not have to integrate with their customers systems. Companies selling to other businesses, however, need to make sure they can communicate without human intervention.

1.20 ARCHITECTURAL FRAMEWORK FOR E-COMMERCE

Architectural framework of e-commerce means the synthesizing of various existing resources like DBMS (Database Management System), data repository, computer languages, software agent-based transactions, monitors or communication protocols to facilitate the integration of data and software for better applications. The architectural framework for e-commerce consists of six layers of functionality or services as follows:

1. Application services.
2. Brokerage services, data or transaction management.
3. Interface and support layers.
4. Secure messaging, security and electronic document interchange.
5. Middleware and structured document interchange, and
6. Network infrastructure and the basic communication services.

1. Applications: In the application layer services of e-commerce, it is decided what type of e-commerce application will be implemented. There are three types of distinct e-commerce applications i.e., consumer to business application, business-to-business application and intra-organizational application.

2. Information brokerage and management Layer: This layer is rapidly becoming necessary in dealing with the voluminous amounts of information on the networks. This layer works as an intermediary providing service integration between customers and information providers, given some constraints such as low price, fast services or profit maximization for a client. For example, suppose a person wants to travel to the USA from India. The person checks the sites of various airlines for the lowest priced ticket with the best available service. For this he must know the URLs (Universal Resource Locators) of all the sites. Secondly, to search the services and the best prices, he also has to feed in the details of the journey again and again on different sites. If there is a site that can work as an information broker and can arrange the ticket as per the need of the person, it will save a lot of time and effort on the part of the person. This is just one example of how information brokerages can add value. Another aspect of the brokerage function is the support for data management and traditional transaction services. Brokerages may provide tools to accomplish more sophisticated, time-delayed updates or future-compensating transactions.

3. Interface and support services: The third layer of the architectural framework is the interface layer. This layer provides an interface for e-commerce applications. Interactive catalogues and directory support services are examples of this layer. Interactive catalogues are the customized interface to customer applications such as home shopping. Interactive catalogues are very similar to paper-based catalogues. The only difference between an interactive catalogue and a paper-based catalogue is that the former has additional features such as the use of graphics and video to make the advertising more attractive. Directory services have the necessary functions for searching for and accessing information. The directories attempt to organize the enormous amount of information and transactions generated to facilitate e-commerce. The main difference between the interactive catalogues and directory services is that former deal with people while directory support services interact directly with software applications.

4. Secure messaging layer: In any business, electronic messaging is an important issue. The commonly used messaging systems like telephone, fax and courier services have certain problems, e.g., the telephone line is dead, one is not able to deliver the urgent messages. In the case of courier services, a message cannot be delivered instantly, it will take some time depending on the distance between the source and destination. The solution for such type of problems is electronic messaging services like e-mail, enhanced fax and EDI.

Electronic messaging has changed the way the businesses operate. The major advantage of electronic messaging is the ability to access the right information at the right time across diverse work groups. The main constraints of electronic messaging are security, privacy and confidentiality through data encryption and authentication techniques.

5. Middleware services: The enormous growth of networks, client server technology and all other forms of communicating between/among unlike platforms is the reason for the invention of middleware services. The middleware services are used to integrate the diversified software programs and make them talk to one another.

6. Network infrastructure: Effective and efficient linkage between the customer and the supplier is a precondition for e-commerce. For this a network infrastructure is required. The early models for networked computers were the local and long distance telephone companies. The telephone company lines were used for connections among the computers. As soon as the computer connection was established, the data travelled along that single path. Telephone company switching equipment (both mechanical and computerized) selected specific telephone lines, or circuits that were connected to create the single path between the caller and the receiver. This centrally-controlled, single connection model is known as **circuit switching.**

However, circuit switching is not really suitable for sending data across a large network. In order to implement circuit switching, point-to-point connections for each pair of senders/ receivers has to be established which is both expensive and difficult to manage. Another technique used by the Internet is called a packet switching network. In this, files and messages are broken down into packets that are labelled electronically with codes that indicate both their origin and destination. Packets travel from computer to computer along the network until they reach their destination. The destination computer collects the packets and reassembles the original data from the pieces in each packet. In packet switching, as the packet passes through various computers on its line the computers determine the best way to move the packet forward to its destination.

1.21 TCP/IP INTERNET PROTOCOL FOR NETWORK INFRASTRUCTURE

A protocol is a collection of rules for formatting, ordering, and error-checking data sent across a network. Protocols determine how the sending device indicates that it has finished sending a message and how the receiving device will indicate that it has received (or not received) the message. The set of protocols that underlie the basic operation of the Internet are transmission control protocols (TCP) and the internet protocol (IP). The TCP/IP is a two-layered program that computers use to make and break communication in a network. TCP controls assembly of the message into smaller packets before it is transmitted over the Internet. It also controls the reassembly of packets at the destination sites. The IP protocol consists of rules for routing individual data packets from their source to their destination. IP ensures that each data packet is labelled with the correct destination address.

1.22 APPLICATIONS OF E-COMMERCE

The following are some of the widely used applications of e-commerce.

Internet Bookshops: This was one of the first applications of e-commerce on the Internet. Books as an item of merchandize have the following significant advantages for online retailers:

- Books can be described well on the Internet. Moreover, they are not items, which require to be checked physically.
- Normally, the books have nominal prices and not too much risk is involved in the online payments.
- Books are small items and can be delivered in the customers letterbox. The customer does not need to be at home. *Amazon.com* is an example of an Internet bookshop. The large online bookstores need a sophisticated website, both to attract and retain the attention of their customers. The facilities of the online bookshop may include:
  - A large database of books. The details available for display include a picture of the cover, description of the book including page numbers, price of the book and reviews of other customers also if possible.
  - The book can be searched with the help of search engines. The search can be made by the author's name, title of the book or the subject etc.
  - There may be software on the site that may records the interests of a particular customer and can inform the customer about new arrivals in that subject.
- Some large online bookshop sites are:
  - www.ebiz.com
  - shopping.indiatimes.com
  - www.homeshop18.com

— www.futurebazaar.com
— www.amazon.com
— www.barnsandnoble.com
— www.bol.com
— www.bookshop.blackwell.co.uk

Grocery Supplies: A person who purchases items from a supermarket will be familiar with some of the similar problems described below.

- The customer has to plan to go to the supermarket, when it is open.
- It may be difficult to find parking.
- The supermarket may be crowded.
- One has to choose the items and wait their turn for billing.
- Items have to be unloaded at the checkout, reloaded into bags, and unloaded at home.
- All these problems may be resolved with the help of an online supermarket. Online supermarkets were set up to meet the needs of persons who cannot go to a supermarket due to physical constraints or constraints of time, or those who simply do not want to go. The online supermarket is similar to any other online shop. The customer has to log-on on to the site and select the groceries that are required. The staff picks the goods, packs and dispatches them. Some of the noteworthy sites for grocery supplies are as follows:
  — shopping.indiatimes.com
  — www.homeshop18.com
  — www.futurebazaar.com
  — www.peapod.com
  — www.homestore.com
  — www.sainsbury.co.uk
  — www.tesco.net

Electronic Newspapers: An electronic newspaper has advantages over both, printed newspapers and the news broadcast on radio and television. As compared to the printed newspaper, the e-newspaper can give up-to-date news similar to broadcast news. Further, the browser could be set to select the news of interest to the reader, leaving out the rest. This is not possible with broadcast news. Despite the said advantages, electronic newspapers are not being very popular due to the following reasons:

- The news on radio and television is often listened to/watched while people are doing other things like eating or driving.
- Printed newspapers may be read on the train or in the park and then may be shared with someone else.
- Printed newspapers give the reader the chance to be selective (the selection depends on the mood and time of the reader).

- There are a number of online newspapers and most of them are web versions of existing newspapers. For example:
  - www.timesofindia.com
  - www.dainikjagran.com

Internet Banking: Sometimes a customer may want to make an urgent payment but cannot visit the bank due to some constraints, or he/she may just want to check the account balance. Internet banking (or telephone banking) can solve these problems. This is also profitable for banks as it reduces their overheads. With the help of online banking a customer can check his or her balance at any time of the day or night. The customer can also pay various bills like telephone, electricity etc., without going to the bank or billing centres. Typical services offered by online banking are as follows:

- A customer can check the account balance at any time.
- The customer can obtain statements regarding any specific debit or credit that has gone through.
- Credit transfers so that bills can be paid online.
- Maintenance of standing orders and direct debits.

The major service that is not provided is cash in and cash out. To withdraw money, a customer has to go to the bank or ATMs.

Some sites related to Internet banking are as follows:

- www.icicibank.com
- www.sbiindia.com
- www.smile.co.uk

One cannot use the services provided by online banks unless one is a customer of the bank.

Electronic Auctions: Auctions have been a well-established market mechanism for trading items at a market negotiated price, based upon demand and supply. The Internet has added a new dimension by creating an online mechanism for implementing the auction process. Traditional auctions had limited participation of people who turned up at the place of auction. Today, the same auction mechanisms can be implemented using e-commerce technologies, allowing people connected through the Internet to bid. Electronic auctions potentially encourage greater participation as Internet users can connect to a web hosting an auction and bid for an item. www.wbay.com <http://www.wbay.com> and www.auctionindia.com <http://www.auctionindia.com> are examples of such sites.

SUMMARY

- Electronic commerce is a modern business methodology that addresses the needs of organizations, merchants and consumers in cutting costs while improving the quality of goods and services and increasing the speed of service delivery.
- The effects of e-commerce are already apparent in all areas of business, from customer service to new product design. It facilitates new types of information based business

processes for reaching out to and interacting with customers, such as on line advertising and marketing, on line order taking and on line customer service, to name a few.

- Many businesses that only used traditional physical methods of trading of goods and currency are jumping on the e-commerce bandwagon. Today, the line between e-commerce and traditional commerce is becoming blurred as more businesses start and continue to integrate the Internet and e-commerce technologies into their business processes.
- The evolution of e-commerce can be attributed to a combination of regulatory reform and technological innovation. Though the Internet (which played an important role in the evolution) appeared in the late 1960s, e-commerce as it exists today really started with the arrival of the World Wide Web and browsers in the early 1990s.
- A broad range of financial and information services are performed over the Internet today and sites that offer them are enjoying rapid growth. These sites are popular because they help consumers, businesses of all sizes and financial institutions to distribute some of their most important information over the Internet more conveniently and thoroughly than can be done using other channels.
- Electronic commerce is forcing companies to rethink the existing ways of target marketing (isolating and focusing on a segment of the population), relationship marketing (building and sustaining a long-term relationship with existing and potential customers), and even event marketing (setting up a virtual booth where interested people can log on and visit).
- E–commerce applications will be built on the existing technology infrastructure – a myriad of computers, communication networks and communication software forming the nascent information superhighway.
- Any successful e-commerce application will require the I-way infrastructure in the same way that regular commerce needs the interstate highway network to carry goods from point to point. One must travel this highway, whether it is an organization purchasing supplies or a consumer ordering a movie on demand.
- An electronic market is an information system that links many buyers and sellers so that they can exchange information, products, services and payments, i.e., a market place that is created by computer and communication technologies linking many buyers and sellers.

REVIEW QUESTIONS

1. Define e-commerce. Name the areas in which companies conduct business online and explain each of them.
2. Discuss the significant issues that are required to implement e-commerce in an organization.
3. How does one purchase or sell items or products on the Internet?
4. Differentiate between traditional commerce and e-commerce.
5. What technologies are required for e-commerce?
6. Discuss the economic potential of e-commerce. How does it affect the marketing and retail industry?

7. List and explain the incentives for engaging in e-commerce.
8. What are the various driving forces behind e-commerce?
9. Discuss the advantages of e-commerce with reference to the following:
   a. Customers
   b. Business
   c. Society
   d. Women
10. Write a short note on the disadvantages of e-commerce.
11. Why is network reliability very important for e-commerce? What factors cause problems for network reliability?
12. What is the effect of cost factors on e-commerce?
13. Discuss the reasons for e-commerce not being very successful.
14. What are the various types of e-commerce? Explain each in one in short.
15. Give the differences between B2C and B2B e-commerce.
16. What do you understand by architectural framework for e-commerce? Explain the various services that form the e-commerce architectural framework.
17. Write short notes on the following:
   a. TCP/IP protocol for network structure
   b. The impact of e-commerce on business
   c. Applications of e-commerce

CHAPTER 2

Network Infrastructure for E-commerce

Electronic commerce needs a network infrastructure to transport the content. The principal short coming of the existing communications infrastructure lies in its inability to provide integrated voice, data and video services.

Companies are upgrading their network infrastructure or creating new products and reorganizing through mergers and acquisitions to be better prepared for life on the I-way. For instance, long distance and local telephone operators are laying new high speed fibre optic links to the home. Cable television providers are either upgrading their coaxial cables or installing fibre optic links.

To access the information, computer companies are making sophisticated PCs with much more functionality, TV manufactures are making television and set top boxes and software companies are competing to build the tools and programs to make it all work together.

The development of the I-way is the next industrial revolution and then the dismissive antithesis. Many people familiar with technology know that constructing the I-way is a painstakingly slow and arduous process.

Most businesses do not understand how the I-way will change the way they advertise, market or sell their products and services how it will change their relationship with customers, what sort of new arrangements will be possible with suppliers and collaborators, how it will affect sharing information between various parts of the organization and how it will impact individual productivity and efficiency. These are the very issues that have been neglected in the media coverage.

2.1 MARKET SOURCES INFLUENCING THE I-WAY

2.1.1 Demand and Requirements of Market Participants

The success or failure of any innovation, product or service is a factor of market forces. It is important to understand the forces that are influencing the construction of the I-way, as e-commerce applications are dependent on the underlying I-way.

Examination of various user roles provides an indication of the market structure and could explain why many companies are merging or realigning themselves. Companies once narrowly focused on one type of user role now seek to broaden their markets and serve as many users as possible. Two points worth considering are:

1. The boundaries among communications, entertainment and information are not absolute. For instance, video is part of information, entertainment and communications (via video conferencing).
2. The boundaries among different pieces of equipment are not absolute. The online services and computer companies want to see an I-way that involves a lot of two way interactions such as electronic mail, information search and retrieval and more forums, chat lines and bulletin boards.

The demands and requirements various participants place on the network infrastructure are bound to be very different. To support as many roles as possible an increasing number of alliances are developing between telecommunication, cable television and entertainment companies.

These partnerships provide the synergy to spur consumer demand for advanced information, entertainment services and the equipment and devices necessary to provide them.

2.1.2 Strategic Alliances and the I-way Infrastructure

To ensure construction of a broadly useful I-way, strategic planning should take into account the needs of the communication, entertainment and information sectors. However, the resources requirements of building these three segments of the I-way are driving companies to make maximum use of existing facilities through alliances to control costs and create test markets.

Alliances, particularly among large firms, are dominant for several reasons. They reduce risks, spread costs and allow firms to acquire costly expertise in different areas instantly. Two aspects of these alliances are worth nothing.

1. They cut across industry lines, a diversity suggesting that member companies will perform different roles within the alliances. For example, studios provide the content,

telephone or cable companies deliver the information and computer hardware and software firms provide the access hardware and applications to use the data.

2. Many alliances are international, signalling that the I-way will be global from the start.

2.2 COMPONENTS OF THE I-WAY

The three major components that make up the I-way infrastructure are:

1. Network access equipment or consumer access equipment.
2. Local on ramps.
3. Global information distribution networks.

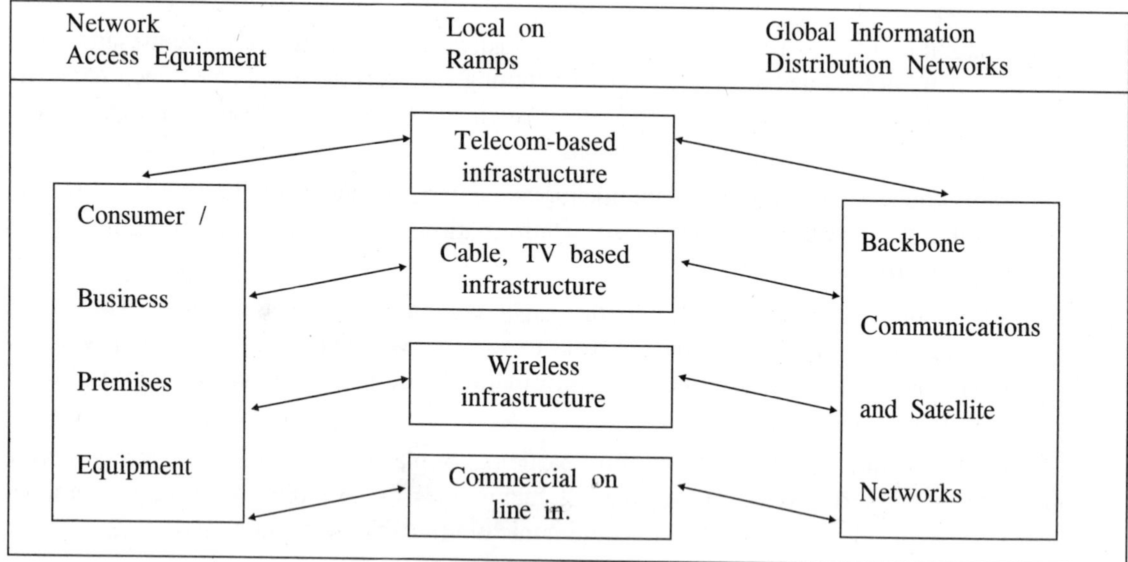

Fig. 2.1: ***Components of the I-way***

2.2.1 Network Access Equipment

One important often-ignored component of the I-way is that the consumer presumes that equipment is a generic term for privately owned communications equipment that is attached to the network. This broad category is divided into three parts.

1. Set top boxes

A key hardware platform for I-way access will be cable converter boxes, also known as set top boxes, converter boxes and converters. These boxes will have greater intelligence and more features than the existing converter boxes, such as enabling users to make phone calls, surf the internet and even plan their viewing schedule for the week. The following is a comparison of the ways of accessing the I-way via a set top versus a PC:

i) The display

ii) The controls

iii) The pipeline

iv) The brains

v) The accessibility

2. **Computer-based telephony**

The largest CPE product sectors are the private branch exchange (PBX), telephones, facsimile products, modems, voice processing equipment and video communication equipment.

3. **Digital switches, routers and hubs**

The digital switches industry has had a major impact on the I-way. A video program, once digitized, looks like any other digital data. In a computer network, data move from one point to their intended destination because they are tagged on the front with a small bundle of identifying digits known as a header.

Like any other data, digital data pass through switches that route them to their intended destination. Since the bundles of data are known as packets and the packets move through a network at very high speeds, this routing technique is known as fast packet switching.

Routers are internet working devices that intelligently connect the local area network (LAN) and wide area network (WAN) of various providers. The major benefits of the Internet include communications between separate networks and access to computing resources distributed throughout an organization.

In contrast to routers, hubs act as the wiring centres for large LANs. They can diagnose line failures, measure and manage traffic flow and greatly simplify reconfiguring large LANs.

2.2.2 Local on Ramps

One of the key forces shaping the dynamics of the I-way infrastructure is the 'last mile wiring linking homes with the backbone. Four types of local on Ramps are:

1. POTS – Plain old telephone system
2. Cable TV coaxial cable
3. Electricity wires
4. Wireless (A radio based cellular or satellite connection)

The 'last mile connections represent a tremendous 'sunken investment that cannot be easily replaced or overlooked in any network strategy.

The huge investment needed for wiring and upgrades will come only after sufficient consumer demand for the e-commerce services.

In sum, companies can expect to upgrade the last mile only once in the next decade due to the tremendous cost. Hence the last mile economics is the most important of the issues that impel a unified vision of the I-way.

2.2.2.1 Telecom-based last mile

The telephone companies are eyeing the last mile and trying to determine the best way of providing a high speed pipe capable of carrying high volumes of interactive voice, data and video homes and businesses.

They also control the world's largest switched distributed network providing point to point voice, fax, data and video conferencing services to hundreds of millions of subscribers. This network appears to be the primary foundation for the I-way for two reasons:

- It is capable of handling millions of simultaneous calls
- It provides accurate usage tracking and billing

However, the telephone network suffers from two problems:

- Lack of digital transmission capability.
- Uneven distribution.

2.2.2.2 Cable TV

Cable is vigorously pushing the concept that high-speed data to the home is best served by running over cable networks not on telephone analogue and more recent ISDN connections.

Cable companies already have high capacity wiring in the form of coaxial cables for broad casting analogue video. However, the cable companies want to provide important business services too, such as voice telephony, data communications and access to online services.

Wireless cable TV

Direct broadcast satellite (DBS), uses super high frequency (SHF) channels to transmit satellite cable programming over the air, instead of through overhead or underground wires.

DBS is a name given to a service that is called multi-channel multipoint distribution services (NMDS). DBS offers two benefits to customers.

- Availability (in rural areas)
- Affordability

2.2.2.3 Radio-based wireless last mile

Radio-based wireless networks are made up of:

- Cellular networks
- Microwave networks
- Specialized mobile radio (SMR) data networks
- Mobile data network

The cellular and satellite networks have advantages over wired networks because they are potentially accessible from any point on the globe without incurring the cost of installing a wire or cable.

The rapid growth of cellular, paging and other wireless services tends to give the false impression that radio technology itself is a recent development.

Two applications of radio technology led to its widespread usage –

- Radio broadcasting
- Warfare

Specialized mobile radio (SMR)

The SMR is a conventional two-way radio system that can be configured in a manner that provides so called "interconnect" service which is functionally very similar to cellular service.

The SMR providers (Dial page, NEXTEL) are known today as the providers of analog, dispatch private radio services. The converted systems, known in the industry as enhanced specialized mobile radio (ESMR) use a digital technology developed by Motorola, known as Motorola integrated radio service (MIRS).

Mobile data networks

Mobile data networks have been built on SMR infrastructure. Advances in portable computers are an important factor that is likely to lead to increased use of mobile data communication.

Wireless data networks have the ability to connect mobile workers to the central data base directly.

2.2.3 Global Distribution Network

Digitizing copyright works and other protected objects, leads to many benefits for the users, especially by simplifying the access. However, for the rights owners it can represent both an opportunity and a threat. Materials can be distributed speedily on the networks, and new markets are opened up, but there is also the danger of loss of sales through unauthorized use and exploitation of these same materials. There are different legal aspects and technologies, which deal with intellectual property rights on the global information network. The two major technologies under pinning high speed global information distribution networks are:

- Fibre optic long distance network
- Satellites network

2.2.3.1 Fibre optic long distance network

Fibre optic communication is a method of transmitting information from one place to another by sending pulses of light through an optical fibre. The light forms an electromagnetic carrier wave that is modulated to carry information. First developed in the 1970s, fibre optic communication systems have revolutionized the telecommunications industry and have played a major role in the advent of the information age. Due to its advantages over electrical transmission, optical fibres have largely replaced copper wire communications in core networks in the developed world.

The process of communicating using fibre optics involves the following basic steps: Creating the optical signal involving the use a transmitter, relaying the signal along the fibre, ensuring that the signal does not become too distorted or weak, receiving the optical signal, and converting it into an electrical signal.

Technology

Modern fibre optic communication systems generally include an optical transmitter to convert an electrical signal into an optical signal to send into the optical fibre, a cable containing bundles of multiple optical fibers that is routed through underground conduits and buildings, multiple kinds of amplifiers and an optical receiver to recover the signal as an electrical signal. The information transmitted is typically digital information generated by computers, telephone systems and cable television companies.

Transmitters

The most commonly-used optical transmitters are semiconductor devices such as light-emitting diodes (LEDs) and laser diodes. The difference between LEDs and laser diodes is that LEDs produce incoherent light, while laser diodes produce coherent light. For use in optical communications, semiconductor optical transmitters must be designed to be compact, efficient and reliable, while operating in an optimal wavelength range, and directly modulated at high frequencies.

In its simplest form, an LED is a forward-biased p-n junction, emitting light through spontaneous emission, a phenomenon referred to as electroluminescence. The emitted light is incoherent with a relatively wide spectral width of 30-60 nm. Transmission of LED light is also inefficient, with only about 1% of the input power, or about 100 microwatts, eventually converted into «launched power» which has been coupled into the optical fibre. However, due to their relatively simple design, LEDs are very useful for low-cost applications.

LEDs used for communications are most commonly made from gallium arsenide phosphide (GaAsP) or gallium arsenide (GaAs). Because GaAsP LEDs operate at a longer wavelength than GaAs LEDs (1.3 micrometers vs. 0.81-0.87 micrometers), their output spectrum is wider by a factor of about 1.7. The large spectrum width of LEDs causes higher fibre dispersion, considerably limiting their bit rate-distance product (a common measure of usefulness). LEDs are suitable primarily for local-area-network applications with bit rates of 10-100 Mbit/s and transmission distances of a few kilometers. LEDs have also been developed that use several quantum wells to emit light at different wavelengths over a broad spectrum, and are currently in use for local-area WDM networks.

A semiconductor laser emits light through stimulated emission rather than spontaneous emission, which results in high output power (~100 mW) as well as other benefits related to the nature of coherent light. The output of a laser is relatively directional, allowing high coupling efficiency (~50 %) into single-mode fibre. The narrow spectral width also allows for high bit rates since it reduces the effect of chromatic dispersion. Furthermore, semiconductor lasers can be modulated directly at high frequencies because of short recombination time.

Laser diodes are often directly modulated, that is the light output is controlled by a current applied directly to the device. For very high data rates or very long distance links, a laser source may be operated in the continuous wave mode, and the light modulated by an external device such as an electroabsorption modulator or Mach-Zehnder interferometer. External modulation increases the achievable link distance by eliminating laser chirp, which broadens the line width of directly-modulated lasers, increasing the chromatic dispersion in the fibre.

Fibre

An optical fibre consists of a core, cladding and a buffer (a protective outer coating), in which the cladding guides the light along the core using the method of total internal reflection. The core and the cladding (which has a lower refractive index) are usually made of high-quality silica glass, although they can both be made of plastic as well. Connecting two optical fibres is done by fusion splicing or mechanical splicing and requires special skills and interconnection technology due to the microscopic precision required to align the fibre cores.

Two main types of optical fibre used in fibre optic communications include multi-mode optical fibres and single-mode optical fibres. A multi-mode optical fibre has a larger core (≥ 50 micrometres), allowing less precise, cheaper transmitters and receivers to connect to it as well as cheaper connectors. However, a multi-mode fibre introduces multi-mode distortion, which often limits the bandwidth and length of the link. Furthermore, because of its higher dopant content, multi-mode fibres are usually expensive and exhibit higher attenuation. The core of a single-mode fibre is smaller (< 10 micrometres) and requires more expensive components and interconnection methods, but allows much longer, higher-performance links.

In order to package fibre into a commercially-viable product, it is typically protectively coated by using ultraviolet (UV), light-cured acrylate polymers, then terminated with optical fibre connectors, and finally assembled into a cable. After that, it can be laid in the ground and then run through the walls of a building and deployed aerially in a manner similar to copper cables. These fibres require less maintenance than common copper cables, once they are deployed.

Amplifiers

The transmission distance of a fibre optic communication system has traditionally been limited by fibre attenuation and by fibre distortion. By using opto-electronic repeaters, these problems can be eliminated. These repeaters convert the signal into an electrical signal, and then use a transmitter to resend the signal at a higher intensity than before. Because of the high complexity of modern wavelength-division multiplexed signals (including the fact that they have to be installed about once every 20 km), the cost of these repeaters is very high.

An alternative approach is to use an optical amplifier, which amplifies the optical signal directly without having to convert the signal into the electrical domain. It is made by doping a length of fibre with the rare-earth mineral erbium, and pumping it with light from a laser with a shorter wavelength than the communications signal (typically 980 nm). Amplifiers have largely replaced repeaters in new installations.

Receivers

The main component of an optical receiver is a photodetector, which converts light into electricity using the photoelectric effect. The photodetector is typically a semiconductor-based photodiode. There are several types of photodiodes including p-n photodiodes, p-i-n photodiodes and avalanche photodiodes. Metal-semiconductor-metal (MSM) photodetectors are also used due to their suitability for circuit integration in regenerators and wavelength-division multiplexers.

The optical-electrical converters are typically coupled with a transimpedance amplifier and a limiting amplifier to produce a digital signal in the electrical domain from the incoming optical signal, which may be attenuated and distorted while passing through the channel. Further signal processing such as clock recovery from data (CDR) performed by a phase-locked loop may also be applied before the data is passed on.

2.2.3.2 Wavelength-division multiplexing

Wavelength-division multiplexing (WDM) is the practice of dividing the wavelength capacity of an optical fibre into multiple channels in order to send more than one signal over the same fibre. This requires a wavelength division multiplexer in the transmitting equipment and a wavelength division demultiplexer (essentially a spectrometer) in the receiving equipment. Arrayed waveguide gratings are commonly used for multiplexing and demultiplexing in WDM. Using the WDM technology now commercially available, the bandwidth of a fibre can be divided into as many as 80 channels to support a combined bit rate in the range of terabits per second.

Bandwidth-distance product

Due to the fact that the effect of dispersion increases with the length of the fibre, a fibre transmission system is often characterized by its bandwidth-distance product, often expressed in units of MHz×km. This value is a product of bandwidth and distance because the bandwidth of the signal and the distance it can be carried are dependant on each other. For example, a common multimode fibre with bandwidth-distance product of 500 MHz×km could carry a 500 MHz signal for 1 km or a 1000 MHz signal for 0.5 km.

Through a combination of advances in dispersion management, wavelength-division multiplexing, and optical amplifiers, modern-day optical fibres can carry information at around 14 Terabits per second over 160 kilometers of fibre. Engineers are always looking at current limitations in order to improve fibre-optic communication, and several of these restrictions are currently being researched.

Dispersion

For modern glass optical fibres, the maximum transmission distance is limited not by attenuation but by dispersion, or spreading of optical pulses as they travel along the fibre. Dispersion in optical fibres is caused by a variety of factors. Intermodal dispersion, caused by the different axial speeds of different transverse modes, limits the performance of a multi-mode fibre. Because a single-mode fibre supports only one transverse mode, intermodal dispersion is eliminated.

In a single-mode fibre, performance is primarily limited by chromatic dispersion (also called group velocity dispersion), which occurs because the index of the glass varies slightly depending on the wavelength of the light, and light from real optical transmitters necessarily has nonzero spectral width (due to modulation). Polarization mode dispersion, another source of limitation, occurs due to the fat that although a single-mode fibre can sustain only one transverse mode, it can carry this mode with two different polarizations, and slight imperfections or distortions in a fibre can alter the propagation velocities for the two polarizations. This phenomenon is called fibre birefringence and can be counteracted by a polarization-maintaining optical fibre. Dispersion limits the bandwidth of the fibre because the spreading optical pulse limits the rate at which pulses can follow one another on the fibre and still be distinguishable at the receiver. Some dispersion, notably chromatic dispersion, can be removed by a 'dispersion compensator'. This works by using a specially prepared length of fibre that has the opposite dispersion to that induced by the transmission fibre. This sharpens the pulse so that it can be correctly decoded by the electronics.

Attenuation

Fibre attenuation, which necessitates the use of amplification systems, is caused by a combination of material absorption, Rayleigh scattering, Mie scattering, and connection losses. Although material absorption for pure silica is only around 0.03 dB/km (modern fibre has an attenuation around 0.3 dB/km), impurities in the original optical fibres cause attenuation of about 1000 dB/km. Other forms of attenuation are caused by physical stresses to the fibre, microscopic fluctuations in density, and imperfect splicing techniques.

Transmission windows

The effects that contribute to attenuation and dispersion depend on the optical wavelength, however wavelength bands exist where these effects are weakest, making these bands, or windows, most favorable for transmission. These windows have been standardized, and the current bands defined are as follows:

Table 2.1: ***Current bands for transmission windows***

Band	Description	Wavelength Range
O band	Original	1260 to 1360 nm
E band	Extended	1360 to 1460 nm
S band	short wavelengths	1460 to 1530 nm
C band	conventional ("erbium window")	1530 to 1565 nm
L band	long wavelengths	1565 to 1625 nm
U band	ultralong wavelengths	1625 to 1675 nm

Note that Table 2.1 shows that current technology has managed to bridge the second and third windows, whereas originally the windows were disjointed.

Historically, the first window used had a width of 800-900 nm; however losses are high in this region and therefore this window is mostly used for short-distance communications. The second window is around 1300 nm, and has much lower losses. The region has zero dispersion. The third window is around 1500 nm, and is the most widely used. This region has the lowest attenuation losses and hence it achieves the longest range. However it has some dispersion, and dispersion compensators are used to eliminate this.

Regeneration

When a communication link has to span a larger distance than existing fibre-optic technology is capable of, the signal must be regenerated at intermediate points in the link by repeaters. Repeaters add substantial cost to a communication system, and so system designers attempt to minimize their use. Recent advances in fibre and optical communications technology have reduced signal degradation so far that regeneration of the optical signal is only needed over distances of hundreds of kilometers. This has greatly reduced the cost of optical networking, particularly over undersea spans where the cost and reliability of repeaters is one of the key factors determining the performance of the whole cable system. The main advances contributing to these improvements in performance are dispersion management, which seeks to balance the effects of dispersion against non-linearity; and solitons, which use nonlinear effects in the fibre to enable dispersion-free propagation over long distances.

Last mile

Although fibre-optic systems excel in high-bandwidth applications, optical fibre systems have been slow in achieving the goal of fibre to the premises or to solve the last mile problem. However, as bandwidth demand increases, more and more progress towards this goal is being observed. In Japan, for instance, fibre-optic systems are beginning to replace wire-based DSL as a broadband Internet source. South Korea's KT also provides a service called fibre to the home (FTTH), which provides 100 percent fibre-optic connections to the subscriber's home. Verizon, a US-based telecom company, provides a service called FiOS which offers TV, high-speed internet, and telephone on a 100 percent fibre-optic network to a junction box mounted in a subscriber's home.

Comparison with electrical transmission

The choice between optical fibre and electrical (or copper) transmission for a particular system is made based on a number of factors to determine the optimum values. Optical fibres are generally chosen for systems requiring higher bandwidths or spanning longer distances than electrical cabling can accommodate. The main benefits of fibre are its exceptionally low loss, allowing long distances between amplifiers or repeaters; and its inherently high data-carrying capacity, such that thousands of electrical links would be required to replace a single high bandwidth fibre cable. Another benefit of fibres is that even when they run alongside each other for long distances, fibre cables experience effectively no crosstalk, in contrast to some types of electrical transmission lines. Fibre can be installed in areas with high electromagnetic interference (EMI), (along the sides of utility lines, power-carrying lines, and railroad tracks). All-dielectric cables are also ideal for areas of high lightning-strike incidence.

While single-line, voice-grade copper systems longer than a couple of kilometers require in-line signal repeaters for satisfactory performance; it is not unusual for optical systems to go over 100 kilometers (60 miles), with no active or passive processing. Single-mode fibre cables are commonly available in 12 km lengths, minimizing the number of splices required over a long cable run. Multi-mode fibre is available in lengths up to 4 km, although industrial standards only mandate 2 km unbroken runs.

Over short distances and relatively low bandwidth applications, electrical transmission is often preferred because of its

- Lower material cost, where large quantities are not required
- Lower cost of transmitters and receivers
- Capability to carry electrical power as well as signals (in specially-designed cables)
- Ease of operating transducers in the linear mode
- Optical fibers are more difficult and expensive to splice
- At higher optical powers, optical fibers are susceptible to fibre fuse wherein too much of light meeting with an imperfection can destroy several meters per second. The installation of fibre fuse detection circuitry at the transmitter can break the circuit and halt the failure to minimize damage.

Due to these benefits of electrical transmission, optical communication is not common in short box-to-box, backplane, or chip-to-chip applications; however, optical systems on these scales have been demonstrated in the laboratory.

In certain situations fibre may be used even for short distances or low bandwidth applications, due to other important features, such as:

- Immunity to electromagnetic interference, including nuclear electromagnetic pulses (although fibre can be damaged by alpha and beta radiation).
- High electrical resistance, making it safe to use near high-voltage equipment or between areas with different earth potentials.
- Need for lighter weight—important, for example, in aircraft.
- No sparks—important in flammable or explosive gas environments.
- Not electromagnetically radiating, and difficult to tap without disrupting the signal—important in high-security environments.
- Much smaller cable size—important where the pathway is limited, such as networking an existing building, where smaller channels can be drilled and space can be saved in existing cable ducts and trays.

Optical fibre cables can be installed in buildings with the same equipment that is used to install copper and coaxial cables, with some modifications due to the small size and limited pull tension and bend radius of optical cables. Optical cables can typically be installed in duct systems in spans of 6000 meters or more depending on the duct's condition, layout of the duct system, and installation technique. Longer cables can be coiled at an intermediate point and pulled farther into the duct system as necessary.

Governing standards

In order for various manufacturers to be able to develop components that function compatibly in fibre optic communication systems, a number of standards have been developed. The International Telecommunications Union publishes several standards related to the characteristics and performance of fibres themselves, including

- ITU-T G.651, "Characteristics of a 50/125 μm multimode graded index optical fibre cable".
- ITU-T G.652, "Characteristics of a single-mode optical fibre cable".

Other standards, produced by a variety of standards organizations, specify performance criteria for fibre, transmitters and receivers to be used together in conforming systems. Some of these standards are as follows:

- 10 Gigabit Ethernet
- FDDI
- Fibre Channel
- Gigabit Ethernet
- HIPPI
- Synchronous Digital Hierarchy
- Synchronous Optical Networking

TOSLINK is the most common format for digital audio cable using plastic optical fibre to connect digital sources to digital receivers.

Applications

Optical fibres are used by many telecommunications companies to transmit telephone signals, Internet communications and cable television signals. Due to much lower attenuation and interference, optical fibres have many advantages over existing copper wire in long-distance and high-demand applications. However, infrastructure development within cities was relatively difficult and time-consuming, and fibre optic systems are complex and expensive to install and operate. Due to these difficulties, fibre optic communication systems have primarily been installed in long-distance applications, where they can be used to their full transmission capacity, offsetting the increased costs. Since the year 2000, the prices for fibre optic communications have dropped considerably. The price for rolling out fibre to the home has currently become more cost-effective than that of rolling out a copper based network. Prices have dropped to $850 per subscriber in the US and lower in countries like the Netherlands, where digging costs are low.

Fig. 2.2: ***A mobile fibre optic splice lab being used to access and splice underground cables***

Since 1990, when optical-amplification systems became commercially available, the telecommunications industry has laid a vast network of intercity and transoceanic fibre communication lines. By 2002, an intercontinental network of 250,000 km of submarine communications cables with a capacity of 2.56 Tb/s was completed, and although specific network capacities are privileged information, telecommunications investment reports indicate that network capacity has increased dramatically since 2002.

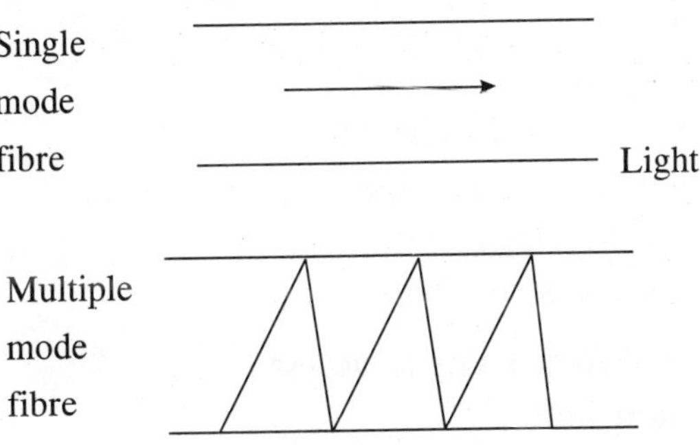

Fig. 2.3: ***Single/Multiple mode fibre***

Satellite networks

Satellite networks do have some advantages over terrestrial networks. They are accessible from any point on the globe, can provide broadcasting digital services, including voice, data and video, to many points without the cost of acquiring right of way and wire installation.

i) **Geo-synchronous satellite - GEO**
- Designed to broadcast a wide beam to ensure wide area coverage
- High orbit satellite
- Provide services to areas that cannot be reached by fibre optic cables

- Earth blanketing satellite services such as Motorola iridium low-earth provide the basic infrastructure to beam data and voice practically anywhere in the world.

ii) Very small aperture terminal - VSAT

- In 1980, industry introduced a new class of satellites using a narrow beam to focus the transmitted energy on small geographic areas.
- VSAT networks are being increasingly used by large corporations to link hundreds of retail sites.
- It is very expensive.

Two technology of VSAT: -

i) **TDM / TDMA** – Time division multiplexing or time division multiple access

- Work on Round Robin also
- Equal slice of time is allocated.

ii) **SCPC** – Single channel per carrier

SCPC is divided into two parts.

a) DAMA – Demand assigned multiple access

b) PAMA – Pre-assigned multiple access

For real time traffic FDMA/FDM (frequency division multiplexing) is used. SCPC is based on FDM technology.

DAMA – Demand assigned multiple access

- There is a central hub
- No specifications for the number of users
- Based on demand/request of users
- Hub allocated frequencies
- A buffer is necessary at the hub

PADA – Permanent/Pre-assigned multiple access

- There is no central hub
- Frequencies are allocated in advance
- It is similar to leased line connections so it is called pre-assigned multiplexing
- There is a permanent rental feature

Advantage: Utilization of resources.

Disadvantage: It is pre-assigned wastage of resources.

Note – In some cases DAMA resembles PAMA, e.g., video conferencing, news channels use central hubs.

DAMA can be converted into PAMA but PAMA cannot be converted into DAMA.

2.3 MULTIMEDIA CONTENT FOR E-COMMERCE APPLICATION

It is important to understand however that applications can be found at all levels of the infrastructure. Not only is multimedia content a part of the infrastructure that will enable consumers to enjoy video on demand but creation of that content is in itself an e-commerce application. Similarly, e-mail can be considered both a messaging infrastructure and a purchasable end product.

- Multimedia content can be considered both fuel and traffic for e-commerce applications.
- The technical definition of multimedia is the use of digital data in more than one format, such as a combination of text, audio, video and graphics in a computer file/document.
- Multimedia mimics the natural way people communicate. Its purpose is to combine the interactivity of a user friendly interface with multiple forms of content.

Multimedia is a combination of computers, television and telephone capabilities in a single device.

- Multimedia systems do much more than conventional database systems. The access to multimedia content depends on the hardware capabilities of the customer. For a long time, the capability of computer hardware was well ahead of the needs of software applications available to run on it.

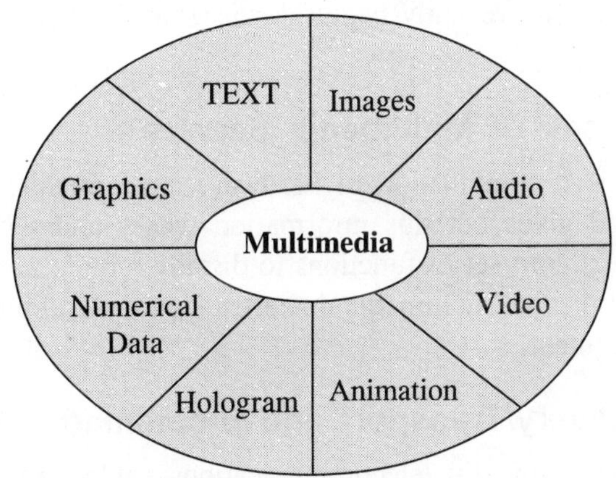

Fig. 2.4: ***Possible components of multimedia***

The success of e-commerce applications also depends on the variety and innovativeness of multimedia content and packaging.

Note: E-Commerce requires robust servers to store and distribute large amounts of digital content to consumers. These multimedia storage servers are large information warehouses capable of handling various content, ranging from books, newspapers, movies, games and X-ray images.

2.4 CLIENT–SERVER ARCHITECTURE IN E-COMMERCE

All e-commerce applications follow the client server model. Clients are devices plus software that request information from servers. The client server model allows the client to interact with the server through a request reply sequence governed by a paradigm known as message passing. The server manages application tasks, handles storage and security and provides scalability, i.e., the ability to add more clients as needed for serving more customers and client devices handle the user interface.

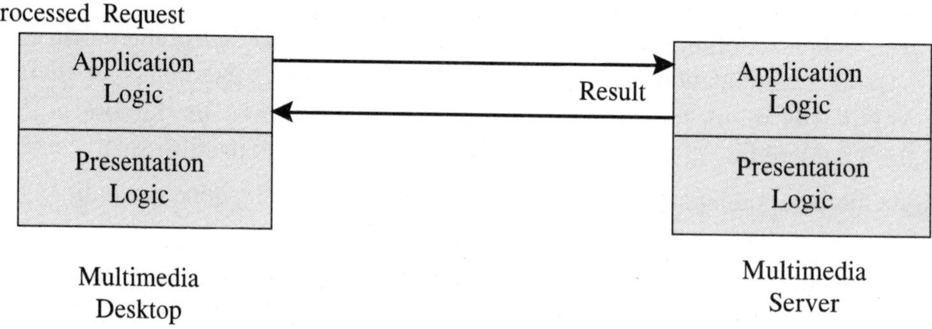

Fig.2.5: ***Distribution of processing in multimedia client server world***

Commercial users have only recently begun downsizing their applications to run on client server network.

2.4.1 Internal Processes of Multimedia Servers

A multimedia server is a combination of hardware and software that converts raw data into usable information and gives out this information where and when users need it. Most multimedia servers provide a core set of functions to display, create and manipulate multimedia documents, to transmit and receive multimedia documents over a computer network and to store and retrieve multimedia content.

2.4.2 Information Delivery/Transport and E-commerce Applications

Transport providers are typically telecommunications cable and wireless industries, and computer networks including commercial networks such as public networks like the Internet.

The distribution of information has become a competitive market with a combination of offence and defence. Playing on the defence are telephone companies and cable television, company providers that have enjoyed monopoly positions for decades.

Transport Providers	Delivery Methods
Telecommunication Companies	Long distance telephone lines, local telephone lines
Cable television companies	Cable TV, coaxial, fibre optic and satellite lines
Computer based on line servers	Internet
Wireless communications	Cellular & radio N/W paging system

Fig. 2.6: ***Transport routes***

2.5 BROADBAND TELECOMMUNICATIONS

2.5.1 Narrowband Versus Broadband Networks

In the analog world, broadband refers to the ability to stalk frequencies on a single transmission medium, providing multiple channels on the same wire. In the digital world, broadband has come to mean any data rate greater than or equal to T-1 speeds (ie. 1.544 Mbps).

With broadband, the physical cabling is conceptually divided into several different channels each with its own unique carrier frequency using a technology called frequency division modulation.

A narrowband network is one that provides a single channel for communication across the physical medium (i.e., cable), so only one device can transmit at a time. Modulation is not used in narrowband.

Note: If the frequency exceeds 1.4 Mbps – broadband.
If the frequency is less than 1.4 Mbps – narrowband.

2.5.2 Integrated Services Digital Network (ISDN)

ISDN stands for integrated services digital network. It is the forerunner of B-ISDN. ISDN was designed to utilize the pre-existing copper wiring that runs from a telephone exchange to telephones on the customer's premises.

ISDN operates by increasing the calling capacity of the existing telephone line.

There are three types of ISDN channels, defined B, D and H.

B channel – is a 64 Kbps clear channel that can carry any digitalized data and voice. A clear channel means that no signalling information is sent and it is meant to be an open communication line. There are two B channels on each ISDN line and so two kinds of information can be exchanged simultaneously.

D channel – used for signalling information, can operate at either 10 Kbps or 64 Kbps. The D channel can be used for what is known as communication signalling, which is useful for synchronization, monitoring and alarm signals. This channel can also transport digital data at speeds up to 9600 bits/second. This channel uses X.25 format for data transfer.

H channel - there are three H channels all providing higher speed transmission than the D channel. The Ho channel operates at 384 Kbps and can be used for video conferencing, high-speed fax or packet switched data. Up to four Ho channels can be multiplexed into a single H1 channel, which operates at 1.544 Mbps. The H1 channel is used for high-speed data communications or LAN interconnections. The H2 channel, which operates at 1.9 Mbps is available only in Europe.

ISDN is used to transmit and receive data at high speeds. ISDN is positioned so as to provide simultaneous voice and data service to the desktops of residential users, home offices and small businesses.

2.5.3 B–ISDN

B-ISDN stands for broadband integrated service digital network. It offers video on demand, live television from many sources, full motion, multimedia, electronic mail, LAN interconnections, high speed data transport and many other services.

The main goal of B-ISDN is integration of audio and video data communication services.

2.5.4 SONET and SDH

A vital component of B-ISDN is called SONET in North America and SDH in the rest of the world.

SONET stands for synchronous optical network; it is a set of standards that govern synchronous fibre optic data transmission at rates ranging from 5.18 Mbps to 2.5 Gbps.

SONET and SDH are not identical because each has features that the other lacks. There is a subnet of mutually compatible specifications that permit the American SONET to interoperate smoothly and nearly effortlessly with the European SDH.

SONET has three advantages:

i) The bandwidth available with fibre optic technology is virtually limitless. SONET's current maximum data rate of 2.5 Gbps is equivalent to 48 T-3 (45 Mbps) lines.

ii) Along with its massive amounts of bandwidth, SONET allows switches to add or drop an individual channel. High speed users generally do not have such access to individual lower speed channels.

iii) It is an international standard.

Since SONET's specifications are universally applicable, SONET equipment from different vendors theoretically should be able to inter operate.

2.5.5 ATM – Asynchronous Transfer Mode

The basic idea behind ATM is to transmit all information in small fixed size packets called calls. The calls are 53 bytes long, of which 5 bytes are header and 48 bytes are data. The ATM uses cell switching technology and is also known as cell (switching) relay service.

The cell switching technology has the following advantages over traditional circuit switching technology :

i) It is highly flexible and can handle both fixed rate and variable rate traffic equally well.

ii) At the high speeds envisioned, digital switching of cells is easier than using traditional multiplexing techniques.

iii) For television distribution broadcasting is essential, cell switching can provide this but circuit switching cannot.

ATM networks are connection oriented. Making a call first requires sending a message to set up the connection. After that subsequent calls follow the same path to the destination. Call delivery is not guaranteed but their order is guaranteed.

The intended speeds for ATM networks are 155 Mbps and 622 Mbps. 155 Mbps speeds are chosen because this is the speed needed to transmit high definition television.

Upper Layers Control Plane	**Upper Layers User Plane**
CS Sub Layer	ATM Adoption Layer
SAR Sub Layer	
ATM Layer	
TC Sub Layer	Physical Layer
PMD Sub Layer	

Fig. 2.7: *B–ISDN ATM reference model*

ATM appears to be the future of high speed networking for several business and technical reasons. ATM has been designed to be independent of the transmission medium. The ATM layer deals with:

1. Transport of cells; it defines the layout of a cell and what the header fields mean.
2. With establishment and release of a virtual circuit.
3. Congestion control.

The ATM adoption layer allows users to send packets larger than a cell. It segments the packet into cells and sends them to the destination. It then re-assembles the cells into packets for delivery to the user.

Note: The ATM scheme is widely used for data communication networks. The ATM network uses the ATM switch which receives the requests for data transfer from different computers. The ATM switch facilitates the data transmission in an asynchronous mode.

Various computers are connected to the ATM switch. It connects the sender's and receiver's computers and transfers the packets to their destination at a high speed. The ATM network is similar to the star network.

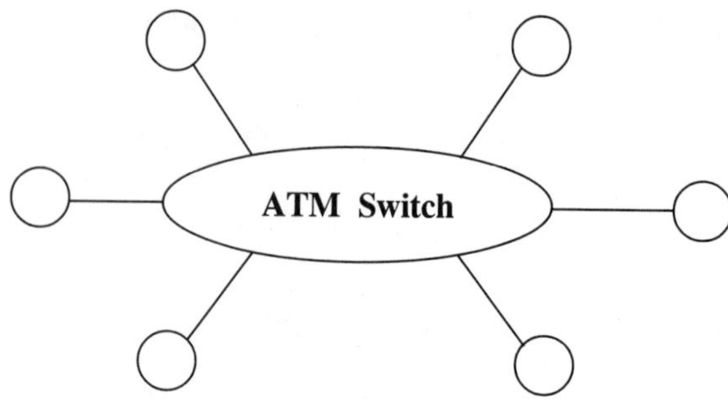

Fig. 2.8: ***ATM switch***

Uses of ATM

An ATM (network) switch is more suitable for multimedia data transfer that contains text, audio and video. The speed of communication between the computers and the ATM switch is 155 Mbps.

SUMMARY

- Electronic commerce needs a network infrastructure to transport the content. The principal shortcoming of the existing communications infrastructure lies in its inability to provide integrated voice, data and video services.
- The success or failure of any innovation, product or service is a factor of market forces. It is important to understand the forces that are influencing the construction of the I-way, because e-commerce applications are dependent on the underlying I-way.
- Examination of various user roles provides an indication of the market structure and could explain why many companies are merging or realigning themselves. Companies that were once narrowly focused on one type of user role now seek to broaden their markets and serve as many users as possible.
- Routers are internet working devices that intelligently connect the LAN and WAN of various providers. The major benefits of internet works include communications between separate networks and access to computing resources distributed throughout an organization.
- In contrast to routers, hubs act as the wiring centres for large LAN – they can diagnose line failures, measure and manage traffic flow and greatly simplify reconfiguring large LANs.
- Cable is vigorously pushing the concept that high-speed data to the home is best served by running over cable networks not on telephone analog and more recent ISDN connections.
- Satellite and direct broadcast satellite (DBS). DBS uses super high frequency (SHF) channels to transmit satellite cable programming over the air, instead of through overhead or underground wires.

- Mobile data networks have been built on SMR infrastructure. Advances in portable computers are an important factor that is likely to lead to increased use of mobile data communication.
- Wireless data networks have the ability to connect mobile workers to the central data base directly.
- All e-commerce applications follow the client server model. Clients are devices plus software that request information from servers. The client server model, allows the client to interact with the server through a request reply sequence governed by a paradigm known as message passing.
- The server manages application tasks, handles storage and security and provides scalability, i.e., the ability to add more clients as needed for serving more customers and client devices that can handle the user interface.

REVIEW QUESTIONS

1. Discuss the network infrastructure for e-Commerce.
2. Discuss the concept of the I-way and also explain the different market forces behind the I-way.
3. Discuss the components of the I-way.
4. Write short notes on the following
   (i) Access equipment
   (ii) Global information distribution network
   (iii) Broadband telecommunication
   (iv) ATM
   (v) ISDN
   (vi) B-ISDN

CHAPTER 3

Mobile Commerce

During the past decade two important technological trends have developed: the extraordinary growth of the Internet and the tremendous development and increased sophistication of mobile technology (Barnes, 2002). The convergence of these two technologies has led to the rise of numerous services delivered via mobile handsets, more commonly referred to as wireless or mobile (m-) commerce. Mobile services have been heralded as the new marketing frontier (Newell & Newell-Lemon, 2001). In reality however, m-commerce is in its incubatory stage, and many challenges remain to be identified (Balasubramanian, Peterson & Jarvenpaa, 2002).

Despite the slow start of m-commerce, vast investments have been made in second-and-a-half and third generation technologies such as GPRS and UMTS to expand business opportunities in this area (*The Economist*, 2000), and telecommunication companies in Germany, the Netherlands, and the USA have introduced i-mode, in an attempt to re-conquer the mobile market.

3.1 DEFINING M-COMMERCE

Repeatedly, m-commerce has been recognized as an extension of e-commerce. Although similarities with e-commerce are recognized, m-commerce should be acknowledged as a business opportunity with its own distinctive characteristics and functions, resulting from the unique advantages that wireless technology have over wired technology. First, wireless devices offer consumers the opportunity of overcoming physical and time limitations through the ubiquity of m-commerce, which is perceived as the most obvious advantage of a wireless service.

Furthermore, the introduction of location-based services (LBS) will allow consumers to obtain context-specific information. This makes mobile devices especially useful for providing time-critical and location-sensitive services. Several authors have stressed this functional value of m-commerce, thereby neglecting the social value that can be derived from mobile services. According to Barwise and Strong (2002), the mobile channel is an extremely personal medium that consumers carry with them at all times. Consequently, it has become part of the consumers social context and everyday life. The unique combination of localization and personalization will generate new opportunities to attract customers. Personalized services allow information tailored to users preferences and the opportunity to create, for example, m-wallets, which are payment applications that create opportunities for personal information storage, abolishing the necessity to supply credit card information with every transaction performed.

Mobile commerce is defined as: Any electronic transaction or information interaction conducted using a mobile device and mobile network (wireless or switched public network) thereby guaranteeing customers virtual and physical mobility; leading to the transfer of real or perceived value in exchange for personalized, location-based information, services, or goods.

3.2 MOBILE SERVICE TYPOLOGY

A variety of mobile services have already been developed and these types of services are likely to expand through the introduction of alleged "third generation" (3G) services that emerge as new wireless technologies such as GRPS and UMTS are implemented to provide a classification of wireless services, distinguishing four major categories: communication, information, transaction and entertainment services.

Mobile Communication	Communication services form the most elementary and well-known type of mobile services. Voice-to-voice application is the primary service in wireless technology (http://www.itweb.co.za).
Mobile Information	Information is developing into an essential service of m-commerce. According to PCIA (2001, http://www.pcia.com/m-userstudy), presently there exists a substantial amount of interest in mobile information regarding daily news, soccer, travelling and weather reports for instance.
Mobile Transaction	Transaction services encompass m-shopping, m-finance and m-payment. Mobile shopping services provide customers the opportunity to purchase anything at any point in time. 'One-click-purchasing possibilities will create convenient shopping experiences for mobile customers. Mobile banking and brokerage are part of m-finance.
Mobile Entertainment	According to the Mobile Entertainment Forum (2001) entertainment will be the 'backbone of wireless value-adding

	services for a substantial time period. Moreover, m-entertainment applications are recognized as a way of exploring new technology. For this reason, Ericsson, Motorola, Nokia, and Siemens launched the Mobile Games Interoperability (MGI) Forum, which aims to specify a global standard and to develop certification procedures to encourage a wide adoption of the standard (http://www.mgif.org), simultaneously enhancing adoption of wireless technology itself.

3.3 MOBILE AND WIRELESS COMPUTING FUNDAMENTALS

Mobile computing means different things to different people. The key feature of the mobile computing environment is that the user need not maintain a fixed position in the network. The terms wireless and mobile are not synonymous. Wireless is a transmission or information transport method that enables mobile computing. It covers many approaches to communications without wires. The goal of wireless is to enable distributed and mobile computing, thus bringing an end to the tyranny of geography.

Growth in several market segments of wireless communications has been explosive and has stimulated activity in all the related areas including technical, regulatory, security, legal and business. Mobile computing on the other hand focuses on the application side. It builds on the concepts of being able to compute no matter where the user is. The goal of mobile computing is to work toward true computing freedom.

3.4 D-COMMERCE

Digital commerce (d-commerce) is the next step of Internet enabled commerce. D-commerce is the management of transactions and workflow associated with digital content to enable commerce. In d-commerce the entire process is digital.

3.4.1 Electronic Buying and Selling of Goods

Technology leaders need to understand that a large share of the market economy is being carried out electronically, through legitimate and legal exchanges. The mainstream availability of Internet purchases of toys, clothing, cars, food, etc. has become commonplace. At the same time, an equal amount of illegal goods and services are surfacing, such as pornography and gambling. Access to almost any product raises the question of legal and illegal acts by the user. Students need to be taught that options in a non-electronic society are also found in an electronic society. The rise of the digital economy does not change the issue of right and wrong, but it does enhance the users access to buying and selling goods, which magnifies the issue of illegal activities.

D-commerce services include content management services, right management services, and transaction management services. It is essential for these services to be well designed, fully-integrated and incrementally deployable to suit business needs.

3.5 MOBILE COMPUTING FRAMEWORK

Mobile computing is expanding in four dimensions –

i) Wireless delivery technology and switching methods
ii) Mobile information access devices
iii) Mobile data internetworking standards and equipment
iv) Mobile computing based business applications

3.5.1 Wireless Delivery Technology and Switching Methods

Wireless communications are evolving in several directions. The many approaches seen in evolution of the wireless industry are aimed at different consumer needs, yet a number of underlying technical concepts are common to the different activities.

The wireless industry is very complicated as it can be split into a number of subsets.

- Radio based (Land based wireless systems and satellite based wireless system)
- Light based wireless systems

Radio based wireless systems

Radio based services can be grouped into two main categories:

- Land based – cellular communications, packet data networks and specialized mobile radio (SMR)
- Satellite based – paging systems and very small aperture terminal (VSAT)

3.5.2 Mobile Information Access Devices

Information can be sent over a coaxial cable or a telephone line in many forms, such as email, data files, video and other information. There are a wide variety of information access devices to utilize this information.

- Portable computers
- Hybrid pen computers
- Personal digital assistants
- Data communication equipment

Portable computers

A **portable computer** is a computer that is designed so that it can be moved from one place to another. Portable computers, by their nature, are microcomputers. Early portables were unkindly referred to as "luggables," referring to their great size and weight (partly due to the need to include a full-blown CRT monitor, as LCD technology was not yet mature). The term "luggable" is today used mainly when speaking of 17" and larger widescreen laptops.

Fig.3.1 ***The Compaq Portable: The first portable IBM PC compatible***

The term portable computer is now almost exclusively used to refer to portable computers that are larger than a laptop, often use conventional parts and usually do not run on batteries. Smaller portable computers are referred to by their more specific terms:

- The laptop (or notebook) with a flat panel display and keyboard, requiring a seated position and both hands. A relatively recently introduced modification has been the Tablet PC, which essentially is a laptop operated with a stylus on a touch-sensitive screen.
- The desktop replacement computer, a large laptop designed to perform all of the functions of a desktop computer.
- The palmtop which is something between a laptop and a PDA (q.v.).
- The pocket computer, which was mostly a phenomenon of the 1980s, and combined the features of an alphanumeric calculator, a small home computer (usually programmable in BASIC), and a PDA (q.v.).
- The personal digital assistant (PDA), usually held in one hand and operated with the other.
- The wearable computer with hands-free interface, and usually some voice capability (speech recognition and speech synthesis).

Portable computers have been increasing in popularity over the past decade, as they do not restrict the user in terms of mobility as a desktop computer would. Wireless Internet, extended battery life and more comfortable ergonomics have been factors driving this increase in popularity.

Portable computers are divided into three distinct types:

- Laptops
- Notebooks
- Hand held

This varies broadly according to the method of entering, storing, playing and processing data.

- **Laptops** are useful for running applications that demand very powerful hardware, such as computer aided design (CAD) and video presentations.

- **Notebooks** serve the more traditional general purpose, user who wants to do a large amount of word processing and manipulate sizable spreadsheets.
- **Hand held** have less powerful versions of these capabilities combined with more intuitive functions such as phone lists and messaging.

It should be noted that the sub-notebooks have become the mainstream of mobile computing, and they provide a close approximation of the desktop computing experience.

Among the more novel approaches to sub-notebook design are those that include Windows software and applications in ROM.

Hybrid pen computers

One of the initial applications envisioned for the pen computer was that of insurance adjusters creating charts of an accident or pointing out which parts of a car were damaged. Pen computers are often equipped with wireless communications.

One of the recent developments in pen based computing systems is the addition of a keyboard, which seeks to harness the best of both worlds. It is provided in two ways, when open, it reveals a full size keyboard and the pen can be used as a mouse. When the display is closed, the user is presented with a tablet size writing pad.

Personal digital assistants (PDAs)

Personal digital assistants (PDAs) are handheld devices that were originally designed as personal organizers, but became much more versatile over the years. PDAs have many uses: calculating, use as a clock and calendar, playing computer games, accessing the Internet, sending and receiving E-mails, use as a radio or stereo, video recording, recording notes, use as an address book, and use as a spreadsheet. Newer PDAs also have both colour screens and audio capabilities, enabling them to be used as mobile phones (smartphones), web browsers or media players. Many PDAs can access the Internet, intranets or extranets via Wi-Fi, or wireless wide-area networks (WWANs). One of the most significant PDA characteristics is the presence of a touch screen.

Touch screen

Many original PDAs, such as the Palm Pilot, featured touch screens for user interaction, having only a few buttons usually reserved for shortcuts to often used programs. Touch screen PDAs, including Windows Pocket PC devices, usually have a detachable stylus that can be used on the touch screen. Interaction is then done by tapping the screen to activate buttons or menu choices, and dragging the stylus to, for example, highlight text.

Text input is usually done in one of two ways:

- Using a virtual keyboard, where a keyboard is shown on the touch screen. Input is done by tapping the letters.
- Using letter or word recognition, where letters or words are written on the touch screen, and then "translated" to letters in the currently activated text field. Despite rigorous research and development projects, this data input method still requires much patience from the user since it tends to be rather inaccurate.

PDAs for business use, including the BlackBerry and Treo, have a full keyboard and scroll wheels or thumb wheels to facilitate data entry and navigation, in addition to supporting touch-screen input. There are also full-size foldable keyboards available that plug directly into the PDA and allow for normal typing.

Synchronization

An important functionality for PDAs is the possibility of synchronizing data with a contact database, such as Microsoft Outlook or ACT!, hosted on a personal computer (PC) or a corporate server or servers. The data synchronized ensures that the PDA has an accurate list of contacts, appointments and e-mail, allowing users to access the same information on the PDA as the host computer.

The synchronizing also prevents the loss of information stored on the device in case it is lost, stolen, or destroyed. Another advantage is that data input is usually a lot quicker on a PC, since text input via a touch screen is still not quite optimal. Transferring data to a PDA via the computer is therefore a lot quicker than having to manually input all data on the handheld device.

Most PDAs come with the ability to synchronize to a PC. This is done through synchronization software provided with the handheld computer, such as HotSync Manager, which comes with Palm OS handhelds, or Microsoft ActiveSync, which comes with Windows mobile handhelds.

These programs allow the PDA to be synchronized with a personal information manager. This personal information manager may be an outside program or a proprietary program. For example, the BlackBerry PDA comes with the Desktop Manager program which can synchronize to both Microsoft Outlook and ACT!. Other PDAs come only with their own proprietary software. For example, some early Palm OS PDAs came only with Palm Desktop while later Palms such as the Treo 650 have the built-in ability to sync to Palm Desktop and/or Microsoft Outlook. Third-party synchronization software is also available for many PDAs. This software synchronizes these handhelds to other personal information managers which are not supported by the PDA manufacturers.

Customization

As with personal computers, it is possible to install additional software on most PDAs. Software can be bought or downloaded from the Internet, allowing users to personalize their PDAs to their liking. Some PDAs also allow for the addition of hardware. The most common is a memory card slot, which allows the users to get additional and exchangeable storage space on their handheld devices. There are also miniature keyboards that can be connected to some PDAs for quicker text input. PDAs with Bluetooth can also use Bluetooth devices like headsets, mouse and foldable keyboards with their PDAs.

Ruggedized PDAs

For many years businesses and government organizations have relied upon rugged PDAs for mobile data applications. Typical applications include supply chain management in warehouses, package delivery, route accounting, medical treatment and record keeping in hospitals, facilities maintenance and management, parking enforcement, access control and security, capital asset maintenance, meter reading by utilities, and "wireless waitress" applications in restaurants and hospitality venues. There are even PDAs designed to take significant amounts of punishment, probably meant for military use. Unfortunately, these devices come with a steep price tag.

Medical and scientific uses

In medicine, PDAs have been proven to aid diagnosis and drug selection and some studies have concluded that their use by patients to record symptoms improves the effectiveness of communication with hospitals during follow-up. The first landmark study in testing the effectiveness of PDAs in a medical setting was conducted at the Brigham & Women's Hospital and Massachusetts General Hospitals in affiliation with Harvard Medical School. Led by the team of Sandeep Shah & Steven Labkoff, MD, the Constellation project used Apple's Newton (first PDA in the market) to cater to the demands of medical professionals. Today, there are a wide range of resources on the market, including drug information, treatment options, guidelines, evidence based information and journal summaries including drug and safety alerts. Other services which are provided today include: drug databases, treatment information and relevant news in formats specific to mobile devices, translation of medical journals into readable formats and updates from journals, organization of medical records to remind doctors making ward rounds of information such as the treatment regimens of patients and programs and tools for conducting research on mobile devices, with a connection back to a central server allowing the user to enter data into a centralized database using their PDA. Recently the development of [sensor web] technology has led to discussion of using wearable bodily sensors to monitor ongoing conditions like diabetes and epilepsy and alerting medical staff or the patients themselves to the treatment required via communication between the web and PDAs.

Educational uses

As mobile technology has become almost a necessity, it is no surprise that personal computing has today become a vital learning tool. Educational institutes have started a trend of integrating PDAs into their teaching practices (mobile learning). With the capabilities of PDAs, teachers are now able to provide a collaborative learning experience for their students. They are also preparing their students for possible practical uses of mobile computing upon their graduation.

PDAs and handheld devices have recently allowed for digital note taking. This has increased students productivity by allowing individuals to quickly spell-check, modify, and amend their class notes or e-notes. Educators are currently able to distribute course material through the use of Internet connectivity or infrared file sharing functions of the PDA. Keeping class material in mind, textbook publishers have begun to release e-books, electronic textbooks, which can be uploaded directly to a PDA. This eliminates the exhausting effort of carrying multiple textbooks at a time.

To meet the instructive needs sought by educational institutes, software companies have developed programs with the learning aspects in mind. Simple programs such as dictionaries, thesauri, and word processing software are important to the digital note taking process. In addition to these simple programs, encyclopedias and digital planning lessons have created added functionality for users.

Sporting uses

PDAs are used by glider pilots for pre-flight planning and to assist navigation in cross-country competitions. They are linked to a GPS to produce moving-map displays showing the tracks to turn-points, airspace hazards and other tactical information.

Currently the major PDA operating systems are:

- Palm OS - owned by PalmSource.
- Windows Mobile (Pocket PC), (based on the Windows CE kernel) - owned by Microsoft.
- IM for the BlackBerry - owned by Research In Motion.
- Many operating systems are based on the Linux kernel - free (not owned by any company). These include:
  - GPE - based on GTK+/X11.
  - OPIE/Qtopia - based on Qt/E Qtopia is developed by Trolltech, OPIE is a fork of Qtopia developed by volunteers.
- Symbian OS (formerly EPOC) owned by Ericsson, Motorola, Panasonic, Nokia, Samsung, Siemens and Sony Ericsson.

Architecture

Many PDAs run using a variation of the ARM architecture (usually denoted by the Intel XScale trademark). This encompasses a class of RISC microprocessors that are widely used in mobile devices and embedded systems, and its design was influenced strongly by a popular 1970s/1980s CPU, the MOS Technology 6502.

Popular consumer PDAs

Fig. 3.2: ***Palm IIIxe PDA***

- Psion
- Amida
- Apple Newton
- BlackBerry
- hp iPAQ Pocket PC (originally Compaq iPAQ until HP merged in 2002)
- hp Jornada Pocket PC (phased out/merged with iPAQ line in 2002)
- Palm Pilot, Tungsten E2, LifeDrive, Treo and Zire
- Sharp Wizard and Zaurus

A PC reduced in size so as to fit inside a coat pocket, PDAs reflect the never-ending quest to build the smallest possible useful computer. The PDA market is dividing up into three functional segments:

Digital assistant: Market segment where the hand held device captures data and digitizes it.

Personal communications: Cellular telephone with an LCD screen integrated into it.

Palmtops: Large storage segment for the user who wants to carry a lot of data and be able to retrieve it easily.

Cellular modems and PCMCIA adapters

Like most computer and communications products, wireless modems have undergone extensive evolution. Originally designed for vehicle installation, the wireless modem has evolved into an integrated transceiver receiver and data modem in a portable compact format.

- It is capable of sending or receiving data
- The cost of using a cellular system for data can be high
- The speed and reliability of a cellular circuit – switched voice channels can vary widely.

There are two major market sectors for cellular modems:

- Industry oriented applications: These include areas such as retailing, warehousing, manufacturing and health care in which products are used for the collection of data. They tend to be slow speed and typically connect hand held devices to a corporate system.
- General purpose applications: These require LAN connectivity while they move from location to location within a given environment and applications are typically used to send and receive electronic mail, access databases and transmit files. They tend to have higher transmission speed.

3.5.3 Mobile Data Internet Working Standards

The phenomenal growth in the cellular industry presents a significant challenge, namely overcoming the inherent capacity and quality limitations of the current analog systems. The specific reasons for the analog to digital transition are as follows:

1. Limited available bandwidth
2. Over crowding

Many feel that digital technology provides the key to spectrum efficiency. Efficient spectrum use is also seen as the key to the creation of the next generation personal communication services.

The current analog system divides the available spectrum into 3-KHz wide channels. This method of channelization (division of the spectrum into multiple channels) is commonly called frequency division multiple access (FDMA)

Alternative means of channelization are being developed to allow more users in the same region of the spectrum. Two dominant methods are:

— Time division multiple access (TDMA)
— Code division multiple access (CDMA)

3.5.3.1 Code division multiple access (CDMA)

Code division multiple access (CDMA) is a form of multiplexing (not a modulation scheme) and a method of multiple access that does not divide up the channel by time (as in TDMA), or frequency (as in FDMA), but instead encodes data with a special code associated with each channel and uses the constructive interference properties of the special codes to perform the multiplexing. **CDMA** also refers to digital cellular telephony systems that make use of this multiple access scheme, such as those pioneered by Qualcomm, and W-CDMA by the International Telecommunication Union or ITU.

CDMA has since been used in many communications systems, including the Global Positioning System (GPS) and in the OmniTRACS satellite system for transportation logistics.

1. Usage in mobile telephony

A number of different terms are used to refer to CDMA implementations. The original U.S. standard defined by QUALCOMM was known as IS-95, the IS referring to an Interim Standard of the Telecommunications Industry Association (TIA). IS-95 is often referred to as 2G or second generation cellular. The QUALCOMM brand name cdmaOne may also be used to refer to the 2G CDMA standard. The CDMA has been submitted for approval as a mobile air interface standard to the ITU International Telecommunication Union.

Whereas the Global System for Mobile Communications (GSM) standard is a specification of an entire network infrastructure, the CDMA interface relates only to the air interface—the radio part of the technology. For example GSM specifies an infrastructure based on internationally approved standard while CDMA allows each operator to provide the network features as suitable. On the air interface, signalling suite work has been progressing to harmonize these.

After a couple of revisions, IS-95 was superseded by the IS-2000 standard. This standard was introduced to meet some of the criteria laid out in the IMT-2000 specifications for 3G, or third generation, cellular. It is also referred to as 1xRTT which simply means "1 times

Radio Transmission Technology" and indicates that IS-2000 uses the same 1.25 MHz shared channel as the original IS-95 standard. A related scheme called 3xRTT uses three 1.25 MHz carriers for a 3.75 MHz bandwidth that would allow higher data burst rates for an individual user, but the 3xRTT scheme has not been commercially deployed. More recently, QUALCOMM has led the creation of a new CDMA-based technology called 1xEV-DO, or IS-856, which provides the higher packet data transmission rates required by IMT-2000 and desired by wireless network operators.

The QUALCOMM CDMA system includes highly accurate time signals (usually referenced to a GPS receiver in the cell base station), so cell phone CDMA-based clocks are an increasingly popular type of radio clock for use in computer networks. The main advantage of using CDMA cell phone signals for reference clock purposes is that they work better inside buildings, thus often eliminating the need to mount a GPS antenna on the outside of a building.

This CDMA system is frequently confused with a similar but incompatible technology called wideband code division multiple access (W-CDMA) which forms the basis of the W-CDMA air interface. The W-CDMA air interface is used in the global 3G standard UMTS and the Japanese 3G standard FOMA, by NTT DoCoMo and Vodafone; however, the CDMA family of US national standards (including cdmaOne and CDMA2000) are not compatible with the W-CDMA family of International Telecommunication Union (ITU) standards.

Another important application of CDMA — predating and entirely distinct from CDMA cellular — is the global positioning system (GPS).

Coverage and applications

The size of a given cell depends on the power of the signal transmitted by the handset, the terrain, and the radio frequency being used. Various algorithms can reduce the noise introduced by variations in terrain, but require extra information be sent to validate the transfer. Hence, the radio frequency and power of the handset effectively determine the cell size. Long wavelengths need less energy to travel a given distance as compared to short wavelengths, so lower frequencies generally result in greater coverage while higher frequencies result in shorter coverage. These characteristics are used by mobile network planners in determining the size and placement of the cells in the network. In cities, many small cells are needed; the use of high frequencies allows sites to be placed more-closely together, with more subscribers being provided service. In rural areas with a lower density of subscribers, use of lower frequencies allows each site to provide broader coverage.

Various companies use different variants of CDMA to provide fixed-line networks using wireless local loop (WLL) technology. Since they can plan with a specific number of subscribers per cell in mind, and these are all stationary, this application of CDMA can be found in most parts of the world.

CDMA is suited for data transfer with bursty behaviour and where delays can be accepted. It is therefore used in wireless LAN applications; the cell size here is 500 feet because of the high frequency (2.4 GHz) and low power. The suitability for data transfer is the reason why

W-CDMA seems to be "winning technology" for the data portion of third-generation (3G) mobile cellular networks.

Code division multiplexing (Synchronous CDMA)

Synchronous CDMA, also known as code division multiplexing (CDM), makes use of the core mathematical properties of orthogonality. Let data signals be represented as vectors. For example, the binary string "1011" would be represented by the vector (1, 0, 1, 1), or the name **a**. An operation on vectors, known as the dot product, is used to "multiply" vectors, by summing the product of the components. The operation is denoted with a dot between the vectors. For example, the dot product of a=(1, 0, 1, 1) and b = (1, –1, –1, 0), written as a·b, would be (1) × (1) + (0) × (–1) + (1) × (–1) + (1) × (0) = 1 + (–1) = 0. For the special case when the dot product of two vectors is identically 0, the two vectors are said to be orthogonal to each other.

The dot product has a number of properties, which will aid in understanding how CDM works. For vectors **a**, **b**, **c**:

$a\cdot(b + c) = a\cdot b + a\cdot c$, and

$a\cdot kb = k(a\cdot b)$., where k is an arbitrary constant, and not a vector

The square root of a·a is a real number, and is called the magnitude of the vector a. It is denoted as

$$||a|| = \sqrt{a\cdot a}.$$

Suppose vectors **a** and **b** are orthogonal. Then:

a. $(a + b) = ||a||^2$ since $a\cdot a + a\cdot b = ||a||^2 + 0$,

a. $(-a + b) = ||a||^2$ since $-a\cdot a + a\cdot b = -||a||^2 + 0$,

b. $(a + b) = ||b||^2$ since $b\cdot a + b\cdot b = 0 + ||b||^2$,

b. $(a - b) = -||b||^2$ since $b\cdot a - b\cdot b = 0 - ||b||^2$.

Example

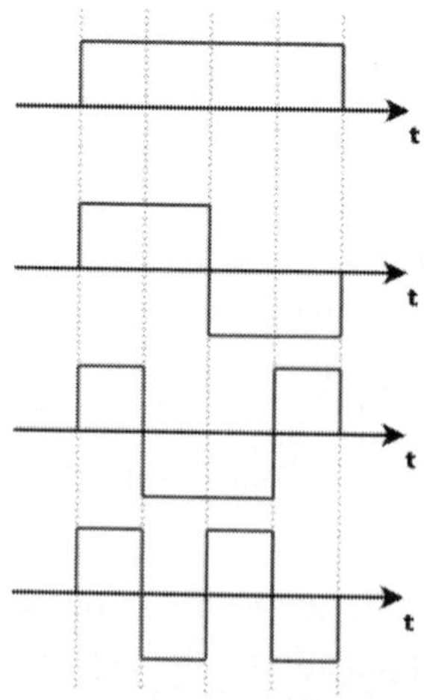

Fig. 3.3: ***An example of 4 orthogonal digital signals***

Suppose there is a set of vectors that are mutually orthogonal to each other. Usually these vectors are specially constructed for ease of decoding—they are columns or rows from Walsh matrices that are constructed from Walsh functions—but strictly mathematically, the only restriction on these vectors is that they are orthogonal. A vector from this set, say **v**, which is called the chip code is associated with one sender. A '0' digit is associated with the vector −**v**, and a '1' digit with the vector **v**. For example, if **v** = (1, −1), then the binary vector (1, 0, 1, 1) would correspond to (1, −1, −1, 1, 1, −1, 1, −1). In this book we call this constructed vector the transmitted vector.

Each sender has a different, unique vector chosen from that set, but the construction of the transmitted vector is identical.

The physical properties of interference also have to be considered. If two signals at a point are in phase, they will "add up" to give twice the amplitude of each signal, but if they are out of phase, they will "subtract" and give a signal that is the difference of the amplitudes. Digitally, this behaviour can be modelled simply by the addition of the transmission vectors, component by component. So, if there are two senders, both sending simultaneously, one with the chip code (1, −1) and data vector (1, 0, 1, 1), and the other with the chip code (1, 1), and data vector (0,0,1,1), the raw signal received would be the sum of the transmission vectors, i.e.,

$$(1,-1,-1,1,1,-1,1,-1) + (-1,-1,-1,-1,1,1,1,1) = (0,-2,-2,0,2,0,2,0).$$

Suppose a receiver gets such a signal, and wants to detect what the transmitter with chip code (1, −1) is sending. The receiver will make use of the property described in the above section, and take the dot product of the received vector in parts. First the first two components of the received vector are considered, i.e., (0, −2), and then (0, −2).(1, −1) = (0)(1) + (−2)(−1) = 2 is considered. Since this is positive, we can deduce that a '1' digit was sent. For the next two components, (−2, 0), (−2, 0).(1,−1) = (−2)(1)+(0)(−1) = −2, the dot products is negative, we can deduce that a '0' digit was sent. Continuing in this fashion, we can successfully decode what the transmitter with chip code (1, −1) was sending: (1, 0, 1, 1).

Likewise, applying the same process with chip code (1, 1): (1, 1).(0,−2) = −2 gives digit 0, (1, 1).(−2,0) = (1)(−2) + (1)(0) = −2 gives digit 0, and so on, to give us the data vector sent by the transmitter with chip code (1, 1): (0, 0, 1, 1).

Asynchronous CDMA

The previous example of orthogonal Walsh sequences describes how two users can be multiplexed together in a synchronous system, a technique that is commonly referred to as code division multiplexing (CDM). The set of 4 Walsh sequences shown in Figure 3.3 will afford up to 4 users, and in general, an NxN Walsh matrix can be used to multiplex N users. Multiplexing requires all the users to be coordinated so that each transmits their assigned sequence **v** (or the complement, −**v**) starting at exactly the same time. Thus, this technique finds use in base-to-mobile links, where all the transmissions originate from the same transmitter and can be perfectly coordinated.

On the other hand, the mobile-to-base links cannot be precisely coordinated, particularly due to the mobility of the handsets, and require a somewhat different approach. Since it is not mathematically possible to create signature sequences that are orthogonal for arbitrarily random starting points, unique "pseudo-random" or "pseudo-noise" (PN) sequences are used in asynchronous CDMA systems. These PN sequences are statistically uncorrelated, and the sum of a large number of PN sequences results in multiple access interference (MAI) that is approximated by a Gaussian noise process (via the theorem of the "law of large numbers" in statistics). If all of the users are received with the same power level, then the variance (e.g., the noise power) of the MAI increases in direct proportion to the number of users.

All forms of CDMA use the spread spectrum process gain to allow receivers to partially discriminate against unwanted signals. Signals with the desired chip code and timing are received, while signals with different chip codes (or the same spreading code but a different timing offset) appear as wideband noise reduced by the process gain.

Since each user generates MAI, controlling the signal strength is an important issue with CDMA transmitters. A CDM (synchronous CDMA), TDMA or FDMA receiver can in theory completely reject arbitrarily strong signals using different codes, time slots or frequency channels due to the orthogonality of these systems. This is not true for asynchronous CDMA, where rejection of unwanted signals is only partial. If any or all of the unwanted signals are much stronger than the desired signal, they will overwhelm it. This leads to a general requirement in any asynchronous CDMA system to approximately match the various signal power levels as seen at the receiver. In CDMA cellular, the base station uses a fast closed-loop power control scheme to tightly control each mobile's transmit power.

Advantages of asynchronous CDMA over other techniques

The main advantage of asynchronous CDMA over CDM (synchronous CDMA), TDMA and FDMA is that it can use the spectrum more efficiently in mobile telephony applications. TDMA systems must carefully synchronize the transmission times of all the users to ensure that they are received in the correct time slot and do not cause interference. Since this cannot be perfectly controlled in a mobile environment, each time slot must have a guard-time, which reduces the probability that users will interfere, but decreases the spectral efficiency. Similarly, FDMA systems must use a guard-band between adjacent channels, due to the random Doppler shift of the signal spectrum which occurs due to the user's mobility. The guard-bands will reduce the probability that adjacent channels will interfere, but decrease the utilization of the spectrum.

Most importantly, asynchronous CDMA offers a key advantage in the flexible allocation of resources. There are a fixed number of orthogonal codes, time-slots or frequency bands that can be allocated for CDM, TDMA and FDMA systems, which remain underutilized due to the bursty nature of telephony and packet data transmissions. There is no strict limit to the number of users that can be supported in an asynchronous CDMA system, only a practical limit governed by the desired bit error probability, since the signal to interference ratio (SIR) varies inversely with the number of users. In a bursty traffic environment like mobile telephony, the advantage afforded by asynchronous CDMA is that the performance (bit error rate) is allowed to fluctuate randomly, with an average value determined by the number of users multiplied by the percentage of utilization. Suppose there are $2N$ users that only talk half of the time, then $2N$ users can be accommodated with the same average bit error probability as N users that talk all of the time. The key difference here is that the bit error probability for N users talking all of the time is constant, whereas it is a random quantity (with the same mean) for $2N$ users talking half of the time.

In other words, asynchronous CDMA is ideally suited to a mobile network where large numbers of transmitters each generate a relatively small amount of traffic at irregular intervals. CDM (synchronous CDMA), TDMA and FDMA systems cannot recover the underutilized resources inherent to bursty traffic due to the fixed number of orthogonal codes, time slots or frequency channels that can be assigned to individual transmitters. For instance, if there are N time slots in a TDMA system and $2N$ users that talk half of the time, then half of the time there will be more than N users needing to use more than N time-slots. Furthermore, it would require significant overhead to continually allocate and deallocate the orthogonal code, time-slot or frequency channel resources. By comparison, asynchronous CDMA transmitters simply send when they have something to say, and go off the air when they don not, keeping the same PN signature sequence as long as they are connected to the system.

Soft handoff

Soft handoff (or soft handover) is an innovation in mobility. It refers to the technique of adding additional base stations (in IS-95 as many as 5) to a connection to be certain that the next base is ready as one moves through the terrain. However, it can also be used to move a call from one base station that is approaching congestion to another with better capacity. As a result, signal quality and handoff robustness is improved compared to TDMA systems.

In TDMA and analog systems, each cell transmits on its own frequency, different from those of its neighbouring cells. If a mobile device reaches the edge of the cell currently serving its call, it is told to break its radio link and quickly tune to the frequency of one of the neighbouring cells where the call has been moved by the network due to the mobile's movement. If the mobile is unable to tune to the new frequency in time the call is dropped.

In CDMA, a set of neighbouring cells all use the same frequency for transmission and distinguish cells (or base stations) by means of a number called the "PN offset", a time offset from the beginning of the well-known pseudo-random noise sequence that is used to spread the signal from the base station. Since all the cells are on the same frequency, listening to different base stations is now an exercise in digital signal processing based on offsets from the PN sequence, not RF transmission and reception based on separate frequencies.

As the CDMA phone roams through the network, it detects the PN offsets of the neighbouring cells and reports the strength of each signal back to the reference cell of the call (usually the strongest cell). If the signal from a neighbouring cell is strong enough, the mobile will be directed to "add a leg" to its call and start transmitting and receiving to and from the new cell in addition to the cell (or cells) already hosting the call. Likewise, if a cell's signal becomes too weak the mobile is directed to drop that leg. In this way, the mobile can move from cell to cell and add and drop legs as necessary in order to keep the call up without ever dropping the link.

It should be noted that this "soft handoff" does not happen via CDMA from cell tower to cell tower. A group of cell sites are linked up with wire and the call is synchronized over wire, over TDM, ATM, or even IP.

When there are frequency boundaries between different carriers or sub-networks, a CDMA phone behaves in the same way as TDMA or analog and performs a hard handoff in which it breaks the existing connection and tries to pick up on the new frequency where it left off.

Features of CDMA

- Narrowband message signal multiplied by wideband spreading signal or pseudonoise code
- Each user has his own pseudonoise (PN) code
- Soft capacity limit: system performance degrades for all users as the number of users increases
- Cell frequency reuse: no frequency planning needed
- Soft handoff increases capacity
- Near-far problem
- Interference limited: power control is required
- Wide bandwidth induces diversity: rake receiver is used

CDMA has been used in military systems for decades because it is secure. Unlike the present analog system and other digital systems, which divide the available spectrum into narrow channels and assign one or more conversations to each channel, CDMA is a wideband spread spectrum technology that spreads multiple conversations across a wide segment of the cellular broadcast spectrum. Each telephone or data call is assigned a unique code that permits it to be distinguished from the multitude of calls simultaneously transmitted over the same broadcast spectrum.

Note: For analog communications frequency division multiple access (FDMA) technology is used, in which the total bandwidth in divided into several parts and each user gets a separate bandwidth.

For digital communication we use technology

- Time division multiple access (TDMA)
- Frequency division multiple access (FDMA)

3.5.3.2 Time division multiple access (TDMA)

In TDMA, the total frequency is combined into band and this total frequency band is given to all users, i.e. one band is shared by a number of users. However this is not a powerful enough technology, so CDMA is preferred, in which each user is given the total bandwidth i.e., each user can access the complete bandwidth. This technology is based on the coding theory.

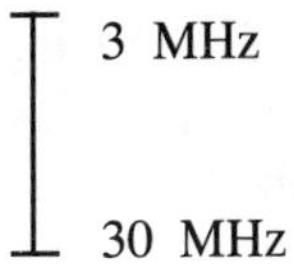

3 MHz

30 MHz

Bandwidth = 30-3 = 27 MHz
i.e., each user can access a bandwidth of 27 MHz

Fig. 3.4: ***Time division multiple access***

Time division multiple access (TDMA) is a technology for shared medium (usually radio) networks. It allows several users to share the same frequency by dividing it into different time-slots. The users transmit in rapid succession, one after the other, each using their own time-slot. This allows multiple users to share the same transmission medium (e.g. radio frequency) while using only the part of the bandwidth they require. TDMA is used in the global system for mobile communications (GSM), personal digital cellular (PDC) and iDEN digital cellular standards, among others. It is also used extensively in satellite systems, local area networks, physical security systems, and combat-net radio systems.

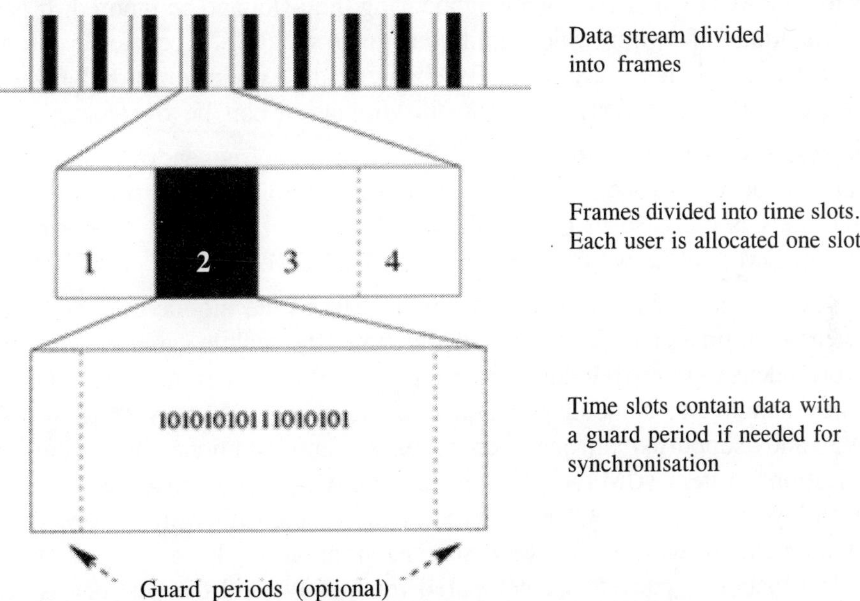

Fig. 3.5: ***TDMA frame structure showing a data stream divided into frames and those frames divided into time-slots***

TDMA is a type of time-division multiplexing, with the special feature that instead of having one transmitter connected to one receiver, there are multiple transmitters. In the case of the uplink from a mobile phone to a base station this becomes particularly difficult because the mobile phone can be moved around and this varies the timing advance required to make its transmission match the gap in transmission from its peers.

In the GSM system, the synchronization of mobile phones is achieved by sending timing advance commands from the base station which instructs the mobile phone to transmit earlier and by how much. This compensates for propagation delay as the speed of radio waves is the same as the speed of light (finite). The mobile phone is not allowed to transmit for its entire time-slot, but there is a guard interval at the end of each time-slot. As the transmission moves into the guard period, the mobile network adjusts the timing advance to synchronize the transmission.

Initial synchronization of a phone requires even more care. Before a mobile phone transmits there is no way of actually knowing the offset required. For this reason, an entire time-slot has to be dedicated to mobiles attempting to contact the network (known as the RACH in GSM). The mobile attempts to broadcast at the beginning of the time-slot, as received from the network. If the mobile is located next to the base station, there will be no time delay and this will succeed. If, however, the mobile phone is at a distance just less than 35 km from the base station, the time delay will mean the mobile's broadcast arrives at the very end of the time-slot. In that case, the mobile will be instructed to broadcast its messages starting nearly a whole time-slot earlier than would be expected otherwise. Finally, if the mobile is beyond the 35 km cell range in GSM, then the RACH will arrive in a neighbouring time-slot and be ignored. It is this feature, rather than limitations of power which limits the range of a GSM cell to 35 kilometers when no special extension techniques are used. By changing the synchronization between the uplink and downlink at the base station, however, this limitation can be overcome.

In radio systems, TDMA is almost always used alongside frequency division multiple access (FDMA) and frequency division duplex (FDD); the combination is referred to as FDMA/TDMA/FDD. This is the case in both GSM and IS-136 for example. The exceptions to this rule include WCDMA-TDD which combines FDMA/CDMA/TDMA and TDD instead.

A major advantage of TDMA is that the radio part of the mobile only needs to listen and broadcast for its own time-slot. For the rest of the time, the mobile can carry out measurements on the network, detecting surrounding transmitters on different frequencies. This allows safe inter frequency handovers, something which is difficult in CDMA systems, not supported at all in IS-95 and supported through complex system additions in a universal mobile telecommunications system (UMTS). This in turn allows for co-existence of microcell layers with macrocell layers. However, CDMA supports "soft hand-off" which allows a mobile phone to be in communication with up to 6 base stations simultaneously, a type of "same-frequency handover". The incoming packets are compared for quality, and the best one is selected. This enables CDMA to perform in areas where TDMA calls would be dropped.

A disadvantage of TDMA systems is that they create interference at a frequency which is directly connected to the time-slot length. This is the irritating buzz which can sometimes be heard if a GSM phone is left next to a radio or speakers. Another disadvantage is that the "dead time" between time-slots limits the potential bandwidth of a TDMA channel. This is why early efforts to incorporate time-slots into UMTS failed, leaving UMTS as a purely CDMA technology. The only country to continue pursuing TD-SCDMA (time division synchronous CDMA) is mainland China.

Features of TDMA

- Shares a single carrier frequency between multiple users
- Non-continuous transmission makes handoff simpler
- Slots can be assigned on demand
- Less stringent power control due to reduced interuser interference
- Higher synchronization overhead
- Equalization is necessary for high data rates
- Frequency/Slot allocation complexity
- Pulsating power envelop: Interference with other devices

Advantages

- Colliding frames are not garbled
- Multiple signals add linearly

This technique is also called spread spectrum i.e., one user is able to call on any bandwidth. Spectrum CDMA can be implemented by various techniques.

3.5.3.3 Frequency division multiple access

Frequency division multiple access or **FDMA** is an access technology that is used by radio systems to share the radio spectrum. The terminology "multiple access" implies the sharing of the resource amongst users, and the "frequency division" describes how the sharing is done by allocating different carrier frequencies of the radio spectrum to users.

In FDMA the given radio frequency (RF) bandwidth is divided into smaller frequency bands called subdivisions. Each subdivision has its own carrier frequency. A control mechanism is used to ensure that two or more earth stations do not transmit in the same subdivision at the same time. Essentially, the control mechanism designates a receive station for each of the subdivisions.

In demand assignment systems, the control mechanism is also used to establish or terminate the voice-band links between the source and destination stations. Consequently, any of the subdivisions is used by any of the participating earth stations at any given time. If each subdivision carries only one 4 KHz voice-band channel, it is known as a single-channel per carrier (SCPC) system.

When several voice-band channels are frequency division multiplexed to form a composite baseband signal comprising groups, super groups or even master groups, a wider subdivision is assigned. This is referred to as multiple-channel per carrier (MCPC).

FDMA also supports demand assignment besides fixed assignment. Demand assignment allows all users a continuous and equal access of the entire transponder bandwidth by assigning carrier frequencies on a temporary basis using a statistical assignment process. The first FDMA demand assignment system for satellites was developed by COMSAT for use on the Intelsat series IVA and V satellites.

In contrast to this methodology with time division multiple access (TDMA), where users are separated in time, other multiple access schemes such as code division multiple access (CDMA), where users are separated by codes; space division multiple access (SDMA); carrier sense multiple access (CSMA) and multi-frequency TDMA (MF-TDMA) also exist.

3.5.4 Applications of Mobile Computing in Business

Today's competitive business climate demands tools that allow users to work and communicate at their own convenience and discretion. It is not enough to have the newest tool. The investment in the new technology should yield an immediate benefit to its buyers without asking them to radically alter the way they live or do their work. This is the vision of mobile computing applications. It results in two alternatives.

- Remote communication
- Data access (Remote data access)

3.5.4.1 Remote communication

Real time communication has required people to structure their work and personal lives around a predetermined meeting place. The business terminology requires communication hubs (where all activities are centralized, e.g., colleges, which act as a communication hub to share knowledge).

When there is no need to be physically present at a particular place the whole time, people have more freedom to be more strategic, creative and flexible about how they make decisions and get things accomplished.

3.5.4.2 Remote data access

An important requirement of mobile computing is to allow workers to be as effective while at remote locations as they are in their usual offices when fully connected. This implies that traditional applications that assumed continuous connectivity must be redesigned to allow a disconnected mode of operation, e.g., a sales representative files an order on her laptop at a customer site. The client software in the laptop should store the transaction until the user is able to reconnect the laptop to the network upon re-connection, the transaction is forwarded to the application server in the network.

A growing list of applications are being built on the mobile computing infrastructure, they include:

1. Point of sale system
2. Inventory tracking and dispatching
3. Sales force automation
4. Package tracking and delivery services
5. Health care
6. Online transaction processing (OLTP)

3.6 MOBILE COMPUTING APPLICATION ISSUES

The programs used in mobile devices like mobile phones, laptops, palm computers, etc. for internet connectivity and other computer related activities are called mobile computing applications. The various issues and designs of mobile computing applications are discussed under the various headings given below.

Technical design

Technical design issues involve network design, capacity planning, response time calculations, data compression considerations, system availability design and security issues. The technical design plays a key role in a mobile computing project and offers unique challenges to the system professionals.

Network design

Issues regarding wireless LAN design and wide area radio network design, which comprise network design, are discussed below.

1. **Wireless LAN design issues**
   - The number of mobile users who will use wireless LAN and the number of them active during the peak period.
   - The types of LAN applications accessed by them. (Keeping in mind that wireless LANs will not be acceptable for the intended users as they operate at much slower speeds than wired LANs).
   - Use of notebook with a wireless NIC as a primary and user device.
   - Roaming areas, location and range of needed access point.
   - Impact of construction materials in single penetration.
   - Preferred technology-spread spectrum or frequency hopping.
   - Radio frequency interference from any other devices in an office, factory or campus etc.
2. **Wide area radio network design issues**
   - The need of building a private radio network.
   - Most appropriate radio network technology for the suite of applications.
   - Matching of user application-usage profiles to a given network capacity.
   - Integration of RNA technology with a radio network infrastructure.
   - Ensuring good coverage and minimum number of dead spots.
   - Managing the way logic networks will be influenced by network design options.

Capacity planning and response time calculations

A mobile computing application transaction has to cover a synchronous set of hardware as well as software components before it reaches the destination server. Diverse physical links, wireless and wired, between the end user's client application software and the information server are present in its reverse path too. So scheduling on a network requires complex rules, which makes it difficult to build a mathematical model to estimate response times. Planning reliable capacities in advance is a still harder task. The network providers give an estimate using complex queuing models or rule-of thumb calculation based on the other customer's experience.

Data compression considerations

As the bandwidth of wireless network is scarce and inexpensive it is necessary to compress data to get the maximum out of this bandwidth. This is usually done in the modem by going beyond the modem hardware in reducing the quantity of traffic on wireless networks using client application programs.

System availability design

Rather than continuing with the general base station hardware and network controllers, redundancy and message switches are typically built on fault-tolerant platforms. Public shared network providers must be approached for details of their redundancies. MCSS is another vital component that badly needs inbuilt redundancy.

Security issues

It is difficult to track whether information is accessed by unauthorized persons. Common security breaches of mobile computing applications include:

- Network by criminal elements.
- Physical breach of security at communication centres mainly unmanned base stations.
- Interception of credit card authorization over wireless network.

Careful security considerations including on-the-air encryption and firewalls must be used.

Other than technical design the next major issue in mobile computing application is ergonomics and logistics design where the designers evaluate the following:

- Form factor of end user device
- Battery life
- Input method - keyboard, pen, touch or voice
- Ruggedness
- Whether portable or fixed
- Safety and health issues

Mobile computing application deals with the future of computer usage and is therefore of great relevance.

3.7 MOBILE COMPUTING SOLUTIONS BENEFITS

Mobile computing solutions have benefits which basically come under two headings, namely tangible benefits and intangible benefits. Tangible benefits include those benefits that are easily quantifiable, while intangible benefits are those that are difficult to quantify.

To be more specific, tangible benefits can be put in quantitative terms, like economic benefits. Mobile computing solutions makes it possible to cut down on the professional's valuable time on administrative work. Boosting industrial productivity and sales per person are a few of the tangible benefits.

Tangible benefits also bring some added benefits like the maintenance of high order fulfilment ratio, considerable reduction in real time inventory cost through the timely placement of orders and the smooth flow of information. Mobile computing has also facilitated service vehicles with on-the-spot invoice production which brings in better cash flow with short payment cycle. The citation/ticketing application with credit card payment is a fine way to illustrate the tangible benefits of mobile computing.

The intangible benefits are difficult to quantify, they include automating sales, improving customer service or gaining competitive advantage. These must be converted into a percentage or should be handled with weights.

The intangible benefits of mobile computing solutions include a wide range of benefits namely,

- Enhanced business productivity through improving work efficiency by accessing more online resources.
- Quick execution of new procedures, pricing etc.
- Bringing PDA and other similar resources on line by unlocking the value in offline devices.
- Boosts information sharing between the workers, customers and partners which results in high quality decision making.
- Allows a firm to keep in touch with customers, which in turn results in sensing and responding to their requirements faster, thus providing better and prompter service.
- Rapid deployment in reaction to an event and fast reaction to adversity through multiple channels, which facilitates business resilience.
- Lowering the cost of ownership and increased productivity, retention of workers along with cultural improvement, by providing work with customized tools for appropriate information and by giving them flexibility to work.

Knowing the tangible and intangible benefits of mobile computing solutions will make decision making much easier.

3.8 MOBILE APPLICATION DEVELOPMENT PLATFORMS

Mobile application development platforms are aided by various specific as well as generic sets of tools. The various choices in development tools are as follows.

- Traditional Microsoft Windows 98 / 2000 / NT / XP tools.
- Palm OS Application Development tools: Java being the standard dominant application development tool for server side programming has made it easier to write safe and reliable code through features, like automatic memorizing and standard exception-handling. Java interfaces are supported by several application servers.

- Modern Application Server Tools offer application server solutions in a web environment based on conventional application servers and this extension is moulded for mobile applications and wireless networks.

3.8.1 Wireless Network Specific Development

Several mobile gateway vendors like IBM, Broad beam, Oracle, Sybase and Telecordia technologies offer mobile application development tool kits. Investigating specialized middleware for wireless and mobile applications are conducted to find the vendors who address all these requirements.

Data synchronization products

Numerous files & DBMS synchronization products are available to solve the problem of synchronizing information in notebook and PDAs with master information in the desktop or the server. Customization can be done through APIs.

With the various choices in development tools being furnished for mobile application development platforms, decisions regarding use of the same, become easier.

3.8.2 Mobile Application Development Strategies and Issues

Care needs to be taken regarding the following mobile application development strategies and issues, while choosing application development tools.

- Application design should be based on the concept of the nature of the users work profile and business process.
- The "client-agent-server" or "thin client-mobile server-enterprise server architectural paradigm should be considered seriously.
- Security matters like leakage, theft and fraud.
- Assess the pros and cons of Java based independent platform development versus platform specific development.
- Mobile applications must be at the foundation of internet development tools and current application servers.

Application development

Modern mobile application server tools

The tools which provide application server solutions in a web environment are based on conventional application servers. Some are extensions, while few others are specifically designed for mobile application and wireless networks.

1. IBMs AS/400 Mobile Application Development tools have their own development environment, which ensures easy and attractive integration.
2. Oracles Mobile Agents and Oracle Lite enable enterprises in developing mobile applications that run over a variety of wireless networks and dial-up LAN connections. Its 3-tiered clients/agents/server architecture replaces session-based connection

oriented computing with an asynchronous, store and forward messaging system. The Oracle mobile agents eliminate the need for constant connection.

3. Sybase's SQL Anywhere Studio is used for developing mobile applications. This software can reside on multiple server and client platforms.
4. Mobile application development strategies and issues and the respective server tools have been discussed briefly above. Being aware of them allows one to understand the various aspects and make decisions accordingly in an intelligent fashion.

3.8.3 Mobile Computing Solutions Costs

Mobile computing solutions costs can only be partly quantified. There are several aspects to it which are impossible to quantify.

1. **One-time capital expenditure**
   a) Hardware
      - Mobile workstation hardware (notebooks, handheld devices, Palm points)
      - Wireless radio modems - wireless LAN adapters, access points
      - Mobile communications server switch (MCSS) hardware and software
      - Hardware upgrade costs

   b) Software purchase or licensing fee
      - Shrink-wrap software license for end user device
      - Software for backend switch, network servers, application servers

   c) Software development or customization
      - Application development tools unique to mobile computing
      - Wireless communication software in the client device and servers
      - Software changes and enhancements

   d) Vertical or horizontal application package costs-per user dollar cost multiplied by the number of users
   e) Mobile application testing costs
   f) External consulting services
   g) End user documentation and training costs
   h) Project implementation - hardware and systems software installation cost
   i) Contingency - no estimate inclusive - allow 10-15% overrun

2. **Ongoing operations**
   a) Telecommunications network services—especially wireless network services.
   b) Computer processing and operation maintenance (hardware/software/equipment).
   c) Technical support (internal/external i.e. outsourced from external vendors) costs.

3. **Other costs (Intangible)**

   The risks of a mobile computing project are difficult to quantify. The actual mobile computing solutions cost is the sum of all the above. While developing a business case for a mobile computing project, both the cost and the benefit from undertaking such a project are analysed. Quantitative as well as qualitative analysis has to be carried out. The costs of hardware and software are much easier to estimate, compared to the application development, application integration and wireless network usage costs, which are difficult to predict.

3.8.4 Defining Mobile Computing Application Server

We define "mobile computing application server (MCAS or simple MAS)" as a software program which runs in a server and provides the following functionality:

- Application level logic that handles business functions involved in a particular organization (e.g. how to handle information requests from sales personnel in the field) and its integration with backend database or business application systems such as mainframe financial accounting systems, manufacturing systems, inventory, enterprise resource planning (ERP) and emerging customer resource management (ERP) systems.
- Presentation services for the mobile client device (handheld computers, notebooks, PDAs, etc) i.e. where the application server takes raw data from database applications/ queries and transforms the data on a specific thin client (or a thick client like a PC) considering its presentation space characteristics and limitations. This is also called graphical user interface (GUI) in some cases though some handheld devices are more like older text terminals than a PC. It includes breaking the messages into smaller chunks, filtering redundant information, and even logically compressing the data, etc.
- Transaction services, in some cases - including multi-threading for heavy volumes and persistency i.e. recovery across session failures.
- Application programming level interfaces (APIs) with specialized communications protocols.

An application server may be considered as part of a multi-tier (mostly three tier) architecture. Conventional tiers are:

1. First tier - A thin client based on handheld devices or a thick client on a PC - typically a browser-based interface in the Web context.
2. Middle tier - Consists of business applications on a set of servers - communications and business applications.
3. Third tier - Backend legacy data base systems and mission-critical ERP systems on a large server or mainframe.

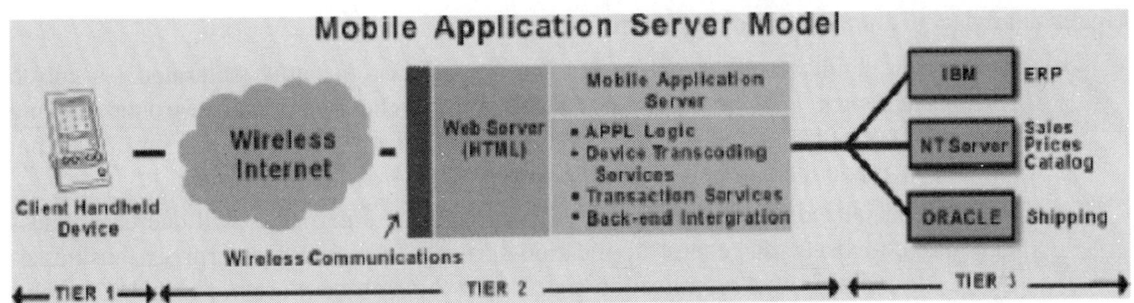

Fig. 3.6 *Mobile application server model*

All application servers are not the same and do not provide the same functionality. The actual implementations of an application server vary from one vendor to another. Some application servers are generic web servers with a systems development kit (SDK) or API capability to pull data from enterprise database systems and send them to a browser-based client software in a handheld device. Other application servers provide a business application with customization capability in a horizontal application, such as e-mail, sales force automation or field service representative computer-aided dispatch applications. Still other mobile application servers are based on WAP protocol. Depending on the heritage of the vendor and their core expertise, application servers can be categorized into the following broad classes:

- Generic application servers with a web-based SDK - e.g. Netscape, Microsoft, Sun, SilverStream, BEA - may have support for handheld devices and wireless networks strapped on (or bolted on) to the basic application server
- Database vendors' application servers - e.g. Oracle 9i and Sybase's iAnywhere Application server
- Data synchronization vendors - e.g. Puma, Synchrologic, Extended Systems
- Specialized mobile or web computing application servers - IBM's Web Sphere
- Mobile specific application servers - e.g. Aligo, Air2Web, Contec Mobile Application server (aimed at carriers), Aether System (aimed at enterprises)
- WAP-centric application servers - Nokia's WAP Server - not a true Application server, in IT sense
- E-mail centric application servers - Microsoft's Mobile Information server, Edge Mail Application Server

It is important to note that not all application servers are strong in all the functions that one may need in a general-purpose application server. Therefore, the key criteria that the application requires should be evaluated. As an example, the application server from Oracle may be strong on integration with databases but not necessarily as strong on interfaces with a variety of handheld devices and wireless networks. It may be the right choice if the environment is primarily Oracle-centric and it supports the particular device and network that has been chosen.

General advisory about mobile application servers

- The mobile application server market has already become quite saturated - a cue to startups is "pick a niche role, and develop the niche functionality around the big players' application servers (IBM, Netscape, Microsoft, Oracle and Sun). Do not become a me-to player and expect to survive" – *Mobile Info Editor*.
- Role of specialized mobile application servers in large enterprises will decrease unless they can co-exist with generic application servers. In medium enterprises businesses (MBE) and SOHO, these application-specific servers will be more popular. Ultimately, they will be grouped under the major generic application servers, MobileInfo.Com thinks.
- Transaction services are the key for future role in pervasive computing model of mobile applications.

List of popular application servers (alphabetical order)

1. **Aether Application Services**

   Aether Systems (merged with Riverbed) is an early leader in the exploding field of wireless data, providing real-time data communications and transactions services that operate over multiple wireless data networks, devices and back-end corporate data systems. In mobile information assessment, they do understand the requirements of a comprehensive and sophisticated application server in the wireless arena. They are now focusing on becoming a wireless application solution provider (ASP).

2. **Airtuit's BlueMoon Application Server**

   BlueMoon - A middleware application server for universal device access and backend application integration

3. **Aligo Application Server**

   Aligo - A Java-based mobile application server - utilities, healthcare, pharmaceutical, mobile workforce automation

4. **Contec's (started in 1999 - had a beta product in 2002) Mobile Application Server - aimed at carriers**

   Hornet - The Hornet carrier-class mobile application server is designed to fit within a mobile operator's network. It connects with all other elements of network infrastructure and can be deployed quickly and cost effectively.

5. **Edge Mail's Wireless Application Server**

   EdgeMail's application server is a Web based software application that provides forms management and improved business process over the Web. It is able to take the majority of business processes that currently require physical information submission and distribution and streamline the processes to online real-time processes conducted over the Web, with no physical exchange of hardcopy and without the time delay associated with the exchange of hardcopy.

6. **Hand Application Development Environment - Primarily a development platform**

   The @hand Mobile Application Server provides core infrastructure and support services including centralized administration, connectivity management, back-end systems integration, and data management. A subset of these core services resides locally on each deployed device through @hand Mobile Clients. The @hand Mobile Developer Studio provides a rapid application development environment that simplifies some of the complexity of creating mobile applications by providing a set of programming and data modelling tools (Visual Studio, Cod Warrior, and Satellite Forms).

7. **IBM's Web Sphere Application Server**

   IBM's Web Sphere Application Server pages are a part of its Enterprise Java Beans (EJB) environment. Mobile Info recommends serious evaluation of this product by users because it has the underpinnings of serious application server for large enterprises. However, user organizations must be ready to allocate enough resources to implement solutions based on this server.

8. **IBM's Domino-based Application Server for Mobile devices -** Domino is an application server that is centred around workgroup and e-mail-centric applications. IBM/Lotus and business partners have built support for handheld and Windows CE devices.

9. **Jacada Presentation Server for Palm**

   This server was announced in the early part of the year 2000 by Jacada, an Atlanta based company with development offices in Israel. It addresses the needs of bringing mission-critical information from enterprise systems to the Web through handheld devices.

10. **Microsoft Mobile Information Server**
11. **Nokia's WAP Application Gateway**
12. **Oracle's Mobile Application Server - A mobile Incarnation of 9i**
13. **Sybase's Mobile Application Studio 7.0**
14. **Every path Mobile Application Server**
15. **Air2Web's Application Server**
16. **Vision Air's Data Routing Engine (DRE)**
17. **Mobile Data Synchronization-Based Application Servers**

    There are a number of vendors who provide limited application server functionality through their synchronization engines. The following vendors are predominant among these:

18. **Extended Systems**

    Extended Systems offer a number of application server related functions

19. **Mobile Application Link (MAL)**

    Mobile Application Link is a communications standard for allowing handheld devices to exchange data and applications directly with centralized applications in the same way. It could be considered server implementation of Hot Synch or Active Synch technologies with the difference that original implementation of the above-mentioned technologies was meant to exchange data with desktop workstations - though enterprise or server-based extension of same technology is either available or will be available soon. Major vendors supporting MAL are AvantGo, Aether Systems, Attachmate, Certicom, Puma and others. Original code was developed by AvantGo but they have put the original version in public domain.

20. **Point Base Data Synchronization Server**

Point Base is offering a small footprint pure Java tools for developing embedded systems data management applications on the Internet. Point Base is headed by ex-Oracle executives. Therefore it has strong database heritage. Point Base Universal Synchronization Option (Point Base UniSynch option and Point Base Device Edition provide the basic framework.

21. **Puma**

Puma is offering MAL based server.

22. **Synchrologic's Application Server**

Synchrologic's iMobile Suite offers data management tools based on their synchronization engine. It provides file distribution, database replication and software distribution with a single interface.

23. **Exchange Lynx Servers from Jas Concepts**

Jas Concepts, Inc. develops middleware for distributed communications systems. They have announced development of Exchange Lynx Server based on Mobile Application Link standard. The Java-based plug-ins will support :

- data collection and routing
- web and software distribution
- connectivity to the back office
- profile management
- session reporting and monitoring

3.8.5 Mobile Computing Horizontal Application Index

While most of the success with mobile computing has, so far, been in the vertical industries, there are now a number of horizontal mobile computing applications that have become very popular among end users, and within all enterprises, large and small, across various vertical industries. Proliferation of the Internet and increasing reliance on the e-mail as the preferred method of communication has made wireless e-mail a major application. In fact, there is more activity in the internet-based horizontal application market now than ever before. We shall list these applications here:

3.8.5.1 Horizontal industry applications

Database query from a mobile device into an information server

The ability to access information from a DBMS server on a LAN, from a minicomputer, or from a mainframe is commonly requested by users of mobile computing.

Mobile data collection

These solutions are based on some sort of handheld device scanning information on an item. It is either stored locally or transmitted to a central processor. A number of vendors have been offering mobile data collection systems in various settings - from simple portable bar code readers to more sophisticated portable data terminals (PDTs) with RF capability that will read information from various devices and send this information automatically through wireless local area networks or wide area networks.

Internet messaging - Email, paging and others

Wireless-network-based e-mail has become a popular application on the various handheld devices, (Rim's Blackberry, Palm Pilot, Handspring's Visor and Pocket PC devices) and smart phones. In order to provide a high level of customer service, mobile workers and professionals must stay in touch with their home, offices and customers. They must respond to urgent e-mails from the field directly. This is possible only through wireless network support.

There are two types of network implementations for wireless e-mail:

- On-request connection - e-mail is pulled by the end user when he/she connects to the ISP or corporate e-mail server where mail resides
- Always-connected - like RIM's Blackberry implementation - e-mail is pushed to the Blackberry device as soon as it is received.

Electronic messaging via paging

One-way paging, text messaging and now two-way interactive paging (from RIM's Blackberry and Motorola's interactive paging devices) are inexpensive ways of keeping in touch with the head office and your corporate e-mail systems.

Instant messaging

Another implementation of wireless e-mail is based on instant messaging where the recipient is on-line and you can interact with him/her in "almost real-time" mode.

Field document distribution

Mobile professionals, especially sales professionals, need to send various documents, sales literature, or standard template-based but personalized letters to their clients while they are still in the field. In the past, this could be done only by coming back to the office. Several vendors have started offering this functionality from the field without the sales professional ever going back to the office. By using specific commands and address information, documents and even e-mail attachments can be sent to the clients without ever going back to the office. The field document distribution is shown in Figure 3.7.

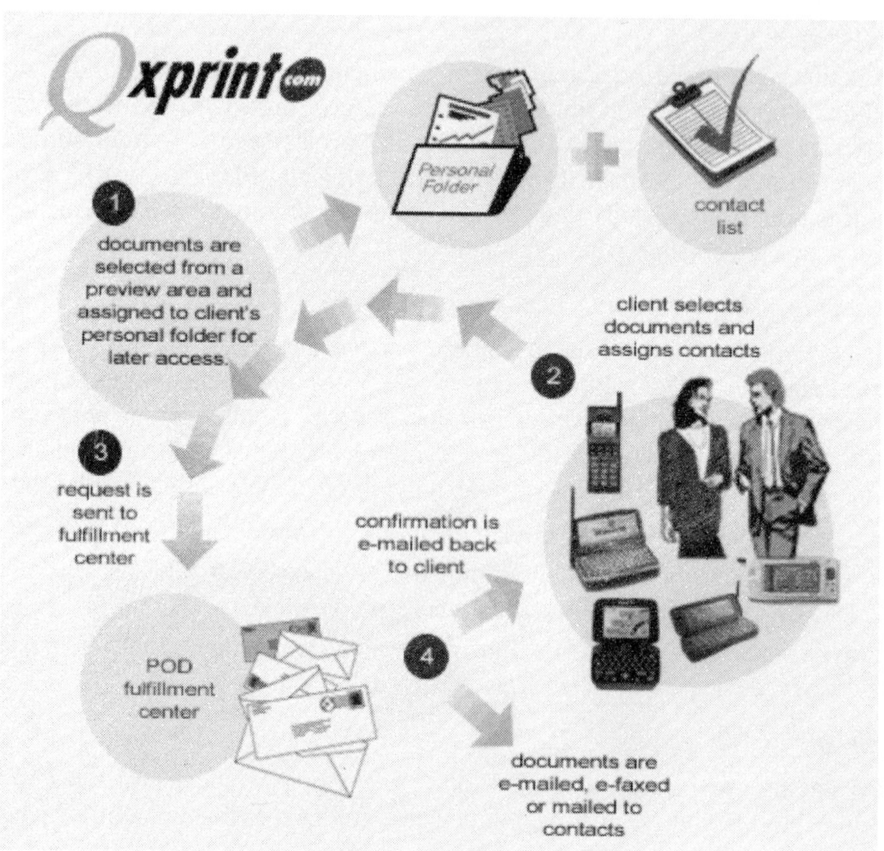

Fig. 3.7: ***Field Document distribution***

Field service dispatch applications

One of the most popular applications of mobile computing is field force automation. Traditional methods of service dispatch rely on receiving service requests at a central service centre and then a service supervisor decides which service representative will service which call. This approach has many problems - lack of responsiveness, inability to change schedules when travelling, delays in ordering parts from the field electronically and having to complete the transaction only on return to the office. A number of companies have relied on computer-aided dispatch for many years.

While pagers and cellular phones have been and are still being used for communication between field service people and the dispatch centre, much greater productivity gains can be achieved by computer-aided dispatch and giving handheld devices to service personnel. Data on work completed, time spent on each job and materials used can be entered into an automated system on the spot. Spare parts can be ordered automatically. Based on this collection of data in the field, the dispatch centre supervisors can keep track of service personnel. They can re-assign personnel to higher priority jobs or where there are customer complaints.

Many classic case studies exist for organizations, such as IBM, Xerox, Sears and others where thousands of service personnel use handheld computers or notebooks to order parts, record work completion details and then transmit this information through wireless networks.

A more recent trend is to equip field force with handheld devices (PDAs) with wireless network connectivity. A number of companies offer complete solutions for this application, which can be employed by any industry.

Field service audit and inspection application

There are many situations where head-office staff needs to carry out on-site field audits. In such a scenario, a field auditor can carry a notebook connected to a client-information database. The following examples illustrate this type of implementation:

- IRS and tax audits by central or state government.
- Financial audits in the field by accounting firms.
- Site inspections by building permit inspectors.
- Environmental control inspections.
- Automobile insurance adjusters.

Field sales force automation

Almost every vertical industry sales force must stay in constant touch with their sales force, access corporate and client information while on the road and submit sales orders without returning to the office. This improves the productivity of the sales force and provides superior customer service because inventory can be committed in real time and the shipping process can start immediately. Process time improvements can result in very significant ROI. There are a number of sales force application packages that have remote access capability - mostly through a wire-line connection but in some cases, through wireless networks as well.

A second field force application that has attracted the attention of mobile computing enthusiasts is the service and dispatch application. The functional objective is to monitor the whereabouts of service representatives, collect information about the completion of the service call wirelessly and then be able to dispatch them electronically to the next call.

A third general application in this area is time and expense entry for field assignments whereby this information can be recorded in the field and sent electronically. Therefore all manual paper-based record entry processes can be replaced by electronic processes - saving time, reducing errors and faster billing.

File transfer, database synchronization and systems management

This is a generic horizontal industry application that enables mobile computers to transfer and synchronize a variety of files with those in the corporate computers. The following are typical examples of synchronizing files between mobile devices (notebooks, PDAs, and handheld devices):

- Application programs have to be updated as new versions come along
- Sales professionals need to update price and rate files on a regular basis

- Insurance professionals need most current rate files
- Update standard documentation in the field

Wireless customer response management (CRM) application (also see sales force automation)

Customer Resource Management (CRM) relates to the IT discipline that deals with keeping track of customers' purchases, preferences, ability to respond to their queries quickly and provide a high level of service using modern technology tools, including a web-interface, e-commerce, data mining, and business intelligence.

Wireless CRM is an enhancement to core CRM applications and systems so that a firm can interact with customers anywhere, any time.

Issues

- Bandwidth network bandwidth limitations. Mobile Information advises careful design of user interface, dialogue and application data flow.
- Support for multiple devices. You can not control the type of devices that customers will buy. Mobile Information recommends that vendors should support most common devices and utilize handheld data transformation software that will support multiple devices.
- Transaction recovery is important.
- Security is extremely important.
- Support for modern payment systems besides conventional credit cards.

Wireless ERP

Enterprise resource management (ERP) systems relate to the IT discipline that deals with keeping fundamental business processes of a company - whether they deal with manufacturing automobiles or providing financial services to its customers.

Wireless ERP is an enhancement to core ERP applications and systems so that mobile sales force and customer service personnel can interact with this information from anywhere, at any time.

Issues

- Bandwidth network bandwidth limitations. Mobile Information advises careful design of user interface, dialogue and application data flow.
- Support for multiple devices. It may not be possible to always control the type of devices that different sets of employees buy. Mobile Information recommends that vendors should support most common devices and utilize handheld data transformation software that will support multiple devices.
- Message and transaction recovery (called message persistency in technical terms) from handheld devices and wireless networks is extremely important.
- Security is extremely important.
- Well-designed integration with in-house ERP systems is extremely important.

Others applications are:

- Mobile data collection
- Online and distance learning using wireless technology
- Wireless phone office applications
- Wireless workgroup applications
- Wireless internet infrastructure services - Content adaptation and delivery

Mobile Computing Vertical Application Index

Airlines and railways

- Access reservation, flight schedules and ticketing information (e.g. changing flight bookings while travelling, frequent-flyer program enquiries) by busy travellers using handheld devices, especially Palm Pilots.
- Virtual check-in for regular customers.
- Airline baggage and cargo control.
- Flight arrival and departure information while travelling to the airport.
- By airline maintenance staff - fuelling and de-icing information and baggage handling information.
- Easier, faster and quicker checking in of baggage by scanning bar-coded information from baggage tickets directly into a database.
- Pen-based work order application using a wireless local area data network.
- Airport security and monitoring

SUMMARY

- M-commerce has been recognized as an extension of e-commerce. Although similarities with e-commerce are recognized, m-commerce should be acknowledged as a business opportunity with its own distinctive characteristics and functions (Müller-Veerse et al., 2001), resulting from unique advantages wireless technology holds over wired technology.
- A variety of mobile services have already been developed and these types of services are likely to expand through the introduction of alleged "third generation" (3G) services that emerge as new wireless technologies such as GRPS and UMTS are implemented.
- Mobile computing means different things to different people. The key feature of the mobile computing environment is that the user need not maintain a fixed position in the network. The terms wireless and mobile are not synonymous. Wireless is a transmission or information transport method that enables mobile computing.
- D- commerce ie. Digital commerce is the next Avatar of Internet enabled commerce. D-commerce is the mgt of transactions and workflow associated with digital content to enable commerce. In d-commerce the entire process is digital.
- **Code division multiple access (CDMA)** is a form of multiplexing (not a modulation

scheme) and a method of multiple access that does not divide up the channel by time (as in TDMA), or frequency (as in FDMA), but instead encodes data with a special code associated with each channel and uses the constructive interference properties of the special codes to perform the multiplexing.

- In TDMA, the total frequency is not divided into separate but it combines into one. And in TDMA the one frequency (total frequency) band is given to all users i.e. One band is shared by *n* number of users. It is not enough powerful technology, so we next use CDMA. Example: Reliance used CDMA technology.
- **Frequency Division Multiple Access** or **FDMA** is an access technology that is used by radio systems to share the radio spectrum. The terminology "multiple access" implies the sharing of the resource amongst users, and the "frequency division" describes how the sharing is done: by allocating users with different carrier frequencies of the radio spectrum.
- Real time communication has required people to structure their work and personal lives around a predetermined meeting place. The business terminology requires communication hubs (where all activity are centralized, example – College act as communication hub, just to share knowledge)

REVIEW QUESTIONS

1. What is different about M-commerce? In particular, what is special about mobile devices that will not only enable new services but also pose challenges in developing these services?
2. What were the key business factors/decisions, technology choices, and country specific factors behind i-Mode's success and why?
3. What were the key challenges for DoCoMo moving forward, both in Japan as well as globally? What would be your recommendations for DoCoMo?
4. Will wireless services take off outside Japan? In particular, what do you see as the main issues that may impede widespread adoption of wireless services worldwide?
5. What are banks' objectives in pursuing a strong mobile presence?
6. What should be CIBC's wireless technology strategy and why? It would help to consider the following questions. What components should CIBC's wireless technology portfolio include? What are the options available in each? What are the advantages/disadvantages of these options?
7. How important are micro-payment systems to mobile commerce? When (and why) would a customer choose to pay through a mobile device instead of other means (e.g., credit card or merchant account)?
8. How do mobile payment solutions create value for various players? What are the impediments to the wholesale adoption of mobile payment solutions?
9. What are the advantages of Paybox in the mobile payment market? What are the impediments to the continued success of Paybox (beyond the issues faced by mobile payment itself)?

CHAPTER 4

Cellular Communication

A cellular mobile communications system uses a large number of low-power wireless transmitters to create cells—the basic geographic service area of a wireless communications system. Variable power levels allow cells to be sized according to the subscriber density and demand within a particular region. As the signals from mobile users travel from cell to cell, the conversations are handed off between cells to maintain seamless service. Channels (frequencies) used in one cell can be reused in another cell some distance away. Cells can be added to accommodate growth, creating new cells in unserved areas or overlaying cells in existing areas.

Cellular radio was originally targeted at vehicular subscribers in urban areas. Today, the industry is moving simultaneously in three directions –

1. Increasing capability and widespread coverage for cordless telephones.
2. Decreasing cell size and power levels for hand-held and vehicular cellular radio.
3. Specialized wireless data systems.

In cellular systems, the areas of coverage are divided into hexagonal cells that overlap at the outer boundaries. Communication takes place through a grid of transmitters and receivers, each one called a cell.

A signal from a cellular hand set is handled by the nearest cell, which passes the signal along normal telephone lines. The average cell is 1-20 km across, with actual size depending on the number of users in the cell. The greater the number of users, the closer the transmitters and hence there is a reduction in cell size. Cellular communication requires careful monitoring and switching of calls from cell to cell as the user moves between them. Without dynamic switching to facilitate a smooth transmission, the calls would be terminated as the user crosses the boundary of a cell.

4.1 PRINCIPLES OF MOBILE COMMUNICATIONS

Each mobile uses a separate, temporary radio channel to talk to the cell site. The cell site talks to many mobiles at once, using one channel per mobile. Channels use a pair of frequencies for communication — one frequency (the forward link) for transmitting from the cell site and one frequency (the reverse link) for the cell site to receive calls from the users. Radio energy dissipates over distance, so mobiles must stay near the base station to maintain communications. The basic structure of mobile networks includes telephone systems and radio services. Where a mobile radio service operates in a closed network and has no access to the telephone system, a mobile telephone service allows interconnection to the telephone network (see *Figure 4.1*).

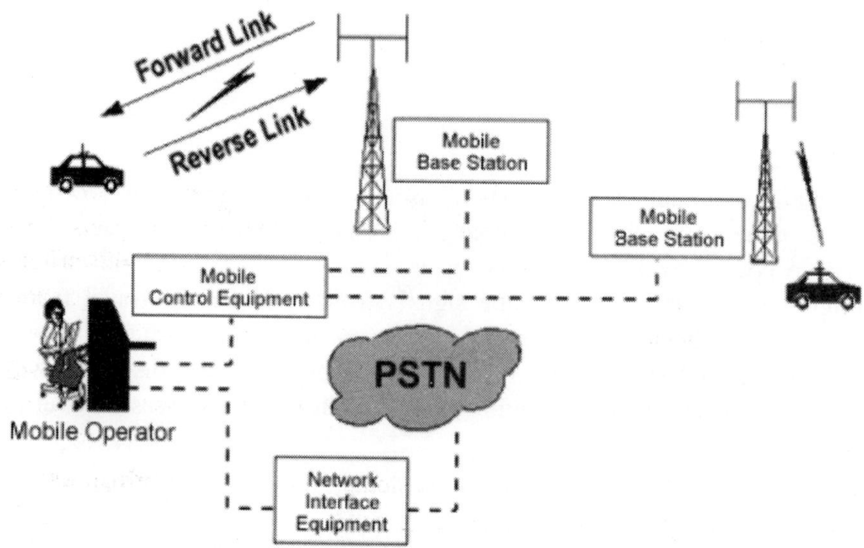

Fig. 4.1: ***Basic mobile telephone service network.***

4.1.1 Early Mobile Telephone System Architecture

Traditional mobile service was structured in a fashion similar to television broadcasting: One very powerful transmitter located at the highest spot in an area would broadcast over a radius of up to 50 km. The cellular concept structured the mobile telephone network in a different way. Instead of using one powerful transmitter, many low-power transmitters were placed throughout a coverage area. For example, by dividing a metropolitan region into one hundred different areas (cells) with low-power transmitters using 12 conversations (channels) each, the system capacity theoretically could be increased from 12 conversations — or voice channels using one powerful transmitter — to 1,200 conversations (channels) using one hundred low-power transmitters. *Figure 4.2* shows a metropolitan area configured as a traditional mobile telephone network with one high-power transmitter.

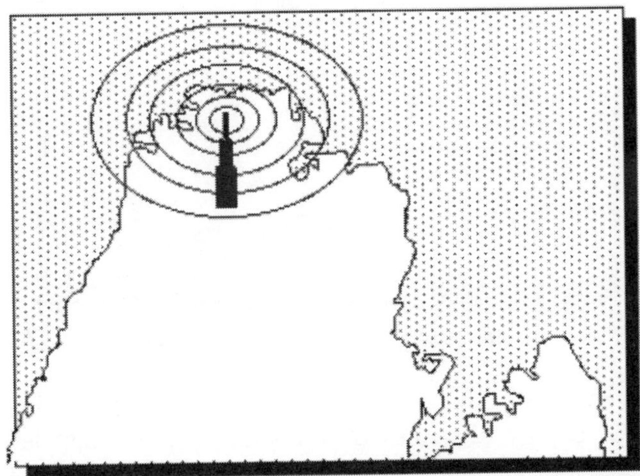

Fig. 4.2: ***Early mobile telephone system architecture***

4.1.2 Mobile Telephone System Using the Cellular Concept

Interference problems caused by mobile units using the same channel in adjacent areas proved that all channels could not be reused in every cell. Areas had to be skipped before the same channel could be reused. Even though this affected the efficiency of the original concept, frequency reuse was still a viable solution to the problems of mobile telephony systems.

Engineers discovered that the interference effects were not due to the distance between areas, but to the ratio of the distance between areas to the transmitter power (radius) of the areas. By reducing the radius of an area by 50 percent, service providers could increase the number of potential customers in an area fourfold. Systems based on areas with a one-kilometre radius would have a hundred times more channels than systems with areas 10 kilometres in radius. Speculation led to the conclusion that by reducing the radius of the areas to a few hundred meters, millions of calls could be served.

The cellular concept employs variable low-power levels, which allow cells to be sized according to the subscriber density and demand of a given area. As the population grows, cells can be added to accommodate that growth. Frequencies used in one cell cluster can be reused in other cells. Conversations can be handed off from cell to cell to maintain constant phone service as the user moves between cells (see *Figure* 4.3).

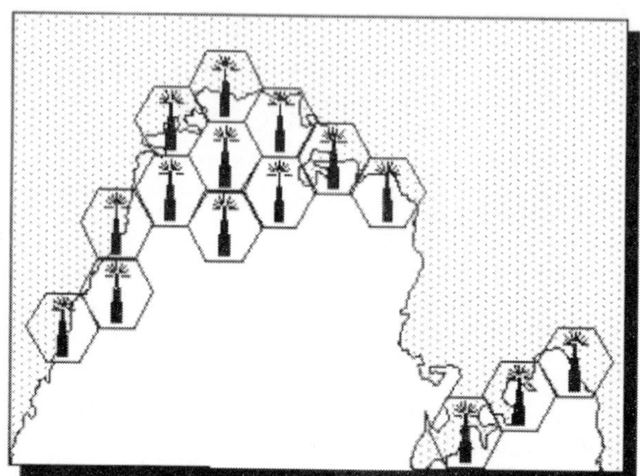

Fig. 4.3: ***Mobile telephone system using a cellular architecture***

The cellular radio equipment (base station) can communicate with mobiles as long as they are within range. Radio energy dissipates over distance, so the mobiles must be within the operating range of the base station. Like the early mobile radio system, the base station communicates with mobiles via a channel. The channel consists of two frequencies, one for transmitting to the base station and one to receive information from the base station.

4.2 CELLULAR SYSTEM ARCHITECTURE

Increases in demand and the poor quality of existing service led mobile service providers to research ways to improve the quality of service and to support more users in their systems. Due to fact that the width of the frequency spectrum available for mobile cellular use was limited, efficient use of the required frequencies was needed for mobile cellular coverage. In modern cellular telephony, rural and urban regions are divided into areas according to specific provisioning guidelines. Deployment parameters, such as amount of cell-splitting and cell sizes, are determined by engineers experienced in cellular system architecture.

Provisioning for each region is planned according to an engineering plan that includes cells, clusters, frequency reuse and handovers.

Cells

A cell is the basic geographic unit of a cellular system. The term *cellular* comes from the honeycomb shape of the areas into which a coverage region is divided. Cells are base stations transmitting over small geographic areas that are represented as hexagons. Each cell size varies depending on the landscape. Because of constraints imposed by natural terrain and man-made structures, the true shape of cells is not a perfect hexagon.

Clusters

A cluster is a group of cells. No channels are reused within a cluster. *Figure 4.4* illustrates a seven-cell cluster.

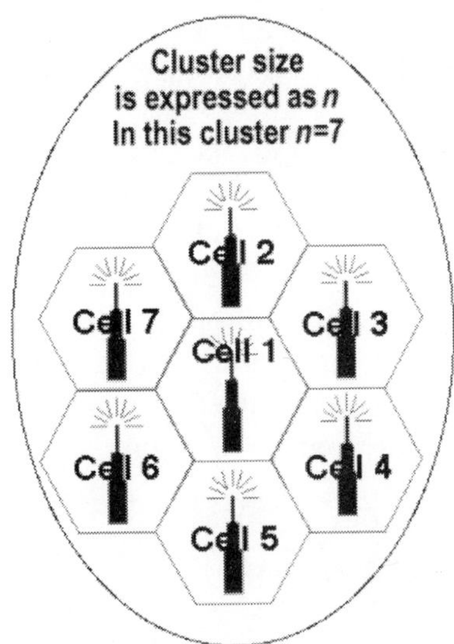

Fig. 4.4: *A seven-cell cluster*

Frequency Reuse

Since only a small number of radio channel frequencies were available for mobile systems, engineers had to find a way to reuse radio channels to carry more than one conversation at a time. The solution the industry adopted was called frequency planning or frequency reuse. Frequency reuse was implemented by restructuring the mobile telephone system architecture into the cellular concept.

The concept of frequency reuse is based on assigning to each cell, a group of radio channels used within a small geographic area. Cells are assigned a group of channels that is completely different from neighbouring cells. The coverage area of cells is called the footprint. This footprint is limited by a boundary so that the same group of channels can be used in different cells that are far enough away from each other so that their frequencies do not interfere (see *Figure 4.5*).

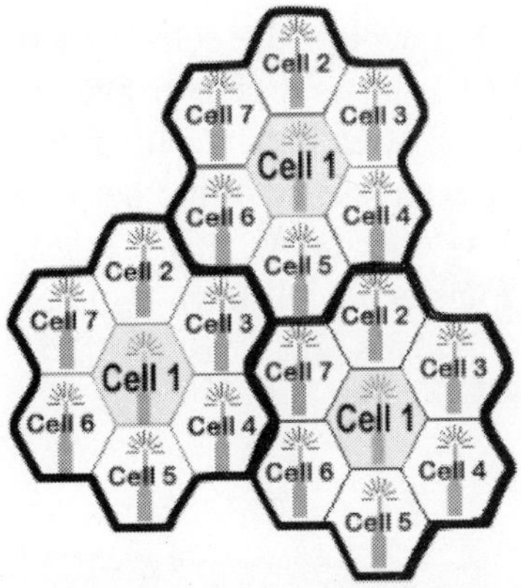

Fig. 4.5: *Frequency reuse*

Cells with the same number have the same set of frequencies. Here, because the number of available frequencies is 7, the frequency reuse factor is 1/7. That is, each cell is using 1/7th of the available cellular channels.

Cell Splitting

Unfortunately, economic considerations made the concept of creating full systems with many small areas impractical. To overcome this difficulty, system operators developed the idea of cell splitting. As a service area becomes full of users, this approach is used to split a single area into smaller ones. In this way, urban centres can be split into as many areas as necessary to provide acceptable service levels in heavy-traffic regions, while larger, less expensive cells can be used to cover remote rural regions (see *Figure 4.6*).

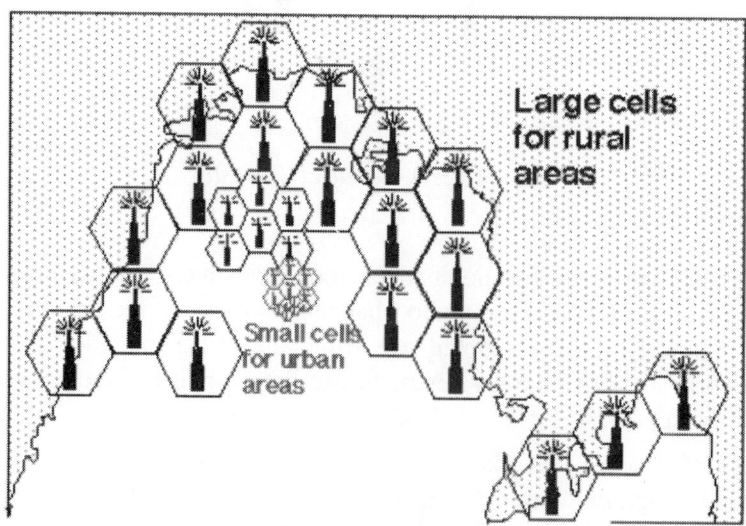

Fig. 4.6: *Cell splitting*

Handoff

The final obstacle in the development of the cellular network involved the problem created when a mobile subscriber travelled from one cell to another during a call. As adjacent areas do not use the same radio channels, a call must either be dropped or transferred from one radio channel to another when a user crosses the line between adjacent cells. Because dropping the call is unacceptable, the process of handoff was created. Handoff occurs when the mobile telephone network automatically transfers a call from radio channel to radio channel as a mobile user crosses adjacent cells (see *Figure 4.7*).

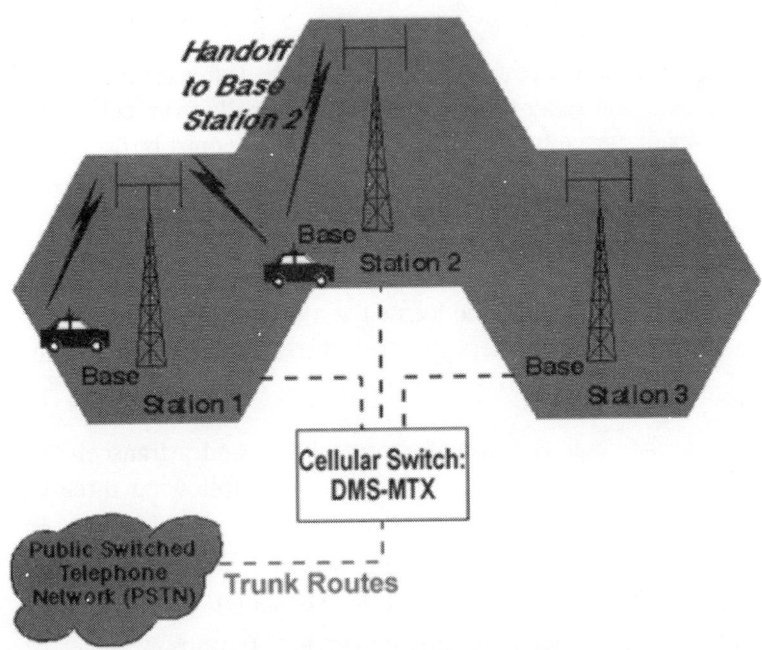

Fig. 4.7: ***Handoff between adjacent cells***

During a call, two parties are on one voice channel. When the mobile unit moves out of the coverage area of a given cell site, the reception becomes weak. At this point, the cell site in use requests a handoff. The system switches the call to a stronger-frequency channel in a new site without interrupting the call or alerting the user. The call continues as long as the user is talking, and the user does not notice the handoff at all.

4.3 CELLULAR SYSTEM COMPONENTS

The cellular system offers mobile and portable telephone stations the same service provided to fixed stations over conventional wired loops. It has the capacity to serve tens of thousands of subscribers in a major metropolitan area. The cellular communications system consists of the following four major components that work together to provide mobile service to subscribers.

- Public switched telephone network (PSTN)
- Mobile telephone switching office (MTSO)
- Cell site with antenna system
- Mobile subscriber unit (MSU)

PSTN

The PSTN is made up of local networks, the exchange area networks, and the long-haul network that interconnects telephones and other communication devices on a worldwide basis.

Mobile Telephone Switching Office (MTSO)

The MTSO is the central office for mobile switching. It houses the mobile switching centre (MSC), field monitoring, and relay stations for switching calls from cell sites to wireline central offices (PSTN). In analogue cellular networks, the MSC controls the system operation. The MSC controls calls, tracks billing information, and locates cellular subscribers.

The Cell Site

The term *cell site* is used to refer to the physical location of radio equipment that provides coverage within a cell. A list of hardware located at a cell site includes power sources, interface equipment, radio frequency transmitters and receivers, and antenna systems.

Mobile Subscriber Units (MSUs)

The mobile subscriber unit consists of a control unit and a transceiver that transmits and receives radio transmissions to and from a cell site. The following three types of MSUs are available:

- The mobile telephone (typical transmit power is 4.0 watts)
- The portable (typical transmit power is 0.6 watts)
- The transportable (typical transmit power is 1.6 watts)

The mobile telephone is installed in the trunk of a car, and the handset is installed in a location convenient to the driver. Portable and transportable telephones are hand-held and can be used anywhere. The use of portable and transportable telephones is limited to the charge life of the internal battery.

4.4 WIRELESS PACKET DATA NETWORKS

Most wireless data schemes use "packet" techniques for transferring data; packet radio is a communication method that transmits packets of data over a network via RF signals. It is the packet radio networks that have become the most closely associated with wireless technology.

Packet radio technology has the following advantages:

i) The frequencies are less susceptible to interference and noise than cellular signals.
ii) Transmission costs are based on data packets.
iii) No connect time.
iv) There are no roaming charges.

Types of wireless: The major types of wireless that are getting the most attention these days include the following:

- Wireless Local Area Networks (LANs)
  - 802.11b (sometimes called wireless Ethernet)
  - 802.11a, HiPerLAN II, and HomeRF (alternatives to 802.11b)
- Fixed Broadband Wireless Multiservice Wide Area Networks (WANs)
  - MMDS and LMDS
  - Small Dish Satellite

- Mobile Wireless (voice/telephony with increasing integration of data and video)
- Wireless Personal Area Networks
  - Based on Bluetooth™ technologies

Wireless LANs are slowly but surely starting to take hold in homes, small businesses and corporations. An 802.11b Network Interface Card (NIC) costs about Rs. 5,000. When compared to the cost of wiring up a cubicle and the inflexibility of that wired connection, it is easy to see why people are gravitating towards wireless LANs. Performance ranges from standard Ethernet performance down to perhaps 2 Mbps if there is significant interference or if the user strays too far away from an access point. If the NIC and access point support roaming, a user can wander around a building or campus and the NIC will automatically switch between access points based on the strength of the beacon signal it receives from nearby access points. The strongest signal prevails. Access points cost anywhere from Rs. 10,000 to Rs. 40,000, depending on features supported. Access points connect to the wired LAN so that users have complete connectivity.

Fixed wireless WANs: With the race on to be the access method of choice for that dreaded last mile of connectivity (sometimes also referred to as first mile and local loop), reaching into a home or office, wireless is fast becoming a viable alternative to (wired) DSL, cable and fibre optic. This avoids the problems of obtaining the right of way from a central office into a house or office, and stringing wires (copper or fibre) across miles and miles of territory. Today, there are technologies emerging that take advantage of line of site transmission capabilities long thought out of date. Whereas line of site technology was more often than not "point to point," today's advances allow for point to multipoint, providing a much more cost effective service. Some of these technologies can even support obstructed transmission paths, more common to typical communities.

The small dish satellite TV: These small businesses have also started offering Internet access. Many of them provide downlink speeds of nearly 1 Megabit per second. Uplinks, in many cases, are provided via a separate telephone line at 56k speeds. The assumption is that much of the traffic is coming from the Internet. The landline helps make up for the delay it would take for keystrokes and mouse clicks to travel all the way up to the satellite and back to the Internet.

Mobile wireless: Another form of wireless involves the ability to move just about anywhere, while still remaining connected to the Internet or the company Intranet. Mobile phones are also becoming portable Internet terminals, with content specifically designed to fit into those little windows. The same principle applied to a PDA or laptop opens up manifold possibilities. People are already using mobile Internet access although the speeds started out as somewhat painfully slow (compared to LAN connections). However, the new 3G (Third Generation) promises mobile speeds of 300 kbps and higher.

Personal area networks (PANs): The term, personal area network (PAN), is used when talking about very small area, low-power radio transmission-based networking systems like Bluetooth. At 1 Megabit per second or below, with distance limits of about 10 metres, and incredibly low power requirements, Bluetooth chips at under Rs. 250 a chip will soon be found in virtually every kind of technology imaginable. Soon a PDA, mobile phone, computer, desktop phone and watch will all be able to share schedule and contact information just by being anywhere near each other, e.g., a PDA will also be able to check out all the services available when a person is in an airport and get instant updates on flight information.

Integrating both mobile and fixed: The hope is that a person will be able to eventually walk around with a machine (laptop, PDA, phone, etc.) and no matter where he or she is, there will always be a connection to "the net." It may eventually be possible to power a laptop at home in the morning, and check one's e-mail from work. Here, there would be a wireless connection from the PC's wireless card connecting through a residential gateway inside the house. It connects to a fixed wireless gateway with a receiver outside a window, which connects the house to an antenna. Since one is connecting to an office, a virtual private network connection is created so that it is possible to securely access the company LAN and one's email. The disadvantage is that communication is slow because all users share bandwidth over a particular network.

4.5 SATELLITE NETWORKS

A satellite communication system, distinguished by its global coverage, inherent broadcast capability, bandwidth-on-demand flexibility, and the ability to support mobility, is an excellent candidate to provide broadband integrated Internet services to globally scattered users. A satellite system, if properly designed, can cover the entire surface of the Earth, making it extremely appealing to aeronautical and maritime users, and to those in remote areas lacking terrestrial communication infrastructure. Even for the densely wired parts of the world, it offers an alternative to the increasingly congested terrestrial links. A satellite network is inherently a broadcast system. It is particularly attractive to point-to-multipoint and multipoint-to-multipoint communications, which are experiencing rapid development, especially in broadband multimedia applications. Satellite networks can serve as broadband access networks, high-speed backbone networks connecting heterogeneous networks, or simply as communication links between users with fixed or mobile terminals.

However, the interoperation between a satellite system and the existing terrestrial Internet infrastructure introduces new challenges. Here, we attempt to survey ongoing research efforts on integrating satellite systems into the global Internet, clarify the crucial technical difficulties and provide insights for further research. In the next section we present the basic background on satellite systems and the satellite-based Internet architectures. Several technical issues in constructing satellite-based Internet and some suggested solutions are discussed. Finally we give a summary and identify some future research directions.

Satellite networks allow global communications and serve thousands of locations all over the world. Satellite networks are ideal for broadcast applications, such as paging, cable TV, news wires and stock tickers.

Satellite networks are useful in any situation where data need to be dispersed to or gathered from many remote nodes and where end-to-end delay is not a primary concern. Two-way satellite links are also an excellent choice when many remote sites need to report into a central database. Satellite communications are reliable. There are no cables that can be dug up or destroyed by fire, flood, earthquakes and solar powered satellites are highly unlikely to fail due to a power failure. Each satellite receives signals on a particular frequency, amplifies them and retransmits them on another frequency.

4.5.1 Fundamentals of Satellite Communication

A satellite system consists of a space segment and a ground segment. The ground segment consists of gateway stations (GSs), a network control centre (NCC), and operation control centres (OCCs). The NCC and OCCs handle overall network resource management, satellite operation, and orbiting control. The GSs act as network interfaces between various external networks and the satellite network. They also perform protocol, address, and format conversions. The space segment is composed of satellites, which may be classified into geostationary orbit (GSO) and nongeostationary orbit (NGSO) satellites, including medium earth orbit (MEO) and low earth orbit (LEO) satellites, according to the orbit altitude above the Earth's surface.

GSO: The majority of satellites in operation nowadays are placed in GSO orbit. The GSO satellite is 35,786 km above the equator, and its revolution around the Earth is synchronized with the Earth's rotation. Therefore, it appears fixed to an observer on the Earth's surface, and may serve as a repeater in the sky. Its high altitude allows each GSO satellite to cover approximately one third of the Earth's surface, excluding the high latitude areas. The area of coverage of a satellite is called its footprint. Three GSO satellites are sufficient for global coverage. However, the cost of launching GSO satellites is high. Due to its high altitude and the inherent signal degradation with distance, large antennas and transmission power are required for both the GSO satellite and ground terminals. The biggest problem is the large propagation delay for GSO satellite links. The typical value of round-trip delay is 250–280 ms, which is undesirable for real-time traffic.

MEO and LEO: MEO's distance from the Earth's surface is from 3000 km up to the GSO orbit with a typical round-trip propagation delay of 110–130 ms. LEOs are located 200–3000 km above the Earth's surface. For a LEO satellite the round-trip delay is 20–25 ms, which is comparable to that of a terrestrial link. Since LEO/MEO satellites are closer to the Earth's surface, the necessary antenna size and transmission power level are much smaller; but their footprints are also much smaller. A constellation of a large number of satellites is necessary for global coverage. The lower the orbit altitude, the greater the number of satellites required. In addition, since satellites travel at high speeds relative to the Earth's surface, a user may need to be handed off from satellite to satellite as they pass rapidly overhead. Therefore, steerable antennas are crucial to maintain continuous service.

Satellite Payload: The satellite payload is responsible for the satellite communication functions. Once the satellite is launched, it is very expensive and almost impossible to upgrade or repair. The space environment, with radiation, rain, and space debris, is harsh for satellites. Therefore, the satellite payload is required to be simple and robust. Traditional satellites, especially GSOs, serve as bent pipes. They act as repeaters between two communication points on the ground. There is no onboard processing (OBP). It is simple and easy to implement. Some satellite systems allow OBP, including demodulation/remodulation, decoding/recoding, transponder/beam switching, and routing to provide more efficient channel utilization. OBP can support high-capacity intersatellite links (ISLs) connecting two satellites within line of sight. By using a sophisticated constellation with ISLs, connectivity in space without any terrestrial resource is possible.

Frequency Bands: The most commonly used satellite frequency bands are the C band (4–8 GHz), Ku band (10–18 GHz), and Ka band (18–31 GHz). With a higher frequency band and a corresponding shorter wavelength, smaller antennas can be used to receive the signal. Some satellite systems use the C band and thus employ large antennas with a minimum diameter of 2–3 m. The majority of direct broadcast satellites use the Ku band for broadcasting as well as for Internet connections from the server to the users, with a terrestrial return link. A Ku band antenna can be as small as 45 cms in diameter. There are proposals to provide a Ka band return link for these systems. A Ka band potentially offers much higher bandwidth than the Ku band, and can use very small antennas, but it suffers from environmental impairments such as fading and rain attenuation. There are also plans to use frequencies beyond the Ka band, but the technologies for using these frequencies are immature and further investigation is needed.

4.5.2 Satellite-Based Internet Architectures

The satellite-based Internet has several architectural options due to the diverse designs of satellite systems, in orbit types (GSO, MEO, LEO), payload choice (OBP or bent pipe), and ISL designs. There are suggestions that multiple satellite types (i.e., GSOs, MEOs, and LEOs) be included in a hybrid GSO/NGSO network to fully utilize the best characteristics of each orbit type.

A satellite network can serve as part of the Internet backbone, a high-speed access network, or both. Using a satellite system as part of the Internet backbone has a long history that dates back to the Atlantic SATNET interconnecting ARPANET with European research networks. However, the idea of using satellites as a solution of the last mile problem (i.e., connecting users to network access points), inspired by the usage of cost-effective, very small aperture terminals (VSAT) and improvements in satellite technologies, is relatively new.

A typical satellite-based Internet scenario with bent-pipe satellites provides Internet access as well as data trunking service. The satellites adopted can be GSO, MEO or LEO. The satellite network interfaces with the ground Internet infrastructure via GSs on the Earth. It may be the only access method for some users (e.g., user A) when no other communication method is available, or a backup connection in addition to an existing terrestrial access network (e.g., user B).

However, the bent-pipe architecture's lack of direct communication paths in space results in low spectrum efficiency and long latency. OBP and ISLs may be used to help construct a network in the sky. This architecture is again a combination access and backbone network.

Teledesic is one such system using a constellation of 288 LEO satellites with ISLs. The rich connectivity in space will provide more flexibility but also bring complex routing issues, which will be discussed later.

In the two aforementioned general architectures, user terminals are assumed to be interactive, which means they can directly transmit data up to the satellite and receive data from the satellite. Although rapid advancements in satellite technology have spawned small user terminals, such as ultra small aperture terminals (USAT) with 60 cm antennas, the interactive terminal is still expensive and thus frustrates direct-to-home implementation. Enlightened by Internet traffic asymmetry where considerably more data are transmitted from the server to the end user than in the reverse direction (e.g., Web browsing), there is a trend to offer Internet access via direct broadcast satellites (DBSs) used for television broadcasting. Each home has a receive-only satellite dish to collect data delivered in the high-speed satellite broadcast channel. The reverse path to the server is provided by a terrestrial link. Hughes's DirecPC system is an example. In order to make full use of the wide bandwidth of satellite broadcast links, DBS is also extended by using the receive-only terminals as gateways to interconnect remote networks.

The above architecture contradicts the traditional symmetric network assumption of a two-way balanced load and identical link characteristics, and causes the so-called unidirectional routing problem elaborated on in the next section.

4.5.3 Technical Challenges

In this section we summarize the technical challenges in designing and implementing the satellite-based Internet. We focus on special requirements unique to satellite systems, and leave out general considerations common to terrestrial networks. Multiple access control schemes, essential for satellite systems, are described first. Then we investigate transmitting IP packets in satellite networks. Finally, transport issues based on TCP modification and satellite-specific transport protocols are presented.

4.5.4 Multiple Access Control

In interactive satellite systems, a large number of user terminals widely scattered within the satellite footprint contend for the satellite uplink channel. Multiple access control (MAC), defined as a set of rules for controlling access to a shared channel among contending users, plays an important role in efficiently and fairly utilizing the limited satellite system resources. MAC protocol performance can significantly affect higher-layer protocols and the QoS provided by the system.

The performance of MAC protocols depends on the characteristics of both the shared communication media and the traffic. The long latency in satellite channels (especially the GSO links) excludes some MAC schemes used in terrestrial local area networks (LANs) such as carrier sense multiple access (CSMA), and the limited power resource in satellites constrains the transponder and computational capacity on board the satellite. Internet traffic turns out to be bursty in nature. Besides the current best-effort service, the Internet is expected to provide diverse QoS guarantees (e.g., on delay, delay jitter, packet loss ratio) for a wide range of traffic types. Thus, a candidate MAC protocol must implement priorities. Real-time traffic with transmission deadlines is usually given higher priority than non-real-time traffic.

Generally speaking, a good MAC scheme for a satellite-based network should be simple to implement, robust and flexible enough to accommodate network reconfiguration. The MAC should be able to achieve high throughput, maintain channel stability, and enjoy low protocol overhead and small access delay.

Depending on how bandwidth is allocated among all contenders, candidate MAC schemes for satellite systems can be categorized into three groups: fixed assignment, random access, and demand assignment.

Fixed assignment: Fixed assignment may be made on a frequency, time or code basis. Major techniques include frequency-division multiple access (FDMA), time-division multiple access (TDMA), and code-division multiple access (CDMA). In FDMA and TDMA systems, each station utilizes its own dedicated channel. They are contention-free, and can provide QoS guarantees. However, this is at the expense of inefficient utilization of resources. Their lack of flexibility and scalability makes them only suitable for small-scale networks with stable traffic patterns. FDMA was the first fixed assignment multiple access method used in satellite systems. TDMA is popular mainly because of its compatibility with the nonlinear nature of transponders and is used in the majority of current satellite systems. In a CDMA system, each user is assigned a unique code sequence which is used to spread the data signal over a wider bandwidth than that required to transmit the data. If code sequences are guaranteed to be orthogonal all other simultaneous transmissions in the same channel act as additive interference to the desired signal and can be removed completely at the receiver side, where a reverse procedure, despread, is carried out to recover original data. Thus, in a CDMA system, the whole bandwidth is used by all users, making it more flexible for system expansion.

Random access: Due to technological advances, small and inexpensive terminals (i.e., VSATs and USATs) with lower data rates are now widely available, thus stimulating home or personal use of satellite access service. The number of stations within a satellite footprint increases from a few to several hundreds or thousands. In addition, the traffic generated by each user is very bursty. Fixed assignment schemes are replaced by contention-based random access (i.e., Aloha and its variations). In random access schemes, each station transmits data regardless of the transmission status of others. Retransmissions after collision increase the average packet delay, and frequent collisions may cause low throughput.

Demand assignment: Although random access may better accommodate a large number of terminals with bursty traffic, it provides no QoS guarantees. Demand assignment multiple access (DAMA) protocols attempt to solve this problem by dynamically allocating system bandwidth in response to user requests. A resource request must be granted before actual data transmission. The transmission of requests is itself a multiple access problem. However, since the request message is typically much shorter than actual data transmission, we can afford to have reservation requests collide and be retransmitted. After a successful reservation, bandwidth is allocated on an overall FDMA or TDMA architecture, and data transmission is guaranteed to be collision-free. This article focuses on the TDMA architecture in which equal-sized time slots are grouped into frames, repeated periodically.

The reservation may be made under centralized or distributed control. The central controller can be located at an Earth station or at a satellite with OBP. For a ground-based controller, the minimum request delay is two round-trip times before the reservation request is granted. The minimum request delay can be halved for a space-based controller, but the satellite payload capacity limits this implementation. Distributed control, in which each station receives all request information from the satellite broadcast channel and makes a decision on its own, is more robust and reliable. The channel overhead associated with reservation announcements is reduced greatly, and the minimum reservation delay is as small as one round-trip time. Although it may put the processing burden on the stations, distributed control is still preferred, considering its overall advantages.

Resource reservation can be made either explicitly or implicitly. Explicit reservation is on a per-transmission basis, and usually a dedicated reservation channel is shared among all stations. Each station sends a short request via the reservation channel specifying the number of time slots needed. Stations access the reservation channel in fixed assignment mode, such as TDMA reservation, or random access mode, such as Aloha reservation. Data are transmitted in the data channel after successful reservation.

In implicit reservation, there is no explicit reservation message, and successful data transmission in a slot serves as an indication of reservation for the corresponding time slot in subsequent frames. Packets belonging to a long transmission can repeatedly occupy the same slot in consecutive frames. An empty slot in a frame indicates the end of the transmission, and other users can then contend for this slot starting in the next frame. This scheme is attractive for relatively steady traffic patterns such as voice and video connections. An example of this scheme is Reservation Aloha, which uses the first data packet as an implicit request unit and accesses the available time slots via the slotted Aloha protocol.

Priority-oriented demand assignment (PODA) and first-in first-out (FIFO) ordered demand assignment (FODA) combine implicit and explicit requests. Each PODA TDMA frame consists of a control part and a data part with an adjustable boundary. Explicit requests contend in the control part by slotted Aloha, while implicit requests are piggybacked on data packets. FODA further divides the data part into stream and datagram subframes. One FIFO stream queue and two FIFO datagram queues, for short interactive traffic and bulky traffic, are maintained with decreasing priorities. Both the latter types of traffic are transmitted in the datagram subframes.

There are proposals to make use of the unreserved resource after the demand assignment. Combined free/demand assignment multiple access (CFDAMA) freely assigns the remaining channels according to some strategy (e.g., round-robin). In combined random access and TDMA-reservation multiple access (CRRMA), the remaining resources are open for random access. By randomly accessing the unreserved channel, some bursty interactive traffic may be transmitted immediately without waiting for the two-hop reservation delay. A hybrid scheme called round-robin reservation (RRR) is based on fixed TDMA. The number of stations is required to be less than or equal to the number of time slots. Each station obtains a dedicated channel, and extra or unused slots are accessed in a round-robin manner or via slotted Aloha. In satellite systems, large GSs interfacing with terrestrial networks function as multiplexers for traffic from those directly connected networks. Gateway stations are usually much more heavily loaded than small terminals, and the number of GSs is much smaller than that of small terminals. The RRR mechanism may be suitable for this scenario. For example, GSs may obtain dedicated time slots, while small terminals contend for the remaining slots in each frame. Similar hybrid methods may combine the advantages of different schemes, but further performance analyses and simulations are needed to demonstrate their feasibility.

4.5.5 Routing Issues in Satellite Systems

Routing issues in a LEO constellation: The significant advantages of LEO with OBP and ISLs, such as small delay and full connectivity, make LEO a very attractive approach to the Internet in the sky. In such networks, the major technical issue is the complex dynamic routing issue due to satellite movements.

Dynamic topology: Due to the relative movement between the LEO satellite and the Earth, a satellite has a very short visible period to motionless users on the ground. To maintain 24-hr continuous coverage, a carefully designed satellite constellation is crucial. At any time there should be at least one satellite within line of sight of a user. When a satellite moves out of a user's visual field and another satellite moves in, intersatellite handover happens. For a satellite with multiple antennae and transponders, the satellite footprint is divided into a number of spotbeams, each covered by an antenna beam. Thus, frequent interbeam handover from spotbeam to spotbeam occurs within a single satellite's visible period.

The ISLs in the constellation form a mesh network topology. Each satellite is typically able to set up 4–8 ISLs. There are two types of ISLs: intraplane ISLs connecting adjacent satellites in the same orbit, and interplane ISLs connecting neighboring satellites in adjoining orbits. Intraplane ISLs are maintained permanently, but some interplane ISLs may be temporarily switched off when the viewing angle or distance between two satellites changes too fast for the steerable antennas to follow. This may occur between two counter-rotating orbits or when two orbits cross. The routing scheme should be able to handle topological variations. Fortunately, although the constellation topology changes frequently, it is highly periodic and predictable because of the strict orbital movements of the satellites.

Some dynamic routing mechanisms popular in the Internet, such as distance vector (DV) and link state algorithm (LSA), are not directly applicable in satellite constellation routing, because frequent topological changes in satellite constellation will cause large overhead and oscillation if these schemes are used. Two new concepts tailored to dynamic satellite constellation are worth mentioning: discrete-time dynamic virtual topology routing (DT-DVTR) and the virtual node (VN).

- **DT-DVTR:** DT-DVTR makes full use of the periodic nature of satellite constellation and works completely offline. It divides the system period into a set of time intervals so that the topology changes only at the beginning of each time interval and remains constant until the next time interval. In each interval, the routing problem is a static topology routing problem that can be solved easily. A number of consecutive routing tables are then stored onboard and retrieved when the topology changes. With this strategy, online computational complexity is transformed into a large storage requirement on the satellites. In order to minimize the storage needed and the intersatellite handover attempts when topology changes, an optimization procedure can be used to choose the best path or a small set of paths from the series of instantaneous routes. Although it can significantly reduce the storage size, some links may become congested while others are underutilized.

- **VN:** The objective of this scheme is to hide the topology changes from the routing protocols. A virtual topology is set up with VNs superimposed on the physical topology of the satellite constellation. Even as satellites are moving across the sky, the virtual topology remains unchanged. Each VN keeps state information, including routing tables and information of users within the VN's coverage area. In a certain period, a VN is represented by a certain physical satellite. As this satellite disappears over the horizon, the VN is represented by the next satellite passing overhead. The state information is also transferred from the first satellite to the second. A routing decision is made on the virtual topology, and the protocols are not aware of the dynamic satellite constellation concealed in state transfers.

Based on these two concepts, some routing schemes are proposed for carrying IP packets through the satellite constellation. Some commercial satellite systems (e.g., Teledesic) use proprietary routing techniques that are highly dependent on explicit orbital and constellation knowledge and optimized for specific designs. Due to their lack of generality, they are not covered in this article.

IP routing at the satellites: To route IP packets through a satellite constellation, it seems straightforward to adopt IP routing at the satellites. This strategy is based on the VN concept. It can seamlessly integrate the space network with the terrestrial Internet, and permits direct support for IP multicast and IP QoS (integrated and differentiated service models). However, how to deal with variable-length IP packets, the scalability problem of onboard routing tables, and computational and processing capacity limitations in space devices are challenging problems. The scheme is still in its infancy, and some practical problems are unsolved in the implementation of the VN concept.

ATM switching at the satellites: Many proposed systems use ATM as the network protocol for the constellation (i.e., Cyberstar, Astrolink, Spaceway, and Skyway) with a satellite-specific signaling protocol and link layer protocol. An ATM version of DT-DVTR is, where all the virtual channel connections between the same pair of ingress and egress satellites are grouped into a virtual path connection (VPC), and onboard switching is done according to the VPC labels. A modified S-ATM packet is suggested to reduce the overhead without changing the cell size. If such a system is adopted to provide Internet service, IP over ATM or other similar technologies will be used.

External routing issues: It is reasonable to assume that the internal routing schemes for satellite constellation will continue to be heterogeneous. Satellite manufacturers and operators will probably select routing methods best suited to their own system designs. The internal protocol should be kept simple. Details of the satellite network should be hidden from the terrestrial Internet as well. Today's Internet achieves this kind of isolation by using the autonomous system (AS) concept. Typically, some external routing schemes are used for inter-AS routing, while internal routing is handled by the AS's own internal routing protocol.

A satellite system can be considered an AS in the Internet. A number of border gateways (BGs) running exterior routing protocols (e.g., Border Gateway Protocol, BGP, used by terrestrial ASs) will communicate with terrestrial ASs. Only BGs on the constellation periphery need be aware of the outside addresses and topological information. All packets going through a satellite constellation enter the satellite AS from one entry BG, which is responsible for determining the exit BG of each packet. If necessary, the entry/exit BGs perform encapsulation/ decapsulation and address resolution. The BGs can be implemented either onboard the satellites or in ground GSs. If space-based BGs are used computational and storage requirements may be too great for the satellites. On the other hand, if terrestrial gateways are used, packets must be bounced back to the ground for IP routing, introducing an extra round-trip delay. However ground BGs are more realistic. Furthermore, external routing protocols popular in terrestrial networks cannot simply be reused in satellite constellations. In terrestrial networks, any internal link within an AS always has smaller cost than an inter-AS link. It is generally true because in terrestrial networks an AS is usually limited to a small geographical area, while an inter-AS link travels a much longer way. But a satellite system extends globally, and routing within a satellite constellation may be as expensive as traversing several ASs. Thus, multiple pairs of BGs should be used from a satellite constellation to a destination in some AS.

Unidirectional routing: As described earlier, Internet access via DBS poses the unidirectional routing problem which cannot be handled by traditional dynamic routing schemes where bidirectional links are assumed. For example, in distance vector routing, a router receiving the distance vector tuple {destination, cost} from its neighbour deduces that it can reach the destination via this neighbour. It is no longer true in the satellite broadcast scenario where the direct reverse link to the satellite does not exist. Multicast routing protocols (e.g., DVMRP) based on the reverse shortest path tree also face such a problem.

There are three ways to handle this problem. Instead of dynamic routing, static routing may be an option; but with thousands of users served by a DBS, it is impossible to manually configure all of the routing entries. The other two methods are routing protocol modification and tunneling, proposed in the Internet engineering task force (IETF) unidirectional link routing (UDLR) working group. They are discussed in the following sections.

Routing protocol modification: In unidirectional routing, the router at one end of a unidirectional link with a send-only interface is referred to as a feeder, while the router at the other end of the unidirectional link with a receive-only interface is called a receiver. The key idea of the modification is twofold. First, the modified protocol should enable a receiver to identify the potential feeders whenever it receives routing updates from them, and to ignore the unusable routing information in those packets while keeping the useful reports to maintain the neighbouring connectivity. Second, the receiver periodically delivers its own routing message to all feeders through the terrestrial reverse channel. Thus, when a feeder gets the routing information, it can update the related routing entries for reachable destinations through the unidirectional link passing the receiver. The idea is used by the UDLR working group in the proposals to modify some popular protocols (i.e., RIP, OSPF, and DVMRP).

Tunnelling: Tunnelling offers a link layer approach to hide the network asymmetry from the routing process. A virtual bidirectional link is set up between a DBS and a user by encapsulation and decapsulation. This virtual link is called a tunnel. Packets destined for the DBS from the user are delivered via the tunnel. The tunnel endpoint at the user side first encapsulates the packet, and then passes it to the routing protocol where it is delivered through the actual terrestrial reverse channel. When the packet arrives at the satellite, the tunnel endpoint captures it, decapsulates it and forwards it to the routing protocol to which it seems to come from a bidirectional link.

The above two approaches are simple, and since tunnelling is transparent to all upper layer protocols, it may be quickly implemented in DBS Internet access architectures. However, the two schemes are designed based on point-to-point unidirectional links, although satellites are point-to-multipoint broadcast systems. Thus, further study is needed to design new approaches optimized for this architecture. The two approaches also focus only on the routing issue within a single AS and fail to address interdomain routing. New interdomain routing schemes that can handle unidirectional links are needed.

4.5.6 Satellite Transport

The TCP/IP and UDP/IP protocol suites form the basis of the Internet. Due to their tremendous legacy, it is unlikely they will be totally discarded in the near future. Therefore, the satellite-based Internet is expected to continue to serve applications based on TCP and UDP. However, the performance of both protocols will be affected by the long latency and error-prone characteristics of satellite links. The impacts on TCP will be much greater, and heated debates have ensued regarding the feasibility of TCP in a satellite environment. Researchers working with NASA's ACTS satellites are performing research regarding TCP/IP over satellite connections. The IETF TCP over Satellite working group is also dedicated to improvement of TCP performance in satellite systems. In this section we first present the main limitations of TCP over satellite links and then summarize the ongoing research efforts on the satellite transport problem.

TCP performance over satellite: TCP uses a positive feedback mechanism to achieve rate control and reliable delivery. The long latency of satellite links (especially GSO links) increases the TCP end-to-end delay and results in sluggish acknowledgments. The slow feedback will weaken the functionality of rate control and congestion avoidance, and thus affect the throughput. In addition, a potential problem is the large fluctuation of measured round-trip time (RTT) that may be caused by dynamic topology in LEO constellation networks. Large variations in RTT measurements may result in false timeouts and retransmissions.

In the initial slow start stage of TCP transmission, although the sending rate increases exponentially, it is still too slow for the high-bandwidth satellite links. One proposed solution is to increase the initial value of the window. TCP originally allows a window size of 64 kbytes, which also limits the maximum sending rate to 64 kbytes/RTT. The satellite link will be underutilized, and a large window scaling up to the bandwidth-delay product of the satellite link is required for higher throughput. A set of window scaling options to TCP implementation are defined in IETF request for comments (RFC) 1323.

Satellite links are subject to various impairments (i.e., interference, fading, shadowing, and rain attenuation). Therefore, a high bit error rate (BER) is expected. Although advanced modulation, coding schemes, and forward error correction (FEC) techniques are used to reduce the BER, in some environments high BER persists. But TCP does not distinguish between corrupted data caused by transmission error and packet loss due to congestion; both are unacknowledged and interpreted as a notification of network congestion. When there is a corrupted packet, the window size is halved even though there is no congestion. Furthermore, transmission errors on a satellite link are bursty in nature, especially under bad weather conditions. Bursty errors in one RTT will dramatically reduce the throughput. The space communications standards-transport protocol (SCPS-TP) defined for the general space environment provides two mechanisms to distinguish the sources of loss and responds differently. In addition, network asymmetry can also impair TCP performance. Satellite network asymmetry occurs in two situations. One is in the asymmetric DBS Internet access architecture described earlier. The other is due to bandwidth asymmetry in some interactive satellite terminals. These terminals may be capable of downloading at tens of megabits per second, but with an uplink speed of only several hundred kilobits per second. The limited reverse link capacity may cause the acknowledgment starvation problem. The backlogged feedback will slow down the window refresh. In addition, acknowledgment loss due to reverse link congestion may trigger unnecessary retransmissions.

Another problem inherent in TCP is the fairness issue between different TCP connections with various RTTs. When those TCP connections share a bottlenecked link, the TCP connections with longer RTTs will suffer unfair bandwidth allocation.

Performance enhancements: The IETF TCP over satellite working group has recently made a number of recommendations to enhance the performance of TCP over satellite links in its RFCs. The last two schemes listed below are non-TCP techniques:

- TCP selective acknowledgment-(SACK) options (RFC2018) allow the receiver to specify the correctly received segments. Thus, the sender needs to retransmit only the lost packets. TCP SACK can recover multiple losses in a transmission window within one RTT.
- TCP for transaction (T/TCP) (RFC1644) attempts to reduce the connection handshaking latency from two RTTs to one RTT, which is a significant improvement for short transmissions.
- Persistent TCP connection, supported in HTTP1.1 (RFC2068), allows multiple small transfers to download in a single persistent TCP connection. It is more efficient.

- The path maximum transfer unit (MTU) discovery mechanism allows TCP to use the largest possible packet size, thus avoiding IP segmentation. It reduces the overhead, and eliminates fragmentation and defragmentation.
- FEC is employed in link layer protocols to improve the quality of satellite links, but it should not be expected to fix all problems associated with manmade noise, such as military jamming, and some natural noise, such as that caused by rain attenuation. Besides FEC, some other link layer approaches (e.g., bit interleaving, link layer automatic repeat request schemes) can also be used to improve packet error rate in transmissions over satellite links.

TCP extensions can solve some of the limitations of standard TCP over satellite links, but other problems such as long end-to-end latency and asymmetry are not effectively addressed. One way to alleviate the effects of large end-to-end latency is to split the TCP connection into two or more parts at the GSs connecting the satellite network and terrestrial networks. There are three approaches to splitting TCP connections over satellite links:

- **TCP spoofing:** The divided connections are isolated by the GSs, which prematurely send spoofing acknowledgments upon receiving packets. The GSs at split points are also responsible for retransmitting any missing data.
- **TCP splitting:** Instead of spoofing, the connection is fully split. A proprietary transport protocol can be used in a satellite network without interference to standard TCP in terrestrial networks. It is more flexible, and some kind of protocol converter should be implemented at the splitting points.
- **Web caching:** In contrast to the above two schemes, the TCP connection is split by a Web cache in the satellite network. Users in the satellite network connected to this Web cache need not set up TCP connections all the way to servers outside if the required contents are available from the cache. Web caching effectively reduces connection latency and bandwidth consumption.

A satellite transport protocol (STP) is designed and used in the TCP splitting approach as well as for traffic management in a satellite network. STP is based on the basic operation of service-specific connection-oriented protocol (SSCOP). The sender periodically requests the receiver to report successful receptions, and retransmission is triggered by explicit selective negative acknowledgment. It uses a hybrid window and rate congestion control mechanism. STP performs well in asymmetric networks since the reverse traffic is significantly reduced, but it does not distinguish between different sources of packet loss and also leaves the fairness problem unsolved.

4.6 PAGING AND SATELLITE NETWORKS

Paging is the oldest form of mobile communications. The paging industry came into existence in 1949, when the FCC allocated some spectrum frequencies for one-way mobile communication services.

Paging is a wide area, wireless communications method in which brief alphanumeric messages are transmitted using radio frequencies to an electronic pager.

When a subscriber's designated telephone number is dialled, the paging switch sends information to a radio transmitter that broadcasts a signal in the service area, which in turn deliver a tone or numeric, alphanumeric or voice message to the subscribers specific pager. The subscriber is alerted either by a beep or by a vibration of the pager itself.

Pagers can also download the messages to a notebook or palm top computers for display messages are transmitted quickly, often in less than one minute users can also receive news, sports, weather and stock information at scheduled intervals.

4.7 INFRARED OR LIGHT BASED MOBILE COMPUTING

Infrared works by sending pulses of light from a light emitting diode to a photo sensor that decodes the signals. Unlike rudimentary infrared devices like TV remote controls, which can only send signals, computing devices typically can both send and receive infrared signals, because the information is carried by light waves, the system will not work if any physical obstruction is placed between the sending and receiving devices.

Most infrared equipment falls into two categories

- Low speed devices which range from 115 Kbps to 250 Kbps
- High-speed devices, which transfer at a rate of about 1.25 Megabytes/second.

Advantages:

- Infrared is low cost.
- Infrared is capable of sending data at many times the speed of radio waves while using very little power.

Disadvantages:

- Not as fast as many cable connections.
- Limited to exchanging small amounts of data between identical devices.

4.8 WIRELESS APPLICATION PROTOCOL (WAP)

Wireless application protocol (WAP) is an application environment and set of communication protocols for wireless devices designed to enable manufacturer-, vendor-, and technology-independent access to the Internet and advanced telephony services Wireless application protocol is a system of protocols and technologies that allow cell phones and other wireless devices with tiny displays, low bandwidth connections and minimal memory, to access web based information and services. WAP is a cross platform (wireless and internet), multi-environment protocol. It defines the communication protocol that links wireless to Internet.

4.8.1 Working of WAP

1. The client generates a request for the information. This information is transmitted in binary code to the WAP gateway through the 'bearer.'
2. WAP gateway processes the requests, translates it into a HTML document and communicates it to the web server across the Internet. The WAP gateway also receives

the information, which is formatted as the wireless markup language (WML), known as a 'deck.'

3. WAP gateway then transmits the compiled request (in binary code) as a 'deck of cards' to the client for display or processing. A card of WML is equivalent to HTML of a web page.
4. The client retrieves the first card of the deck and displays it.

'Deck of card' is designed for small, low-resolution screens on digital handheld devices. Each request results in the presentation of data in a deck of one or more cards.

4.8.2 Benefits of WAP

Operators

For wireless network operators, WAP promises to decrease churn, cut costs, and increase the subscriber base both by improving existing services, such as interfaces to voice-mail and prepaid systems, and facilitating an unlimited range of new value-added services and applications, such as account management and billing inquiries. New applications can be introduced quickly and easily without the need for additional infrastructure or modifications to the phone. This will allow operators to differentiate themselves from their competitors with new, customized information services. WAP is an interoperable framework, enabling the provision of end-to-end turnkey solutions that will create a lasting competitive advantage, build consumer loyalty, and increase revenues.

Content providers

Applications will be written in wireless markup language (WML), which is a subset of extensible markup language (XML). Using the same model as the Internet, WAP will enable content and application developers to grasp the tag-based WML that will pave the way for services to be written and deployed within an operator's network quickly and easily. As WAP is a global and interoperable open standard, content providers have immediate access to a wealth of potential customers who will seek such applications to enhance the service offerings given to their own existing and potential subscriber base. Mobile consumers are becoming more eager to receive increased functionality and value-addition from their mobile devices, and WAP opens the door to this market.

End users

End users of WAP will benefit from easy, secure access to relevant Internet information and services such as unified messaging, banking and entertainment through their mobile devices. Intranet information such as corporate databases can also be accessed via WAP technology. Because a wide range of handset manufacturers already support the WAP initiative, users will have significant freedom of choice when selecting mobile terminals and the applications they support. Users will be able to receive and request information in a controlled, fast, and low-cost environment, a fact that renders WAP services more attractive to consumers who demand more value and functionality from their mobile terminals.

As the initial focus of WAP, the Internet will set many of the trends in advance of WAP implementation. It is expected that the Internet service providers (ISPs) will exploit the true potential of WAP. Web content developers will have great knowledge of and direct access to the people they attempt to reach. In addition, these developers will realise the huge potential of the operators' customer bases; thus, they will be willing and able to offer competitive prices for their content. WAP's push capability will enable weather and travel information providers to use WAP. This push mechanism affords a distinct advantage over the WWW and represents tremendous potential for both information providers and mobile operators.

4.8.3 Why Choose WAP?

In the past, wireless Internet access has been limited by the capabilities of handheld devices and wireless networks.

WAP utilizes Internet standards such as XML, user datagram protocol (UDP), and Internet protocol (IP). Many of the protocols are based on Internet standards such as hypertext transfer protocol (HTTP) and TLS that have been optimized for the unique constraints of the wireless environment: low bandwidth, high latency, and less connection stability.

Internet standards such as hypertext markup language (HTML), HTTP, TLS and transmission control protocol (TCP) are inefficient over mobile networks, requiring large amounts of mainly text-based data to be sent. Standard HTML content cannot be effectively displayed on the small-size screens of pocket-sized mobile phones and pagers.

WAP utilizes binary transmission for greater compression of data and is optimized for long latency and low bandwidth. WAP sessions cope with intermittent coverage and can operate over a wide variety of wireless transports.

WML and wireless markup language script (WMLScript) are used to produce WAP content. They make optimum use of small displays, and navigation may be performed with one hand. WAP content is scalable from a two-line text display on a basic device to a full graphic screen on the latest smart phones and communicators.

The lightweight WAP protocol stack is designed to minimize the required bandwidth and maximize the number of wireless network types that can deliver WAP content. Multiple networks will be targeted, with the additional aim of targeting multiple networks. These include global system for mobile communications (GSM) 900, 1,800, and 1,900 MHz; interim standard (IS)–136; digital European cordless communication (DECT); time-division multiple access (TDMA), personal communications service (PCS), FLEX, and code division multiple access (CDMA). All network technologies and bearers will also be supported, including short message service (SMS), USSD, circuit-switched cellular data (CSD), cellular digital packet data (CDPD), and general packet radio service (GPRS).

As WAP is based on a scalable-layered architecture, each layer can develop independently of the others. This makes it possible to introduce new bearers or to use new transport protocols without major changes in the other layers.

Mobile-Originated Example of WAP Architecture

WAP will provide multiple applications, for business and customer markets such as banking, corporate database access, and a messaging interface (see Fig. 4.8).

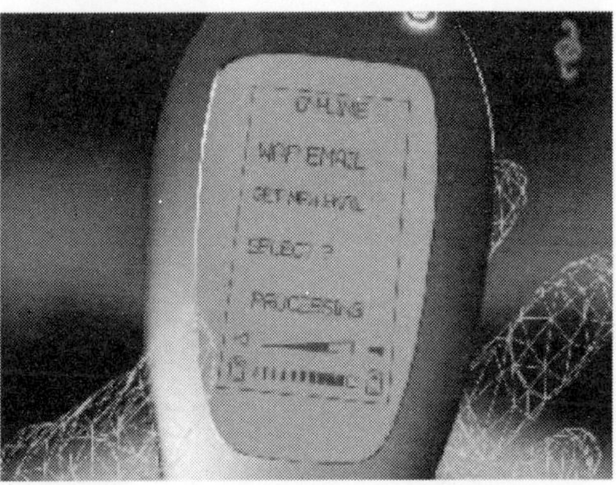

Fig. 4.8: *Messaging interface*

The request from the mobile device is sent as a URL through the operator's network to the WAP gateway, which is the interface between the operator's network and the Internet (see Fig. 4.9).

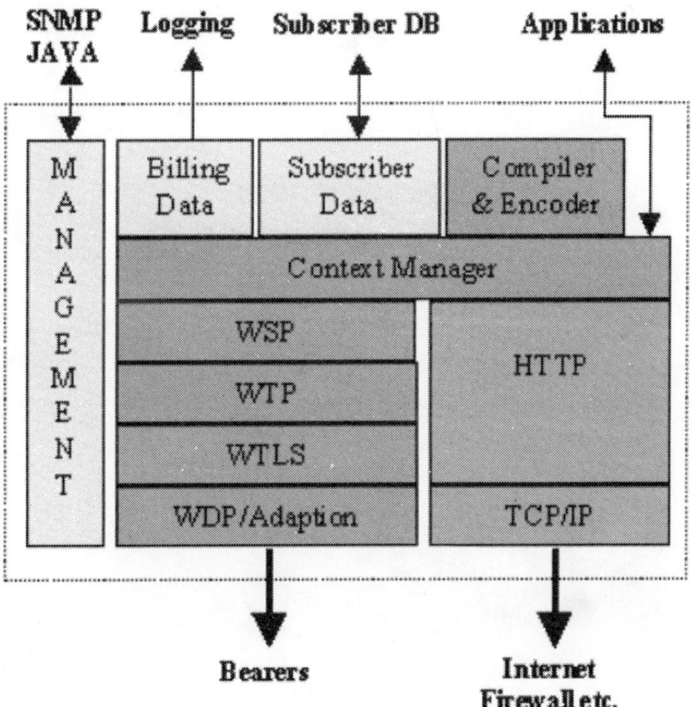

Fig. 4.9 *Architecture of the WAP gateway*

Architecture of the WAP Gateway

WDP

The WAP datagram protocol (WDP) is the transport layer that sends and receives messages via any available bearer network, including SMS, USSD, CSD, CDPD, IS–136 packet data, and GPRS.

WTLS

The wireless transport layer security (WTLS), an optional security layer, has encryption facilities that provide the secure transport service required by many applications, such as e-commerce.

WTP

The WAP transaction protocol (WTP) layer provides transaction support, adding reliability to the datagram service provided by WDP.

WSP

The WAP session protocol (WSP) layer provides a lightweight session layer to allow efficient exchange of data between applications.

HTTP Interface

The HTTP interface serves to retrieve WAP content from the Internet as requested by the mobile device.

WAP content (WML and WMLScript) is converted into a compact binary form for transmission over the air (see Fig. 4.10).

Fig. 4.10: ***WAP content in compact binary form***

The WAP microbrowser software within the mobile device interprets the byte code and displays the interactive WAP content (see Fig. 4.8).

4.8.4 The Future of WAP

The tremendous surge of interest and development in the area of wireless data in recent times has caused worldwide operators, infrastructure and terminal manufacturers, and content developers to collaborate on an unprecedented scale, in an area notorious for the diversity of standards and protocols. The collaborative efforts of the WAP Forum have devised and continue to develop a set of protocols that provide a common environment for the development of advanced telephony services and Internet access for the wireless market. If the WAP protocols were to be as successful as transmission control protocol (TCP)/Internet protocol (IP), the boom in mobile communications would be phenomenal. Indeed, the WAP browser should do for mobile Internet what Netscape did for the Internet.

As mentioned earlier, industry players from content developers to operators can explore the vast opportunity that WAP presents. As a fixed-line technology, the Internet has proved highly successful in reaching the homes of millions worldwide. However, mobile users until now have been forced to accept relatively basic levels of functionality, over and above voice communications and are beginning to demand that the industry move from a fixed to a mobile environment, carrying the functionality of a fixed environment with it.

Initially, services are expected to run over the well-established SMS bearer, which will dictate the nature and speed of early applications. Indeed, GSM currently does not offer the data rates that would allow mobile multimedia and Web browsing. With the advent of GPRS, which aimed at increasing the data rate to 115 kbps, as well as other emerging high-bandwidth bearers, the reality of access speeds equivalent or higher to that of a fixed-line scenario became evermore believable. GPRS is seen by many as the perfect partner for WAP, with its distinct time slots serving to manage data packets in a way that prevents users from being penalized for holding standard circuit-switched connections.

4.8.5 Handset Manufacturers and WAP Services

It is expected that mobile terminal manufacturers will experience significant change as a result of WAP technology—a chance that will impact the look and feel of the hardware they produce. The main issues faced by this arm of the industry concern the size of mobile phones, power supplies, display size, usability, processing power, and the role of personal digital assistants (PDAs) and other mobile terminals.

With over 75 percent of the world's key handset manufacturers already involved in the WAP Forum and announcing the impending release of WAP–compatible handsets, the drive toward new and innovative devices is quickly gathering pace. The handsets themselves will contain a micro browser that will serve to interpret the byte code (generated from the WML/WMLS content) and display interactive content to the user.

The services available to users will be wide-ranging in nature, as a result of the open specifications of WAP, their similarity to the established and accepted Internet model, and the simplicity of the WML/WMLS languages with which the applications will be written. Information will be available in push-and-pull functionality, with the ability for users to interact with services via both voice and data interfaces. Web browsing as experienced by the desktop user, however, is not expected to be the main driver behind WAP as a result of time and processing restraints.

Real-time applications and services demand small and key pieces of information that will fuel the success of WAP in the mobile marketplace. Stock prices, news, weather, and travel are only some of the areas in which WAP will provide services for mobile users. Essentially, the WAP application strategy involves taking existing services that are common within a fixed-line environment and tailoring them to be purposeful and user-friendly in a wireless environment.

Empowering the user with the ability to access a wealth of information and services from a mobile device will create a new battleground. Mobile industry players will fight to provide their customers with sophisticated, value-added services. As mobile commerce becomes a more secure and trusted channel by which consumers may conduct their financial affairs, the market for WAP will become even more lucrative.

4.8.6 WAP in the Competitive Environment

Competition for WAP protocols could come from a number of sources:

- **Subscriber identity module (SIM) toolkit:** The use of SIMs or smart cards in wireless devices is already widespread and used in some of the service sectors.
- **Windows CE:** This is a multitasking, multithreaded operating system from Microsoft designed for including or embedding mobile and other space-constrained devices.
- **Java Phone™:** Sun Microsystems is developing Personal Java™ and a Java Phone™ API, which is embedded in a Java™ virtual machine on the handset. NEPs will be able to build cellular phones that can download extra features and functions over the Internet; thus, customers will no longer be required to buy a new phone to take advantage of improved features.

The advantages that WAP can offer over these other methods are the following:

- Open standard, vendor independent
- Network-standard independent
- Transport mechanism–optimised for wireless data bearers

Application downloaded from the server, enabling fast service creation and introduction, as opposed to embedded software.

4.9 COMPONENTS OF WAP

1. Hand held device/Micro-browser (client)
2. WAP server
3. Proxy server or WAP gateway
4. WTA (Wireless telephony application) server

4.9.1 Micro-browser

A **micro-browser** (sometimes called a **mini-browser** or **mobile browser**) is a web browser designed for use on a handheld device such as a PDA or mobile phone. Micro-browsers are optimized so as to display Internet content most effectively for small screens on portable devices and have small file sizes to accommodate the low memory capacity and low-bandwidth of wireless handheld devices. A browser in the wireless Internet environment is called a micro-browser, because it performs limited functions in comparison to the browser in the Internet environments. The micro-browser software is embedded within the digital hand held device and interprets information exchanged with WAP gateway.

Underlying technology

The micro-browser usually sets up the cellular networks itself and gets content written in XHTML Mobile Profile (WAP 2.0), or WML (WAP 1.3 which was based on HDML). WML and HDML are stripped-down formats suitable for transmission across limited bandwidth, and wireless data connection called WAP. In Japan, DoCoMo defined the i-mode service based on i-mode HTML, which is an extension of Compact HTML (C-HTML), a simple subset of HTML.

WAP 2.0 specifies XHTML Mobile Profile plus WAP CSS, subsets of the W3C's standard XHTML and CSS with minor mobile extensions.

Newer microbrowsers are full-featured Web browsers capable of HTML, WML, i-mode HTML, cHTML, CSS, ECMAScript, and plug-ins such as Macromedia Flash.

Pioneers

The so-called micro-browser technologies such as WAP, NTTDocomo's i-mode platform and Openwave's HDML platform have fuelled the first wave of interest in wireless data services.

A British company, STNC Ltd., developed a micro-browser (HitchHiker) intended to present the entire device UI in 1997. The demonstration platform for this micro-browser (Webwalker) had 1 MIPS total processing power. This was a single core platform, running the GSM stack on the same processor as the application stack. In 1999 STNC was acquired by Microsoft and HitchHiker became Microsoft Mobile Explorer 2.0, not related to the primitive Microsoft Mobile Explorer 1.0. HitchHiker is believed to be the first micro-browser with a unified rendering model, handling HTML and WAP along with EcmaScript, WMLScript, POP3 and IMAP mail in a single client. Although it was not used, it was possible to combine HTML and WAP in the same pages although this would render the pages invalid for any other device.

The communication between a micro-browser and WAP gateway is based on client-server computing. The micro-browser is the client and the WAP gateway the server. The micro-browser communicates with two servers on the network.

1. The WAP gateway or proxy server
2. Wireless telephony application (WTA) server

Popular micro-browsers

The following are some of the more popular micro-browsers. Some micro-browsers are really miniaturized Web browsers, so some micro-browser companies also provide browsers for the PC. Default browsers used by major mobile phone and PDA vendors are:

- NetFront by ACCESS Co., Ltd.
- Nokia Series 40 Browser by Nokia.
- Nokia web browser by Nokia.
- Novarra nWeb.
- Web Browser for S60 by Nokia.
- Obigo Browser by Obigo AB (Sweden), 100% owned by Teleca AB
- Openwave (Redwood, CA) (formerly Phone.com, formerly Unwired Planet).
- Opera Mobile by Opera Software ASA (Norway). - Capable of reading HTML and reformat for small screens
- Pocket Internet Explorer by Microsoft Inc.
- Wapaka Browser Java micro-browser by Digital Airways.
- Picsel Browser by Picsel Technologies (Scotland).
- Blazer by Palm.

4.9.2 WAP Server

The WAP server is the server with which the WAP gateway interacts directly. The WAP server is just a normal web server and a WAP gateway-type device built into one. People assume that it is necessary to have a WAP server in order to serve WAP content, but this is not so. WAP content is servable from any normal web server. While focusing on WAP security, the WAP server can help plug some few holes, which are unplugged in the WAP environment.

As the WAP server contains a gateway, the 3rd party gateway usually hosted by the cellular operator can be skipped, and WAP content host will have full control on the entire encrypted stream.

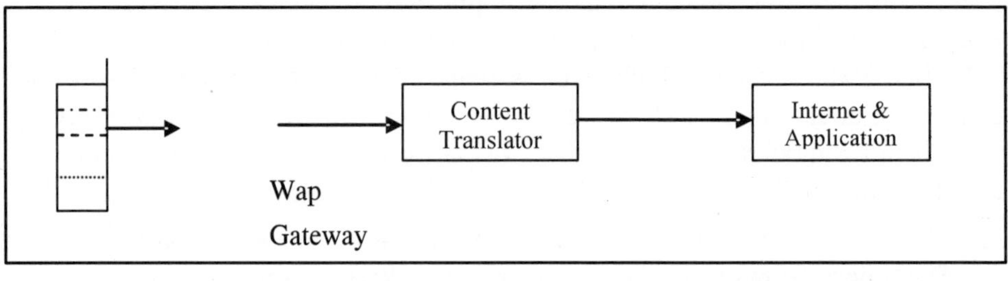

Network operator Enterprise

Fig. 4.11: ***Secured model of WAP in WAE***

The information between the user and the enterprise is secured because of the WAP protocols.

4.9.3 Proxy Server or WAP Gateway

A server between a client application, such as a Web browser, and a real server is called a proxy server. It intercepts all requests to the real server to see if it can fulfil the requests itself. If not, it forwards the request to the real server WAP gateway. It is essentially a piece of middle ware, performing the functions of an intermediary and protocol translator between the WAP gateway, the client (i.e. Micro-browser) and the web server. WAP gateway is therefore also called a 'proxy server' because it is not the server but only a 'proxy'.

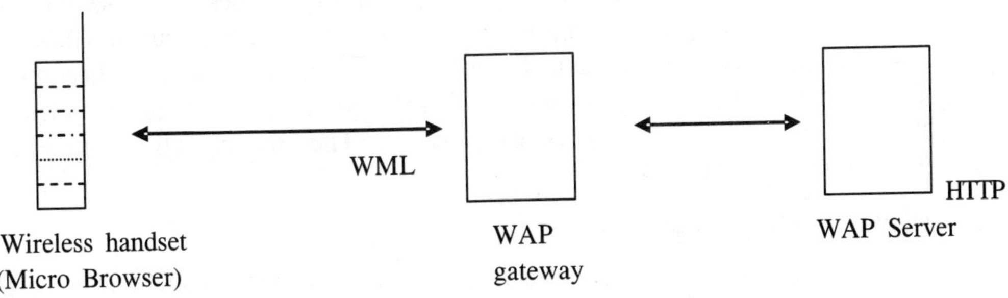

Fig. 4.12: ***Proxy server or WAP gateway***

Proxy servers have two main purposes:

1. **To improve performance:**

   A proxy server can dramatically improve performance for groups of users. This is because it saves the results of all requests for a certain amount of time. Consider the case where both user X and user Y access the World Wide Web through a proxy server. First user X requests a certain Web page, which we will call Page 1. Sometime later, user Y requests the same page. Instead of forwarding the request to the Web server where Page 1 resides, which can be a time-consuming operation, the proxy server simply returns the Page 1 that it already fetched for user X. Since the proxy server is often on the same network as the user, this is a much faster operation. Real proxy servers support hundreds or thousands of users. The major online services such as America Online, MSN and Yahoo, for example, employ an array of proxy servers.

2. **To filter requests:**

   Proxy servers can also be used to filter requests. For example, a company might use a proxy server to prevent its employees from accessing a specific set of Web sites.

A WAP gateway performs the following functions:

1. Conversion of HTML document into a WML deck.
2. Compression of the VML pages into a more compact form to save bandwidth.

4.9.4 WTA Servers

WTA includes a client-side programming library and a WTA server, allowing WAP sessions to control the voice channel. Voice calls can be placed, DTMF can be sent along the voice channel and the client can initiate conference calls. The WTA server generates WTA events, which are interpreted by the WAP gateway, which sends the resulting WML to the WAP mobile phone. The WTA server controls the voice connections. WTA currently is a challenging task to implement; vendors are unsure of customers' requirements for this functionality and find it challenging to implement computer telephony integration (CTI) equipment without network operators' support. Another limitation is that current GSM networks only support either one voice or data channel at a time, and thus WTA will not become feasible before the availability of GPRS networks and terminals, supporting simultaneous voice and data transmission. These servers represent a telephone switch. They handle call signalling and user interfaces to conference calls, etc.

Wireless telephony applications interface

The wireless telephony applications interface (WTAI) enables applications to perform typical functions of a mobile telephone with WML (Version 1.2 and higher) or WMLScript (where this introduction tries to shed some light on), but aims for a more elaborate goal: To make the user interface and processing of the mobile device programmable and customizable.

Security

The WTA security model demands from the WAP gateway to allow only requests from trusted WTA servers to pass. The user also can inhibit access to the functions of his mobile device.

Concept

The client must have a repository, memory that is, in which channels, basically links to WML decks and WMLScript functions, can be stored persistently (otherwise the phone has to establish a connection to the WTA server on every ring).

Functionality of WAP network environment

The functionality of the basic components of WAP network environment requires an understanding of WAP stack and its following two substructures:

1. Wireless Application Environment (WAE)
2. Wireless Telephony Application (WTA)

4.10 COMMUNICATION BETWEEN THE WAP GATEWAY'S CLIENTS AND SERVER

The architecture of the WAP stack follows the OSI layering model. It is implemented via a layered approach and consists of the following:

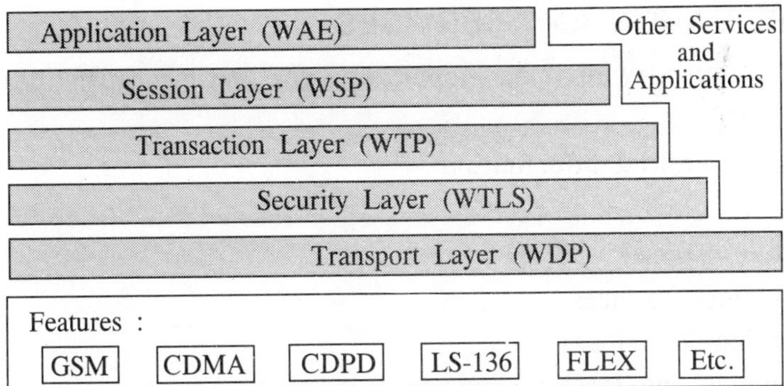

Fig. 4.13: ***WEB and WAP architecture***

Note: - The WAP stack is a set of protocols that cover the complete process of wireless content delivery, from the definition of WML and WML script for the creation and layout of the actual content.

WAL – Wireless application layer
– Interact with end user

WSL – Wireless session layer
– Establishing, maintaining and terminating session

WTL – Wireless transaction layer
– Providing three types of services

1. Non dependable one way message
2. Dependable one way message – SMS (mobile)
3. Dependable two way message – query & response

- Assembling and dissembling is also carried out at the transaction layer.

WTSL – Wireless transport security layer

- Contains security S/W (i) to ensure security of data transmission, (ii) to provide data compression service; public key encryption technology is not able to open the web page, because the S/W density is high. We use private key Algo rather than public key but all the Algo's may be utilized.
- WTSL is an optional layer based on SSL. WTSL is not as secure as SSL.

Note: An IP layer is not planned here, because no IP address is required before the gateway.

WTL – Wireless transport layer

This has two protocols:

1. WCMP – Wireless control message protocol – in comparison TCP/IP is an Internet control message protocol (ICMP).
2. WDP – Wireless datagram protocol – in comparison to WDP (user Datagram Protocol).

Note: There is no physical layer here.

4.11 WAP APPLICATION AND SERVICES

Services that are presented with finite graphic text can use the capabilities of WAP's WAE feature. For example,

1. **Exchanging limited information –**

   Examples would include access to
   - Address books
   - Directory services
   - Driving directions
   - Mapping and locator services.
   - Message notification.
   - Receiving news, business, sports or information services
   - Scanning or reading selected e-mail
   - Weather and traffic alerts
   - Travel schedules: Air, rail and other

2. **M and E-commerce transactions**

   Examples would include access to
   - Book travel reservations
   - Credit card purchases
   - Money transfer
   - Online banking
   - Stock trading

4.12 WAP AND COOKIES

Cookies are used on the Internet to identify the web browser and thereby assist in providing customized and stream lines service. The cookies' information is transmitted via HTTP headers. HTTP on the Internet is a stateless protocol.

WAP specification has not specified how Internet and WAP protocols are required to work together regarding sessions. Thus, so far there are no 'cookies' for session management as there is no support by WML.

Cookie

A cookie is a message given to a Web browser by a Web server. The browser stores the message in a text file. The message is then sent back to the server each time the browser requests a page from the server.

Session cookie

A session cookie, also called a transient cookie, is a cookie that is erased when the user closes the Web browser. The session cookie is stored in the temporary memory and is not retained after the browser is closed. Session cookies do not collect information from the users computer. They will typically store information in the form of a session identification that does not personally identify the user.

Persistent cookie

This is also called a permanent cookie, or a stored cookie. It is a cookie that is stored on a users hard drive until it expires (persistent cookies are set with expiration dates) or until the user deletes the cookie. Persistent cookies are used to collect identifying information about the user, such as Web surfing behaviour or user preferences for a specific Web site.

The main purpose of cookies is to identify users and possibly prepare customized Web pages for them. When you enter a Web site using cookies, you may be asked to fill out a form providing such information as your name and interests. This information is packaged into a cookie and sent to your Web browser, which stores it for later use. The next time you go to the same Web site, your browser will send the cookie to the Web server. The server can use this information to present you with custom Web pages. So, for example, instead of seeing just a generic welcome page you might see a welcome page with your name on it.

The name cookie derives from UNIX objects called magic cookies. These are tokens that are attached to a user or program and change depending on the areas entered by the user or program.

4.13 LIMITATIONS OF WIRELESS NETWORK

Wireless network is a constrained communication environment. Its features are as follows:

1. Limitation of power.
2. The latency is higher, in comparison to the raditional world network.
3. Far less bandwidth is available than on the Internet environment.
4. Spectrum limitation due to limited network capacity.
5. Network availability is less predictable due to network congestion.

SUMMARY

- A cellular mobile communications system uses a large number of low-power wireless transmitters to create cells—the basic geographic service area of a wireless communications system. Variable power levels allow cells to be sized according to the subscriber density and demand within a particular region.
- Cellular communication requires careful monitoring and switching of calls from cell to cell as the user moves between them without dynamic switching to facilitate a smooth transmission, the calls would be terminated as the user crosses the boundary of a cell.
- A satellite communication system, distinguished by its global coverage, inherent broadcast capability, bandwidth-on-demand flexibility, and the ability to support mobility, is an excellent candidate to provide broadband integrated Internet services to globally scattered users.

- Wireless application protocol (WAP) is an application environment and set of communication protocols for wireless devices designed to enable manufacturer-, vendor-, and technology-independent access to the Internet and advanced telephony services.
- Wireless application protocol is a system of protocols and technologies that allows cell phones and other wireless devices with tiny displays, low bandwidth connections and minimal memory, to access web based information and services. WAP is a cross platform (wireless and internet), multi-environment protocol. It defines the communication protocol that links wireless to Internet.
- A micro-browser (sometimes called a mini-browser or mobile browser) is a web browser designed for use on a handheld device such as a PDA or mobile phone. Micro-browsers are optimized so as to display Internet content most effectively for small screens on portable devices and have small file sizes to accommodate the low memory capacity and low-bandwidth of wireless handheld devices.
- A WAP server is the server with which the WAP gateway interacts directly. It is just a normal web server and a WAP gateway-type device built into one. People assume that it is necessary to have a WAP server in order to serve WAP content, but this is not so.
- A server between a client application, such as a Web browser, and a real server is called a proxy server. It intercepts all requests to the real server to see if it can fulfil the requests itself. If not, it forwards the request to the real server. A WAP gateway is essentially a piece of middle ware, performing the functions of an intermediary and protocol translator between the WAP gateway, the client (i.e. micro-browser) and the web server.
- WTA includes a client-side programming library and WTA server, allowing WAP sessions to control the voice channel. Voice calls can be placed, DTMF can be sent along the voice channel and the client can initiate conference calls. The WTA server generates WTA events, which are interpreted by the WAP gateway, which sends the resulting WML to the WAP mobile phone.

REVIEW QUESTIONS

1. Discuss the wireless application protocol stacks in detail.
2. Differentiate between WEB and WAP.
3. Discuss the role of WTA and WTA Server in WAP.
4. Discuss the four principal components of WAP.
5. Discuss the role of proxy server in World Wide Web.

CHAPTER 5

Web Security and Network Security

The W3 conventions form a powerful tool for bringing together a widespread academic community. These conventions will allow current and future software systems to work together harmoniously across different platforms. Software is available, and continually being contributed, to allow information to be presented to a world audience, and read by anyone. If the need arises, restricted access to particular servers can be implemented easily.

5.1 WEB SECURITY

The primary security issue on the web is confidentiality. Web sites can access a considerable amount of information about the person visiting their pages, as shown for example at the following sites:

- Network-Tools.net
- 404 Research Lab Supersleuth

While a computer communicates a lot of technical data when a person visits web sites, the browser is built to safeguard the person's name, email address, and other personal data. The information that web sites can access is described below:

- IP address confidentiality. Web sites can and often do record the IP addresses of visitors. For most dial-up users a new IP address is dynamically assigned every time they sign on, so the most that it reveals about the user is the Internet Service Provider that they are using. This is a confidentiality risk only if the service provider provides their logs to others, which is unlikely unless they are under a court order. However, if one uses an office computer or a high speed connection where the IP address is permanently assigned, then the address can be used to uniquely identify a machine, and a web site can use this information to track repeat visits.

- **Cookies:** Cookies are often used to store information on a computer to track a user's browsing patterns on a particular site.
- **Configuration:** Web servers can record the operating system and browser being used, the plugins the user has installed, and the pages the user accesses on their site.
- **Previous address:** When a user clicks on a web page link, the HTTP protocol sends the URL of the current page to the new page, so the new page can tell where the link came from. The destination web server can capture this information and store it in their logs. If a user does not want a web site to be able to tell where they accessed it, then they should manually copy and paste the link they want to access into the URL field of their browser and then press return, so there is no sending page to transmit. This feature can also lead to a particular vulnerability when clicking on web page links from a web email service.
- **Next address**: A site could include code that will tell it which link is chosen when a person leaves the site, so it knows where they are going, although normal links to other sites do not return this sort of information.

Resources: The following resources can help with web security issues:

- If one is concerned about confidentiality risks, one can consider the use of an Anonymizer.
- There are a range of programs to filter adult content from the Internet, so that children can be protected from undesirable content.

5.2 NETWORK SECURITY

A security threat is defined as a circumstance, condition or event with the potential to cause economic hardship to data or network resources in the form of destruction, disclosure, modification of data, denial of service and fraud waste and abuse.

Security concerns in e-commerce can be divided into two broad types:

1. **Client server security:** This uses various authorization methods to make sure that only valid users and programs have access to information resources as databases. Such a mechanism includes password protection, encrypted smart cards, biometrics and firewalls.
2. **Data and transaction security:** This ensures the privacy and confidentiality in electronic messages and data packets, including the authentication of remote users in network transactions for activities such as online payments. Preventive measures include data encryption using various cryptographic methods.

5.3 CLIENT–SERVER NETWORK SECURITY

Network security on the Internet is a major concern for commercial organizations, especially top management. Recently the Internet has raised many new security concerns. By connecting to the internet, a local network organization may be exposing itself to the entire population on the Internet.

An Internet connection effectively breaches the physical security perimeter of the corporate network and opens itself to access from other network comprising the public Internet.

For many commercial operations, security will simply be a matter of making sure that existing system features, such as password and privileges are configured properly. They need to audit all access to the network.

Hackers can use password guessing, password trapping, security holes in programs, or common network access procedures to impersonate users and thus pose a threat to the server.

Client server network security problems manifest themselves in three ways:

1. **Physical security holes:** These result when individuals gain unauthorized physical access to a computer. A good example would be a public workstation room, where it would easy for a wandering hacker to reboot a machine into single user mode and tamper with the files, if precautions are not taken. On the network, this is also a common problem, as hackers gain access to network systems by guessing passwords of various users.
2. **Software security holes:** These result when badly written programs or privileged software are compromised into doing things they should not be doing; the most famous example of this category is the send mail hole. This is the highest level of access possible and could be used to delete the entire file system or create a new account or password file resulting in incalculable damage.
3. **Inconsistent usage holes:** They result when a system administrator assembles a combination of hardware and software such that the system is seriously flawed from a security point of view. The incompatibility of attempting two unconnected but useful things creates the security holes. Problems like this are difficult to isolate once a system is set up and running, so it is better to carefully build the system with them in mind. This type of problem is becoming common as software becomes more complex.

To reduce these security threats, various protection methods are used:

- Trust based security
- Security through obscurity
- Password schemes
- Biometric systems

5.3.1 Trust Based Security

Trust based security means to trust everyone and do nothing extra for protection. It is possible not to provide access restriction of any kind and to assume that all users are trust worthy and competent in their use to the shared network. This approach worked in the past, when the system administrator only had to worry about a limited threat.

5.3.2 Security Through Obscurity

Any network can be secure as long as nobody outside its management group is allowed to find out anything about its operational details and users are provided information on a need to know basis. Hiding account passwords in binary files or scripts with the presumption that "nobody will ever find them" is a prime case of STO.

In short, STO provides a false sense of security in computing systems by hiding information. In reality, however, if an employee leaves a firm, the knowledge goes with the employee, reducing the effectiveness of the method.

Many users today have advanced knowledge of how their operating system works and through experience can guess at the bits of knowledge considered confidential. This bypasses the whole basis of STO and makes this method of security useless.

5.3.3 Password Schemes

This scheme often works because users tend to choose relatively simple or familiar word as passwords. To beat the dictionary comparison method, experts often recommend using a minimum of eight-character length mixed case passwords containing at least one non-alphanumeric character and changing passwords every 60 to 90 days.

Because passwords in a remote log-in session usually pass over the network in unencrypted form, any eavesdropper on the network can simply record the password any time it is used.

Having distinct passwords for distinct devices is sometimes a problem, because people will write them down, share them or include them in automatic scripts.

5.3.4 Biometric System

Biometric systems, the most secure level of authorization, involve some unique aspects of a person's body. Past biometric authentication was based on comparisons of fingerprints, palm prints, retinal patterns or on signature verification or voice recognition.

Disadvantages

Biometric systems are very expensive to implement. They may be better suited for controlling physical access – where one biometric unit can serve for many workers – than for network or workstation access.

5.4 EMERGING CLIENT–SERVER SECURITY THREATS

Other security threats that are emerging in the electronic commerce world are mobile code (software agent), which in many ways resembles the more traditional virus threats.

Mobile code is an executable program that has the ability to move from machine to machine and also to invoke itself without external influence.

These threats can be divided into two major categories:

1. Threats to the local computing environment from mobile software.
2. Access control and threats to servers that include impersonation, denial of service, packet relay and packet modification.

5.4.1 Software Agents and Malicious Code Threat

The major threats to security from running client software result because of the nature of the Internet as client programs interpret data download from arbitrary servers on the internet.

The security threat arises when the downloaded data passes through local interpreters on the client system without the user's knowledge that the potential security breach has been plugged in most of the new mail system.

The client threats arise from malicious data or code. Malicious code refers to viruses, worms, Trojan horses and other deviant software programs. Clients must scan for malicious data and executable program fragments that are transferred from the server to client.

5.4.2 Threats to Servers

Threats to servers consist of authorized modification of server data, unauthorized eavesdropping or modification of incoming data packets and compromise of a server system by exploiting bugs in the server software.

Compared to stand alone systems, network servers are much more susceptible to attacks where legitimate users are impersonated.

For example, hackers have potential access to a large number of systems. Hackers can use popular Unix programs liker finger, rsh or ruser to discover account names and then try to guess simple passwords using a dictionary or more sophisticated password guessing methods.

Note: - Hackers can use electronic eavesdropping to trap user names and unencrypted passwords sent over the network. They can monitor the activity on a system continuously and impersonate a user when the impersonation attack is less likely to be detected.

Hackers can eavesdrop using software that monitors packets sent over the network. Many networks programs, such as Telnet and ftp are vulnerable to eavesdroppers who obtain passwords, which are often sent across the network encrypted.

Three types of effects are:

- Service overloading
- Message overloading
- Packet overloading

5.5 FIREWALLS AND NETWORK SECURITY

The most commonly accepted network protection is a barrier – a firewall between the corporate network and the outside world.

The term firewall can mean many things to many people, but basically it is a method of placing a device - a computer or a router between the network and the Internet to control and monitor all traffic between the outside world and the local network.

In the context of the Internet - "A firewall is a system - a router, a personal computer, a host or a collection of hosts - set up specifically to shield a site or subnet from protocols and services that can be abused from hosts on the outside of the subnet".

A firewall system is usually located at a gateway point, such as a site's connection to the Internet, but can be located at internal gateways to provide protection for a smaller collection of hosts or subnets. Firewalls come in several types and offer various levels of security.

The firewall can be thought of as a mechanism:

1. To block incoming traffic
2. To permit outgoing traffic

Without a firewall, network security is a function of each host on the network and all hosts must cooperate to achieve a uniformly high level of security. The larger, the subnet, the less manageable it is to maintain all hosts at the same level of security.

In practice firewalls range from simple traffic logging systems, that record all network traffic flowing through the firewall in a file or database for auditing purposes to more complex method.

1. **Service overloading**

   Servers are especially vulnerable to service overloading. One can easily overload a www server by writing a small loop that sends requests continually for a particular file. Example - home page.

2. **Message overloading**

   Message overloading occurs when someone sends a very large file to a user's message box every few minutes. The message occupies all the space on the disk and increases the number of receiving processes on the recipient machine trying it even more and often causing a disk crash.

   The best way to avoid message overloading is to provide separate areas for different programs and to make provisions for graceful failures.

3. **Packet overloading**

   The packet relay refers to the recording and retransmission of message packets in the network. This is a significant threat for programs that require authentication sequences because a hacker could replay legitimate authentication sequence messages to gain access to a secure system.

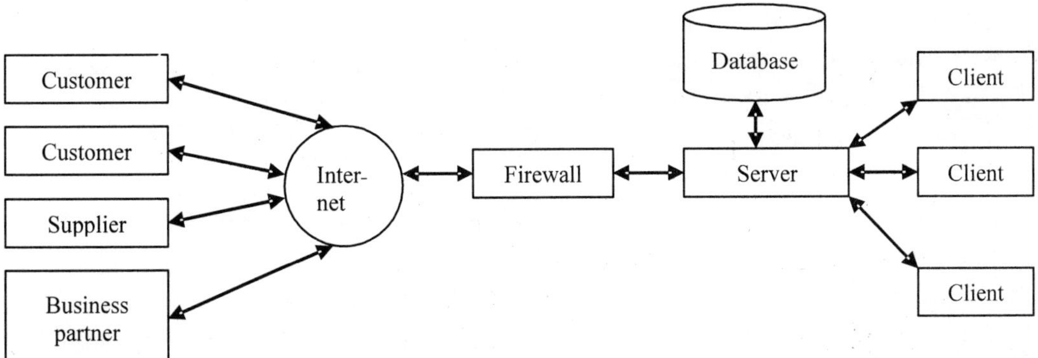

Fig. 5.1: ***Firewall***

A firewall could be:

1. IP Packet screening routers
2. Hardened firewall hosts
3. Proxy application gateways

The simplest firewall is a packet-filtering gateway or screening router, application gateways are more complex and secure.

5.5.1 IP Packet Screening Routers

This is a static traffic routing service placed between the network service provider's router and the internal network. The traffic routing service may be implemented at an IP level via screening rules in a router or at an application level via proxy gateways and services.

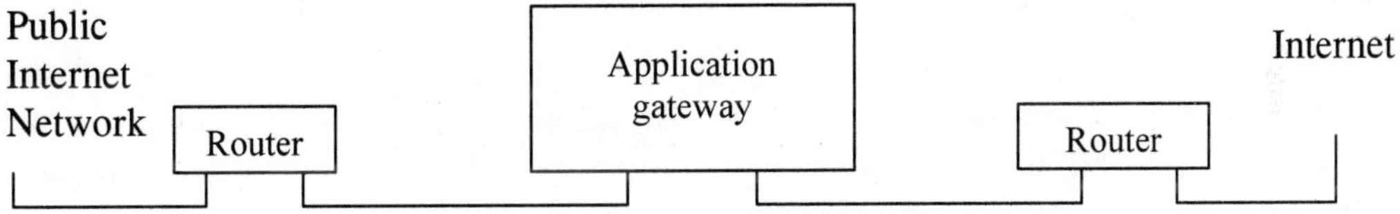

Fig. 5.2

The firewall router filters incoming packets to permit or deny IP packets based on several screening rules. These screening rules, implemented into the router are automatically performed.

Rules include target interface to which the packet is routed, known source IP address and incoming packet protocol (TCP, UDP, ICMP).

5.5.2 Hardened Firewall Hosts

A hardened firewall host is a stripped down machine that has been configured for increased security. This type of firewall requires inside or outside users to connect to the trusted applications on the firewall machine before connecting further.

These firewalls are configured to protect the computer against unauthenticated interactive logins from the external world.

Creating a hardened host requires:

- Removing all user accounts except those necessary for operation of the firewall i.e., if users cannot log-in to the firewall host, they cannot subvert the security measures.
- Removing all non crucial and executable files, especially network server programs and client programs like FTP and telnet.
- Extending traffic logging and monitoring to check remote access.
- Disabling IP forwarding to prevent the firewall from forwarding unauthorized packets between the internet and the enterprise network.

Advantages:

1. Provide a greater level of audit and security
2. Hide information
3. Centralized and simplified management of network services

Disadvantages:

1. Increased configuration cost
2. Decreased level of service

5.5.3 Proxy Application Gateways

A proxy application gateway is a special server that typically runs on a firewall machine. Its primary use is access to applications such as the World Wide Web from within a secure parameter.

Instead of talking directly to external www servers, each request from the client would be routed to a proxy on the firewall that is defined by the user.

The proxy knows how to get through the firewalls. An application level proxy makes a firewall safely permeable for users in an organization, without creating a potential security hole through which hackers can get into corporate networks.

The proxy waits for a request from inside the firewall, forwards the request to the remote server outside the firewall, reads the response and then returns it to the client. All clients within a given subnet use the same proxy.

Advantages of proxies

1. Allow browser programmers to ignore the complex networking code necessary to support every firewall protocol
2. Concentrate on important client issues
3. They can manage network functions
4. Control access to services for individual methods, host and domain, etc.
5. The proxy must be in a position to filter dangerous URLS and malformed commands.

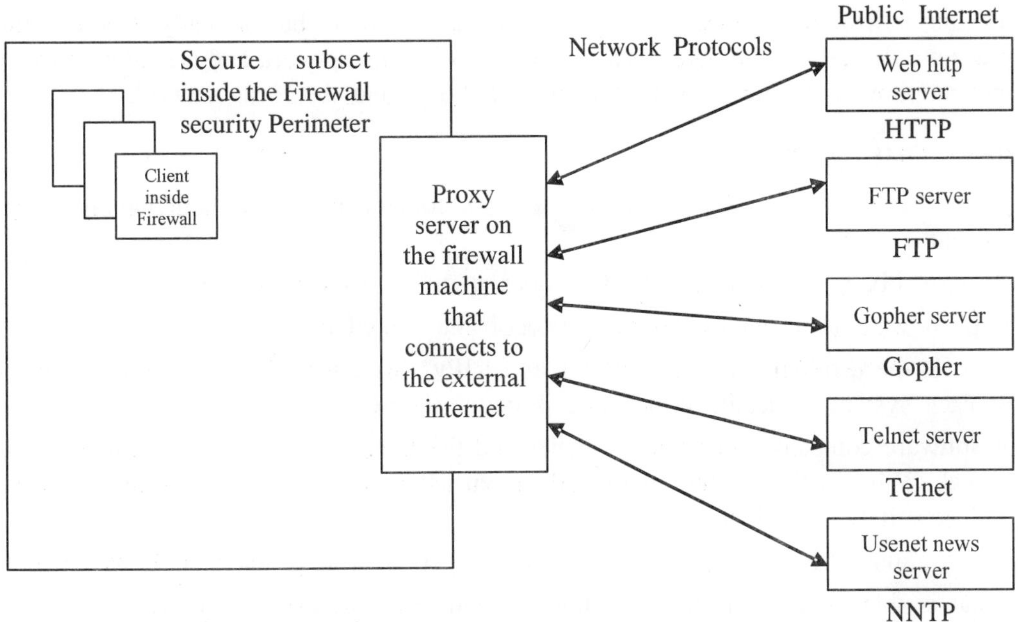

Fig. 5.3: ***Proxy servers on the World Wide Web***

SUMMARY

- The W3 conventions form a powerful tool for bringing together widespread academic communities. These conventions will allow current and future software systems to work together harmoniously across different platforms. Software is available, and continually being contributed, to allow information to be presented to a world audience, and read by anyone.
- A security threat is defined as a circumstance, condition or event with the potential to cause economic hardship to data or network resources in the form of destruction, disclosure or modification of data, denial of service and fraud waste and abuse.
- Network security on the Internet is a major concern for commercial organizations, especially top management. Recently the Internet has raised many new security concerns. By connecting to the Internet, a local network organization may be exposing itself to the entire population on the Internet.
- Other security threats that are emerging in the electronic commerce world are mobile code (software agent), which in many ways resembles the more traditional virus threats.
- Mobile code is an executable program that has the ability to move from machine to machine and also to invoke itself without external influence.
- The most commonly accepted network protection is a barrier – a firewall – between the corporate network and the outside world.

- The term firewall can mean many things to many people, but basically it is a method of placing a device – a computer or a router - between the network and the Internet to control and monitor all traffic between the outside world and the local network.

REVIEW QUESTIONS

1. What allows us to access the shared network folders quickly without having to browse the entire network?
2. What is Pix Firewall Security? How does it differ from a firewall?
3. Explain what is meant by routing protocol and routed protocol?
4. What is the difference between RIPv1 and RIPv? State the advantages and disadvantages of each system in detail. Which one is better to use?
5. A software company owns four branches and the Internet connection is available at every branch. What will be required to build a virtual private network between the branches and how it will be done.
6. Suppose in a LAN, one host does not get a connection, what problem could have occurred?
7. What is domain controller? Show how it manages a network security.
8. How should one create a trust relationship between two different forests.

CHAPTER 6

Electronic Commerce and the World Wide Web

The need for electronic commerce stems from the demand within business and the government to make better use of computing i.e., to better apply computer technology to improve business processes and information exchange both within an enterprise and across organizations.

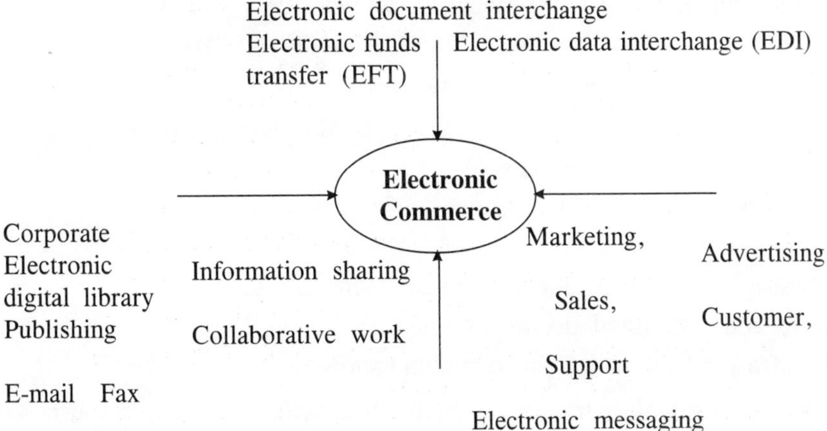

Fig. 6.1: ***Convergence of previously disparate functions around electronic commerce***

Electronic commerce applications are quite varied. In its most common form, e-commerce is also used to denote the paperless exchange of business information using EDI, e-mail, electronic bulleting boards, electronic funds transfer and other similar technologies.

The term electronic commerce is used to describe a new on-line approach to performing traditional functions such as payment and funds transfer, order entry and processing, invoicing, inventory management, cargo tracking electronic catalogs, and point of sale data gathering.

More recently, companies have realized that the advertising, marketing and customer support functions are also part of domain of the electronic commerce applications.

In short, what we are witnessing is the use of the term electronic commerce as an umbrella concept to integrate a wide range of new and old applications.

At first glance, it appears that messaging based technologies such as EDI and mail enabled applications combined with database and information management services form the technical foundation for effective electronic commerce solutions. However, no single one of these technologies can deliver the full potential of electronic commerce.

This integrated architecture is emerging in the form of the World Wide Web. As electronic commerce becomes more mature, we are beginning to see sophisticated applications being developed on the WWW technically and commercially, the WWW client server model seems poised to become a dominant technology. In short, the Web provides the functionality necessary for electronic commerce.

6.1 ARCHITECTURAL FRAMEWORK OF E-COMMERCE

A framework is intended to define and create tools that integrate the information found in today's closed systems, and allow the development of e-commerce applications. The aim of the architectural framework itself is not to build a new database management system, data repository, computer languages, software agent based transaction monitors or communication protocols. Rather, the architecture should focus on synthesizing the diverse resources already in place in corporations to facilitate the integration of data and software for better applications.

Electronic commerce application architecture consists of six layers of functionality or services such as:

1. Applications services
2. Brokerage services, data or transaction management
3. Interface and support layers
4. Secure messaging, security and electronic document interchange.
5. Middleware and structured document interchange
6. Network infrastructure and basic communication services

These layers provide a seamless transaction between today's computing resources and those of tomorrow by transparently integrating information access and exchange within the context of the chosen applications. Figure 5.2 shows that electronic commerce applications are based on several elegant technologies. But only when they are integrated do they provide uniquely powerful solutions.

Layer	Examples
Application Services	Consumer to business, business to business, intra-organizational
Brokerage and data Management	order processing-mail order houses, payment schemes – e-cash, clearing house or virtual mall
Interface Layer	interactive catalogs, directory support functions software agents
Secure Messaging	secure hypertext transfer protocol, encrypted E-mail, EDI, remote programming (RPC)
Middleware Service	structured document (SGML, HTML) compound documents (OLE, Open doc)
Network Infrastructure	wireless – cellular, radio, PCS wireline – POTS, coaxial fiber optic

Fig. 6.2: ***E-commerce: A conceptual framework***

6.2 ELECTRONIC COMMERCE APPLICATION SERVICES

The application services layer of e-commerce comprises existing and future applications built on the innate architecture. Three distinct classes of electronic commerce applications are:

1. Consumer to business
2. Business to business
3. Intra organization

6.2.1 Consumer to Business

This is known as marketplace transaction. In a market place transaction, customers learn about products differently through electronic publishing, buy them differently using electronic cash and secure payment systems and have them delivered differently.

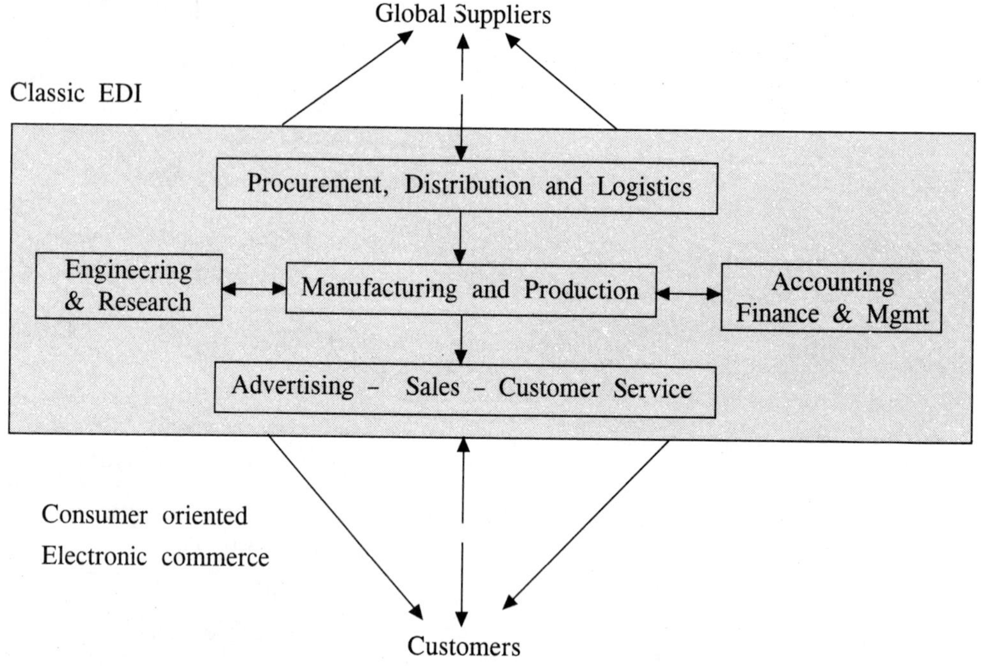

Fig. 6.3: ***Different types of electronic commerce applications***

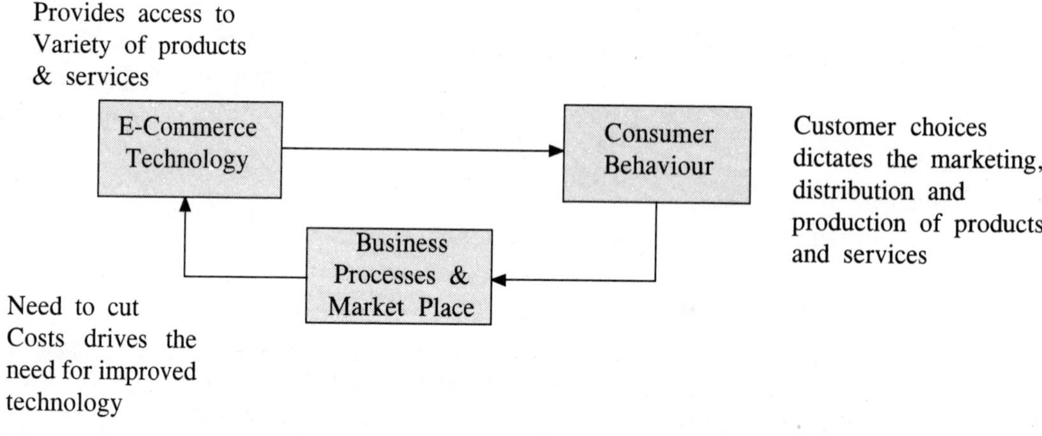

- Consumer behaviour changes in accordance with e-commerce technology i.e., technology revolution changes the behaviour of consumers.
- Business processes change in accordance with the demands of consumers. Business to consumers is highly dynamic compared to business to business transactions and changes very regularly.

    1. Performance and services
    2. Personalization

3. Socialization
4. Look and feel
   — B2B is less of multimedia feature but in B2C we look and feel.
5. Incentive - As when we purchase a certain product and get another product as an incentive
6. Security and reliability

6.2.2 Business to Business Transactions

This is called as market link transaction. Here businesses, governments and other organizations depend on computer-to-computer communication as a fast, economical and dependable way to conduct business transactions.

Business to business transactions include the use of EDI and electronic mail for purchasing goods and services, buying information and consulting services, submitting requests for proposals and receiving proposals.

Intra-organisational

This is known as market driven transactions. A company becomes market driven by dispersing information about its customers and competitors throughout the firm, by spreading strategic and tactical decision making so that all units can participate.

A market driven business develops a comprehensive understanding of its customers' business and how customers in the immediate and down stream market perceive value.

Three major components of market place transactions are

- Customer orientation through product and service customization
- Cross-functional coordination through enterprise integration
- Advertising, marketing and customer services

6.3 SUPPLY CHAIN MANAGEMENT (SCM)

A supply chain is a network of facilities and distribution options that performs the functions of procurement of materials, transformation of these materials into intermediate and finished products, and the distribution of these finished products to customers. Supply chains exist in both service and manufacturing organizations, although the complexity of the chain may vary greatly from industry to industry and firm to firm. Supply chain management is typically viewed to lie between fully vertically integrated firms, where the entire material flow is owned by a single firm and those where each channel member operates independently. Therefore coordination between the various players in the chain is the key to its effective management.

Many firms have been seeking ways of increasing profits through better management of their supply chain (network of partnership) using technology and avoiding the extremes of either internalizing it or of outsourcing most functions.

Supply chain management is an interesting process based on the flawless delivery of basic and customized services. SCM plays an important role in the management of processes that cut across functional and departmental boundaries.

Objectives

1. Get the right product to the right place at the least cost.
2. Keep the inventory as low as possible and consumer satisfaction maximum.
3. Reduce cycle time (order payment cycle).

In electronic commerce, supply chain management has the following characteristics:

1. The ability to source raw material or finished goods from anywhere in the world.
2. A centralized, global business and management strategy with flawless local execution.
3. On line, real time distributed information processing to the desktop, providing total supply chain information visibility.
4. The ability to manage information not only within a company but across industries and enterprises.
5. The seamless integration of all supply chain processes and measurements including third party suppliers, information systems, cost accounting standards and measurement system.
6. The development and implementation of an accounting model such as activity based costing that links cost to performance, which is used as a tool for cost reductions.
7. Reconfiguration of the supply chain organization into high performance teams from the shop floor to senior management.

6.3.1 Supply Chain Decisions

The decisions for supply chain management are classified into two broad categories – strategic and operational. As the term implies, strategic decisions are typically made over a longer time horizon. These are closely linked to the corporate strategy, and guide supply chain policies from a design perspective. On the other hand, operational decisions are short term, and focus on activities on a day-to-day basis. The effort in these types of decisions is to effectively and efficiently manage the product flow in the "strategically" planned supply chain.

There are four major decision areas in supply chain management: i) location, ii) production, iii) inventory and iv) transportation (distribution), and there are both strategic and operational elements in each of these decision areas.

Location decisions

The geographic placement of production facilities, stocking points, and sourcing points is the natural first step in creating a supply chain. The location of facilities involves a commitment of resources to a long-term plan. Once the size, number and location of these are determined, so are the possible paths by which the product flows through to the final customer. These decisions are of great significance to a firm since they represent the basic strategy for accessing customer markets, and will have a considerable impact on revenue, cost and level of service. These decisions should be determined by an optimization routine that considers production costs, taxes, duties and duty drawback, tariffs, local content, distribution costs, production limitations, etc. Although location decisions are primarily strategic, they also have implications on an operational level.

Production decisions

Strategic decisions include what products to produce, and which plants to produce them in, allocation of suppliers to plants, plants to distributors and distributors to customer markets. As before, these decisions have a big impact on the revenues, costs and customer service levels of the firm. These decisions assume the existence of the facilities, but determine the exact path(s) through which a product flows to and from these facilities. Another critical issue is the capacity of the manufacturing facilities, which largely depends on the degree of vertical integration within the firm. Operational decisions focus on detailed production scheduling. These decisions include the construction of the master production schedules, scheduling production on machines, and equipment maintenance. Other considerations include workload balancing, and quality control measures at a production facility.

Inventory decisions

These refer to the means by which inventories are managed. Inventories exist at every stage of the supply chain as either raw material, semi-finished or finished goods. They can also be in process between locations. Their primary purpose is to act as a buffer against any uncertainty that might exist in the supply chain. Since holding of inventories can cost anywhere between 20 to 40 percent of their value, their efficient management is critical in supply chain operations. It is strategic in the sense that top management sets goals. However, most researchers have approached the management of inventory from an operational perspective. These include deployment strategies (push versus pull), control policies, i.e., the determination of the optimal levels of order quantities and reorder points, and setting safety stock levels, at each stocking location. These levels are critical, since they are primary determinants of customer service levels.

Transportation decisions

Strategic decisions regarding the choice of mode of transport have to be taken. These are closely linked to the inventory decisions, since the best choice of mode of transport is often found by trading-off the cost of using the particular mode of transport with the indirect cost of inventory associated with that mode. While air shipments may be fast, reliable and warrant lesser safety stocks, they are expensive. Meanwhile shipping by sea or rail may be much cheaper, but they necessitate holding relatively large amounts of inventory to buffer against the inherent uncertainty associated with them. Therefore customer service levels and geographic location play vital roles in such decisions. Since transportation is more than 30 percent of the logistics costs, operating efficiently makes good economic sense. Shipment sizes (consolidated bulk shipments versus lot-for-lot), routing and scheduling of equipment are key in effective management of the firm's transport strategy.

6.3.2 Supply Chain Modelling Approaches

Clearly, each of the above two levels of decisions require a different perspective. The strategic decisions are, for the most part, global or "all encompassing" in that they try to integrate various aspects of the supply chain. Consequently, the models that describe these decisions are huge, and require a considerable amount of data. Often due to the enormity of data requirements, and the broad scope of decisions, these models provide approximate solutions to the decisions they describe. The operational decisions, meanwhile, address the day-to-day operation of the supply chain. Therefore the models that describe them are often very specific in nature. Due to their narrow perspective, these models often consider great detail and provide very good, if not optimal, solutions to the operational decisions.

To facilitate a concise review of the literature, and at the same time attempt to accommodate the above polarity in modelling, we divide the modelling approaches into three areas - network design, "rough cut" methods, and simulation based methods. The network design methods, for the most part, provide normative models for the more strategic decisions. These models typically cover the four major decision areas described earlier, and focus more on the design aspect of the supply chain; the establishment of the network and the associated flows on them. "Rough cut" methods, on the other hand, give guiding policies for the operational decisions. These models typically assume a "single site" (i.e., ignore the network) and add supply chain characteristics to it, such as explicitly considering the sites relation to the others in the network. Simulation methods are methods by which a comprehensive supply chain model can be analyzed, considering both strategic and operational elements. However, as with all simulation models, one can only evaluate the effectiveness of a pre-specified policy, rather than developing new policies. It is the traditional question of "What if?" versus "What is best?"

6.3.3 Network Design Methods

As the very name suggests, these methods determine the location of production, stocking, and sourcing facilities, and paths the product(s) take through them. Such methods tend to be large scale, and are generally used at the inception of the supply chain.

Clearly, these network-design based methods add value to the firm in that they lay down the manufacturing and distribution strategies far into the future. It is imperative that firms at one time or another make such integrated decisions, encompassing production, location, inventory and transportation, and such models are therefore indispensable. Although there is considerable potential for these models as strategic determinants in the future, they are not without their shortcomings. Their very nature forces these problems to be on a very large scale. They are often difficult to solve to optimality. Furthermore, most of the models in this category are largely deterministic and static in nature. Additionally, those that consider stochastic elements are very restrictive in nature. In sum, there does not seem to yet be a comprehensive model that is representative of the true nature of material flows in the supply chain.

Rough cut methods

These models form the bulk of supply chain literature, and typically deal with the more operational or tactical decisions. Most of the integrative research (from a supply chain context) in the literature seems to take on an inventory management perspective. In fact, the term "supply chain" first appears in the literature as an inventory management approach. The thrust of the rough cut models is the development of inventory control policies, considering several levels or echelons together. These models have come to be known as "multi-level" or "multi-echelon" inventory control models.

Multi-echelon inventory theory has been very successfully used in industry. Cohen *et al.* [1990] describe "OPTIMIZER", one of the most complex models to date, to manage IBM's spare parts inventory. They develop efficient algorithms and sophisticated data structures to achieve large-scale systems integration.

Although current research in multi-echelon based supply chain inventory problems shows considerable promise in reducing inventories with increased customer service, the studies have several notable limitations. First, these studies largely ignore the production side of the supply chain. Their starting point in most cases is a finished goods stockpile, and policies are given to manage these effectively. Since production is a natural part of the supply chain, there seems to be a need for models that include the production component in them. Second, even on the distribution side, almost all published research assumes an arborescence structure, i. e. each site receives re-supply from only one higher level site but can distribute to several lower levels. Third, researchers have largely focused on the inventory system only. In logistics-system theory, transportation and inventory are primary components of the order fulfilment process in terms of cost and service levels. Therefore, companies must consider important interrelationships among transportation, inventory and customer service in determining their policies. Fourth, most of the models under the "inventory theoretic" paradigm are very restrictive in nature, i.e., they mostly restrict themselves to certain well-known forms of demand or lead-time or both, often quite contrary to what is observed.

6.3.4 Model of Supply Chain Management

The two primary models of supply chain management are as follows:

1. **Push based model (Traditional model)**

   Manufacturer

   ↓

   Distribution centre

   ↓

   Retailer

   ↓

   Consumers purchase merchandise

Advantages of SCM

i) Lower operating costs through reduced inventory requirements.
ii) Improve customer satisfaction of maintaining adequate stock.
iii) Improve productivity through more efficient use of resources, better data integrity.

2. Pull based model (Present model)

Consumers purchase merchandise
↓
Retailer
↓
Distribution centre
↓
Manufacturer

6.3.5 Components of SCM (Features of SCM)

The term, components of SCM, means the programming model, which has been incorporated. Supply chain management systems can be built using intranets, extranets or special supply chain management software. The major entities in SCM use the flow of information to coordinate the activities involved in buying, making and moving a product.

Capacity, inventory level, delivery schedule, payment terms

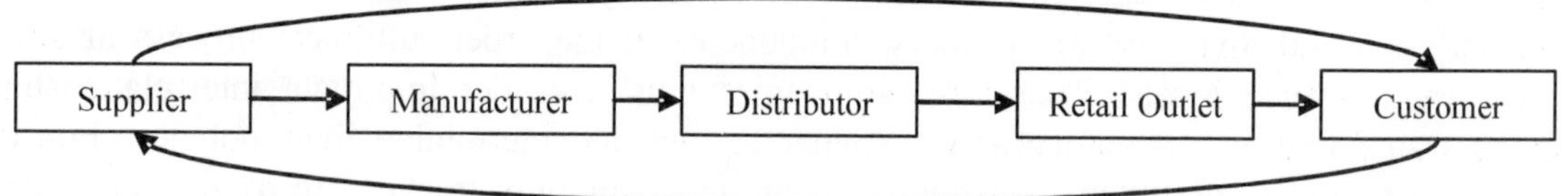

Orders, return requests, repair and service requests, payments

Fig. 6.4: ***Supply chain management***

1. Supplier management
2. Inventory management
3. Distribution management
4. Channel management
5. Payment management – using EFT
6. Financial management
7. Sales force management

6.4 INFORMATION BROKERAGE AND DATA MANAGEMENT

The information brokerage and management layer provides service integration through the motion of information brokerages, the development of which is necessitated by the increasing fragmentation of information resource.

Brokers are required because information is highly fragmented. A broker in e-commerce means mobile software, software agent. They are also called healthy viruses. Viruses have a certain level of intelligence.

Information brokerage does more than just search for another aspect of the brokerage function is the support for data management and traditional services.

6.5 INTERFACE AND SUPPORT SERVICES

The interface and support services will provide interfaces for electronic commerce applications such as interactive catalogues and will support directory services, i.e. functions necessary for information search and access.

1. **Interactive catalogues** – Interactive catalogues are the customized interface to consumer applications such as home shopping. An interactive catalogue is an extension of paper based catalogues and incorporates additional features such as sophisticated graphics and video to make the advertising more attractive.
2. **Directories** – Operate behind the scenes and attempt to organize the enormous amount of information and transactions generated to facilitate electronic commerce.

   Directory services are data based and make data from any server appear as a local file. For example, telephone white pages, which allow us to locate people and telephone numbers.

In the case of electronic commerce, directories would play an important role in information management functions.

6.6 SECURE MESSAGING

- **Security** – Achieved through digital signature, secure socket layer.
- **Messaging** – Messaging a frame work for the total implementation of portable applications, divorcing the user from the architectural primitives of their system. In general, messaging products are not applications that solve problems; rather they are enablers of the applications that solve problems. Messaging can be synchronous and asynchronous. In synchronous messaging messages are delivered immediately. Synchronous messaging is used in real life, e.g. steel plant.

In asynchronous messaging, messages are immediately forwarded. It is based on the store and forward techniques, e.g. e-mail.

Note : The security of messages which are transmitted from one place to another is known as secure messaging.

6.7 MIDDLEWARE SERVICES

Middleware is the ultimate mediator between diverse software programs that enables them talk to one another. Another reason for middleware is the computing shift from application centric to data centric. To achieve data centric computing, middleware services focus on three elements:

- Transparency
- Transaction security and management
- Distributed object management and services

Note : Middleware services deal with structured and unstructured documents.

- Unstructured document – there is no fixed structure. This is done by using protocols FTP and SMTP, e.g. e-mail.
- Structured document – there is a fixed structure, e.g. application form.

6.8 ELECTRONIC COMMERCE ON THE WORLD WIDE WEB: A CASE STUDY

This short case study is intended to introduce students to the world of electronic commerce as currently conducted on the World Wide Web (WWW) and the Internet. It does not focus on any particular firm, though it will be referenced by other cases. The case provides students who have access to Mosaic, or other Web browsers, with guided assistance in learning about the WWW's applicability to electronic commerce. Those without access to a browser will still gain a solid understanding of the possibilities. The case has three main sections. In the first, we look at an exciting new technological opportunity – the World Wide Web. Here we introduce the Internet, the Internet communications protocols (TCP/IP), the World Wide Web, and Web browsers such as Mosaic. In the second, we see how both small and large organizations are learning to harness this new opportunity to electronic commerce. The final section is intended to provide students with a high level understanding of how Web applications are constructed.

Introduction

Businesses throughout much of the world have begun to show considerable interest in the development of electronic data highways. Many feel that these two-way electronic communications pathways will provide dramatic innovations in education, shopping, financial services, entertainment, and many other fields. Although it is not yet clear what technology or technologies will provide the communications backbone for these highways, there is at least one such environment in place that provides an inexpensive early testing grounds. That technology is the Internet and in particular the World Wide Web.

This case study first introduces the Internet and the World Wide Web and then discusses some of the early attempts to use these technologies for electronic commerce. It concludes by providing an introduction to developing applications for the World Wide Web.

What is the Internet and the World Wide Web?

This section includes a brief history of the Internet, the TCP/IP communications protocols, the World Wide Web (WWW or 'Web') and Mosaic, a tool for accessing the Web.

The Internet

The Internet is not a single computer network, such as one that might interconnect the computers in an office or building. Rather it is a network of networks – a network that spans much of the earth. All these networks have in common their use of the Internet protocols which are described below. Computers, acting as smart switches, serve as gateways connecting the various networks together. They can also translate messages to and from computers that use different communications protocols. The gateways use the Internet addressing scheme to move packets of information (text, graphics, audio) back and forth. Packets are passed from one computer (or node) to another until the final destination is reached. If a pathway is unavailable, the packet is rerouted automatically by the switches. Upon arriving at their final destination, the packets are automatically reassembled (packets are often too small to contain entire messages or graphics) and provided to the requestor. Typically, only a few seconds will pass from the time the request is initiated until it completed.

The Internet provides a conduit for electronic mail, including mail sent to LISTSERVS of people with some shared interest. The file transfer protocols, or FTP, are used for sending files from one computer to another. Normally a user must have a password for the computer you wish to exchange files with, but there are also many anonymous FTP sites which permit anyone to log on and retrieve specific files. Telnet is an internet protocol permitting a user to log on to one computer by accessing it from another (for instance, if you are visiting a friend in Chennai you might log on to his account and use it to sign on to your own back in Mumbai). Usenet News, another feature of the Internet, are bulletin boards containing discussions on any conceivable topic – for instance, specialists in environmental accounting. A variety of other special services have been developed for the Internet. Several, including Archie and WAIS are search services, capable of locating files or articles from throughout the world. Gopher, developed at the University of Minnesota, is a relatively easy to use navigation tool for finding and retrieving information on the net. In 1994 the most exciting Internet capability was the World Wide Web, which is described below.

In July of 1994 there werc an estimated 10 million users accessing the Internet from 20,000 unique networks. Growth has been tremendous, with a near doubling in subscribers reported each year. Although the Internet had long been in use on college campuses, much recent growth was in commercial accounts. However, many of those commercial subscribers, fearing security breaches, had chosen to either isolate their commercial networks or to establish very limited access between them and the Worldwide Web.

The Internet is not an organization with stockholders, president, and a board of directors. Instead it can be thought of as a set of communications protocols, as functions users can perform, as a great inventory of available information, or as a scheme for intelligently connecting the people of the world into one fast learning organism. The governance structure for the Internet, thus far, has been fairly loose. Net etiquette (or Netiquette) and a strong culture had provided some discipline in the past, but the massive growth and increased commercial exploitation of the Web have created clashes of the old and new cultures. Among the most notorious such clash in 1994 was the transmission of a law firm s advertisement to several thousand listserv participants.

TCP/IP Communications Protocols

At its simplest the Internet was little more than a set of communications protocols that many people had agreed to use in connecting computers to a network and in connecting networks to each other. The Transmission Control Protocol/Internet Protocol (TCP/IP) had come out of work started by the U.S. Department of Defence in 1969. The intention was to design a communications network that could survive nuclear war. TCP/IP was designed to support a distributed network architecture. That is, there were multiple pathways between computers, no central point of vulnerability, and intelligence in the network that could make corrections as necessary.

TCP/IP is in marked contrast to, for instance, the systems network architecture of IBM which assumed that a mainframe computer would control communications routings. Furthermore TCP/IP was a non-proprietary standard that provided for open competition across the hardware platforms of various computer and communications equipment providers. The decreasing costs of both workstations and communications bandwidth had, in the early 1990s, spurred intense customer interest in the so called client-server computer and communications architecture that TCP/IP represented. In such an environment the workstation (or client) was in control while larger computers acted as servers for those clients. In the past information was pushed to users; now it could be pulled.

The World Wide Web

The World Wide Web (WWW) began as an attempt by high-energy physicists at the CERN research centre in Switzerland to share files with colleagues around the world. Its subsequent use has probably far exceeded their expectations. Essentially, the WWW or Web provides easy to use access to an ever expanding cornucopia of information sources located throughout the world. Files to be shared can be in a variety of formats (text, audio or video) and from many sources. The intelligence of the user s desk top workstation (or client) coupled with the intelligence of the computers that provide the information to servers to ensure that incompatibility problems are automatically resolved.

Electronic Commerce on the Worldwide Web

In this section we explore electronic commerce on the Worldwide Web (WWW) by a brief discussion of The Future Fantasy Bookstore and other online retailers. We then explore publishing activities on the Web, and other electronic services including electronic malls. The section concludes with a discussion of the opportunities and challenges to be faced as firms seek to reengineer commerce with the Worldwide Web.

The Future Fantasy Bookstore

The Future Fantasy Bookstore was an early commercial enterprise on the Web. Future Fantasy carries science fiction and fantasy books as well as posters, statuary, and related side lines. Future Fantasys, walk-in store, located near Stanford University in Palo Alto, had long served mail order customers, but mail order business increased dramatically when the store went up on the WWW. This was done with the assistance of Digital Equipment Corporation's Palo Alto-based Network Systems Laboratory. The owner, Jean Schroeter, or members of her staff, now spent several hours a day packing up orders for non-U.S. customers. Previously these new customers had to wait months and pay large premiums to get these books in their own country – if they were able to get them at all.

Increases in the mail order business tended to track the increased use of the Internet. Incidental mentions of the store on the various news groups and bulletin boards that shared the Internet with the WWW also provoked a flurry of new sales. For instance, web surfers are occasionally reminded that the bookstore carries the Darwin Fish, a popular adornment for car bumpers. Another stimulus to sales has been the mutual electronic links Schroeter has established with other web businesses such as The Lysator Science Fiction & Fantasy Archive in Linkoping, Sweden.

Other book stores have now begun to appear on the Web for, among others, technical subjects, college text books, and general interest books. Book sellers are also beginning to appear for books in languages such as German. Some book sellers provide electronic catalogues while others are little more than online advertisements. Lists of bookstores on the WWW make it easy to browse in many stores. Entrepreneurs are also beginning to establish electronic markets for used text books.

Stores were also springing up on the web to sell other products. Nordic Track, for instance has an advertisement on the Web while Earrings by Lisa provides color pictures of their merchandise. In an August of 1994 press release, Pizza Hut and Santa Cruz Operation Inc. announced a pizza store on the Web, but one that would only serve computer literate customers in Santa Cruz, California. This had prompted one wag to worry that, 'I'll order pizza Saturday night but not get it until Sunday morning'.

Publishers on the Web

The risk to book publishers on the web comes from more than just a new distribution channel for used textbooks. The Gutenberg Project, for instance, is building an electronic library with titles such as Alice's Adventures In Wonderland, that are no longer covered by copyright protection. Selections of cartoonist Gary Trudeau's Doonesbury is on line. Steven King, the popular suspense writer, has been selling a short story directly to consumers on the Web and electronic books are also being written specifically for distribution over the WWW. Among the publishers on the WWW are The Palo Alto Weekly, Wired Magazine, and The Internet Poetry Archive. Most of these ventures are free of charge, with expenses usually paid for by subsidies from other ventures or advertisers. Wired magazine, for instance, waits until the next issue hits the bookstands and then releases the previous month's issue, without ads, to the Internet. But organizations such as Softlock Services are offering software tools and services to support the online sale of published merchandise. Softlock clients provide prospective customers with teasers from their works and then, if they wish the entire document, they obtain an encryption key from Softlock in exchange for a credit card number. The Encylcopedia Britannica has taken another approach to selling access to its online encyclopedia. University campuses subscribe for $1 per student per year, where access is limited by the addresses of the requestors. If your university is a subscriber, your workstation will be provided access by the server computers.

Many electronic publishers have yet to free themselves from 'the tyranny of the printed page', that is the inability to view hypertext from a perspective that was different than print.

Hypertext documents are more easily digested when broken into short, relatively self-contained segments that fit on one or two workstation screens. Hypertext linkages can then take you from a general, high level view of the topic to the more detailed and specific, but only if you want to. For instance, the press release accompanying a new product introduction can be made available on the Web. It might include a link to further information on the product, technical details, user manual, et cetera. The individual modules of a document, if carefully written, can also then be easily linked to from another document or even documents written at some later point by another author, acting without permission of the original writer. The modular style of hypertext documents, coupled with the ease of linking to others written by different authors, without their permission or knowledge, presents a variety of copyright issues.

WWW-based publishing faces electronic competition of its own. CDROM has become, a common means of publication. Although the Web offers advantages for keeping information current, bandwidth limitations makes it a poor second choice for the display of graphics as well as the use of audio. The Web also shares the Internet with a variety of electronic publishing alternatives. Newsletters are commonly circulated by electronic mail and Gopher files provide a less sophisticated, but simpler, means to retrieve documents in a relatively nonformatted manner.

Electronic Malls

The Internet competes to some extent with organizations such as Prodigy, America Online, and CompuServe. Such organizations have a management structure and bureaucracy in place that makes them appear considerably better organized internally than the Internet. Anyone with the relatively low price of admission can join the Internet, but without the initial advantage of a hierarchical menu structure that would immediately lead customers to your door. Instead a number of directories such as Commercial Sites on the Internet have sprung up to help make order out of the Internet chaos. Some of these, called electronic malls, often provide additional services to help retailers set up storefronts on the web. Among these are such unfamiliar names as The Internet Mall, Downtown Anywhere, and Branch Information Services. Some such as The Global Network Navigator are beginning to carry advertising from firms such as Digital Equipment.

Other Electronic Services on the Web

Many other services are now becoming available over the world wide web, with new additions listed almost daily on the web pages of the popular Whats New in Commercial Sites on the Web? During the first two weeks of July 1994, for instance, 40 new commercial ventures were listed. Among the larger were Intel, Dell Computer, and Microsoft. Already on the Web were such computer companies as Apple Computer, Digital Equipment, Hewlett Packard, IBM, Silicon Graphics, and Sun Microsystems, as well as communication suppliers such as AT&T (Bell Labs), Novell, and Nippon Telegraph and Telecphone Corporation. Conspicuous by their absence in the summer of 1994 were such big systems integration consulting firms as Andersen Consulting, Computer Science Corporation, and EDS.

But the bulk of the organizations with listings on the WWW are small and entrepreneurial. For instance, in the first two weeks of July both the city of Staunton, Virginia and Scottso the Clown came on board. Other services increasingly available on the WWW include software developers, real estate, lawyers, home mortgages, and even a company offering incorporation services.

Reengineering Commerce

Although many new firms are joining the web, their presence varies considerably in sophistication. Even among some of the larger firms, the activities seem to be grass roots activities rather than major marketing presences. Several firms have begun small initial experiments with online ordering, although usually not with their own primary product line. One supplier of computer equipment, for instance, established a gift shop carrying items such as shirts and hats. This provided a relatively easy way to gain an introductory understanding of electronic commerce.

One participant in some of these early tests observed:

Barriers to entry on the internet are very low. As the cartoonist said, 'nobody knows you're a dog on the Internet'. But if you are going to displace paper catalogs with electronic ones they better provide things paper can't. Customization has to be a big piece of this. Retailers will bring your attention to things you want – items like those you have bought before, rather than things they want to sell you. Retailers will be better able to manage their inventory. If it doesn't sell the first day, it probably isn't going to. Or, if you are about to sell out, take it off the electronic shelf immediately. Imagine the power of Consumer Reports if there was a hypertext link directly from their best product designation and that firm's electronic catalog.

Free samples, demonstration software, or trial subscriptions are increasingly being used to attract customers. In July of 1994, Silicon Graphics announced the availability of a 30 day trial subscription to its conferencing software. Similarly, Digital Equipment Corporation let customers demo Alpha server computers from their own desktops. Free recipes from Le Cordon Bleu, similarly might attract new students or full screen color images of paintings might lure buyers to the works of Haitian artists displayed in the Electric Gallery.

Advertising on the Internet would also follow a different set of rules than most businesses were used to. Historically, advertising has been 'active', with advertisers filling subscribers' mailboxes, newpapers, and televisions with unsolicited materials. Unsolicited materials delivered via electronic mail could, however, quickly cripple the Internet. Internet advertising was more passive, with customers seeking out information they required at the moment. Mart Nisenholtz, of Ogilvy and Mather Direct offered New York Times readers (August 3rd, page D16) several suggestions for advertising on the Internet. Among them were:

- No unsolicited commercial messages
- Don't sell mailing lists without the user's express permission
- Focus advertising to appropriate news groups and listservs.
- Display the full rules for any promotions.

- Make sure that consumers understand when you are conducting market research
- Don't surreptitiously collect data from unsuspecting users.

Electronic commerce requires changes to internal processes as well as the invention of some new ones. For instance, the exchange of merchandise for money is difficult when the identity of neither the supplier nor the customer can be confirmed by the other. Bad press attached to early failings in Internet security as well as misconceptions about advertising on the Internet have made many managers wary of establishing a web presence. Another concern is the perception (and the reality) of the Internets unreliability. The lack of a central management structure coupled with the Internets rapid growth provides little reassurance. Furthermore, most internal information system managers still know little about the Internet and, because of security concerns, generally have isolated themselves from it. Among their real or imagined concerns are the vulnerability of electronic mail transactions to hackers, the possibility of computer viruses coming in over the network, unprofessional behavior on the part of their own employees, as well as the fear that external access could expose vulnerabilities in their own internal networks and systems.

The unique problems of electronic commerce are beginning to be explored by such organizations as Commerce Net, a group of Silicon Valley firms that were working together to promote and develop electronic commerce. Commerce Net's committees are exploring these and related issues and the minutes of various deliberations, such as that for network services are distributed over the world wide web.

Developing Applications for the World Wide Web

In this section we provide a very basic introduction to the hyper text mark-up language, and related HTML documentation and tools. We then describe what a homepage is and how they are located with uniform resource locators. We then discuss the value of hypertext maps and forms. Last, we explain what it is like developing HTML applications for the World Wide Web.

Hyper Text Markup Language

Before documents can be effectively displayed on the network, they have to be first marked up in the hypertext markup language (also commonly referred to by the letters in its abbreviation – html or HTML). Such documents can then be attractively and consistently displayed by web readers or, as they are sometimes called, browsers. An example is the National Center for Supercomputer Applications Mosaic browser. Html documents are formatted in a very structured manner. Paragraph headers, for instance, are surrounded by special notation as in: <H1>This is a Demonstration Header</H1>. Paragraphs ended with <P> while blank lines in the source text are ignored by html browsers. Similar formatting is available for producing indented lists (ordered or unordered), lists within lists, italics, et cetera. Documents also can include embedded links to other documents or to other locations within the same document. The text pointing to these other locations is highlighted in a different color or, for black and white monitors, underlined.

Other html commands are used to insert graphics, previously recorded sound, or full motion video clips into the text. In these instances, if the web reader is capable of handling the material, an icon would be inserted on the displayed screen, indicating that there was a graphic available. Non text-based documents require far more memory and communications bandwidth than do text and therefore considerably reduce system responsiveness. A video of 10 seconds, which would appear only in a small corner of the screen might consume several minutes to download from the server.

HTML Documentation & Tools

Extensive online documentation exists for the Windows, Macintosh, and workstations versions of Mosaic as well as for the WWW, and the NCSA. Developers will also find useful information in web sites such as the WWW and HTML Developers Jump Station, W3 and HTML Tools, and the Web Developers Work Bench. Foreign language versions of some documentation is available on the Web including a Japanese guide to the Hyper Text Markup Language. English language hypertext documentation is also available for introductory, intermediate, and advanced capabilities. But, despite the extensive documentation available online, one of the best ways to learn html is to look at the html for screens developed by others. Each workstation needs to have a copy of the marked up code to present the attractive screen images. That same html code is available in the workstation so the user can see how a particular effect was achieved. Web Browsers had various ways, some easy and some less so, to make that source html code available for inspection.

The hypertext mark up language will probably eventually be produced automatically by word processors, but most web users in 1994 are still marking up their own documents with the html commands. Specialized software called hypertext editors and converters are available via the web to assist with big conversion efforts. But projects are still time consuming.

Home Pages

Home pages are used to provide information on individuals, enterprises, organizations. They are also used to point to collections of related home pages such as The Web's Edge, an Index to Multimedia Sources, a list of Commercial Services on the Web or The California Virtual Tourist (a compendium of web home pages in California). Usually a home page contains the broadest set of information about the entity with hypertext links branching down into subordinant pages. For instance, Digital Equipment Corporations Corporate Research home page provides links to individual research labs, publications of those labs, projects underway, and web servers that had been constructed with Digital's assistance. Despite this hierarchical arrangement, links can be readily established to connect any location on the Web to any other location.

Uniform Resource Locators

Establishing a link from one document to another requires that you know its location or URL (uniform resource locator). Just as an electronic mail address is required to send someone a message over the internet, URLs are necessary to access information. When Mosaic or another web reader is provided with a URL, either by the user keying it in or clicking on highlighted hypertext, the reader initiates a request to the server named in the URL to provide a copy of the file designated. In 1994, URLs were beginning to show up on business cards, advertisements, letterhead, and in the trailers (called 'signatures') to electronic mail messages.

Maps

In addition to text and graphics, users can specify in html a map. Maps are graphics that contain links to textual information or to other graphics. A Texan planning a trip to Palo Alto, for instance, scanned a Web-based map of the city of Palo Alto, provided by the Chamber of Commerce, and identified an accommodation close to the site of his meeting. The proprietor of the bed and breakfast, although unaware that their name appeared on a listing on the Web, was delighted by the prospect of this new distribution channel.

Forms

Html also supports the use of data capture forms. For instance, The Management Information Systems Quarterly, a journal of research on information systems management, and Grant's Florist and Greenhouse both used the forms fill-in capability to take orders for their merchandise. Customers with web readers that were incapable of handling forms could instead print out the text-based versions of the web documents which they could then complete and fax to the supplier; thus the customer still gets fast turnaround and a greater likelihood of availability, but with no requirement for the supplier to modify current business practices. Other web merchandisers rely on electronic mail addresses for ordering. An example is the Electric Gallery, that displayed and sold original paintings by Haitian artists such as Fernand Pierre's painting entitled, "Arbre de vie" (Tree of life). Images such as those displayed by the Electric Gallery or sound recordings required additional software on the user's computer. Once available, however, these programs could be automatically started up and run by web readers such as Mosaic. Much of this software was itself downloadable from the internet often at little or no charge.

Developing Web Applications with HTML

Although time consuming, the html documentation syntax is relatively simple. It is also relatively easy to spread the burden of creating web documents across different parts of the country or world. The hierarchical nature of related documents, coupled with the ability to observe one another's work, makes it very easy to work cooperatively or to quickly blend two projects together even across continents. But users of the web commonly encounter under construction notices or file not found error messages in the web pages of even the most sophisticated web developers. Moreover, the web is a very dynamic force with new homepages or changes in old ones occurring daily. But it is also common for web data to be poorly maintained, for servers not to be operating, for homepages to relocate to new servers (and therefore new addresses), or to disappear completely.

SUMMARY

- Electronic commerce applications are quite varied. In its most common form, e-commerce is also used to denote the paperless exchange of business information using EDI, e-mail, electronic bulleting boards, electronic funds transfer and other similar technologies.
- A framework is intended to define and create tools that integrate the information found in today's closed systems and allow the development of e-commerce applications. The aim of the architectural framework itself is not to build a new database management system, data repository, computer languages, software agent based transaction monitors or communication protocols.
- A supply chain is a network of facilities and distribution options that performs the functions of procurement of materials, transformation of these materials into intermediate and finished products, and the distribution of these finished products to customers.
- The term, components of SCM, means the programming model, which has been incorporated. Supply chain management systems can be built using intranets, extranets or special supply chain management software. The major entities in SCM use the flow of information to coordinate the activities involved in buying, making and moving a product.

REVIEW QUESTIONS

1. What opportunities does the World Wide Web offer in reaching customers? Discuss the architectural framework.
2. Which industries seem most likely to benefit first from those opportunities? Why?
3. How will marketing on the World Wide Web differ from traditional marketing?
4. Who will be the key players in supplying the technology for this emerging market?
5. Who is most threatened by the opportunities offered by the World Wide Web?
6. Explain the supply chain management and its components in details.
7. Discuss the advantages and disadvantages of SCM.

CHAPTER 7

Encryption

A technique widely used in computer networks to enhance security is encryption. Encryption makes plain text unintelligible by means of some type of reversible encoding scheme developed around a private key known only to the transmitter and receiver. It is the conversion of data into a form, called a cipher text that cannot be easily understood by unauthorized people. The reverse of encryption is decryption, in which the cipher text is reversed to the original plain text so that it can be understood. Encryption normally occurs at the transmitting site, decryption occurs at the receiving site.

The use of encryption/decryption is as old as the art of communication. In wartime, a cipher, often incorrectly called a code, can be employed to keep the enemy from obtaining the contents of transmissions. (Technically, a code is a means of representing a signal without the intent of keeping it secret; examples are Morse code and ASCII.) Simple ciphers include the substitution of letters for numbers, the rotation of letters in the alphabet, and the "scrambling" of voice signals by inverting the sideband frequencies. More complex ciphers work according to sophisticated computer algorithms that rearrange the data bits in digital signals.

In order to easily recover the contents of an encrypted signal, the correct decryption key is required. The key is an algorithm that undoes the work of the encryption algorithm. Alternatively, a computer can be used in an attempt to break the cipher. The more complex the encryption algorithm, the more difficult it becomes to eavesdrop on the communications without access to the key.

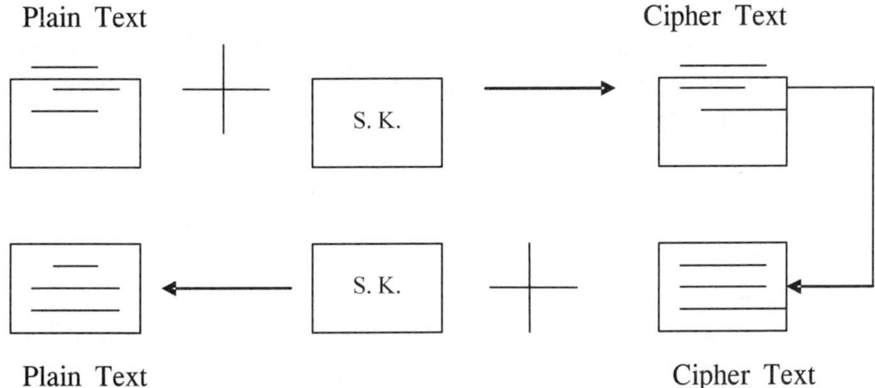

Fig. 7.1: ***The process of encryption***

Encryption/decryption is especially important in wireless communications. This is because wireless circuits are easier to tap than their hard-wired counterparts. Nevertheless, encryption/ decryption is a good idea when carrying out any kind of sensitive transaction, such as a credit-card purchase online, or the discussion of a company secret between different departments in the organization. In general, the stronger the cipher - that is, the harder it is for unauthorized people to break it - the better. However, as the strength of encryption/decryption increases, so does the cost.

In recent years, a controversy has arisen over so-called strong encryption. This refers to ciphers that are essentially unbreakable without the decryption keys. While most companies and their customers view it as a means of keeping secrets and minimizing fraud, some governments view strong encryption as a potential vehicle by which terrorists might evade authorities. These governments, including that of the United States, want to set up a key-escrow arrangement. This means that everyone who uses a cipher would be required to provide the government with a copy of the key. Decryption keys would be stored in a supposedly secure place, used only by authorities, and used only if backed up by a court order. Opponents of this scheme argue that criminals could hack into the key-escrow database and illegally obtain, steal or alter the keys. Supporters claim that while this is a possibility, implementing the key escrow scheme would be better than doing nothing to prevent criminals from freely using encryption/decryption.

There are many factors to consider when it comes to data encryption and classification in practical cryptography. Understanding all aspects of corporate database encryption can be daunting. It is necessary to obtain information and advice on database encryption before attempting the task, including encryption for media protection and for separation of duties.

Windows BitLocker disk encryption technology, which enables disk encryption for data protection, can be an essential tool for organizational data protection. One should obtain information about what the technology can and cannot do and how it can help to avoid a data breach.

When it comes to encryption, it often seems that IT administrators are constantly repeating bad practices. One should learn how to avoid and prevent some of the biggest encryption mistakes, such as using WEP encryption, failing to encrypt laptops and ignoring patches and updates. For a hacker, a misplaced or stolen laptop can serve as an open door into a world of personal data. One should learn how laptop encryption can help to achieve strong laptop security strategy and prevent data or identity theft.

7.1 DATA ENCRYPTION TECHNIQUES

Often there has been a need to protect information from 'prying eyes'. In the electronic age, information that could otherwise benefit or educate a group or individual can also be used against such groups or individuals. Industrial espionage among highly competitive businesses often requires that extensive security measures be put into place. And, those who wish to exercise their personal freedom, outside of the oppressive nature of governments, may also wish to encrypt certain information to avoid suffering the penalties of going against the wishes of those who attempt to control. The methods of data encryption and decryption are relatively straightforward, and easily mastered.

Traditionally, several methods can be used to encrypt data streams, all of which can easily be implemented through software, but not so easily decrypted when either the original or its encrypted data stream are unavailable. (When both source and encrypted data are available, code-breaking becomes much simpler, though it is not necessarily easy). The best encryption methods have little effect on system performance, and may contain other benefits (such as data compression) built in. The well-known 'PKZIP®' utility offers both compression and data encryption in this manner. Also DBMS packages have often included some kind of encryption scheme so that a standard 'file copy' cannot be used to read sensitive information that might otherwise require some kind of password to access. They also need 'high performance' methods to encode and decode the data.

Fortunately, the simplest of all of the methods, the 'translation table', meets this need very well. Each 'chunk' of data (usually 1 byte) is used as an offset within a 'translation table', and the resulting 'translated' value from within the table is then written into the output stream. The encryption and decryption programs each use a table that translates to and from the encrypted data. In fact, the 80x86 CPU's even have an instruction 'XLAT' that lends itself to this purpose at the hardware level. While this method is very simple and fast, the disadvantage is that once the translation table is known, the code is broken. Further, such a method is relatively straightforward for code breakers to decipher - such code methods have been used for years, even before the advent of the computer. Still, for general "unread ability" of encoded data, without adverse effects on performance, the 'translation table' method lends itself well.

A modification to the 'translation table' uses 2 or more tables, based on the position of the bytes within the data stream, or on the data stream itself. Decoding becomes more complex, since the same process has to be reliably reversed. However, the use of more than one translation table, especially when implemented in a 'pseudo-random' order, makes code breaking relatively difficult. An example of this method might use translation table 'A' on all of the 'even' bytes, and translation table 'B' on all of the 'odd' bytes. Unless a potential code breaker knows that there are exactly 2 tables, even with both source and encrypted data available the deciphering process is relatively difficult.

Similar to using a translation table, 'data repositioning' lends itself to use by a computer, but takes considerably more time to accomplish. A buffer of data is read from the input, then the order of the bytes (or other 'chunk' size) is rearranged, and written 'out of order'. The decryption program then reads this back in, and puts them back 'in order'. Often such a method is best used in combination with one or more of the other encryption methods mentioned here, making it even more difficult for code breakers to determine how to decipher encrypted data. As an example, consider an anagram. The letters are all there, but the order has been changed. Some anagrams are easier than others to decipher, but a well written anagram is a brain teaser nonetheless, especially if it is intentionally misleading.

Other methods involve something that only computers can do: word/byte rotation and XOR bit masking. If the words or bytes within a data stream are rotated using multiple and variable direction and duration of rotation, in an easily reproducible pattern, a stream of data can rapidly be encoded with a method that is nearly impossible to break. Further, the use of an 'XOR mask' in combination with this ('flipping' the bits in certain positions from 1 to 0, or 0 to 1) makes the code breaking process even more difficult. The best combination would also use 'pseudo random' effects, the easiest of which would involve a simple sequence like Fibbonaci numbers. The sequence '1,1,2,3,5,...' is easily generated by adding the previous 2 numbers in the sequence to get the next. Carrying out modular arithmetic on the result (i.e. Fibbonaci sequence mod 3 to get rotation factor) and operating on multiple byte sequences (using a prime number of bytes for rotation is usually a good guideline) will make the code breaker's job even more difficult, adding the 'pseudo-random' effect that is easily reproduced by the decryption program.

In some cases, one may want to detect whether data has been tampered with. In this case some kind of 'checksum' is encrypted into the data stream itself. This is useful not only for authorization codes but for programs themselves. A virus that infects such a 'protected' program would no doubt neglect the encryption algorithm and authorization/checksum signature. The program could then check itself each time it loads, and thus detect the presence of file corruption. Naturally, such a method would have to be kept very secret, as virus programmers represent the worst of the code breakers: those who wilfully use information to do damage to others. As such, the use of encryption is mandatory for any good anti-virus protection scheme.

A cyclic redundancy check is a typically used checksum method. It uses bit rotation and an XOR mask to generate a 16-bit or 32-bit value for a data stream, such that one missing bit or 2 interchanged bits are more or less guaranteed to cause a 'checksum error'. This method has been used for file transfers for a long time, such as with XMODEM-CRC. The method is somewhat well documented, and standard. But, a deviation from the standard CRC method might be useful for the purpose of detecting a problem in an encrypted data stream, or within a program file that checks itself for viruses.

7.2 KEY-BASED ENCRYPTION ALGORITHMS

One very important feature of a good encryption scheme is the ability to specify a 'key' or 'password' of some kind, and have the encryption method alter itself such that each 'key' or 'password' produces a different encrypted output, which requires a unique 'key' or 'password' to decrypt. This can either be a 'symmetrical' key (both encrypt and decrypt use the same key) or 'asymmetrical' (encrypt and decrypt keys are different). The popular 'PGP' public key encryption, and the 'RSA' encryption that it is based on, uses an 'asymmetrical' key. The encryption key, the 'public key', is significantly different from the decryption key, the 'private key', such that attempting to derive the private key from the public key involves many hours of computing time, making it impractical at best.

There are few operations in mathematics that are truly 'irreversible'. In nearly all cases, if an operation is performed on 'a', resulting in 'b', an equivalent operation can be performed on 'b' to get 'a'. In some cases this may yield the absolute value (such as a square root), or the operation may be undefined (such as dividing by zero). However, in the case of 'undefined' operations, it may be possible to base a key on an algorithm such that an operation like division by zero would prevent a public key from being translated into a private key. As such, only 'trial and error' would remain, which would require a significant amount of processing time to create the private key from the public key.

The RSA encryption algorithm uses very large prime numbers to generate the public key and the private key. Although it would be possible to factor out the public key to get the private key (a trivial matter once the 2 prime factors are known), the numbers are so large as to make it very impractical to do so. The encryption algorithm itself is also very slow, which makes it impractical to use RSA to encrypt large data sets. What PGP does (and most other RSA-based encryption schemes do) is encrypt a symmetrical key using the public key, then the remainder of the data is encrypted with a faster algorithm using the symmetrical key. The symmetrical key itself is randomly generated, so that the only way to get it would be by using the private key to decrypt the RSA-encrypted symmetrical key.

Example

Suppose one wants to encrypt data (e.g. a Web page) with a key of 12345. Using the public key, the 12345 is RSA-encrypted, and put at the front of the data stream (possibly followed by a marker or preceded by a data length to distinguish it from the rest of the data). Then the 'encrypted key' data are followed with the encrypted Web page text, encrypted using one of the above methods and the key '12345'. Upon receipt, the decrypt program looks for (and finds) the encrypted key, uses the 'private key' to decrypt it, and gets back the '12345'. It then locates the beginning of the encrypted data stream, and applies the key '12345' to decrypt the data. The result is a very well protected data stream that is reliably and efficiently encrypted, transmitted, and decrypted.

Source files for a simple RSA-based encryption algorithm can be found at the address ftp://ftp.funet.fi/pub/crypt/cryptography/asymmetric/rsa

It is somewhat difficult to write a front-end to get this code to work, but for the sake of illustration, the method actually does work and by studying the code it is possible to understand the processes involved in RSA encryption.

7.3 TYPES OF ENCRYPTION

7.3.1 Symmetric Encryption

Symmetric encryption is the oldest and best-known technique. A secret key, which can be a number, a word, or just a string of random letters, is applied to the text of a message to change the content in a particular way. This might be as simple as shifting each letter by a number of places in the alphabet. As long as both sender and recipient know the secret key, they can encrypt and decrypt all messages that use this key.

Symmetric encryption is also known as secret key encryption. The concept behind encryption is simple: To protect data so that only certain people can unprotect it. The simplest way to do this with computers - where data is represented in bits of 1's and 0's - is to shuffle the bits around.

Although this is an extremely over-simplistic view of encryption, it is worthwhile keeping the 'shuffler' point of view in mind, because no matter how complex the process is and how much work has gone into it, it is really just moving bits around or replacing bits according to preset substitution tables.

7.3.1.1 Data encryption standard (DES)

DES is one of the oldest computer based encryption methods. Designed by IBM in 1977, DES is considered breakable due to its fairly small key size of 56 bits. Although the algorithm was broken in 1998, it took a dedicated machine costing 250 thousand dollars and 3 days to crack it. "On Tuesday, January 19, 1999, Distributed.Net, a worldwide coalition of computer enthusiasts, worked with EFF's DES Cracker and a worldwide network of nearly 100,000 PCs on the Internet, to win RSA Data Security's DES Challenge III in a record-breaking 22 hours and 15 minutes. The worldwide computing team deciphered a secret message encrypted with the United States government's data encryption standard (DES) algorithm using commonly available technology. From the floor of the *RSA Data Security Conference & Expo*, a major data security and cryptography conference being held in San Jose, Calif., EFF's DES Cracker and the Distributed.Net computers were testing 245 billion keys per second when the key was found."

To put things into perspective, DES is breakable but it took a series of dedicated custom built DES cracking CPUs some effort to do so. Maybe less effort would be needed now; however, DES is fairly difficult to crack and still has its uses depending on security needs and the sensitivity of the data.

A simplified overview of the DES encryption algorithm

As it is very difficult to discuss how encryption works without getting into the mathematics, this overview is not a complete picture.

The steps to DES encryption are given below:

1. Take the plain text input and break it into blocks of 64 bits. For this reason, DES is a block based encryption method. This blocking is fairly important, as will be seen later.
2. Derive - from the 56 bit encryption key - 16 sub keys of length 48 bits. This is again based on bit shuffling. The process is fairly straight forward. For generating each sub key, the previous sub key is halved and the bits of each half are moved one bit to the left. The first bits are wrapped around to the end. The two new halves are rejoined to make a new key. The 56 bit key that you provide to the encryption method is only used to generate the first sub key, and isn't directly used to encrypt the data.
3. Once the plain text has been broken up into a series of 64 bit blocks, it is shuffled (a process also called permutation) based on a known 'shuffle' table that specifies how the bits are shuffled. That is, bit 1 is placed in bit 40, bit 2 is placed in bit 23 and so on. This does not actually help to make the encryption any more secure. In fact, it makes the process more difficult to achieve using a software based algorithm.
4. Once this shuffle has been done, the bits then are passed through 16 steps, or rounds, using one of the generated 16 sub keys.
5. The shuffled 64 bits created in step 3 are passed to a round, where it is split into two blocks of 32 bits each and processed against the corresponding key for that round. The process conducted in the round is covered later.
6. Step 4 is repeated 16 times, once for each sub key. The output of each round is fed into the following round.
7. Once the 16th round is complete, the resulting two 32 bit halves are switched and then rejoined back into a 64 bit block.
8. Finally, the 64 bit block is then reshuffled (permutated) using the inverse shuffle that was applied in step 3. Again, this does not make any great difference to the effectiveness of the encryption method.

All the blocks of the plain text go through this process. Once all the blocks have been processed they are combined to give the encrypted cipher text.

Figure 7.2 shows the process, but it only gives the overall picture, most of the complexity occurs within each of the rounds.

An overview of a DES round

There are 16 rounds to the DES encryption algorithm and the 64 bit outcome from one round becomes the input of the next round. Each round also has an associated 48 bit key that was derived from the master 56 bit key. Within each round the following process occurs.

The 64 bit block is halved. The right hand half is copied down and makes up the left hand side of the output block. The right hand half also goes through a mangler function before being exclusively OR'd with the left hand half to make up the right hand half of the output block.

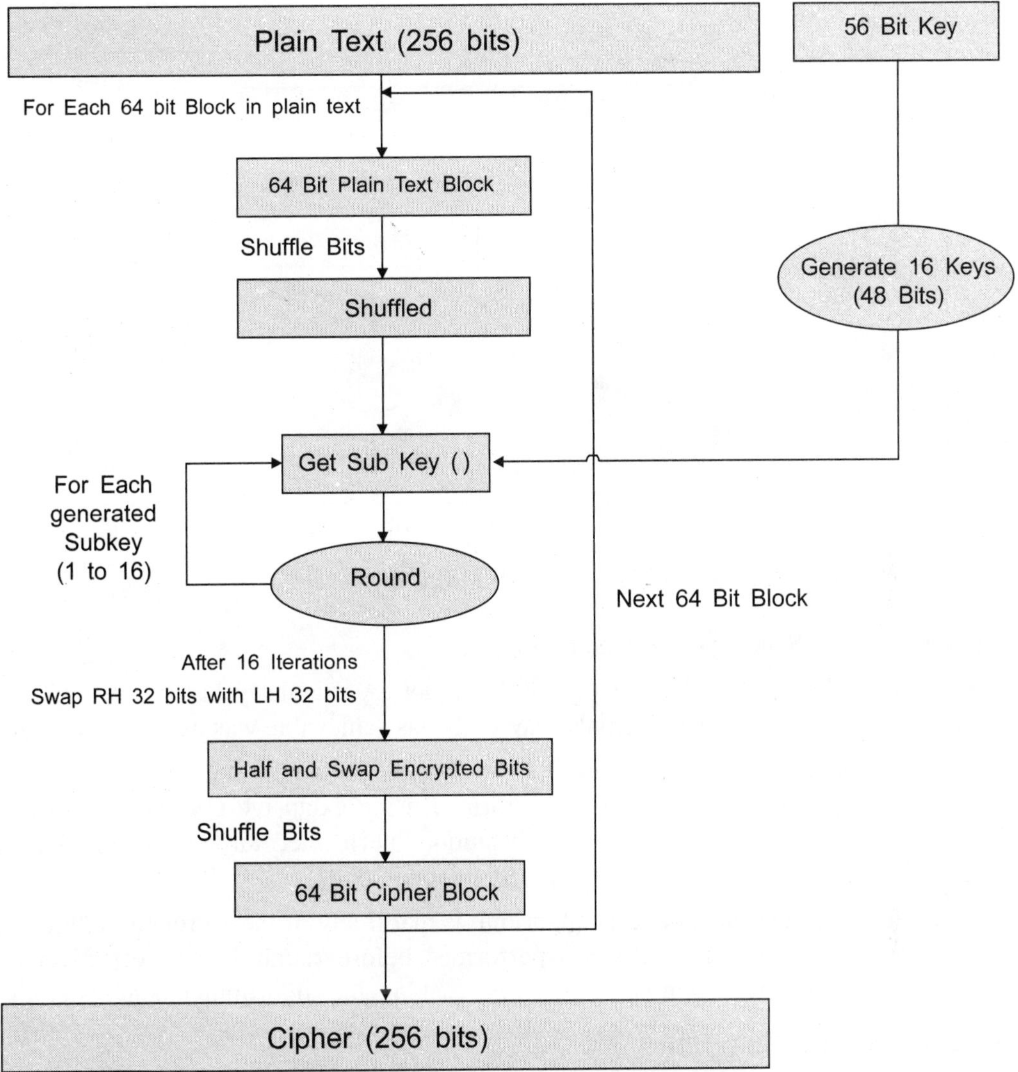

Fig. 7.2: *DES symmetric encryption*

The mangler function is a substitution algorithm, which is another full process in itself. The substitution involves rather a large number of look up substitution tables.

Basically, the right hand 32 bits are expanded to 48 bits before being broken down into 8 chunks of 6 bits. The rounds key, which is 48 bits, is also broken down into 8 chucks of 6 bits. The chunks of the data is exclusively OR'd with the chucks of the key.

The resulting 48 bits are then passed through the substitution method - also known as an s-box - which produces a 32 bit block of data. This data block is exclusively OR'd with the left hand half of the block passed into the round, as shown in Fig. 7.3.

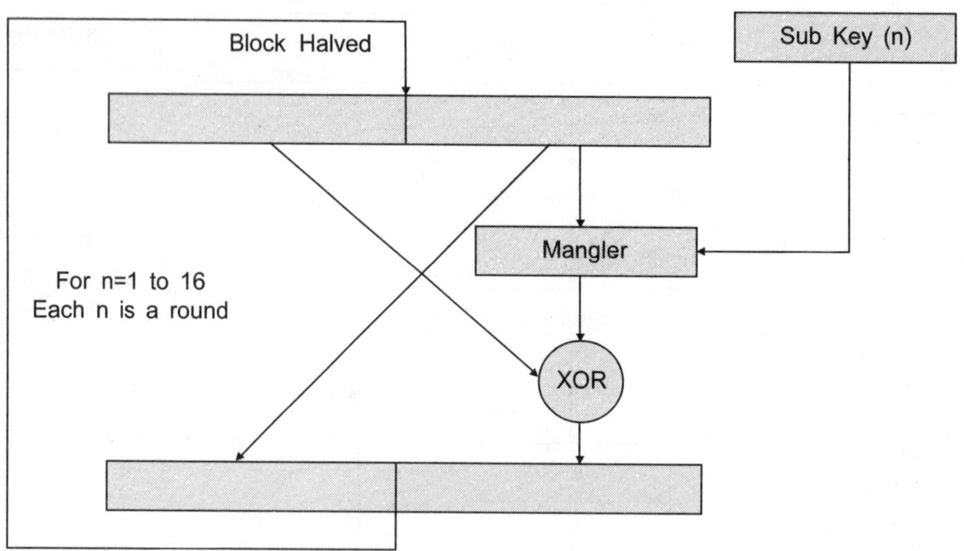

Fig. 7.3: ***DES round process***

Review of the DES encryption algorithm

Prior to modern CPUs, DES encryption was not a particularly fast process. Coupled with some unnecessary data shuffles, the only way DES was achievable was using custom built CPUs.

That has changed thanks to modern CPUs. Since DES uses an unusual and small key size, it is fast as most of the bit shuffling is performed using exclusive ORs, which are extremely fast. However with all the shuffles and substitutions performed throughout the algorithm, the whole DES encryption process is completely reversible.

Another interesting fact about the algorithm is that if any of the 16 rounds where performed in a different order - say round 3 was performed before round 1 - the effectiveness of the algorithm is reduced by a number of factors, making the algorithm much easier to crack.

7.3.1.2 Block based encryption

DES, as well as many other encryption algorithms, works by breaking the data into blocks. With DES, this block size can only be 64 bits. In some other encryptions, the block size can be changed. It is very unlikely that the data being encrypted will be a multiple of 64 bits, which results in the last block not being large enough for the process. Usually, the last block is padded so that it fills the required size.

Breaking the data into blocks creates a problem. If two 64 bit blocks happen to contain the same data, then the cipher text of each block will also be the same and this leaks information to a potential attacker.

An attacker can also easily copy a cipher block and use it anywhere in the cipher to replace another cipher block. When the cipher is decoded, no error will occur and an attacker has essentially altered the original data.

To solve this problem, there are a couple of approaches that can be used. Each of the approaches has certain advantages and disadvantages. Which approach is chosen depends on various factors. These approaches are called modes of operation.

This approach should be avoided. It does not change the behaviour of the encryption. Identical blocks produce identical cipher text resulting in the above problem. It does have one advantage, though. Only the key needs to be known in order to decrypt the message. In other modes of operation, an initialization vector (iv) is required, which means two pieces of information - the key and iv - need to be known to encrypt and decrypt.

7.3.1.3 Cipher block chaining (CBC)

This is the most common mode of operation. In this approach, an initialization vector (**iv**) is used along with the key to encrypt the initial block. The produced cipher block is then used as an (**iv**) for encrypting subsequent blocks. The previous cipher block effects the encryption of the current block, which effects the encryption of the next block.

The advantage of this approach is that it removes the problem of duplicate cipher blocks. Another advantage is the (**iv**). By changing the (**iv**), the same message can be encrypted to a complete different cipher, which means that the same data can be sent a number of times without this being apparent to a potential attacker.

The disadvantages of this approach are that the cipher cannot be decrypted unless one has all the cipher blocks. Also, if there are any damaged bits in one of the blocks, it results in garbled output in the subsequent block.

7.3.1.4 Output feedback mode (OFM)

In this mode of operation the encryption process is altered slightly. Instead of the message being directly encrypted, the initialization vector (**iv**) is encrypted. If the original message is 256 bits long (4 blocks of 64 bits) then the (**iv**) is encrypted 4 times to produce a similar size piece of information, called the one-time pad. The original message is then exclusively OR'd with this one-time pad to produce the cipher text. The encryption process remains the same but the (**iv**) is encrypted rather than the data.

Similar to the CBC approach, the previous (**iv**) encryption block influences the current (**iv**) blocks encryption. However, only a certain number of bits are used. In CBC, the whole block is used to alter the encryption of the next block. In ORM, only a certain number of bits are used.

The advantages are that the one-time pad can be created at any time, meaning that only a portion of the cipher can be decrypted at a time. In other words, the whole cipher is not needed to be able to decrypt.

The disadvantage is that if an attacker has a copy of the original data and a copy of the cipher they can work out the one-time pad, meaning they can replace the original data with whatever replacement data they want.

7.3.1.5 Cipher feedback mode (CFM)

This mode is similar to OFM and CBC. As with OFM, the initialization vector is encrypted and the plain text message is exclusively OR'd with the result to produce the cipher. However, as with CBC, it is the resulting cipher that is used to alter the next (iv) block's encryption.

In other words, the (**iv**) is encrypted and exclusively OR'd with *n*-bits of the plain text, which produces a cipher. Part of this cipher is then used to alter the next (**iv**) encryption process. That result is then exclusively OR'd with the next *n*-bits of the plain text, and so on.

7.3.1.6 Choice of a symmetric encryption method

There are two important considerations of symmetric encryption. The first one, and the most important, is the key. The second is the mode of operation and how cipher blocks are used to alter subsequent cipher blocks.

In the case of the key, one has to choose between the size of the key, its performance, and the nature of the data. A larger key size means better security but at a cost of reduced performance.

DES with the smallest key is the fastest encryption method but the 56 bit key size means it is not necessarily the most secure. Consider the nature of the data. If the data needing protection only has a 'shelf-life' of a couple of hours and contains reasonably insensitive data, then DES is still a valid choice. If the data have a longer 'shelf life', are fairly sensitive and do not belong to the user (for example, a customer's credit card details) then it is best to sacrifice performance in favour of a larger key.

In the case of the blocks, the choice is between functionality and performance. Using ECB is the fastest mode of operation but is not advisable if the data uses more than 64 bits of information (more than one block).

CBC is the most common process. For the most part is generally suitable, but it is slightly slower than the CFM method, especially in larger data sets. If the data set is of a reasonable size then either CBC or OFM mode is the better choice. If it is necessary to decrypt the cipher before receiving all the cipher text, then OFM should be used; otherwise, CFM is a better choice.

7.3.2 Asymmetric Encryption

The problem with secret keys is exchanging them over the Internet or a large network while preventing them from falling into the wrong hands. Anyone who knows the secret key can decrypt the message. One answer is asymmetric encryption, in which there are two related keys - a key pair. What one key encrypts, only the other can decrypt.

A public key is made freely available to anyone who might want to send you a message. A second, private key is kept secret, so that only the user knows it. Frequently (but not necessarily), the keys are interchangeable, in the sense that if key A encrypts a message, then B can decrypt it, and if key B encrypts a message, then key A can decrypt it. While common, this property is not essential to asymmetric encryption.

Asymmetric encryption is also known as public key cryptography, since users typically create a matching key pair, and make one public while keeping the other secret.

Users can "sign" messages by encrypting them with their private keys. This is effective since any message recipient can verify that the user's public key can decrypt the message, and thus prove that the user's secret key was used to encrypt it. If the user's secret key is, in fact, secret, then it follows that the user, and not some impostor, really sent the message.

Users can send secret messages by encrypting a message with the recipient's public key. In this case, only the intended recipient can decrypt the message, since only that user should have access to the required secret key.

The key to successful use of asymmetric encryption is a key management system, which implements a public key infrastructure. Without this, it is difficult to establish the reliability of public keys, or even to conveniently find suitable ones.

Any messages (text, binary files or documents) that are encrypted by using the public key can only be decrypted by applying the same algorithm, but by using the matching private key. Any message that is encrypted by using the private key can only be decrypted by using the matching public key. This means that one does not have to worry about passing public keys over the Internet (the keys are supposed to be public). A problem with asymmetric encryption, however, is that it is slower than symmetric encryption. It requires far more processing power to both encrypt and decrypt the content of the message.

7.3.2.1 Digital certificates

To use asymmetric encryption, there must be a way for people to discover other public keys. The typical technique is to use digital certificates (also known simply as certificates). A certificate is a package of information that identifies a user or a server, and contains information such as the organizations name, the organization that issued the certificate, the user's e-mail address and country, and the user's public key.

When a server and client require a secure encrypted communication, they send a query over the network to the other party, which sends back a copy of the certificate. The other party's public key can be extracted from the certificate. A certificate can also be used to uniquely identify the holder.

7.3.2.2 Encryption with private keys (Secret key algorithms)

A principle disadvantage of any type of private key structure is that all sites of the network must have knowledge of the common keys. Some administrative and logistic problems arise in the distribution of keys.

The idea of the private key has been the dominant approach for providing network cryptography.

7.3.2.3 Encryption with public keys (Public key algorithms)

Many commercial systems use public key encryption/decryption systems. Separate keys are used to encipher and decipher data. The encrypting key and algorithms can be known to anyone, only the deciphering key is kept secret.

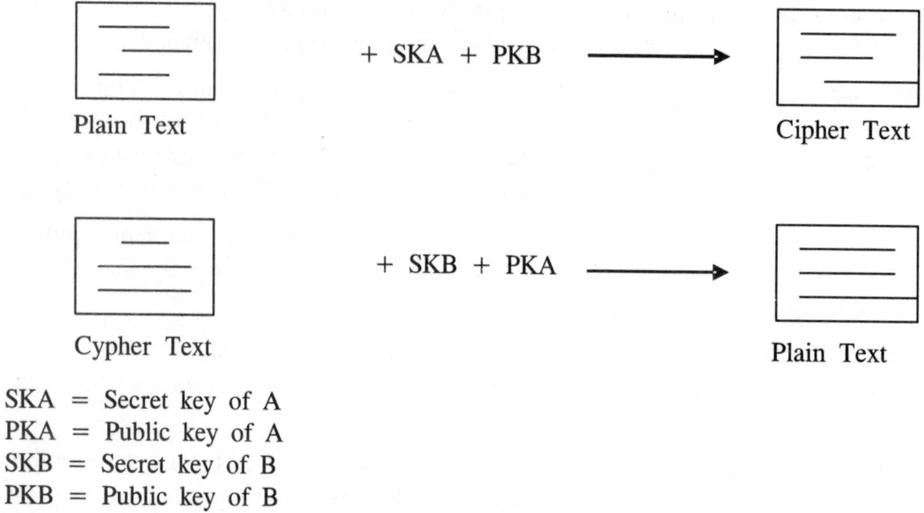

Fig. 7.4: *Public key encryption/decryption systems*

If once closed by public key of B and secret key of A then it is opened by secret key of B and public key of A and if it is closed by public key of A and secret key of B then opened by secret key of A and public key of B.

Fig. 7.5

A public key encryption system can be viewed as a series of public and private keys that lock data when they are transmitted and unlock them when they are received. The sender locates the recipients public key in a directory and uses it to encrypt a message. The message is sent in encrypted form over the Internet or a private network. When the encrypted message arrives the recipient uses his private key to decrypt the data and read the message.

7.3.3 Digital Signatures

In the case of business transactions, authentication refers to the use of digital signatures, which have the same function for digital documents as hand written signatures have for printed documents. A digital signature is a code that can be attached to an electronically transmitted message to uniquely identify its contents and the sender.

The signature is an unforgettable piece of data declaring that a named person wrote or otherwise agreed to the document to which the signature is attached. Unlike encryption, digital signatures are a recent development, the need for which has arisen with the proliferation of e-commerce.

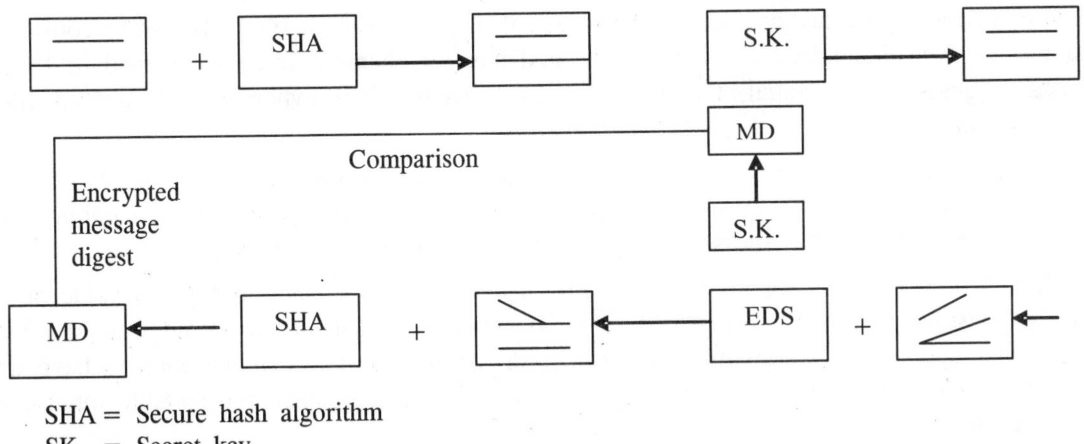

SHA = Secure hash algorithm
SK = Secret key
MD = Message digest

Fig. 7.6

The recipient, as well as a third party can verify that the document did indeed originate from the person whose signature is attached and that the document has not been altered since it was signed.

A secure digital signature system thus consists of two parts –

1. A method of signing a document such that forgery is unfeasible.
2. A method of verifying that a signature was actually generated by whomever if represents.

A digital signature actually provides a greater degree of security than a handwritten signature. The recipient of a digitally signed message can verify both that the message originated from the person whose signature is attached and that the message has not been altered either intentionally or accidentally since it was signed. Furthermore, secure digital signatures cannot be repudiated; the signer of a document cannot later disown it by claiming the signature was forged. In other words, digital signatures enable "authentication" of digital messages, assuring the recipient of a digital message of both the identity of the sender and the integrity of the message.

How is a digital signature used for authentication?

Suppose 'A' wants to send a signed message to 'B'. 'A' creates a message digest by using a hash function on the message. The message digest serves as a "digital fingerprint" of the message; if any part of the message is modified, the hash function returns a different result. 'A' then encrypts the message digest with her private key. This encrypted message digest is the digital signature for the message.

'A' sends both the message and the digital signature to 'B'. When 'B' receives them, he decrypts the signature using A's public key, thus revealing the message digest. To verify the message, he then hashes the message with the same hash function 'A' used and compares the result to the message digest he received from 'A'. If they are exactly equal, 'B' can be confident that the message did indeed come from 'A' and has not changed since she signed it. If the message digests are not equal, the message either originated elsewhere or was altered after it was signed.

It should be noted that using a digital signature does not encrypt the message itself. If 'A' wants to ensure the privacy of the message, she must also encrypt it using B's public key, only then can 'B' read the message by decrypting it with his private key.

It is not feasible for anyone to either find a message that hashes to a given value or to find two messages that hash to the same value. If either were feasible, an intruder could attach a false message onto A's signature. Specific hash functions have been designed to have the property that finding a match is not feasible, and are therefore considered suitable for use in cryptography.

One or more digital certificates can accompany a digital signature. If a digital certificate is present, the recipient (or a third party) can check the authenticity of the public key.

How long do digital signatures remain valid?

Normally, a key expires after some period of time, such as one year, and a document signed with an expired key should not be accepted. However, there are many cases where it is necessary for signed documents to be regarded as legally valid for much longer than two years; long-term leases and contracts are examples. By registering the contract with a digital time-stamping service at the time it is signed, the signature can be validated even after the key expires.

If all parties to the contract keep a copy of the time-stamp, each can prove that the contract was signed with valid keys. In fact, the time-stamp can prove the validity of a contract even if one signer's key is compromised at some point after the contract was signed. Any digitally signed document can be time-stamped, assuring that the validity of the signature can be verified after the key expires.

What is a digital time-stamping service?

A digital time-stamping service (DTS) issues time-stamps which associate a date and time with a digital document in a cryptographically strong way. The digital time-stamp can be used at a later date to prove that an electronic document existed at the time stated on its time-stamp. For example, a physicist who has a brilliant idea can write about it with a word processor and have the document time-stamped. The time-stamp and document together can later prove that the scientist deserves the Nobel Prize, even though an arch rival may have been the first to publish.

One way such a system could work would be that suppose 'A' signs a document and wants it time-stamped. She computes a message digest of the document using a secure hash function and then sends the message digest (but not the document itself) to the DTS, which sends to her in return a digital time-stamp consisting of the message digest, the date and time it was received at the DTS, and the signature of the DTS. Since the message digest does not reveal any information about the content of the document, the DTS cannot eavesdrop on the documents it time-stamps. Later, 'A' can present the document and time-stamp together to prove when the document was written. A verifier computes the message digest of the document, makes sure it matches the digest in the time-stamp, and then verifies the signature of the DTS on the time-stamp. To be reliable, the time-stamps must not be forgeable. The requirements for a DTS of the type just described are as follows:

- The DTS itself must have a long key if the time-stamps are to be reliable for, say, several decades.
- The private key of the DTS must be stored with utmost security, as in a tamper proof box.
- The date and time must come from a clock, also inside the tamper proof box, which cannot be reset and which will keep accurate time for years or perhaps for decades.
- It must be infeasible to create time-stamps without using the apparatus in the tamper proof box.

A cryptographically strong DTS using only software has been implemented by Bellcore; it avoids many of the requirements just described, such as tamper proof hardware. The Bellcore DTS essentially combines hash values of documents into data structures called binary trees, whose "root" values are periodically published in a newspaper. A time-stamp consists of a set of hash values which allow a verifier to recompute the root of the tree. Since the hash functions are one-way, the set of validating hash values cannot be forged. The time associated with the document by the time-stamp is the date of publication.

The use of a DTS would appear to be extremely important, if not essential, for maintaining the validity of documents over many years. Suppose a landlord and tenant sign a twenty-year lease. The public keys used to sign the lease are set to expire after two years. Solutions such as recertifying the keys or resigning every two years with new keys require the cooperation of both parties several years after the original signing. If one party becomes dissatisfied with the lease, he or she may refuse to cooperate. The solution is to register the lease with the DTS at the time of the original signing; both parties would then receive a copy of the time-stamp, which can be used years later to enforce the integrity of the original lease.

In the future, it is likely that a DTS will be used for everything from long-term corporate contracts to personal diaries and letters. Today, if an historian discovers some lost letters of Mark Twain, their authenticity is checked by physical means. But a similar find 100 years from now may consist of an author's computer files; digital time-stamps may be the only way to authenticate the find.

What is the legal status of documents signed with digital signatures?

If digital signatures are to replace handwritten signatures they must have the same legal status as handwritten signatures, i.e., documents signed with digital signatures must be legally binding. The Australian Government and most states and territories in Australia have already enacted legislation that gives electronic communications the same status as written communications in law (both criminal and civil). These are known as the electronic transactions acts. There are some limitations as to when electronic communications are effective, but the basic principle is that transactions are not invalid because they took place electronically. However, since the validity of documents with digital signatures has never been challenged in court, their legal status is not yet well-defined. Through such challenges, the courts will issue rulings that collectively define which digital signature methods, key sizes, and security precautions are acceptable for a digital signature to be legally binding.

Digital signatures have the potential to possess greater legal authority than handwritten signatures. If a ten page contract is signed by hand on the tenth page, one cannot be sure that the first nine pages have not been altered. However, if the contract was signed with digital signatures, a third party can verify that not one byte of the contract has been altered.

Currently, if two people want to digitally sign a series of contracts, they might first sign a paper contract in which they agree to be bound in the future by any contracts digitally signed by them with a given signature method and minimum key size.

7.3.4 Digital Signature Standard (DSS) or Digital Certificate

An attachment to an electronic message to verify the identity of the sender and to provide the receiver with the means to encode a reply is known as a digital certificate. It plays a valuable role in authentication. Digital certificates are data files used to establish the identity of people and electronic assets for protection of on line transactions.

It is an attachment to an electronic message used for security purposes. The most common use of a digital certificate is to verify that a user sending a message is who he or she claims to be, and to provide the receiver with the means to encode a reply.

An individual wishing to send an encrypted message applies for a digital certificate from a certificate authority (CA). The CA issues an encrypted digital certificate containing the applicant's public key and a variety of other identification information. The CA makes its own public key readily available through print publicity or perhaps on the Internet.

The recipient of an encrypted message uses the CA's public key to decode the digital certificate attached to the message, verifies it as issued by the CA and then obtains the sender's public key and identification information held within the certificate. With this information, the recipient can send an encrypted reply.

The most widely used standard for digital certificates is X.509. It was selected to be the digital authentication standard. Criticism of DSS has focused on a few main issues:

1. It lacks key exchange capability.
2. The underlying cryptosystem is too recent and has been subjected to too little security for users to be confident of its strength.
3. Verification of signatures with DSS is too slow.
4. The existence of a second authentication standard will cause hardship to computer hardware and software vendors.
5. In the DSS system, signature generation is faster than signature verification.

6. The most serious criticism of DSS involves security. DSS was originally proposed with a fixed S/2 bit key size, but after much criticism that this is not secure enough.

What is a digital certificate?

Digital certificates are the electronic counterparts of drivers licenses, passports and membership cards. A digital certificate can be presented electronically to prove a persons identity or right to access information or services online.

Digital certificates bind an identity to a pair of electronic keys that can be used to encrypt and sign digital information. A digital certificate makes it possible to verify someone's claim that they have the right to use a given key, helping to prevent people from using false keys to impersonate other users. Used in conjunction with encryption, digital certificates provide a more complete security solution, assuring the identity of all parties involved in a transaction.

A digital certificate is issued by a certification authority (CA) and signed with the CA's private key.

A digital certificate typically contains the:

- Owner's public key
- Owner's name
- Expiration date of the public key
- Name of the issuer (the CA that issued the digital certificate)
- Serial number of the digital certificate
- Digital signature of the issuer

The most widely accepted format for digital certificates is defined by the CCITT X.509 international standard; thus certificates can be read or written by any application complying with X.509. Further refinements are found in the PKCS standards and the PEM standard.

What are digital certificates used for?

Digital certificates can be used for a variety of electronic transactions including e-mail, electronic commerce, groupware and electronic funds transfers. Netscape's popular Enterprise Server requires a digital certificate for each secure server. For example, a customer shopping at an electronic mall run by Netscape's server software requests the digital certificate of the server to authenticate the identity of the mall operator and the content provided by the merchant. Without authenticating the server, the shopper should not trust the operator or merchant with sensitive information like a credit card number. The digital certificate is instrumental in establishing a secure channel for communicating any sensitive information back to the mall operator.

Why is a digital certificate necessary?

Virtual malls, electronic banking, and other electronic services are becoming more commonplace, offering the convenience and flexibility of round-the-clock service directly from the home. However, concerns about privacy and security might prevent a person from taking advantage of this new medium for their personal business. Encryption alone is not enough, as it provides no proof of the identity of the sender of the encrypted information. Without special safeguards, there is a risk of being impersonated online. Digital certificates address this problem, providing an electronic means of verifying someone's identity. Used in conjunction with encryption, digital certificates provide a more complete security solution, assuring the identity of all parties involved in a transaction.

Similarly, a secure server must have its own digital certificate to assure users that the server is run by the organization that it claims to be affiliated with and that the content provided is legitimate.

How is a digital certificate used?

On receipt of digitally signed messages, the signer's digital certificate is used to determine that no forgery or false representation has occurred.

When messages are sent, the sender can sign the messages and enclose their digital certificate to assure the recipient of the message that the message was actually sent by the intended sender. Multiple digital certificates can be enclosed with a message, forming a hierarchical chain, wherein one digital certificate testifies to the authenticity of the previous digital certificate. At the end of a digital certificate hierarchy is a top-level certification authority, which is trusted without a digital certificate from any other certification authority. The public key of the top-level certification authority must be independently known, for example by being widely published. The more familiar the receiver is to the recipient of the message, the less need there is to enclose a digital certificate.

7.4 SECURE SOCKETS LAYER (SSL)

Security of data in transit over the Internet becomes increasingly necessary because of the steadily growing volume and importance or importance. Nowadays, every user of a public network sends various types of data, from email to credit card details daily, and he would therefore like them to be protected when in transit over a public network. SSL protocol has been adopted for protection of data in transit that encompasses all network services that use TCP/IP to support typical application tasks of communication between servers and clients.

The SSL protocol was originally developed by Netscape, to ensure security of data transported and routed through HTTP, LDAP or POP3 application layers. SSL is designed to make use of TCP as a communication layer to provide a reliable end-to-end secure and authenticated connection between two points over a network (for example between the service client and the server). Notwithstanding this SSL can be used for protection of data in transit in situations related to any network service, it is used mostly in HTTP server and client applications. Today, almost each available HTTP server can support an SSL session, whilst IE or Netscape Navigator browsers are provided with SSL-enabled client software.

Electronic commerce applications
Secure hypertext transfer protocol (S-HTTP)
TCP – based application protocol (HTTP, SMTP, NNTP)
Secure sockets layer (SSL)
Internet protocol (IP)

Fig. 7.7: *Web security layers*

SSL is layered beneath application protocols such as HTTP, SMTP, TELNET, FTP, Gopher and NNTP and above the Internet connection protocol TCP/IP.SSL provides a security 'handshake' to initiate the TCP/IP connection. Its only role is to encrypt and decrypt the message stream.

7.4.1 SSL Objectives and Architecture

The main objectives of SSL are:

- **Authenticating the client and server to each other:** SSL protocol supports the use of standard key cryptographic techniques (public key encryption) to authenticate the communicating parties to each other. Though the most frequent application consists in authenticating the service client on the basis of a certificate, SSL may also use the same methods to authenticate the client.
- **Ensuring data integrity:** During a session, data cannot be either intentionally or unintentionally tampered with.
- **Securing data privacy:** Data in transport between the client and the server must be protected from interception and be readable only by the intended recipient. This prerequisite is necessary for both the data associated with the protocol itself (securing traffic during negotiations) and the application data that is sent during the session itself. SSL is in fact not a single protocol but rather a set of protocols that can additionally be further divided in two layers:

1. The protocol to ensure data security and integrity: This layer is composed of the SSL record protocol.
2. Protocols that are designed to establish an SSL connection: Three protocols are used in this layer: the SSL Handshake Protocol, the SSL ChangeCipher SpecProtocol and the SSL Alert Protocol.

This protocol fully encrypts all the information in both the HTTP request and HTTP response, including the URL the client is requesting, any submitted form contents (including things like credit card numbers), any HTTP access authorization information (user names and passwords) and all the data returned from the server to the client.

SSL provides encryption that creates a secure channel to prevent third parties on the network from being able to tamper with and read messages being exchanged between the client and server and authentication that uses a digital signature to verify the legitimacy of the server.

The server implements server side support for HTTP over SSL, including support for acquiring a server certificate and communicating securely with SSL enabled browsers. To provide security, the Netscape navigator supports a new URL access method, http for connecting to http servers.

7.4.2 SSL Session and Connection

The concepts as mentioned above are fundamental for a connection between the client and the server, and they also encompass a series of attributes. Some more details are given below:

- **Connection:** this is a logical client/server link, associated with the provision of a suitable type of service. In SSL terms, it must be a peer-to-peer connection with two network nodes.
- **Session:** this is an association between a client and a server that defines a set of parameters such as algorithms used, session number etc. An SSL session is created by the Handshake Protocol that allows parameters to be shared among the connections made between the server and the client. Sessions are used to avoid negotiation of new parameters for each connection. This means that a single session is shared among multiple SSL connections between the client and the server. In theory, it may also be possible that multiple sessions are shared by a single connection, but this feature is not used in practice. The concepts of a SSL session and connection involve several parameters that are used for SSL-enabled communication between the client and the server. During the negotiations of the Handshake Protocol, the encryption methods are established and a series of parameters of the session state are subsequently used within the session. A session state is defined by the following parameters:
    - Session identifier: this is an identifier generated by the server to identify a session with a chosen client
    - Peer certificate: X.509 certificate of the peer
    - Compression method: a method used to compress data prior to encryption
    - Algorithm specification termed CipherSpec: specifies the bulk data encryption algorithm (for example DES) and the hash algorithm (for example MD5) used during the session.
    - Master secret: 48-byte data being a secret shared between the client and server
    - "is resumable": this is a flag indicating whether the session can be used to initiate new connections.

According to the specification, the SSL connection state is defined by the following parameters:

- Server and client random: random data generated by both the client and server for each connection.
- Server write MAC secret: the secret key used for data written by the server.
- Client write MAC secret: the secret used for data written by the client.

- Server write key: the bulk cipher key for data encrypted by the server and decrypted by the client.
- Client write key: the bulk cipher key for data encrypted by the client and decrypted by the server.
- Sequence number: sequence numbers maintained separately by the server for messages transmitted and received during the data session.

The abbreviation MAC used in the above definitions means message authentication code that is used for transmission of data during the SSL session. The role of MAC will be explained further when discussing the record protocols. A brief description of the terms was necessary to be able to explain the next issues connected with the functioning of the SSL protocol, namely the SSL record protocol.

7.4.3 The SSL Record Protocol

The SSL record protocol is used to transfer any data within a session - both messages and other SSL protocols (for example the Handshake Protocol), as well as for any application data.

It involves using SSL in a secure manner and with message integrity ensured. To this end it is used by upper layer SSL protocols. The purpose of the SSL record protocol is to take an application message to be transmitted, fragment the data which needs to be sent, encapsulate it with appropriate headers and create an object called a record, which is encrypted and can be forwarded for sending under the TCP protocol. The first step in the preparation of transmission of the application data consists in its fragmentation i.e. breaking up the data stream to be transmitted into 16Kb (or smaller) data fragments followed by the process of their conversion in a record. These data fragments may be further compressed, although the SSL 3.0 protocol specification includes no compression protocol, thus at present, no data compression is used.

At this moment, creation of the record is started for each data portion by adding a header to it, possible information to complete the required data size and the MAC. The record header that is added to each data portion contains two elementary pieces of information, namely the length of the record and the length of the data block added to the original data. In the next step, the record data constructed consists of the following elements:

- Primary data
- Some padding to complete the datagram as required
- MAC value.

MAC is responsible for the verification of integrity of the message included in the transmitted record. It is the result of a hash function that follows a specific hash algorithm, for example MD5 or SHA-1. MAC is determined as a result of a hash function that receives the following data:

MAC = Hash function [secret key, primary data, padding, sequence number].
A secret key in creation of MAC is either a client write MAC secret or a server write MAC secret respectively, it depends on which party prepares the packet.

After receiving the packet, the receiving party computes its own value of the MAC and compares it with that received. If the two values match, this means that data has not been modified during transmission over the network. The length of the MAC obtained in this way depends on the method used for its computing. Next, the data plus the MAC are encrypted using a preset symmetric encryption algorithm, for example DES or triple DES. Both data and MAC are encrypted. This prepared data is attached with the following header fields:

- Content type: identifies what payload is delivered by the packet to determine which higher protocols are to be used for processing of data included in the packet. The possible values are change_cipher_spec, alert, handshake, and application_data that refer to the appropriate protocols.
- Major version: establishes the main portion of the protocol version to be used. For SSL 3.0, the value is 3,
- Minor version: establishes the additional portion of the used version of the protocol. For SSL 3.0 the value is 0.

With the addition of fields, the process of record preparation is completed. Afterwards, the record is sent to the targeted point. The entire process of preparation of the packet to be sent is illustrated in Figure 7.8.

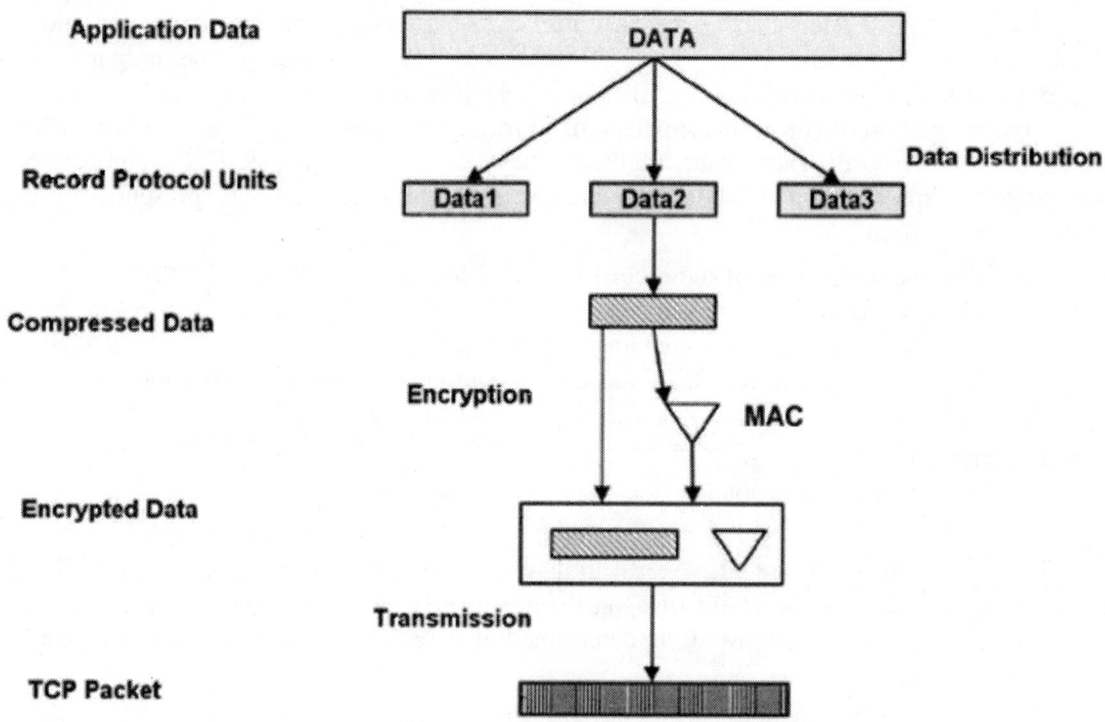

Fig. 7.8: ***Creating a packet under SSL record protocol***

7.4.4 The Alert Protocol

The Alert Protocol is used by parties to convey session messages associated with data exchange and functioning of the protocol. Each message in the alert protocol consists of two bytes. The first byte always takes a value, "warning" (1) or "fatal" (2), that determines the severity of the message sent. Sending a message having a "fatal" status by either party will result in an immediate termination of the SSL session. The next byte of the message contains one of the defined error codes, which may occur during an SSL communication session.

7.4.5 The ChangeCipher Spec Protocol

This protocol is the simplest SSL protocol. It consists of a single message that carries the value 1. The sole purpose of this message is to cause the pending session state to be established as a fixed state, which results, for example, in defining the used set of protocols. This type of message must be sent by the client to the server and vice versa. After exchange of messages, the session state is considered agreed. This message and any other SSL messages are transferred using the SSL record protocol.

7.4.6 The Handshake Protocol

The Handshake Protocol constitutes the most complex part of the SSL protocol. It is used to initiate a session between the server and the client. Within the message of this protocol, various components such as algorithms and keys used for data encryption are negotiated. Due to this protocol, it is possible for the parties to authenticate each other and negotiate appropriate parameters of the session between them.

The process of negotiations between the client and the server is illustrated in Figure 6.9. It can be divided into 4 phases separated with horizontal broken lines. During the first phase, a logical connection must be initiated between the client and the server followed by the negotiation on the connection parameters. The client sends the server a client_hello message containing data such as:

- Version: the highest SSL version supported by the client
- Random: data consisting of a 32-bit timestamp and 28 bytes of randomly generated data. These data are used to protect the key exchange session between the parties of the connection.
- Session ID: A number that defines the session identifier. A nonzero value of this field indicates that the client wishes to update the parameters of an existing connection or establish a new connection on this session. A zero value in this field indicates that the client wishes to establish a new connection.
- CipherSuite: A list of encryption algorithms and key exchange methods supported by the client or a new session. The server uses this field to send a single set of protocols selected by the server from those proposed by the client. The first element of this field is a chosen method of exchange of cryptographic keys between the client and the server. The next element is the specification of encryption algorithms and hash

functions, which will be used within the session being initiated, along with all specific parameters.

The set of encryption algorithms and key exchange method sent in the CipherSuite field establishes three components:

1. The method of key exchange between the server and client
2. The encryption algorithm for data encryption purposes
3. A function used for obtaining the MAC value

The server begins the next phase of negotiations by sending its certificate to the client for authentication. The message sent to the client contains one or a chain of X509 certificates. These are necessary for authentication of both the server and the certification path towards a trusted certification official of the certificating body for the server. This step is not obligatory and may be omitted, if the negotiated method of key exchange does not require sending the certificate (in the case of the anonymous Diffie-Hellman method). Depending on the negotiated method of key exchange, the server may send an additional server_key_exchange message, which is however not required in the case when the fixed Diffie-Hellman method or RSA key exchange technique has been negotiated. Moreover, the server can request a certificate from the client. The final step of Phase 2 is the server_done message, which has no parameters and is sent by the server merely to indicate the end of the server messages. After sending this message, the server waits for a client response. Upon receipt of the message, the client should verify the server's certificate, the certificate validation data and path, as well as any other parameters sent by the server in the server_hello message. The client's verification consists of:

- Validation date check of the certificate and comparison with the current date, to verify whether the certificate is still valid.
- Checking whether the certifying body is included in the list of trusted certifying authorities in possession of the client. If the CA, which has issued the server's certificate is not included in the CA's list, the client attempts to verify the CA signature. If no information about the CA can be obtained, the client terminates the identification procedure by either returning the error signal or signaling the problem for the user to solve it.
- Identifying the authenticity of the public key of the CA which has issued the certificate: if the certifying authority is included in the clients list of trusted CAs, the client checks the CA's public key stated in the servers certificate with the public key available from the list. This procedure verifies the authenticity of the certifying body.
- Checking whether the domain name used in the certificate matches the server name shown in the server's certificate.

Upon successful completion of all steps the server is considered authenticated. If all parameters are matched and the servers certificate correctly verified, the client sends the server one or multiple messages. Next the client_key_exchange message must be sent to deliver the keys. The content of this message depends on the negotiated method of key exchange. Moreover, at the servers request, the clients certificate is sent along with the message enabling verification of the certificate. This procedure ends Phase 3 of the negotiations. Phase 4 is to confirm the messages so far received and to verify whether the pending data are correct. The client sends a change_cipher_spec message (in accordance with the pending SSL ChangeCipher Spec), and then sets up the pending set of algorithm parameters and keys into the current set of the same. Then the client sends the finished message, which is first protected with just negotiated algorithms, keys and secrets. This is to confirm that the negotiated parameters and data are correct. The server in response to the client sends the same message sequence. If the finished message is correctly read by either party this confirms that the transmitted data, negotiated algorithms and the session key are correct. This indicates that the session has been terminated and that it is possible to send the application data between the server and the client, via SSL. At this point the TCP session between the client and the server is closed however a session state is maintained, allowing it to resume communications within the session using the retained parameters.

7.4.7 Implementation of SSL

- SSL protocol is implemented at the host station.
- Instead of http clients lie with https.
- Typing the address that the client/server understand.
- The client request from the server.
- Server sends its digital certification to client, digital certificate contain public key and digital signature.
- Client can verify that digital certification is carried out. Now the client will recommend a list of algorithms from the client to server.
- Based on the client request, the server selects the best algorithms.
- Now client generates a secret key (any random number). All the keys generated by clients are not the same (= secret key of client + public key of server). Encrypted secret key sends to the server. Now servers open this using a secret key called the session key. All should take the through session key.

If the client has secret key algorithms the server has public key algorithms.

7.5 TRIPLE ENCRYPTION (DES ENCRYPTION)

In 1972, the National Institute of Standards and Technology (called the National Bureau of Standards at the time) decided that a strong cryptographic algorithm was needed to protect non-classified information. The algorithm was required to be cheap, widely available, and very secure. NIST envisioned something that would be available to the general public and could be used in a wide variety of applications. So they asked for public proposals for such an algorithm. In 1974 IBM submitted the Lucifer algorithm, which appeared to meet most of NIST's design requirements.

NIST enlisted the help of the National Security Agency to evaluate the security of Lucifer. At the time many people distrusted the NSA due to their extremely secretive activities, so there was initially a certain degree of scepticism regarding the analysis of Lucifer. One of the greatest worries was that the key length, originally 128 bits, was reduced to just 56 bits, weakening it significantly. The NSA was also accused of changing the algorithm to plant a "back door" in it that would allow agents to decrypt any information without having to know the encryption key. But these fears proved unjustified and no such back door has ever been found.

The modified Lucifer algorithm was adopted by NIST as a federal standard on November 23, 1976. Its name was changed to the data encryption standard (DES). The algorithm specification was published in January 1977, and with the official backing of the government it became a very widely employed algorithm in a short time.

Unfortunately, over time various shortcut attacks were found that could significantly reduce the amount of time needed to find a DES key by brute force, and as computers became progressively faster and more powerful, it was recognized that a 56-bit key was simply not large enough for high security applications. As a result of these serious flaws, NIST abandoned their official endorsement of DES in 1997 and began work on a replacement, to be called the advanced encryption standard (AES). Despite the growing concerns about its vulnerability, DES is still widely used by financial services and other industries worldwide to protect sensitive on-line applications.

To highlight the need for stronger security than a 56-bit key can offer, RSA Data Security has been sponsoring a series of contests to crack DES since early 1997. In 1998 the Electronic Frontier Foundation won the RSA DES Challenge II-2 contest by breaking DES in less than 3 days. EFF used a specially developed computer called the DES Cracker, which was developed for under $250,000. The encryption chip that powered the DES Cracker was capable of processing 88 billion keys per second. In early 1999, Distributed.Net used the DES Cracker and a worldwide network of nearly 100,000 PCs to win the RSA DES Challenge III in a record breaking 22 hours and 15 minutes. The DES Cracker and PCs combined were testing 245 billion keys per second when the correct key was found. In addition, it has been shown that for a cost of one million dollars a dedicated hardware device can be built that can search all possible DES keys in about 3.5 hours. This just serves to illustrate that any organization with moderate resources can break through DES with very little effort these days.

DES encrypts and decrypts data in 64-bit blocks, using a 64-bit key (although the effective key strength is only 56 bits, as explained below). It takes a 64-bit block of plaintext as input and outputs a 64-bit block of ciphertext. Since it always operates on blocks of equal size and it uses both permutations and substitutions in the algorithm, DES is both a block cipher and a product cipher.

DES has 16 rounds, meaning the main algorithm is repeated 16 times to produce the ciphertext. It has been found that the number of rounds is exponentially proportional to the amount of time required to find a key using a brute-force attack. So as the number of rounds increases, the security of the algorithm increases exponentially.

Key scheduling

Although the input key for DES is 64 bits long, the actual key used by DES is only 56 bits in length. The least significant (right-most) bit in each byte is a parity bit, and should be set so that there are always an odd number of 1s in every byte. These parity bits are ignored, so only the seven most significant bits of each byte are used, resulting in a key length of 56 bits.

The first step is to pass the 64-bit key through a permutation called permuted choice 1, or PC-1 for short (Table 7.1). Note that in all subsequent descriptions of bit numbers, 1 is the left-most bit in the number, and n is the rightmost bit.

TABLE 7.1: ***PC-1: Permuted choice 1***

PC-1: Permuted Choice 1							
Bit	**0**	**1**	**2**	**3**	**4**	**5**	**6**
1	57	49	41	33	25	17	9
8	1	58	50	42	34	26	18
15	10	2	59	51	43	35	27
22	19	11	3	60	52	44	36
29	63	55	47	39	31	23	15
36	7	62	54	46	38	30	22
43	14	6	61	53	45	37	29
50	21	13	5	28	20	12	4

For example, we can use the PC-1 table to figure out how bit 30 of the original 64-bit key transforms to a bit in the new 56-bit key as follows: Find the number 30 in Table 7.1 and notice that it belongs to the column labelled 5 and the row labelled 36. Add up the value of the row and column to find the new position of the bit within the key. For bit 30, 36 + 5 = 41, so bit 30 becomes bit 41 of the new 56-bit key. Note that bits 8, 16, 24, 32, 40, 48, 56 and 64 of the original key are not in the table. These are the unused parity bits that are discarded when the final 56-bit key is created.

Now that we have the 56-bit key, the next step is to use this key to generate 16 48-bit sub keys, called K[1]-K[16], which are used in the 16 rounds of DES for encryption and decryption. The procedure for generating the sub keys - known as key scheduling - is fairly simple, and is given below:

1. Set the round number R to 1.
2. Split the current 56-bit key, K, up into two 28-bit blocks, L (the left-hand half) and R (the right-hand half).
3. Rotate L left by the number of bits specified in the table below, and rotate R left by the same number of bits as well.
4. Join L and R together to get the new K.
5. Apply Permuted Choice 2 (PC-2) to K to get the final K[R], where R is the round number we are on.

6. Increment R by 1 and repeat the procedure until we have all 16 subkeys K[1]-K[16].

The tables (Tables 7.2 and 7.3) involved in these operations are given below:

TABLE 7.2: Subkey rotation

Subkey Rotation Table																
Round Number	1	2	3	4	5	6	7	8	9	10	11	12	13	14	15	16
Number of bits to rotate	1	1	2	2	2	2	2	2	1	2	2	2	2	2	2	1

TABLE 7.3: Permuted choice 2

PC-2: Permuted Choice 2						
Bit	**0**	**1**	**2**	**3**	**4**	**5**
1	14	17	11	24	1	5
7	3	28	15	6	21	10
13	23	19	12	4	26	8
19	16	7	27	20	13	2
25	41	52	31	37	47	55
31	30	40	51	45	33	48
37	44	49	39	56	34	53
43	46	42	50	36	29	32

Plaintext preparation

Once the key scheduling has been performed, the next step is to prepare the plaintext for the actual encryption. This is done by passing the plaintext through a permutation called the initial permutation, or IP for short. This table also has an inverse, called the inverse initial permutation, or IP^(-1). Sometimes IP^(-1) is also called the final permutation. Both of these tables are shown below (Tables 7.4 and 7.5).

TABLE 7.4: Initial permutation

IP: Initial Permutation								
Bit	0	1	2	3	4	5	6	7
1	58	50	42	34	26	18	10	2
9	60	52	44	36	28	20	12	4
17	62	54	46	38	30	22	14	6
25	64	56	48	40	32	24	16	8
33	57	49	41	33	25	17	9	1
41	59	51	43	35	27	19	11	3
49	61	53	45	37	29	21	13	5
57	63	55	47	39	31	23	15	7

TABLE 7.5: Inverse initial permutation

IP^(-1): Inverse Initial Permutation								
Bit	**0**	**1**	**2**	**3**	**4**	**5**	**6**	**7**
1	40	8	48	16	56	24	64	32
9	39	7	47	15	55	23	63	31
17	38	6	46	14	54	22	62	30
25	37	5	45	13	53	21	61	29
33	36	4	44	12	52	20	60	28
41	35	3	43	11	51	19	59	27
49	34	2	42	10	50	18	58	26
57	33	1	41	9	49	17	57	25

These tables are used just like PC-1 and PC-2 were for the key scheduling. By looking at the table it becomes apparent why one permutation is called the inverse of the other. For example, let us examine how bit 32 is transformed under IP. In Table 7.4, bit 32 is located at the intersection of the column labelled 4 and the row labelled 25. So this bit becomes bit 29 of the 64-bit block after the permutation. Now applying IP^(-1). In IP^(-1), bit 29 is located at the intersection of the column labelled 7 and the row labelled 25. So this bit becomes bit 32 after the permutation. And this is the bit position that we started with before the first permutation. So IP^(-1) really is the inverse of IP. It does the exact opposite of IP. If you run a block of plaintext through IP and then pass the resulting block through IP^(-1), you will end up with the original block.

DES core function

Once the key scheduling and plaintext preparation have been completed, the actual encryption or decryption is performed by the main DES algorithm. The 64-bit block of input data is first split into two halves, L and R. L is the left-most 32 bits, and R is the right-most 32 bits. The following process is repeated 16 times, making up the 16 rounds of standard DES. We call the 16 sets of halves L[0]-L[15] and R[0]-R[15].

1. R[I-1] - where I is the round number, starting at 1 - is taken and fed into the E-Bit Selection Table, which is like a permutation, except that some of the bits are used more than once. This expands the number R[I-1] from 32 to 48 bits to prepare for the next step.
2. The 48-bit R[I-1] is XORed with K[I] and stored in a temporary buffer so that R[I-1] is not modified.
3. The result from the previous step is now split into 8 segments of 6 bits each. The left-most 6 bits are B[1], and the right-most 6 bits are B[8]. These blocks form the index into the S-boxes, which are used in the next step. The Substitution boxes, known

as S-boxes, are a set of 8 two-dimensional arrays, each with 4 rows and 16 columns. The numbers in the boxes are always 4 bits in length, so their values range from 0-15. The S-boxes are numbered S[1]-S[8].

4. Starting with B[1], the first and last bits of the 6-bit block are taken and used as an index into the row number of S[1], which can range from 0 to 3, and the middle four bits are used as an index into the column number, which can range from 0 to 15. The number from this position in the S-box is retrieved and stored away. This is repeated with B[2] and S[2], B[3] and S[3], and the others up to B[8] and S[8]. At this point, you now have 8 4-bit numbers, which when strung together one after the other in the order of retrieval, give a 32-bit result.
5. The result from the previous stage is now passed into the P Permutation.
6. This number is now XORed with L[I-1], and moved into R[I]. R[I-1] is moved into L[I].
7. At this point we have a new L[I] and R[I]. Here, we increment I and repeat the core function until I = 17, which means that 16 rounds have been executed and keys K[1]-K[16] have all been used.

When L[16] and R[16] have been obtained, they are joined back together in the same fashion they were split apart (L[16] is the left-hand half, R[16] is the right-hand half), then the two halves are swapped, R[16] becomes the left-most 32 bits and L[16] becomes the right-most 32 bits of the pre-output block and the resultant 64-bit number is called the pre-output.

Tables 7.6 to 7.15. are used in the DES core function.

TABLE 7.6

E-Bit Selection Table						
Bit	**0**	**1**	**2**	**3**	**4**	**5**
1	32	1	2	3	4	5
7	4	5	6	7	8	9
13	8	9	10	11	12	13
19	12	13	14	15	16	17
25	16	17	18	19	20	21
31	20	21	22	23	24	25
37	24	25	26	27	28	29
43	28	29	30	31	32	1

TABLE 7.7

P Permutation				
Bit	**0**	**1**	**2**	**3**
1	16	7	20	21
5	29	12	28	17
9	1	15	23	26
13	5	18	31	10
17	2	8	24	14
21	32	27	3	9
25	19	13	30	6
29	22	11	4	25

TABLE 7.8

S-Box 1: Substitution Box 1																
Row/Column	**0**	**1**	**2**	**3**	**4**	**5**	**6**	**7**	**8**	**9**	**10**	**11**	**12**	**13**	**14**	**15**
0	14	4	13	1	2	15	11	8	3	10	6	12	5	9	0	7
1	0	15	7	4	14	2	13	1	10	6	12	11	9	5	3	8
2	4	1	14	8	13	6	2	11	15	12	9	7	3	10	5	0
3	15	12	8	2	4	9	1	7	5	11	3	14	10	0	6	13

TABLE 7.9

S-Box 2: Substitution Box 2																
Row/Column	**0**	**1**	**2**	**3**	**4**	**5**	**6**	**7**	**8**	**9**	**10**	**11**	**12**	**13**	**14**	**15**
0	15	1	8	14	6	11	3	4	9	7	2	13	12	0	5	10
1	3	13	4	7	15	2	8	14	12	0	1	10	6	9	11	5
2	0	14	7	11	10	4	13	1	5	8	12	6	9	3	2	15
3	13	8	10	1	3	15	4	2	11	6	7	12	0	5	14	9

TABLE 7.10

S-Box 3: Substitution Box 3																
Row/Column	**0**	**1**	**2**	**3**	**4**	**5**	**6**	**7**	**8**	**9**	**10**	**11**	**12**	**13**	**14**	**15**
0	10	0	9	14	6	3	15	5	1	13	12	7	11	4	2	8
1	13	7	0	9	3	4	6	10	2	8	5	14	12	11	15	1
2	13	6	4	9	8	15	3	0	11	1	2	12	5	10	14	7
3	1	10	13	0	6	9	8	7	4	15	14	3	11	5	2	12

TABLE 7.11

S-Box 4: Substitution Box 4																
Row/Column	**0**	**1**	**2**	**3**	**4**	**5**	**6**	**7**	**8**	**9**	**10**	**11**	**12**	**13**	**14**	**15**
0	7	13	14	3	0	6	9	10	1	2	8	5	11	12	4	15
1	13	8	11	5	6	15	0	3	4	7	2	12	1	10	14	9
2	10	6	9	0	12	11	7	13	15	1	3	14	5	2	8	4
3	3	15	0	6	10	1	13	8	9	4	5	11	12	7	2	14

TABLE 7.12

S-Box 5: Substitution Box 5																
Row/Column	**0**	**1**	**2**	**3**	**4**	**5**	**6**	**7**	**8**	**9**	**10**	**11**	**12**	**13**	**14**	**15**
0	2	12	4	1	7	10	11	6	8	5	3	15	13	0	14	9
1	14	11	2	12	4	7	13	1	5	0	15	10	3	9	8	6
2	4	2	1	11	10	13	7	8	15	9	12	5	6	3	0	14
3	11	8	12	7	1	14	2	13	6	15	0	9	10	4	5	3

TABLE 7.13

S-Box 6: Substitution Box 6																
Row/Column	**0**	**1**	**2**	**3**	**4**	**5**	**6**	**7**	**8**	**9**	**10**	**11**	**12**	**13**	**14**	**15**
0	12	1	10	15	9	2	6	8	0	13	3	4	14	7	5	11
1	10	15	4	2	7	12	9	5	6	1	13	14	0	11	3	8
2	9	14	15	5	2	8	12	3	7	0	4	10	1	13	11	6
3	4	3	2	12	9	5	15	10	11	14	1	7	6	0	8	13

TABLE 7.14

S-Box 7: Substitution Box 7																
Row/Column	**0**	**1**	**2**	**3**	**4**	**5**	**6**	**7**	**8**	**9**	**10**	**11**	**12**	**13**	**14**	**15**
0	4	11	2	14	15	0	8	13	3	12	9	7	5	10	6	1
1	13	0	11	7	4	9	1	10	14	3	5	12	2	15	8	6
2	1	4	11	13	12	3	7	14	10	15	6	8	0	5	9	2
3	6	11	13	8	1	4	10	7	9	5	0	15	14	2	3	12

TABLE 7.15

S-Box 8: Substitution Box 8																
Row/Column	**0**	**1**	**2**	**3**	**4**	**5**	**6**	**7**	**8**	**9**	**10**	**11**	**12**	**13**	**14**	**15**
0	13	2	8	4	6	15	11	1	10	9	3	14	5	0	12	7
1	1	15	13	8	10	3	7	4	12	5	6	11	0	14	9	2
2	7	11	4	1	9	12	14	2	0	6	10	13	15	3	5	8
3	2	1	14	7	4	10	8	13	15	12	9	0	3	5	6	11

How to use the S-boxes

The purpose of this example is to clarify how the S-boxes work. Suppose we have the following 48-bit binary number:

011101000101110101000111101000011100101101011101

In order to pass this through steps 3 and 4 of the core function as outlined above, the number is split up into 8 6-bit blocks, labelled B[1] to B[8] from left to right:

011101 000101 110101 000111 101000 011100 101101 011101

Now, eight numbers are extracted from the S-boxes - one from each box:

B[1] = S[1](01, 1110) = S[1][1][14] = 3 = 0011
B[2] = S[2](01, 0010) = S[2][1][2] = 4 = 0100
B[3] = S[3](11, 1010) = S[3][3][10] = 14 = 1110
B[4] = S[4](01, 0011) = S[4][1][3] = 5 = 0101
B[5] = S[5](10, 0100) = S[5][2][4] = 10 = 1010
B[6] = S[6](00, 1110) = S[6][0][14] = 5 = 0101
B[7] = S[7](11, 0110) = S[7][3][6] = 10 = 1010
B[8] = S[8](01, 1110) = S[8][1][14] = 9 = 1001

In each case of S[*n*][row][column], the first and last bits of the current B[*n*] are used as the row index, and the middle four bits as the column index.

The results are now joined together to form a 32-bit number which serves as the input to stage 5 of the core function (the P Permutation):

00110100111001011010010110101001

Cipher text preparation

The final step is to apply the permutation IP^(–1) to the pre-output. The result is the completely encrypted cipher text.

Encryption and decryption

The same algorithm can be used for encryption or decryption. The method described above will encrypt a block of plaintext and return a block of cipher text. In order to decrypt the cipher text and obtain the original plaintext again, the procedure is simply repeated but the sub keys are applied in reverse order, from K [16]-K[1]. That is, stage 2 of the core function as outlined above changes from R[I-1] XOR K[I] to R[I-1] XOR K[17-I]. Other than that, decryption is performed exactly the same as encryption.

Modes of operation

ECB (Electronic code book)

This is the regular DES algorithm, exactly as described above. Data is divided into 64-bit blocks and each block is encrypted one at a time. Separate encryptions with different blocks are totally independent of each other. This means that if data are transmitted over a network or phone line, transmission errors will only affect the block containing the error. It also means, however, that the blocks can be rearranged, thus scrambling a file beyond recognition, and this action would go undetected. ECB is the weakest of the various modes because no additional security measures are implemented besides the basic DES algorithm. However, ECB is the fastest and easiest to implement, making it the most common mode of DES seen in commercial applications. This is the mode of operation used by Private Encryptor.

CBC (Cipher block chaining)

In this mode of operation, each block of ECB encrypted ciphertext is XORed with the next plaintext block to be encrypted, thus making all the blocks dependent on all the previous blocks. This means that in order to find the plaintext of a particular block, you need to know the ciphertext, the key, and the ciphertext for the previous block. The first block to be encrypted has no previous ciphertext, so the plaintext is XORed with a 64-bit number called the initialization vector, or IV for short. So if data are transmitted over a network or phone line and there is a transmission error (adding or deleting bits), the error will be carried forward to all subsequent blocks since each block is dependent upon the last. If the bits are just modified in transit (as is the more common case) the error will only affect all of the bits in the changed block, and the corresponding bits in the following block. The error does not propagate any further. This mode of operation is more secure than ECB because the extra XOR step adds one more layer to the encryption process.

CFB (Cipher feedback)

In this mode, blocks of plaintext that are less than 64 bits long can be encrypted. Normally, special processing has to be used to handle files whose size is not a perfect multiple of 8 bytes, but this mode removes that necessity (Private Encryptor handles this case by adding several dummy bytes to the end of a file before encrypting it). The plaintext itself is not actually passed through the DES algorithm, but merely XORed with an output block from it, in the following manner: A 64-bit block called the shift register is used as the input plaintext to DES. This is initially set to some arbitrary value, and encrypted with the DES algorithm. The ciphertext is then passed through an extra component called the M-box, which simply selects the left-most M bits of the ciphertext, where M is the number of bits in the block to be encrypted. This value is XORed with the real plaintext, and the output of that is the final ciphertext. Finally, the ciphertext is fed back into the shift register, and used as the plaintext seed for the next block to be encrypted. As with CBC mode, an error in one block affects all subsequent blocks during data transmission. This mode of operation is similar to CBC and is very secure, but it is slower than ECB due to the added complexity.

OFB (Output feedback)

This is similar to the CFB mode, except that the ciphertext output of DES is fed back into the shift register, rather than the actual final ciphertext. The shift register is set to an arbitrary initial value, and passed through the DES algorithm. The output from DES is passed through the M-box and then fed back into the shift register to prepare for the next block. This value is then XORed with the real plaintext (which may be less than 64 bits in length, like CFB mode), and the result is the final ciphertext. Note that unlike CFB and CBC, a transmission error in one block will not affect subsequent blocks because once the recipient has the initial shift register value, it will continue to generate new shift register plaintext inputs without any further data input. However, this mode of operation is less secure than the CFB mode because only the real ciphertext and DES ciphertext output is needed to find the plaintext of the most recent block. Knowledge of the key is not required.

7.6 VPN – VIRTUAL PRIVATE NETWORK

A **virtual private network** (**VPN**) is a private communications network often used within a company, or by several companies or organizations, to communicate confidentially over a publicly accessible network. VPN message traffic can be carried over a public networking infrastructure (e.g. the Internet) on top of standard protocols, or over a service provider's private network with a defined service level agreement (SLA) between the VPN customer and the VPN service provider.

A virtual private network is a logical concept to make a private connection between two stations over a public network. A virtual private network is implemented using the following three technologies.

- Authentication
- Tunnelling
- Encryption

7.6.1 Authentication

This is used to verify the legitimacy of the server. For this, the digital signature and secure socket layer are used.

Authentication mechanism

VPN involves two parts: the protected or "inside" network, which provides physical and administrative security to protect the transmission; and a less trustworthy, "outside" network or segment (usually through the Internet). Generally, a firewall sits between a remote user's workstation or client and the host network or server. As the user's client establishes the communication with the firewall, the client may pass authentication data to an authentication service inside the perimeter. A known trusted person, sometimes only when using trusted devices, can be provided with appropriate security privileges to access resources not available to general users.

Many VPN client programs can be configured to require that all IP traffic must pass through the tunnel while the VPN is active, for better security. From the user's perspective, this means that while the VPN client is active, all access outside their employer's secure network must pass through the same firewall as would be the case while physically connected to the office ethernet. This reduces the risk that an attacker might gain access to the secured network by attacking the employee's laptop, other computers on the employee's home network, or on the public internet; it is as though the machine running the VPN client simply does not exist. Such security is important because other computers local to the network on which the client computer is operating may be untrusted or partially trusted. Even with a home network that is protected from the outside internet by a firewall, people who share a home network may be simultaneously working for different employers over their respective VPN connections from the shared home network. Each employer would therefore want to ensure their proprietary data are kept secure, even if another computer in the local network gets infected with malware. If a travelling employee uses a VPN client from a Wi-Fi access point in a public place, such security is even more important. However, the use of IPX/SPX is one way users might still be able to access local resources.

7.6.2 Tunnelling

In tunnelling there is one to one communication, e.g. PPTP Protocol. E-mail is read by using protocol post office protocol (POP3) in which there is point to point protocol (PPP) which is in the data link layer. Tunnelling is the transmission of data through a public network in such a way that routing nodes in the public network are unaware that the transmission is part of a private network. Tunnelling is generally done by encapsulating the private network data and protocol information within the public network protocol data so that the tunnelled data is not available to anyone examining the transmitted data frames. Tunnelling allows the use of public networks (e.g. the Internet), to carry data on behalf of users as though they had access to a 'private network', hence the name. Port forwarding is one aspect of tunnelling in particular circumstances. In tunnelling, the point to point (PPTP) tunnelling protocol is used.

7.6.3 Encryption

This is the coding and scrambling of messages to prevent their being read or accessed without authorization.

The most important part of a VPN solution is security. The very nature of VPNs — putting private data on public networks — raises concerns about potential threats to that data and the impact of data loss. A virtual private network must address all types of security threats by providing security services in the areas of:

Authentication (access control): This is the process of ensuring that a user or system is who they claim to be. There are many types of authentication mechanisms, but they all use one or more of the following approaches:

- something you know (e.g. a login name, a password, a PIN)
- something you have (e.g. a computer readable token (e.g. a Smartcard), a card key)
- something you are (e.g. fingerprint, retinal pattern, iris pattern, hand configuration, etc)

What is generally regarded as weak authentication makes use of one of these components, usually a login name/password sequence. Strong authentication is usually taken to combine at least two authentication components from different areas (i.e. two-factor authentication). However, the use of weak and strong in this context can be misleading. A stolen SmartCard and a shoulder-surfed login name/PIN sequence is not hard to achieve and will pass a strong authentication two-factor text handily. More seriously, stolen or lost security data (e.g. on a backup tape, a laptop, or stolen by an employee) dangerously furthers many such attacks on most authentication schemes. There is no fully adequate technique for the authentication problem, including biometric ones.

7.6.4 Types of VPN

Secure VPNs use cryptographic tunnelling protocols to provide the intended confidentiality (blocking snooping and thus Packet sniffing), sender authentication (blocking identity spoofing), and message integrity (blocking message alteration) to achieve privacy. When properly chosen, implemented and used, such techniques can provide secure communications over unsecured networks. This has been the usually intended purpose for VPN for some years.

Because such choice, implementation, and use are not trivial, there are many insecure VPN schemes available on the market.

Secure VPN technologies may also be used to enhance security as a "security overlay" within dedicated networking infrastructures.

Secure VPN protocols include the following:

- IPsec (IP security) - commonly used over IPv4, and an obligatory part of IPv6.
- SSL used either for tunnelling the entire network stack, as in the OpenVPN project, or for securing what is, essentially, a web proxy. Although the latter is often called a "SSL VPN" by VPN vendors, it is not really a fully-fledged VPN in the usual sense.
- PPTP (point-to-point tunnelling protocol), developed jointly by a number of companies, including Microsoft.
- L2TP (Layer 2 Tunnelling Protocol), which includes work by both Microsoft and Cisco.
- L2TPv3 (Layer 2 Tunnelling Protocol version 3), a new release.
- VPN-Q The machine at the other end of a VPN could be a threat and a source of attack; this has no necessary connection with VPN designs and has been usually left to system administrative efforts. There has been at least one attempt to address this issue in the context of VPNs. On Microsoft ISA Server, an application called QSS (Quarantine Security Suite) is available.

Some large ISPs now offer "managed" VPN service for business customers who want the security and convenience of a VPN but prefer not to undertake administering a VPN server themselves. In addition to providing remote workers with secure access to their employer's internal network, other security and management services are sometimes included as part of the package. Examples include keeping anti-virus and anti-spyware programs updated on each client's computer.

Trusted VPNs do not use cryptographic tunnelling, but instead rely on the security of a single provider's network to protect the traffic. In a sense, these are an elaboration of traditional network and system administration work.

- Multi-protocol label switching (MPLS) is often used to build trusted VPN.
- L2F (Layer 2 forwarding), developed by Cisco, can also be used.

7.6.5 Category of VPN

- Remote access VPN
- Site to site VPN or network to network VPN

7.6.5.1 Types of remote access VPN

- Client initiated remote access VPN
- Server initiated remote access VPN

In client initiated remote access VPN, clients have certain software, so it is normal to call the remote access server through a server connected head-office. The complete software make tunnel is available to the client so this is called client initiated remote access VPN.

In server initiated remote access VPN, the clients may not have any software, e.g. ordinary mobile clients dial a number and request for VPN services. The client is verified by the server and then the server connects the head office.

The server makes tunnel with the client and head office, so this called server initiated remote access VPN.

7.6.5.2 Site to site VPN

In site to site VPN, the server has a permanent connection, such as a leased line, with its clients. ISP should have VPN facilities to provide VPN services.

VPN is substitute for VSAT, and has the following benefits:

- Diverse geographic base or diverse consumer base head office, branch office
- Mobile work force
- Extranets applications
- Virtual leased line
- Lost cost communication

Characteristics in application

A well-designed VPN can provide great benefits for an organization. It can:

- Extend geographic connectivity
- Improve security where data lines have not been ciphered
- Reduce operational costs versus traditional WAN
- Reduce transit time and transportation costs for remote users
- Simplify network topology in certain scenarios
- Provide global networking opportunities
- Provide telecommuter support
- Provide broadband networking compatibility
- Provide faster ROI (return on investment) than traditional carrier leased/owned WAN lines
- Show a good economy of scale
- Scale well, when used with a public key infrastructure

However, since VPNs extend the "mother network" by such an extent (almost every employee) and with such ease (no dedicated lines to rent/hire), there are certain security implications that must receive special attention:

- Security on the client side must be tightened and enforced, lest security be lost at any of a multitude of machines and devices. This has been termed, central client administration, and security policy enforcement. It is common for a company to require that each employee wishing to use their VPN outside company offices (e.g. from home) first install an approved firewall (often hardware). Some organizations with especially sensitive data, such as healthcare companies, even arrange for an employee's home to have two separate WAN connections: one for working on that employer's sensitive data and one for all other uses.
- The scale of access to the target network may have to be limited.
- Logging policies must be evaluated and in most cases revised.

A single breach or failure can result in the privacy and security of the network being compromised. In situations in which a company or individual has legal obligations to keep information confidential, there may be legal problems, even criminal ones, as a result. Two examples are the HIPPA regulations in the US with regard to health data, and the more general European Union data privacy regulations which apply to even marketing and billing information and extend to those who share that data elsewhere.

Encryption key management issues

Ideally, it should not be necessary to manage the keys, i.e. key management should be as automated as possible. An application should do this for the user, so there should be no need to copy it anywhere. For example, a backup product like Tivoli Storage Manager is fully integrated with IBM's LTO-4, so the backup product takes care of key management. This is an ideal set up since another component is not needed to take care of the keys.

One of the main drawbacks to encryption is losing the keys, so there must be a back up.

However, the keys should not be backed up to encrypted media and must be backed up somewhere where they can be retrieved.

Unlocking encryption management

As encryption technology becomes more user-friendly and manageable, more businesses are adding standalone encryption platforms to their IT security. Someday, encryption features built into a wide range of IT products - from operating systems and messaging gateways to hard drives and storage systems - may work in concert to offer central policy enforcement across different types of network assets and devices.

Until that day arrives, however, companies embracing the tools have become dependent on standalone encryption platforms to give them distributed control and policy enforcement across their IT systems.

Long known as much for their complexity and demand for hands-on care and feeding as they have been valued for their protective qualities, encryption platforms are finally finding their way into a number of large businesses.

This growth in adoption has been driven by the proliferation of data protection regulations and based on the availability of products that address the hardest elements of encryption technology - policy enforcement and key management.

"*The performing of the encryption itself is something that generally belongs close to whatever type of data you are trying to encrypt, whether that is e-mail, network traffic, or a database, but companies are buying into technologies today that allow them to do centralized policy enforcement and key management,*" said Paul Stamp, analyst with Forrester Research.

"*It's great in theory to say that all of this activity needs to happen in the infrastructure components themselves,*" he said, "*But that's not a reality yet in terms of allowing for centralized management, so customers are turning to these platforms in the meantime.*"

End-users agree that encryption has long been a security process they desired to implement but avoided because of its complexity. The arrival of more usable encryption technology over the last few years has helped eliminate some of the traditional roadblocks, according to some corporate users.

"*From my previous experience with e-mail encryption, I had two major concerns with using the tools: Key management and any dependence on the end-user to make the systems work right,*" said Michael Gabriel, corporate information security officer for Career Education Corporation (CEC) a higher-education provider that operates more than 75 colleges, schools, and universities in the US.

"*I haven't ever seen an encryption project where management wasn't a major sticking point, that has been the history of the technology, but it seems that the vendors are finally getting it right,*" Gabriel said. "*Compared to mapping the business process, putting the technology in place was a breeze. The only real sticking point was getting the data flow.*"

CEC is using encryption tools made by PGP in cooperation with its data leakage prevention and e-mail filtering systems to protect sensitive information being passed among its employees.

Gabriel said that PGP's embedded key management capabilities may be the most valuable aspect of the system - a feature that simply did not exist in the past.

Other PGP users echoed those sentiments, saying that encryption tools have advanced significantly over the past several years in terms of eliminating the management headaches that have made it challenging to deploy the systems on a wider basis.

SUMMARY

- Encryption is the conversion of data into a form, called a ciphertext, that cannot be easily understood by unauthorized people. Decryption is the process of converting encrypted data back into its original form, so it can be understood. The use of encryption/decryption is as old as the art of communication.
- Traditionally, several methods can be used to encrypt data streams, all of which can easily be implemented through software, but not so easily decrypted when either the original or its encrypted data stream are unavailable. (When both source and encrypted data are available, code-breaking becomes much simpler, though it is not necessarily easy). The best encryption methods have little effect on system performance, and may contain other benefits (such as data compression) built in.
- Symmetric encryption is the oldest and best-known technique. A secret key, which can be a number, a word, or just a string of random letters, is applied to the text of a message to change the content in a particular way. This might be as simple as shifting each letter by a number of places in the alphabet. As long as both sender and recipient know the secret key, they can encrypt and decrypt all messages that use this key.
- The problem with secret keys is exchanging them over the Internet or a large network while preventing them from falling into the wrong hands. Anyone who knows the secret key can decrypt the message. One answer is asymmetric encryption, in which there are two related keys - a key pair. A public key is made freely available to anyone who might want to send you a message. A second, private key is kept secret, so that only the user knows it.
- A digital code is a code that can be attached to an electronically transmitted message to uniquely identify its contents and the sender.
- The signature is an unforgettable piece of data asserting that a named person wrote or otherwise agreed to the document to which the signature is attached. Unlike encryption, digital signatures are a recent development, the need for which has arisen with the proliferation of e-commerce.
- A digital certificate is an attachment to an electronic message to verify the identity of the sender and to provide the receiver with the means to encode a reply. Digital certificates play a valuable role in authentication. Digital certificates are data files used to establish the identity of people and electronic assets for protection of on line transactions.
- Digital certificates are the electronic counterparts to drivers licenses, passports and

membership cards. A digital certificate can be presented electronically to prove the users identity or right to access information or services online.

- SSL is layered beneath application protocols such as HTTP, SMTP, TELNET, FTP, Gopher and NNTP and above the Internet connection protocol TCP/IP.SSL provides a security 'handshake' to initiate the TCP/IP connection. Its only role is to encrypt and decrypt the message stream.
- A virtual private network (VPN) is a private communications network often used within a company, or by several companies or organizations, to communicate confidentially over a publicly accessible network.

REVIEW QUESTIONS

1. What is encryption?
2. Why should organizations use encryption?
3. What are encryption algorithms?
4. What encryption method does Blue Scale Encryption use?
5. Have any data encryption solutions been hacked successfully?
6. How does AES AES-256 work?
7. How does encryption make it easier to dispose of data?
8. What kind of encryption solutions are available?
9. Which category of encryption does Spectra Blue Scale encryption match?
10. Why does everyone not already encrypt data using existing solutions?
11. What about encrypting data on my network (that is, using the network network-based solution)?

CHAPTER 8

Electronic Payment Systems

Electronic payment systems are becoming central to the on line business process innovation as companies look for ways to serve customers faster and at lower cost. Electronic payment systems and e-commerce are intricately linked given that on line customers must pay for products and services.

8.1 A LAYERED PROTOCOL MODEL

A three-layer model is used to compare payments schemes.

Policy

The semantics of the payment scheme include refund policies, and the liabilities incurred by customers, merchants and financial institutions.

Data flow

This is the requirement for storage of data by and communications between the parties. This includes not only the data flows for payments themselves but also for refunds, account enquiries and settlement.

Mechanism

These are the methods by which the necessary security requirements for messages and stored data are achieved.

All three abstraction levels are tightly coupled since policy makes requirements of data flow and data flow makes requirements of mechanism.

8.1.1 Payment Protocol Models

Cash

Cash consists of a token, which may be authenticated independently of the issuer. This is commonly achieved through use of self-authenticating tokens or tamper proof hardware.

Cheque

Cheques are payment instruments whose validity requires reference to the issuer.

Card

Card payment schemes provide payment mechanisms through the existing credit card payment infrastructure. Such schemes have many structural similarities to cheque models except that solutions are constrained by that structure. A key feature of card payment systems is that every transaction carries insurance.

8.2 TYPES OF ELECTRONIC PAYMENT SYSTEMS

Electronic payment systems are proliferating in banking, retail, health care, on line markets and even in the government – in fact, anywhere money needs to change hands. Organizations are motivated by the need to deliver products and services more cost effectively and to provide a higher quality of service to customers.

In the early 1970's, the emerging electronic payment technology was labelled electronic funds transfer (EFT). EFT is defined as – "any transfer of funds initiated through an electronic terminal, telephonic instrument or computer or magnetic tape so as to order, instruct or authorize a financial institution to debit or credit an account."

Work on EFT can be segmented into three broad categories:

1. Banking and financial payments:
   a. Large scale or wholesale payments, e.g. bank to bank transfer.
   b. Small scale or retail payments, e.g. automated teller machines and cash dispensers.
   c. Home banking, e.g. bill payment.
2. Retailing payments:
   a. Credit cards
   b. Private label credit/debit cards
   c. Charge cards

3. Online electronic commerce payments:
   a. Token based payment systems
      i. Electronic cash, e.g. Digicash
      ii. Electronic check, e.g. net cheque)
      iii. Smart cards or debit cards, e.g. Mondex electronic currency cards
   b. Credit card based payment systems
      i. Encrypted credit cards, e.g. World Wide Web from based encryption.
      ii. Third party authorization numbers, e.g. first virtual.

8.3 DIGITAL TOKEN BASED ELECTRONIC PAYMENT SYSTEMS

Electronic tokens are designed as electronic analogues of various forms of payment backed by a bank or financial institution. Simply stated, electronic tokens are equivalent to cash that is backed by a bank.

Electronic tokens are of three types:

1. **Cash or real time:** Transactions are settled with the exchange of electronic currency. An example of on line currency exchange is e-cash.
2. **Debit or prepaid:** Users pay in advance for the privilege of getting information, e.g. smart cards and electronic purses that store electronic money.
3. **Credit or postpaid:** The server authenticates the customers and verifies with the bank that funds are adequate before purchase, e.g. credit/debit cards and electronic checks.

8.3.1 Electronic Cash (E-Cash)

Electronic cash is a new concept in on-line payment systems because it combines computerized convenience with security and privacy that improve on paper cash. E-Cash focuses on replacing cash as the principal payment vehicle in consumer oriented electronic payment systems. Cash is the dominant form of payment for three reasons:

- Lack of trust in the banking system
- Inefficient clearing and settlement of non-cash transactions
- Negative real interest rate paid on bank deposits

E-cash presents some interesting characteristics that should make it an attractive alternative for payment over the Internet.

- Acceptable to all people i.e. creditability
- Cash is a legal tender i.e. no one can reject it
- Cash is negotiable i.e. it can be exchanged anywhere
- Cash is a bearer instrument i.e. the person who physically holds the cash is the owner of cash
- No risk on acceptance

Properties of electronic cash

E-cash must have the following properties:

- **Monetary value:** E-cash must have a monetary value, it must be backed by cash, bank authorized credit, or a bank–certified cashier's check.
- **Interoperability:** E-cash must be interoperable i.e. exchangeable as payment for other e-cash, paper cash, goods or services, lines of credit, deposits in banking accounts, bank notes, electronic benefits transfer, etc.
- **Retrievability:** E-cash must be storable and retrievable. Remote storage and retrieval would allow users to exchange e-cash from their home or office while travelling. The cash could be stored on a remote computer's memory, in smart cards or in other easily transported standard or special purpose devices.
- **Security:** The following security feature are available on e-cash
  - Denomination required
  - Digital signature
  - Backed by a bank

How E-cash is generated

E-cash is based on cryptographic systems called digital signatures. This method involves a pair of numeric keys one for locking and the other for unlocking.

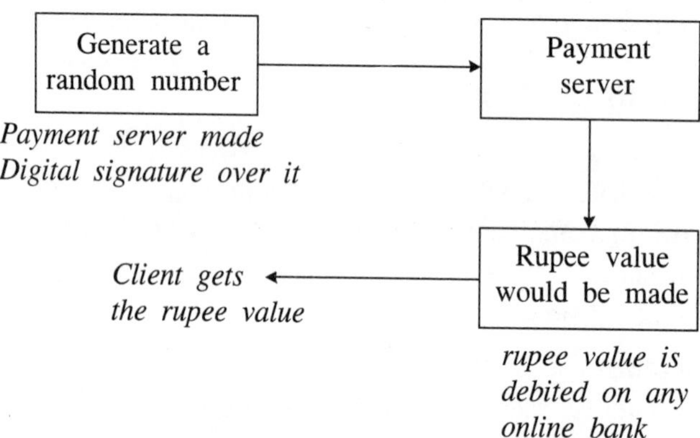

Fig. 8.1: ***Schematic for generation of e-cash***

By supplying all customers with its public keys, a bank enables customers to decode any message (or currency) encoded with the bank's private key. If decoding by a customer yields a recognizable message, the customer can be fairly confident that only the bank could have encoded it. These digital signatures are as secure as the mathematics involved and have proved. Before the e-cash can be used to buy products or services it must be procured from a currency server.

The purchase of e-cash from an on-line currency server involves:

- Establishment of an account
- Maintaining enough money in the account to back the purchase

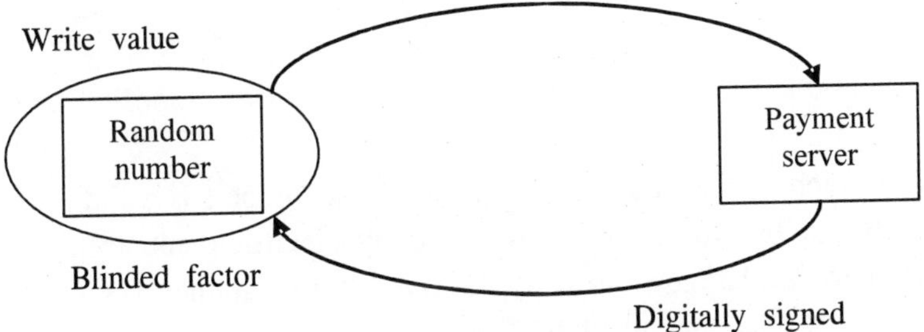

Fig. 8.2: ***How Algo works***

1. When an e-cash withdrawal is made, the PC of the e-cash user calculates how many digital coins of what denominations are needed to withdraw the requested amount.
2. Random numbers for those coins will be generated and the blinding factor will be included.
3. The result of these calculations will be sent to the digital bank.
4. The bank will encode the blinded numbers with its secret key (digital signatures) and at the same time debit the account of the client for the same amount.
5. The authenticated coins are sent back to the user and finally the user will take out the blinding factor that he introduced.
6. The serial numbers pulls their signatures are now digital coins their value is guaranteed by the bank.

Many business transactions are not feasible because of double spending, which is equivalent to a bounced check. Double spending becomes possible because it is very easy to make copies of e-cash, forcing banks or merchants to take extra precautions.

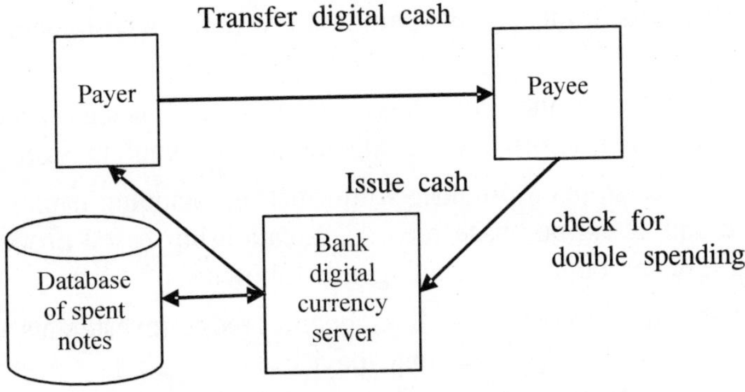

Fig. 8.3: ***Detection of double spending***

To uncover double spending, banks must compare the note passed to it by the merchant against a database of spent notes. Just as paper currency is identified by a unique serial number, digital cash can also be identified.

One drawback of e-cash is its inability to be easily divided into smaller amounts.

Operational risk and e-cash

Operational risk associated with e-cash can be mitigated by imposing constraints such as limits on:

1. The time period for which the given electronic money is valid
2. How much can be stored and transferred by electronic money
3. The number of exchanges that can take place before money needs to be re-deposited with a bank or financial institution
4. The number of such transactions that can be made during a given period of time

The objective of imposing constraints is to limit the issuer's liability.

8.3.2 Smart Cards and Electronic Payment Systems

Smart cards have been in existence since the early 1980s and hold promise for secure transactions using existing infrastructure. Smart cards are credit and debit cards and other card products enhanced with microprocessors capable of holding more information than the traditional magnetic strip.

The smart card technology is widely used in countries such as France, Germany, Japan and Singapore to pay for public phone calls, transportation and shopper loyalty programs. Smart cards are basically of two types:

- Relationship based smart credit card
- Electronic purses (which replace money, also known as debit cards and electronic money)

Relationship based smart cards

A relationship-based smart card is an enhancement of existing card services and/or the addition of new services that a financial institution delivers to its customers via chip based card or other device.

These new services may include access to multiple financial accounts, value–added marketing programs or other information cardholders may want to store on their card.

Enhanced credit cards store card-holder's information including name, birth date, personal shopping preference and actual purchase records. Relationship based products are expected to offer customers far greater options, including the following:

1. Access to multiple accounts, such as debit, credit, investments or stored value for e-cash on one card or an electronic device.
2. A variety of functions such as cash access, bill payment, balance inquiry or funds transfer for selected accounts.

3. Multiple access options at multiple locations using multiple device types, such as an automated teller machine (ATM), a screen phone, a personal computer, a personal digital assistant or interactive TVs.

Companies are trying to incorporate these services into a personalized banking relationship for each customer. They can package financial and non financial services with value added programs to enhance convenience, build loyalty and retention and attract new customers.

Electronic purses and debit cards

Despite their increasing flexibility, relationship based cards are credit based and settlement occurs at the end of the billing cycle. There remains a need for a financial instrument to replace cash.

The electronic purses are wallet-sized smart cards embedded with programmable microchips that store sums of money for people to use instead of cash for everything from buying food, to making photocopies, to paying subway fares.

The electronic purse works in following manner: After the purse is loaded with money, at an ATM or through the use of an inexpensive special telephone, it can be used to pay for, say candy in a vending machine equipped with a card reader.

The vending machine need only verify that a card is authentic and there is enough money available for a chocolate bar. In one second, the value of the purchase is deducted from the balance on the card added to the e-cash box in the vending machine. The remaining balance on the card is displayed by the vending machine or can be checked at an ATM or with a balance reading device.

This allows customers to pay for rides and calls with a prepaid card that remembers each transaction and when the balance on an electronic purse is depleted, the purse can be recharged with more money.

8.3.3 E-Checks

Electronic checks are another form of electronic tokens. They are designed to accommodate the many individuals and entities that might prefer to pay on credit or through some mechanism other than cash.

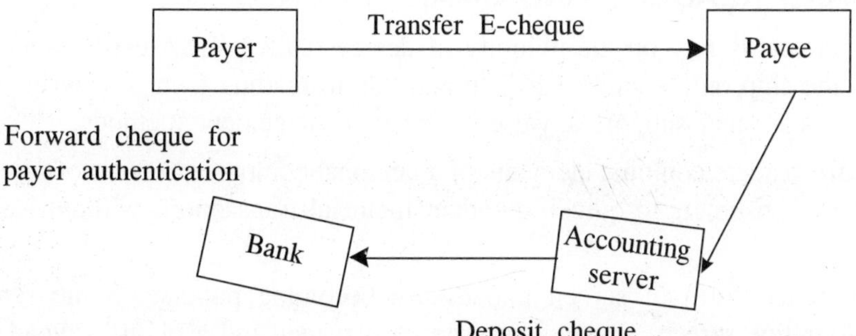

Fig. 8.4: ***Payment transaction sequence in an e-cheque system***

The buyers must register with a third party account server before they are able to write an e-cheque. The accounting server acts as a billing server. The registration procedure can vary depending on the particular account server and may require a credit card or a bank account to back the cheques.

E-checks were deliberately created to work in much the same way as conventional paper checks. An account holder will issue an electronic document that contains the name of the payer, the name of financial institution, the payer's account number, the name of payee and the amount of the check. An e-check will bear the digital equivalent of a signature and will need to be endorsed by the payee, using another electronic signature, before the check can be paid.

Kerberos algorithms are used for the implementation of e-checks.

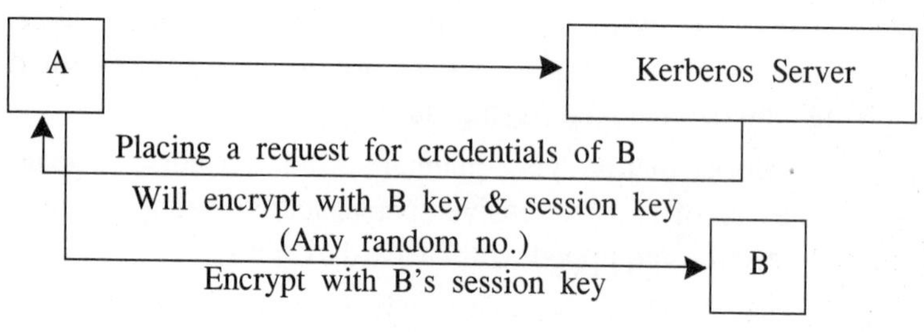

Fig. 8.5

On receiving the check, the seller presents it to the accounting server for verification and payment. The accounting server verifies the digital signature on the check using Kerberos authentication scheme.

Suppose 'A' wants to communicate with 'B', i.e. 'A' is going to send the session key to 'B'. 'A' encrypts the session key with B's secret key, so that the communication reaches 'B'. Now 'B' will be able to open the communication and both parties will able to generate more secure new keys. Communication is done with the new secure keys.

Note – All the clients are supposed to have a connection with the Kerberos server, which is known as the payment server.

8.4 SMART CARD READERS AND SMART PHONES

The benefits of smart cards rely on the ubiquity of devices called smart card readers that can communicate with the chip on the smart card. In addition to reading from and writing to smart cards, these devices can also support a variety of key management methods.

Some smart card readers combine elements of a personal computer, a point of sale terminal, and a phone to allow consumers to quickly conduct financial transactions without leaving their homes.

Card readers in the form of screen phones are becoming popular. Some screen-based phones feature a four line screen, a magnetic strip card reader and a phone keypad that folds away to reveal a keyboard for use in complex transactions.

Many bankers maintain that screen based phones are more convenient to use than pc-based home banking applications, which require users to boot up their systems and establish a modem connection before conducting a transaction.

Smart card readers can be customized for specific environments. The operating environment allows programmers to use the C programming language to create and modify applications without compromising the device's security functions.

Note: Smart cards are plastic cards which contain some memory and a processor chip. They differ from debit/credit cards, which use magnetic chips while smart cards use PROM, EPROM, EEPROM memory chips.

Smart cards have all the technical features of debit/credit cards along with some extra memory features. They mostly use EEPROM. Flash memory is also used for smart cards.

The various types of smart cards are:

1. Contact – insert it
2. Contact less – Flash it (EISRO)
3. Combination cards (combi card) – either you insert or flash it.

The various applications of smart cards depend on the memory usage and can be classified as –

1. Read only – (ROM chip used) used for authentication
2. Add only – Bank places
3. Modify only – Bank places
4. Execution only – complex operation authorizing

Smart cards are basically of two types

- Relationship based smart cards
- Electronic purses

8.5 CREDIT CARD BASED ELECTRONIC PAYMENT SYSTEMS

If consumers want to purchase a product or service, they simply send their credit card details to the service provider involved and the credit card organization will handle this payment like any other. Credit card payment on on-line networks can be broken down into three basic categories:

1. Payments using plain credit card details

   The disadvantages are:

   - Low level security
   - Authentication problems

2. Payments using encrypted credit card details
3. Payments using third party verification

8.5.1 Payments Using Plain Credit Cards

To avoid the complexity associated with digital cash and electronic checks, consumers and vendors are also looking at credit card payments on the Internet as one possible time tested alternative. There is nothing new in the basic process. If consumers want to purchase a product or service, they simply send their credit card details to the service provider involved and the credit card organization will handle this payment like any other.

Credit card payments on on-line networks can be divided into three basic categories:

1. **Payments using plain credit card details:** The easiest methods of payment are the exchange of unencrypted credit cards over a public network such as telephone lines or the Internet. The low level of security inherent in the design of the Internet makes this method problematic. Authentication is also a significant problem, and the vendor is usually responsible for ensuring that the person using the credit card is its owner. Without encryption there is no way to do this.
2. **Payments using encrypted credit card details:** It would make sense to encrypt the credit card details before sending them out, but even then it is necessary to consider the cost of a credit card transaction itself. Such costs would prohibit low value payments by adding costs to the transactions.
3. **Payments using third party verification:** One solution to security and verification problems is the introduction of a third party that collects and approves payments from one client to another. After a certain period of time, one credit card transaction for the total accumulated amount is completed.

8.5.2 Encryption and Credit Cards

Encryption is initiated when credit card information is entered into a browser or other electronic commerce device and sent securely over the network from buyer to seller as an encrypted message.

To make a credit card transaction truly secure and non refutable, the following sequence of steps must occur before actual goods, services or funds flow:

1. A customer presents his credit card information securely to the merchant.
2. The merchant validates the customer's identity as the owner of the credit card account.
3. The merchant relays the credit card charge information and signature to its bank or on-line credit card processors.
4. The bank or processing party relays the information to the customer's bank for authorization approval.
5. The customer's bank returns the credit card data, charge authentication, and authorization to the merchant.

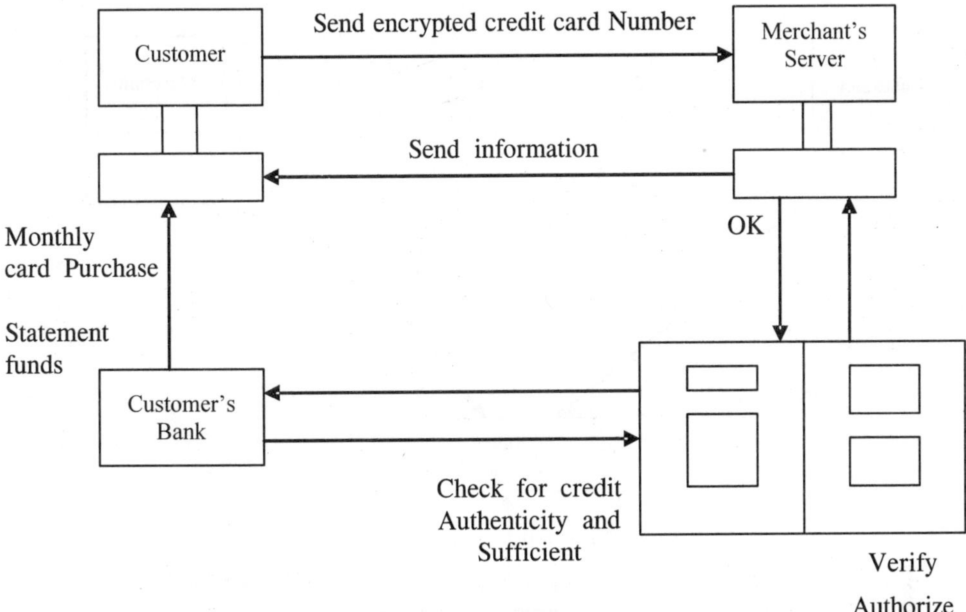

Fig. 8.6: ***Processing payments using encrypted credit cards***

8.5.3 Third Party Processors and Credit Cards

In third party processing, consumers register with a third party on the Internet to verify electronic micro-transactions. The verification mechanisms can be designed with many of the attributes of electronic tokens, including anonymity. They differ from electronic token systems in that:

1. They depend on existing financial instruments.
2. They require the on-line involvement of at least one additional party and in some cases, multiple parties to ensure extra security.

Payments can be made by credit card or by debiting a demand deposit account via the automated clearing house. For the sake of brevity, we refer to them as on-line third party processors since both methods are fairly similar in nature.

1. The consumer acquires an OTPP account number by filling out a registration form. This will give the OTPP a customer information profile that is backed by a traditional financial instrument such as a credit card.
2. To purchase an article, software or other information on line, the consumer requests the item from the merchant by quoting his/her OTPP account number.
3. The merchant contacts the OTPP payment server with the customer's account number.
4. The OTPP payment server verifies the customer's account number for the vendor and checks for sufficient funds.

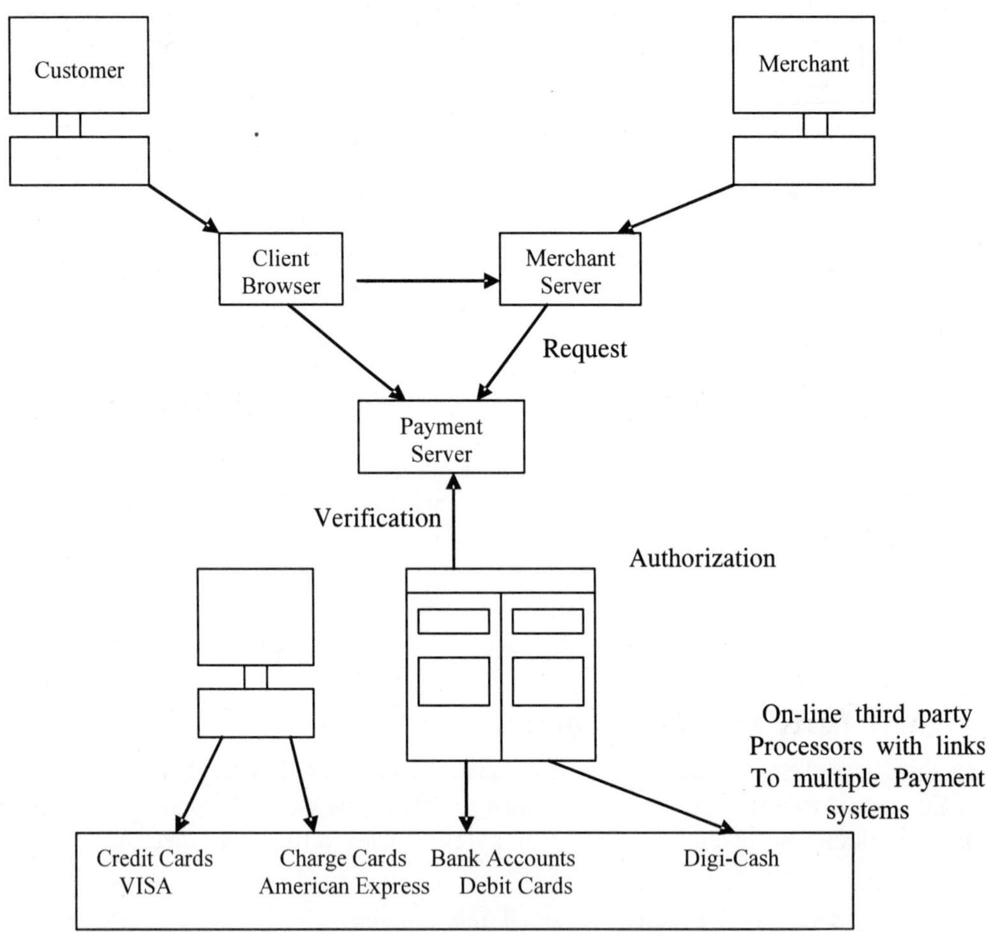

Fig. 8.7: ***On-line payment process using a third party processor***

5. The OTPP server sends an electronic message to the buyer. The buyer responds to the form.
6. If the OTPP payment server gets a yes from the customer, the merchant is informed and the customer is allowed to download the material immediately.
7. The OTPP will not debit the buyer's account until it receives confirmation of completion of the purchase. Abuse by a buyer who receives information or a product and declines to pay can result in account suspension.

8.6 BUSINESS PROS AND CONS OF CRED!T CARD BASED PAYMENT

Third party processing for credit card entails a number of pros and cons. These companies are chartered to give credit accounts to individuals and act as bill collection agencies for business. Consumers use credit cards by presenting them for payment and then paying an aggregate bill once a month, consumers either pay a flat fee or individual transaction charges for this service. Merchants get paid for the credit card drafts that they submit to the credit card company. Businesses get charged a transaction charge ranging from 1 percent to 3 percent for each draft submitted.

Credit cards have advantages over checks in that the credit card company assumes a larger share of financial risk for both buyer and seller in a transaction. Buyers can sometimes dispute a charge retroactively and have the credit card company act on their behalf. Sellers are ensured that they will be paid for all their sales so that they need not worry about fraud. This is convenient for the buyer, in that credit card transactions are usually quicker and easier than check transactions. One disadvantage of credit cards is that their transactions are not anonymous and credit card companies do in fact compile valuable data about spending habits.

Record keeping with credit cards is one of the features consumers value most because of disputes and mistakes in billing. Disputes may arise because different services may have different policies. The complexity of credit card processing takes place in the verification phase, a potential bottle neck. If there is a lapse in time between the charging and the delivery of goods or services, the customer verification process is simple because it does not have to be done in real time. In fact, all the relaying and authorizations can occur after the customer merchant transaction is completed, unless the authorization request is denied. If the customer wants a report, it can be down loaded into a personal computer or other information appliance immediately at the time of purchase, however, many message relays and authorizations take place in real time while the customer waits. Such exchanges may require many sequence specific operations such as staged encryption and decryption and exchanges of cryptographic keys.

8.6.1 Infrastructure for Online Credit Card Processing

Competition among the service providers of credit cards is based on service quality, price, processing system speed, customer support and reliability. Most third party processors market their services directly to large regional or national merchants rather than through financial institutions or independent sales organizations. Barriers to entry include:

1. Large initial capital requirements
2. Ongoing expenses related to establishing and maintaining an electronic transaction processing network.
3. The ability to obtain competitively priced access to an existing network
4. The reluctance of merchants to change processors

Many companies are developing advanced electronic services for home based financial transactions and software companies are increasingly allying with banks to sell home banking. Eventually, the goal would be to offer everything from mutual funds to brokerage services over the network. Many banks are concerned about this prospect and view it as an encroachment on their turf. After years of dabbling, mostly unsuccessfully, with remote banking, banking is receiving a jarring message: Get wired or lose customers.

8.6.2 Credit Cards for People with Bad Credit

Credit cards for people with bad credit aim at strengthening and rebuilding the credit history that is currently poor. Initially there was only a very limited number of lenders and hence there was a demand for them. Today, there are numerous lenders in the field, who are willing to offer credit cards to a person with a poor credit history, bad credit record holder or even people with no previous credit history.

This has become more common now, as at least one in four persons face such problems. They also find it difficult in applying for a credit, and one has to search for lenders willing to help. A credit problem in the past limits one's options in finding a lender, as when assessing an application for credit, lenders consider the person's credit history and their credit score.

An adverse credit history amounts to a low or poor credit rating. That does not mean a clean credit history, or even none, is considered a good credit score either.

However, today a history of defaults or arrears, CCJs or bankruptcy does not prevent a person from restoring their credit rating using a credit card.

8.6.3 Directory of Companies

There is a long list of companies who sympathize with people with bad credit. At least one in four of the adult population in the UK is estimated to experience some form of bad credit. It shows that nobody can escape bad credit. But there is always a chance given to them to escape from it. This is done by a few companies who are generous enough to help such people. Having difficulty in getting a credit card, personal loan or mortgage is this due to poor credit history, but there are an increasing number of companies to help people who had credit problems in the past.

8.6.4 Various Applications for Credit

An application for a card, personal loan or a store card, involves a credit search by the lender. A search makes a mark on the applicant's credit record. Though not necessarily an issue, too many such marks generate a sort of warning for the lenders.

8.6.5 High Rates of Interest

It goes without saying, that a poor credit rating will cost a person, money. Only when credit scorings meet the requirements set by the lenders can a person make the best credit card deals. A person with a poor credit score is not entitled to mainstream credit cards.

Bad credit-credit cards

If a person has or has had bad credit but still require a credit card, then he/she must know how to repair on his/her credit rating. If a person feels there is a chance of their being turned down for a credit card, they should write to the credit reference agencies, who will send the person a copy of their report.

Unsecured credit cards

Such cards are issued to persons with a high income or an excellent credit history. A bank deposit amount is not required for security and annual fees are not charged. The interest charged on the amount lent is low.

High risk credit cards

If a person has a low paid job, or poor credit history and credit score; then the credit cards lenders charge an activation fee upon activation, and also charge an annual fee. The interest rates charged are also higher.

Secured credit cards

Cards issued to people with low paid jobs and/or a very bad credit history and credit score are to be secured. This is because the card providers face a greater risk in issuing credit cards to such persons. Hence these card holders need to have a deposit in a bank account, where the deposit equals the credit amount available on the card. They are normally charged an annual fee and very high interest rates too. Charges are very high for late fees, and over-the-limit fees.

Credit card scams

There are agencies who offer a guaranteed secured credit card, however these agencies are often out to cheat people and one should not get carried away by such scams. These agencies target people who have a poor credit history or no credit at all. Their advertisements are mostly for secured credit cards. Secured credit cards are an efficient way to build or re-establish credit history; yet there are some marketers of secured cards who make unreliable advertising claims just to convince people to apply for a secured credit card. One should avoid falling for such secured credit card scams. The following points should be looked for:

- Guaranteed credit. A guarantee to get a person credit is not possible.
- A claim of "No credit check." Genuine credit providers, even of secured cards, will always check a person's credit report while assessing the risk of extending credit.
- A legitimate creditor will not charge for calls to obtain information about their product.
- Credit cards offered by "credit repair" companies or "credit clinics".

Such offers that seem too good to be true probably are.

Limitations of different types of credit cards

There are various types of credit cards available, each having their own limitations. In order to find the best credit card deals, one has to have the time to find the lender most suitable to them before applying. One or two late payments on a credit card is not a problem. Lenders on their part will only contact credit reference agencies.

8.7 ONLINE BUSINESS ADMINISTRATION PROGRAM

The dynamics of global business operations have witnessed a massive change in the last few decades. With the advancement of the Internet and telecommunications the system of information delivery has become fast and more accurate. Electronic communication has become indispensable and without the use of the Internet it is now next to impossible to carry out certain business operations. In this era it has become mandatory for the business professionals to upgrade their knowledge.

Many students who want to enter the world of business need to be aware of the latest business scenario and the global business trends. There are several universities who are offering online business degrees to students, with the up-to-date business skills. The business administration degrees have attained immense popularity with the growth of global businesses. As the global business players are aiming to explore unexplored international markets, to initiate the business policies, these houses are seeking skilled and experienced managers.

It is indeed a good idea to be aware of the business trends and the managerial tactics required in the business world. The online business administration programs are tailored to meet the industry's requirements. The universities upgrade the course curricula and the syllabi on a regular basis. Since many professionals do not have the time to participate in the regular courses; these courses are especially helpful to them.

Effective selection: Before taking up a course it is necessary to enquire about the education provider. Often it is difficult to select the proper education provider. There are plenty of education counsellors who offer advice and who are aware of the educational institutes and can give effective suggestions. Online business administration degrees are often worthwhile, as there are several education providers that offer the latest case studies etc. It is a good idea to see the course curriculum and the syllabus before finally enrolling.

The students are given a unique student identity number and e-mail id. Using the student number one can access information related to the course. In several cases special video conferencing facilities are also provided for the participants' convenience. Students are sent course material through the mail, which has to be followed. For effective completion of the course it is necessary to take part in the discussion forums. Universities provide special discussion forums for the students.

There are several case studies provided to the students. The education providers attempt to provide the best course material to make the courses more oriented towards industry's needs. There are several universities that offer fast track online business administration courses and these courses are highly effective for students who want to complete the courses earlier. There are certain programs that offer courses as per the present industry's needs and it is best to search for these. After successful completion of these courses it is easier to get a job.

The nature of online business course: There are certain common subjects offered within the online business administration courses. These courses provide a vivid idea about the present needs of the business industry's needs. It is helpful to check all the papers before starting the course. The students are provided with a wide range of databases and it is necessary to visit these databases regularly to complete the assignments effectively. There are online assignment submission boxes and each student needs to submit the assignments to successfully complete the course. Again there are several courses that offer online examinations.

Knowledge management, business background, business information systems, system analysis are some popular papers. The demand for these courses is extremely high, as with the advancement of information technology all business houses and transnational corporations need these courses. The students are requested to send e-mails to the course coordinators in case of any requirement. Feedback is taken from the students and the courses are altered as per the students requirements.

Professionals find these courses extremely helpful as professional experience helps a lot when the students seek jobs. For this reason many working professionals take part in these online business administration courses. There are several accreditations given to the education providers, as per the standards of the courses. There are many universities whose courses are not accredited but are designed as per the industry's needs.

Importance of self study: These days there are numerous online business administration degree providers. So, to select the right one it is necessary to be aware of these degrees. Today it is simple to carry out research using the Internet and the World Wide Web. Plenty of web portals are available that focus on information related to degrees and it is best to search for the best business schools using a good search engine. Certain business schools do not offer online programs.

There are several business schools that offer courses which are greatly in demand and it is prudent to select such a course. There are also many online articles and journals; by going through them one can take a final decision. Many institutions offer live chat facilities, which prospective participants can avail of. All the institutes have toll free numbers and the customer care executives can provide effective suggestions. It is also possible to communicate directly with the students who have already participated in these courses, and many people prefer to do so, as it gives a clear idea about the realities of the course.

8.8 CREDIT CARD DEBT RELIEF

Credit, whether in the form of a credit card or a bank loan, is not necessarily bad and need not be totally avoided. Credit cards offer a convenient means to make purchases without having to carry large sums of money. However, too much credit can quickly put a person in heavy debt that might take seemingly forever to get out of.

The best use of credit is to purchase assets that will grow in value over time, like a house. But, the purchase of expensive consumer goods, such as a car, would not be possible for most people without the use of credit. Purchasing consumables, including furniture, clothes, sporting goods, vacations or anything else that loses its value after purchase, is a dangerous use of credit.

One should ask oneself whether the object is one that is really needed or is just wanted, as these are two totally different things. One should not spend more than they earn.

The most common types of credit are: (i) Open-end credit – This includes credit cards, cash advance credit cards and lines of credit, which can be used up to a pre-approved limit. Credit cards might have annual fees, while some lines of credit will charge maintenance or usage fees. (ii) Closed-end credit - This is the kind of loan used to buy a house or a car. Unlike a credit card, the interest rate, amount financed and payment schedule are all agreed upon by the lender and the borrower. (iii) Incidental credit - This is what professionals (like doctors) grant. One is charged for a service after it is availed of. Usually, there is no fee charged. (iv) Public utility credit - This is used by utilities such as telephone, electricity and cable companies. How these are granted depends on the lending institution and the income, credit rating, character and collateral of the borrower.

Someone with a good credit history, who always pays their bills, will be able to borrow more. This is possible because the lending institution knows the member is not going to swindle them. A local bank or credit union might also offer a credit card with a lower interest rate to customer who has a good credit history.

Credit is not free. It costs something to borrow money. Interest is always charged on any balance maintained. Major credit cards vary in how they compute this rate, but it is usually much higher than what a financial institution would charge for a loan. Plus, credit cards also add on finance charges just for maintaining a balance, for cash advances and for late fees.

Unfortunately, some people just cannot put down their plastic money, and they wind up with debt in the thousands if not tens of thousands of rupees. Although there are ways to get help in this situation, the first thing to do is change one's behaviour. There are measures that can be taken to improve things such as contacting the lending institution and asking if they have any kind of credit counselling services. They may also verify the debt and request the creditors for a lower interest rate. Most creditors are willing to charge a lower rate if it means they will eventually get their money.

To avoid getting heavily into debt one should:

- Prioritize debts; e.g. mortgage and car payments should come first.
- Budget living expenses based on earnings and ensure all minimum monthly payments are met on all debts.
- Pick the credit card with the lowest balance and begin "power payments." These are made with whatever is left over after all expenses and minimum payments are budgeted. Paying the credit card with the smallest bill, similar to what a financial institution would do, allows one to see success sooner and move on to bigger bills.

Of course, as they say, prevention is the best medicine. 'If you don't need it, don't charge it'. Credit can be a useful tool to help a person realize their dreams, but one should not give in to the temptation to over-use the card, or else there will be a credit crunch.

8.9 SET PROTOCOL ALGORITHMS FOR CREDIT CARDS

SET Protocol — Financial Information
First Virtual — Non Financial Information

SET protocol having four characteristics

- Higher secure – for this security Algo like public key Algo is used.
- Low visibility – not shown to everybody.

- Recognized standard – set is formed by master or VISA cards; it has a recognized standard.
- Non-repudiation – nobody can display; it is implemented by public key Algo.

There are two problems when dealing with credit cards, namely:

- Hackers' problems
- Merchant problems

Hacker's problems arise due to the fact that the credit card information is transferred to different places. To avoid these two problems set protocol Algo is used. By using SET protocol Algo, the merchant problem is totally solved, but the hacker's problem is not totally solved.

To use this protocol a wallet software is installed at the client's end. After entering a number into it the client gets digital certification, and is able to use his credit card for any e-commerce transaction.

Wallet software is installed at the client's end and Merchant software at the server's end.

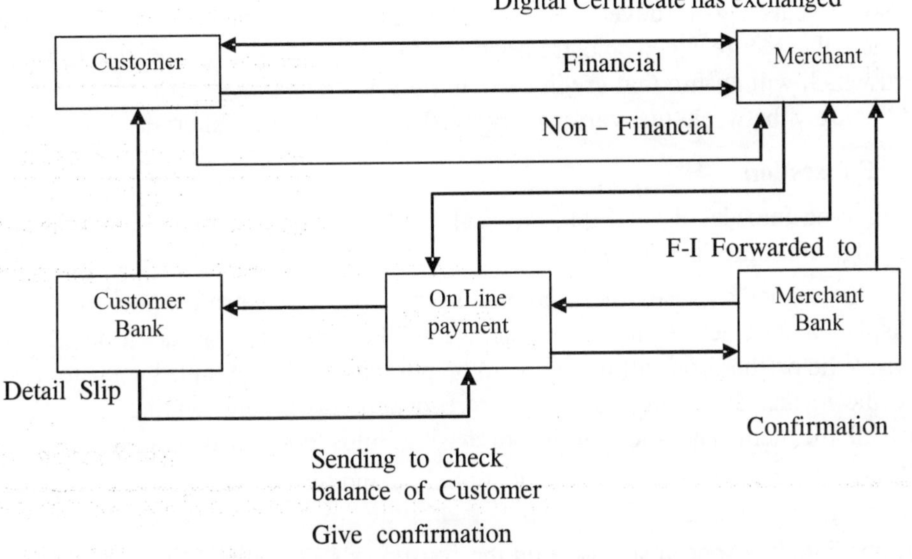

Fig. 8.8: ***Schematic for digital certification***

- Customer places a request and verifies that this is a genuine merchant and the merchant also verifies that this is a genuine customer.
- Financial information will be encrypted with the online payment server's public key and sent to the merchant. The merchant cannot read it but simply forwards it to the on line payment server, so that problem of merchant fraud is totally eliminated.
- On line payment server sends a query to the customer's bank requesting confirmation to the on line payment server.
- After receiving confirmation from the customer's bank, the online payment server sends this to merchant's bank.

- Merchant's bank sends confirmation to the on line payment server.
- Finally, the online payment server sends confirmation to the merchant.

Note – Non financial information will be encrypted using the public key of the merchant, so that the latter is able to open the message using the secret key and is able to deliver goods to the customer.

The growth of the Internet over the past few years has been explosive. It is also changing its character from merely being a purveyor of information to being a complete transaction enabler. Thus, today a surfer can purchase a variety of goods on the Internet, as opposed to merely accessing information. However, what is impeding rapid growth of this business is the consumer perception of poor security on the Net. Most payment methods revolve around the credit card, and consumers remain hesitant to reveal their card information on the Internet. Also, not surprisingly, credit card frauds on the Internet have registered a dramatic increase.

To address these growing security concerns and pave the way for uninhibited growth of electronic commerce on the Net, the two leading credit card brands, Visa and MasterCard, teamed up some years ago to develop a common standard to process card transactions on the Internet, called the secure electronic transaction (SET) standard. As the name implies, SET is a standard which will ensure that credit card and associated payment order information travels safely and securely between the various involved parties on the Internet.

A sample SET session

Before getting into details of SET, we shall take a simple example to describe how SET works from the consumer's perspective.

1. The consumer accesses the merchant's web site, goes through the various goods on display and selects what he or she wants. Perhaps there is a virtual shopping cart where he or she drops all the items to be purchased. At the end, the customer proceeds to the virtual checkout counter. A screen pops up giving details, including the cost of all the items the shopper is purchasing, plus taxes and shipping costs.
2. Then the screen asks for the payment method and the consumer chooses to pay through a credit card using SET.
3. Immediately, a special software on the consumer's PC called Digital Wallet is invoked, and it asks the customer to choose one credit card from the many he or she possesses.
4. The consumer chooses a card, and the electronic transaction using SET is underway. A few seconds later, there is a confirmation that this order has been processed.

Objectives of SET

SET addresses seven major business requirements:

1. It provides confidentiality of payment information and enables confidentiality of order information that is transmitted along with the payment information.
2. Ensures the integrity of all transmitted data.
3. Provides authentication that a cardholder is a legitimate user of a branded payment card account.

4. Provides authentication that a merchant can accept branded payment card transactions through its relationship with an acquiring financial institution.
5. Ensures the use of the best security practices and system design techniques to protect all legitimate parties in an electronic commerce transaction.
6. Creates a protocol that neither depends on transport security mechanisms nor prevents their use.
7. Facilitates and encourages interoperability among software and network providers.

Point 1 ensures that card information cannot be viewed by unauthorized parties. Point 2 ensures that the information cannot be changed or tampered with. Points 3 and 4 ensure that the cardholder and merchant are really who they claim they are. Hence, in essence, this framework, if implemented effectively, will allow both buyers and sellers to transact in total confidence over an open network.

SET principally uses cryptography to meet its objectives.

Mechanics of SET

What happens in an actual SET transaction is a bit more involved. The method has been developed keeping in mind the basic objectives of SET: confidentiality, integrity and authentication of both sender and receiver.

To ensure integrity, a one-way hashing algorithm is used on the message to generate a message digest. This algorithm uses statistical methods to compute a checksum (or message digest) from the characters in the message. If the content or position of even a single character is changed, the message digest will not match. To secure the message digest itself from tampering, the digest is encrypted using the sender's private key. The encrypted form of the message digest is called the digital signature of the sender. The receiver can decrypt the digest using the sender's public key, regenerate the digest and compare them. This also ensures that the message has really come from the sender (nobody else knows the sender's private key) and hence accomplishes the objective of authenticating the sender.

To ensure confidentiality, the entire message is encrypted. Since the message could be large, the more efficient symmetric encryption is used. A random symmetric key is generated and used to encrypt the message. To secure the symmetric key itself, it is encrypted using the public key of the receiver.

Finally, the symmetrically encrypted message and the random symmetric key encrypted using the receiver's public key are sent to the receiver. Only the receiver can decrypt the symmetric key, since only he possesses the private key of the receiver. Thus authentication of the receiver is achieved.

The receiver uses his private key to decrypt the random symmetric key. Then he uses the random symmetric key to decrypt the main message. He locates the sender's digital signature and using the public sender's key, he decrypts it and retrieves the message digest. He regenerates the message digest using the known hashing function and compares it to the retrieved digest. If they match, he is assured that the message has not been tampered with and has indeed originated from the sender.

SET implementation

Before this is applied to an actual implementation of SET, we examine how a credit card transaction is processed in the physical non-SET world.

1. The cardholder presents the card to the merchant, who in turn swipes the card on a POS terminal.
2. An electronic message containing the card number and amount is then sent to the acquiring bank, with whom the merchant is associated.
3. The acquiring bank, in turn, forwards the message to the card brand's (Visa or MasterCard) central computer.
4. The card brand forwards the message to the issuing bank, which initially issued the card to the cardholder.
5. The issuing bank checks the available credit limit on the card and sends back an authorization.
6. This authorization travels all the way back, until it reaches the merchant's POS terminal.

How the transaction will progress in an SET environment has been described earlier. Here it is described in more detail, in the light of the mechanics of SET, (in the interest of clarity, some details have been omitted/simplified).

1. The cardholder goes to a merchant's web site and selects the items he or she wants to purchase. The cardholder then clicks on the virtual checkout button or its equivalent.
2. This triggers wallet software to be invoked on the cardholder's PC. The software presents several credit cards which the cardholder possesses, and one is chosen. The wallet software also receives the digital certificates of two entities: the merchant and the acquiring bank (also called a payment gateway). These two certificates are validated by traversing the hierarchy of trust, through messages sent on the Internet to all the entities on the trust chain.
3. The wallet software then generates a message containing two parts: the order information and the payment information. The order information contains information confirming the order, whereas the payment information contains the card number and the amount. The payment information is encrypted using a random symmetric key, which, in turn, is encrypted with the payment gateway's public key, so that only the payment gateway can decrypt it. In other words, the merchant will never know the details of the card number of its customer. This data are sent automatically to the merchant's web site.
4. The merchant's computer will first validate the cardholder's digital certificate. Then it will send the payment information to the payment gateway (which is the acquiring bank's computer).
5. The payment gateway will verify the digital certificates of both the merchant and the card holder and decrypt the message to access the card number and the amount.
6. Then the payment gateway will interface with the legacy systems of the acquiring bank

to send the transaction to the card brand, which will then send it to the issuing bank for authorization.

7. This authorization response is then encrypted in the usual fashion and sent to the merchant, who, in turn, will validate the message and store the response. Then the merchant will arrange to ship the goods.

All of these transactions happen on the Internet and are quite transparent to the cardholder.

Practical requirements for SET

SET has been introduced and is working successfully in several European countries. The prerequisites for SET are:

1. The issuing bank will need to request that its cardholders acquire digital certificates. Typically, it will supply a wallet software, which will set up a digital certificate for the cardholder automatically.
2. There has to be a reasonable number of merchant web sites which support SET. For this to happen, the merchants' acquiring banks have to implement payment gateways. Payment gateway software is now available from several certified leading software vendors. Currently the number of SET-enabled web sites is small; however, this is expected to grow substantially in the near future. A list of SET-enabled sites is available from the web sites of MasterCard (www.mastercard.com) and Visa (www.visa.com).

Net Cash

Net Cash will enable new types of services on the Internet by providing a real-time electronic payment system that satisfies the diverse requirements of service providers and their users. Among the properties of the Net Cash framework are: security, anonymity, scalability, acceptability, and interoperability.

Net Cash was designed to facilitate anonymous electronic payments over an unsecured network without requiring the use of tamper-proof hardware. Net Cash provides secure transactions in an environment where attempts at illegal creation, copying, and reuse of electronic currency are likely. In order to protect the privacy of parties to a transaction, Net Cash implements financial instruments that prevent tractability and preserve the anonymity of users.

Net Cheque

At present the implementation is a research prototype and is available for licensing by companies implementing commercial payment service. It is not presently supported as a consumer product or service. Small companies and individuals looking for a way to accept payment on the web may find the tutorial material on this site useful, but until the Net Cheque system is offered as a commercial service, it is not an option available for their use.

Users registered with Net Cheque accounting servers are able to write electronic checks to other users. These checks may be sent through e-mail or as payment for services provided through other network protocols. When deposited, the check authorizes the transfer of account balances from the account against which the check was drawn to the account to which the check was deposited.

The strengths of the Net Cheque system are its security, reliability, scalability, and efficiency. Signatures on checks are authenticated using Kerberos. Reliability and scalability are provided by using multiple accounting servers. The Net Cheque system is well suited for clearing micro payments; its use of conventional cryptography makes it more efficient than systems based on public key cryptography. The Net Cheque system will enable creation of new Internet services that charge small fees, on the order of pennies, for access to information, processing queries, and consumption of resources. Such services are a critical component of electronic commerce.

When used in combination with Net Cheque, service providers and their users are able to select payment mechanisms based on the level of anonymity desired, ranging from non-anonymous and weakly anonymous instruments that are scalable, to unconditionally anonymous instruments that require more resources of the currency server.

Net Cash provides scalable electronic currency that is accepted across multiple administrative domains. Currency issued by a currency server is backed by account balances registered with Net Cheque to the currency server itself. Net Cash currency servers also use the Net Cheque system to clear payments across servers, and to convert electronic currency into debits and credits against customer and merchant accounts. Though payments using Net Cheque originate from named accounts, with Net Cash the account balances are registered in the name of the currency server, and not the end user.

Since the introduction of the Net Cash research prototype, there have been several other payment systems that have used the Net Cash name. Over time, various systems have operated at netcash.com. No other systems are affiliated with the Net Cash research prototype.

SUMMARY

- Electronic payment systems are becoming central to on line business process innovation as companies look for ways to serve customers faster and at lower cost. Electronic payment systems and e-commerce are intricately linked given that on line customers must pay for products and services.
- Cash consists of a token, which may be authenticated independently of the issuer. This is commonly achieved through use of self-authenticating tokens or tamper proof hardware.
- Card payment schemes provide payment mechanisms through the existing credit card payment infrastructure. Such schemes have many structural similarities to cheque models except that solutions are constrained by that structure. A key feature of card payment systems is that every transaction carries insurance.
- Electronic tokens are designed as electronic analogs of various forms of payment backed by a bank or financial institution. Simply stated, electronic tokens are equivalent to cash that is backed by a bank.

- Electronic cash is a new concept in on-line payment systems because it combines computerized convenience with security and privacy that improve on paper cash. E-cash focuses on replacing cash as the principal payment vehicle in consumer oriented electronic payment systems.
- Smart cards have been in existence since the early 1980s and hold promise for secure transactions using existing infrastructure. Smart cards are credit and debit cards and other cards product enhanced with microprocessors capable of holding more information than the traditional magnetic stripe.
- Electronic checks are another form of electronic tokens. They are designed to accommodate the many individuals and entities that might prefer to pay on credit or through some mechanism other than cash.
- The benefits of smart cards will rely on the ubiquity of devices called smart card readers that can communicate with the chip on the smart card. In addition to reading from and writing to smart cards, these devices can also support a variety of key management methods.
- In third party processing, consumers register with a third party on the Internet to verify electronic micro-transactions. Verification mechanism can be designed with many of the attributes of electronic tokens, including anonymity.
- Net Cash will enable new types of services on the Internet by providing a real-time electronic payment system that satisfies the diverse requirements of service providers and their users. Among the properties of the Net Cash framework are: security, anonymity, scalability, acceptability, and interoperability.
- Net Cash provides scalable electronic currency that is accepted across multiple administrative domains. Currency issued by a currency server is backed by account balances registered with Net Cheque to the currency server itself.

REVIEW QUESTIONS

1. Which of the following is not a common use of smart cards?
   (a) Loyalty programs (b) PC replacement
   (c) Transportation identification (d) Financial cards
2. Which of the following is not an example of an e-payment?
   (a) Smart cards (b) Cash
   (c) Digital checks (d) Electronic billing
3. Which of the following is not one of the parties usually associated with electronic payments?
   (a) Issuer (b) Customer/payer/buyer
   (c) Enforcer (d) Regulator
4. Business A provides a system of credits that allow other businesses to make online purchases. What role is Business A performing?
   (a) Issuer (b) Customer/payer/buyer
   (c) Merchant/payee/seller (d) Regulator

5. An ACS System:
   (a) Is used to authenticate contact-less cards.
   (b) Is a subset of a firewall.
   (c) Verifies addresses against purchasers.
   (d) Issues p-cards.
6. A CVN:
   (a) Is used to authenticate contact-less cards.
   (b) Is a subset of a firewall.
   (c) Verifies addresses against purchasers.
   (d) Compares the verification number on a card to issuer records.
7. Which of the following is not one of the major types of payment cards?
   (a) Credit cards (b) Charge cards
   (c) Flip cards (d) Debit cards
8. EIPP is used for:
   (a) B2C micropayments
   (b) Smart card payments
   (c) Presenting and paying B2B invoices online
   (d) Uploading catalogue data
9. 'A' has an e-card that she uses to purchase office supplies for the company she works for. What type of smart card is she using?
   (a) Credit card (b) Purchase card
   (c) Smart card (d) Contact card
10. 'B' has an e-card that he uses to access different parts of his company's R&D offices. What type of smart card is he using?
    (a) Credit card (b) Purchase card
    (c) Smart card (d) Contact card
11. Which of the following is not a limitation of e-cash?
    (a) Lack of potential uses (b) Software installation
    (c) Adopting merchants (d) Adopting individuals
12. Which of the following is not characteristic of an e-check?
    (a) Same information as a standard check
    (b) Can be used where paper checks are used
    (c) Work under a new, enhanced legal framework
    (d) Work in essentially the same way paper checks work
13. Virtual credit cards are used to:
    (a) Use in place of actual CC numbers online for security
    (b) Make retail purchases when a credit card does not exist
    (c) Replace existing cards
    (d) Defraud online sellers.

CHAPTER 9

Electronic Data Interchange

9.1 EDI: ELECTRONIC DATA INTERCHANGE

EDI is the transfer of data between different companies using networks, such as VANs or the Internet. It is defined as the inter-process communication (computer application to computer application) of business information in standardized electronic forms. As more and more companies get connected to the Internet, EDI is becoming increasingly important as an easy mechanism for companies to buy, sell, and trade information. ANSI has approved a set of EDI standards known as the X12 standards.

Electronic data interchange (EDI) is the computer-to-computer exchange of structured information, by agreed message standards, from one computer application to another by electronic means and with a minimum of human intervention. In common usage, EDI is understood to mean specific interchange methods agreed upon by national or international standards bodies for the transfer of business transaction data, with one typical application being the automated purchase of goods and services.

Despite being relatively unheralded, in this era of technologies such as XMLservices, the Internet and the World Wide Web, EDI is still the data format used by the vast majority of electronic commerce transactions in the world.

Standards

The EDI standards were designed from the beginning to be independent of lower level technologies and can be transmitted using Internet protocols as well as private networks. It is important to differentiate between the EDI documents and the methods for transmitting them. While comparing the bisynchronous 2400 bit/s modems and value-added network to the Internet some people predicted erroneously that EDI would be replaced. These older transmission methods are being replaced by internet protocols such as FTP, telnet and email, although standards for these media are still emerging.

EDI documents contain the same data that would normally be found in a paper document used for the same organizational function. For example an EDI 940 ship-from-warehouse order is used by a manufacturer to tell a warehouse to ship a product to a retailer. It typically has a ship to address, bill to address, a list of product numbers and quantities. It may have other information if the parties agree to include it. However, EDI is not confined to just business data related to trade but encompasses all fields such as medicine (patient records, laboratory results, etc.), transport (container and modal information, etc.), engineering and construction, etc.

There are two major sets of EDI standards. UN/EDIFACT is the only international standard (in fact, a United Nations recommendation) and is predominant in all areas outside of North America. ANSI ASC X12 (X12) is popular in North America and is used worldwide.

These standards prescribe the formats, character sets, and data elements used in the exchange of documents and forms, such as purchase orders and invoices.

The standard says which pieces of information are mandatory for a particular document, which pieces are optional and give the rules for the structure of the document. The standards are like building codes. Just as two kitchens can be built "to code" but look completely different, two EDI documents can follow the same standard and contain different sets of information. For example a food company may indicate an expiration date for a particular product while a clothing manufacturer would choose to send colour and size information.

Organizations that send or receive documents from each other are referred to as "trading partners" in EDI terminology. The trading partners agree on the specific information to be transmitted and how it should be used. This is done in human readable specifications (also called specs or spec sheets). While the standards are analogous to building codes, the specifications are analogous to blue prints. (The specification may also be called a mapping but the term mapping is typically reserved for specific machine readable instructions given to the translation software.) Larger companies have existing specification sheets and are usually unwilling to negotiate. Often in a large company these sheets will be written to be used by different branches or divisions and therefore will contain information not needed for a particular exchange.

Service providers provide global platforms to connect and integrate "business partners" around the world. They provide integration platforms that make the exchange of EDI (or XML) documents transparent and easy between diverse constituents. These providers will track and reconcile documents to reduce errors and improve supply chain performance.

Interpreting data

Often real world descriptions of how the data should be interpreted are missing from the specifications. This is particularly important when specifying quantities. For example, suppose candy is packaged in a large box that contains 5 display boxes and each display box contains 24 boxes of candy packaged for the consumer. If an EDI document says to ship 10 boxes of candy it may not be clear whether to ship 10 consumer packaged boxes, 240 consumer packaged boxes or 1200 consumer packaged boxes. It is not enough for two parties to agree to use a particular qualifier indicating case, pack, box or each; they must also agree on what that particular qualifier means.

EDI translation software provides the interface between the internal system and the common standards. For an "inbound" document it typically takes the variable length fields of the EDI document, translates the individual pieces of data and then creates a file of fixed length fields. For an "outbound" document the translation software queries the internal system, as in the case of an SQL database, or it translates a fixed width file exported by the internal software. Translation software may also utilize other methods or file formats. The mechanism of translation is not part of the standard.

(In EDI terminology "inbound" and "outbound" refer to the direction of transmission of an EDI document in relation to a particular system, not the direction of merchandise, money or other things represented by the document. For example, an EDI document that tells a warehouse to perform an outbound shipment is an inbound document in relation to the warehouse computer system. It is an outbound document in relation to the manufacturer or dealer that transmitted the document.)

9.1.1 Overview of EDI Benefits and Drawbacks

The EDI process has many benefits. Computer-to-computer exchange of information is much less expensive than handling paper documents. Studies have shown that manually processing a paper-based order can cost over Rs. 3,000 while processing an EDI order costs less than Rs. 50. Much less labour time is required and fewer errors occur because computer systems process the documents rather than processing by hand.

EDI transactions between companies flow faster and more reliably than paper documents. Faster transactions support reduction in inventory levels, better use of warehouse space, fewer out-of-stock occurrences and lower freight costs through fewer emergency expedites.

Paper purchase orders can take up to 10 days from the time the buyer prepares the order to when the supplier ships it. EDI orders can take as little as one day.

However, there are a few drawbacks, e.g. companies choosing to implement both paper and EDI processes must manage both of these processes. As stated before, using EDI is much more efficient than using paper, lending strength to the argument against paper documents. Also, companies must ensure that they have the resources in place to make an EDI program work; however, the need for these resources (or their hiring) may be offset by the increased efficiency that EDI provides.

9.1.2 Example of EDI

In this section we give an example of how the electronic data interchange process works. A buyer prepares an order in his purchasing system and has it approved. Next, the EDI order is translated into an EDI document format called an 850 purchase order.

The EDI 850 purchase order is then securely transmitted to the supplier either via the internet or through a value added network (VAN). The buyer's VAN is a like an electronic post office that interconnects with the supplier's VAN. The VANs make sure that EDI transactions are sent and received. The supplier's VAN ensures that the supplier receives the order. The supplier's computer system then processes the order. Only internet access and email are needed.

Data security and control are maintained throughout the transmission process using passwords, user identification and encryption. Both the buyer's and the supplier's EDI applications edit and check the documents for accuracy.

9.1.3 Requirements of EDI

Each trading partner has unique EDI requirements. These will include the specific kinds of EDI documents to be processed, such as the 850 purchase order used in the example above, 856 advance ship notices and 810 invoices. The fact is that almost any business document that one company would exchange with another company can be sent via EDI. However each EDI document must be exchanged with the partner in exactly the format they specify.

Many partners will have an EDI implementation guide or kit that explains their specific requirements. Maps are required to translate the EDI documents from the trading partner's format into the format that is useable by the receiving party.

EDI capability involves either buying or outsourcing the following components:

- Software for communications
- VAN service for EDI transmission
- Mail boxing of EDI transactions
- Mapping
- Translation

VAN, ASYNC, BISYNC, FTP and AS/2 Internet communications will be required by various partners. A server or PC, communication devices and peripherals will be needed as well as secured office space, monitored security, backups and redundant power. Additional software will be needed if integration of the EDI transactions with back office systems is desired. A VAN will need to be contracted for transmissions. Personnel must be trained in how to use the software and communication devices. Maps will then need to be developed.

9.1.4 Advantages vs. Disadvantages of using EDI

Advantages

There are several advantages of using EDI all of which provide distinct benefits to the user. One of the most notable benefits to using EDI is the time-saving capability it provides. By eliminating the process of distributing hard copies of information throughout the company, easy access to electronic data simplifies inter-department communication. Also, another time-savings advantage is the ability to track the origin of all information, thereby significantly reducing time spent on corresponding with the source of the information.

Another benefit for the user of this information system is the ultimate savings in costs for the company. Although the initial set-up costs may seem high, the overall savings in the long run ensures its value. For any business, regardless of its size, hard-copy print outs and document shipping costs add up. EDI allows for a paper-less exchange of information reducing handling costs and worker productivity that is involved with the organization of paper documents.

Electronic data interchange has another strong advantage over paper-based information exchange which has to do with accuracy of information. When the information is already stored electronically, it speeds up an organization's ability to check for accuracy and make any necessary corrections as data are already input in the system. Also, unlike paper-based methods, EDI allows for the ability to send and receive information at any time thereby tremendously improving an organization's ability to communicate quickly and efficiently.

Disadvantages

There are a few barriers to using electronic data interchange. One of the most significant barriers is the accompanying process change. Existing processes built around slow paper handling may not be suited for EDI. For example, a business may receive the bulk of their goods by 1 or 2 day shipping and all of their invoices by mail. The existing process may therefore assume that goods are typically received before the invoice. With EDI, the invoice will typically be sent when the goods ship and will therefore require a process that handles large numbers of invoices whose corresponding goods have not yet been received.

Another significant barrier is the initial set-up. The preliminary expenses and time that arise from the implementation, customization and training can be costly and therefore may discourage some users.

The primary benefit of EDI to business is a considerable reduction is transaction costs by improving the speed and efficiency of filling orders, however it is not widely used.

Electronic commerce is often equated with EDI, so it is important to clarify that electronic commerce embraces EDI and much more. EDI is one well known example of structured document inter change, which enables data in the form of document content to be exchanged between software applications that are working together to process a business transaction.

9.2 EDI LAYERED ARCHITECTURE

EDI architecture specifies four layers, the semantic layer (application layer), the standard translation layer, the packing (or transport) layer and the physical network infrastructure layer.

EDI Semantic layer	Application level services	
EDI Standard layer	EDI business from standard	
	ANSI x 12 business from standard	
EDI Transport layer	Electronic mail	X.435, NIME
	Point to point	FTP, TELNET
	World Wide Web	HTTP
Physical layer	Dial up lines, Internet, I-way	

Fig. 9.1: ***Layered architecture of EDI***

9.2.1 Semantic Layer

The EDI semantic layer describes the business application that is driving EDI. This layer is specific to a company and the software it uses. In other words, the user interface and content visible on the screen are tailored or customized to local environments.

When a company receives the document, their EDI translation software automatically changes the standard format into the proprietary format of their document processing software so that the company can manipulate the information in whatever way it chooses to.

9.2.2 EDI Standard Layer

EDI standards specify business form structure and to some extent influence the content seen at the application layer. For instance, a purchase order name field in an X12 standard might be specified to hold a maximum of 50 characters. An application using 75 character field lengths will produce name truncation during the translation from the application layer to standard layer.

In short, the EDI standards and application levels, although separate are closely intertwined.

9.2.3 Transport Layer

The EDI transport layer corresponds closely with the non-electronic activity of sending a business form from company A to company B. The business form could be sent via regular postal service, registered mail, certified mail or private carrier such as united parcel service (UPS) or simply faxed between the companies. In other words, the content and structure of the form are separated from the transport carrier. EDI documents are exchanged rapidly over electronic networks using the existing email programs and infrastructure. EDI document transport is far more complex than simply sending email messages or sharing files through a network. These EDI documents are more structured than email.

9.3 EDI Vs E-MAIL

- EDI is a structured document whereas e-mail is an unstructured document, there is no fixed structure in e-mail.

- In EDI, the interchange is composed by one software for interpretation by another software. If a reply is involved it is composed by a software to be interpreted by another software i.e. EDI is a software to software interface.
- In e-mail, the message is composed by a human and or interpreted by a human and/or a reply is composed by a human and interpreted by a human. i.e. software cannot understand an e-mail document.
- In EDI, there is typically no human involvement in the processing of the information. Whereas in e-mail human involvement is necessary. A human-to-software interface is involved at least at one end of the interchange.

Note: EDI - structured document, software to software interface. E-mail - unstructured document, human to software interface.

9.4 EDI IN ACTION

The idea behind EDI is very simple. EDI seeks to take what has been a manually prepared form or a form from a business application, translate the data into a standard electronic format and transmit them. At the receiving end, the standard format is "un-translated" into a format that can be read by the recipient applications. Hence output from one application becomes input to another through computer to computer exchange of information.

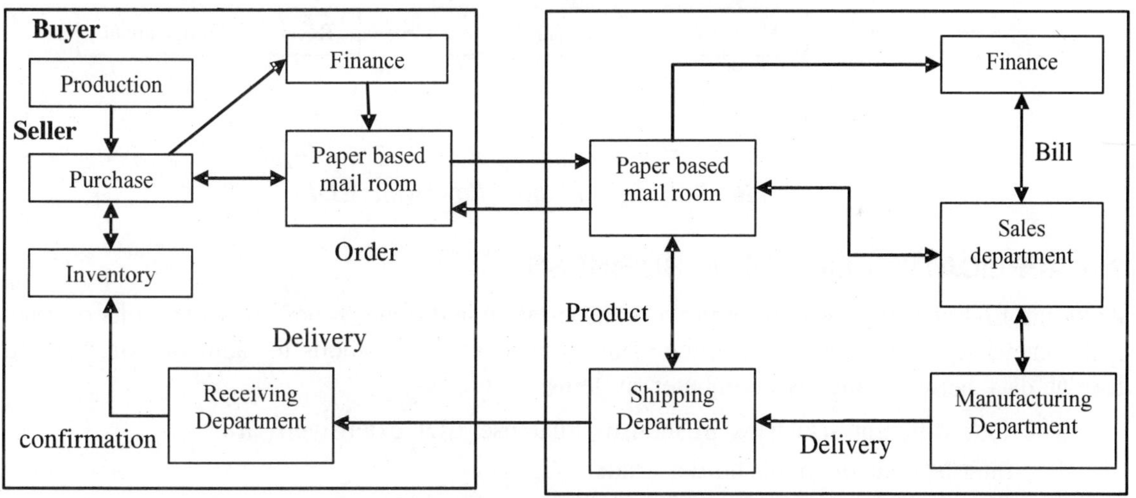

Fig. 9.2: ***Information flow without EDI***

When the buyer sends a purchase order to a seller, the relevant data must be extracted from the internal database and recorded on a hard copy. This hard copy is then forwarded to the seller after passing through several intermediate steps. Sellers receive information in the form of letters and in some cases a vast number of facsimiles. This information is manually entered into the internal information systems of the recipient by data entry operators. This process generates a considerable amount of overhead in labour costs and time delays, such as:

- Overheads in labour costs
- Time delays
- Increased risk of errors

9.5 BENEFITS OF EDI

- Paperless exchange
- Improved problem resolution and services
- Less time in comparison of manuals
- Reduce costs
- Decreased risk of errors
  - Transmission error: 1299 - 1929
  - Transcription error: 1299 - 12992
  - Expanded customer base/supplier

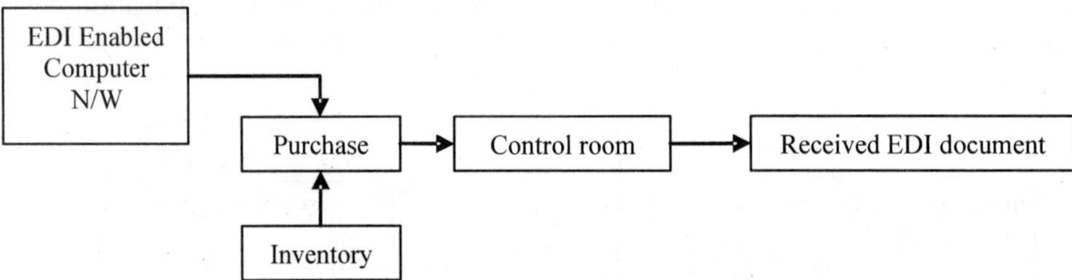

Fig. 9.3: ***Information flow with EDI***

9.6 APPLICATION OF EDI IN BUSINESS

Although EDI was developed to improve transportation and trade, it has grown from its original and somewhat limited use as expediter of the transfer of trade goods to facilitator of standard format data between any two-computer systems.

The four different scenarios in industry that use EDI extensively are:

1. International or cross border trade
2. Electronic funds transfer (EFT)
3. Health care EDI for insurance claim processing
4. Manufacturing and retail procurement

Companies have applied a number of EDI-based solutions to improve business processes for both strategic and competitive advantages. EDI has shaped a company's marketing and distribution efforts by helping to create new distribution channels, introduce new market research methods and introduce better customer services.

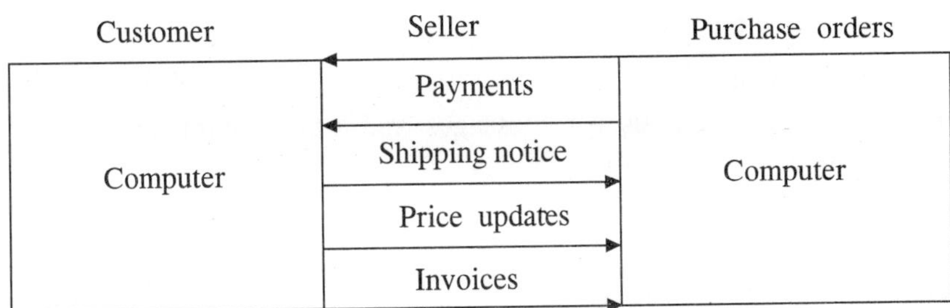

Fig. 9.4: ***Electronic data interchange***

Companies can use EDI to automate electronic commerce applications. Purchase orders and payments can be transmitted directly from the customer's computers to the seller's computer. The seller can transmit shipping notices, price changes and invoices electronically back to the customer.

9.7 EDI AND VALUE ADDED NETWORK (VAN)

In EDI, information is organized according to a specified format set by both parties, allowing a "hands-off" computer transaction that requires no human intervention or re-keying on either end. All information contained in an EDI transaction set is, for the most part, the same as on a conventionally printed document. Organizations have adopted EDI for the same reasons they have embraced much of today's modern technology-enhanced efficiency and increased profits. Benefits of EDI include: reduced cycle time, better inventory management, increased productivity, reduced costs, improved accuracy, improved business relationships, enhanced customer service, increased sales, minimized paper use and storage and increased cash flow.

Industries currently using EDI include retail, insurance, education, entertainment and banking. However, this list is far from complete, as more and more businesses are turning to EDI.

A value-added network (VAN) is a private network provider (sometimes called a turnkey communications line) that is hired by a company to facilitate electronic data interchange (EDI) or provide other network services. Before the arrival of the World Wide Web, some companies hired value-added networks to move data from their company to other companies. With the arrival of the World Wide Web, many companies found it more cost-efficient to move their data over the Internet instead of paying the minimum monthly fees and per-character charges found in typical VAN contracts. In response, contemporary value-added network providers now focus on offering EDI translation, encryption, secure e-mail, management reporting, and other extra services for their customers.

Value added networks are an essential part of business to business (B2B) e-commerce as they provide a common EDI platform connecting various participating organizations of trade partners and take care of various technical network management and communication issues involved in EDI so that the trading partners can concentrate on their core business rather than worrying about conforming to the EDI standards.

VANs in EDI play a vital role in:

- EDI program management
- Alternative delivery methods for messages and EDI documents
- EDI consulting
- EDI software management

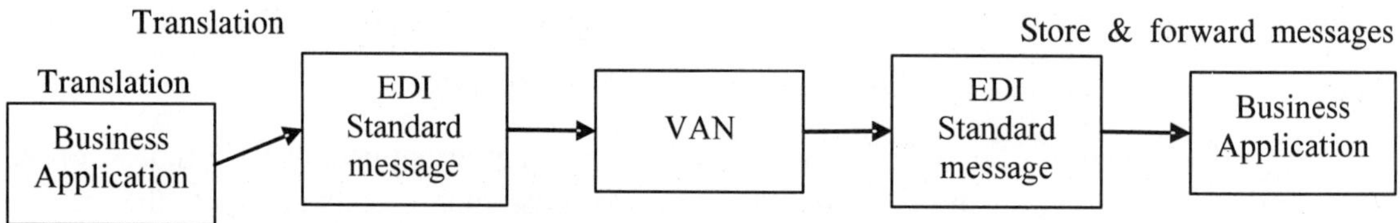

Fig. 9.5: *VAN in EDI*

VANs are mostly provided by third party service providers like ISPs. the advantages of VANs to EDI are:

- Flexibility and scalability
- Adherence to local rules and regulations governing communication and transactions
- Infra-structure allocation, development and sharing

There are three basic components of VANs.

Technical - Message formatting/Communication protocols
Mail - Maintaining e-mail boxes and buffering to support EDI transactions
Links - Between various VAN networks

VANs in EDI business offer additional peripheral services other than just direct connections, for example:

- Direct communication links between trading partners
- Maintenance of the EDI standards and technologies by the VAN service provider
- VAN support to multiple data format standards
- Store and forward systems
- Varied protocol/Access support

Round the clock availability

- VANs dial up services to connect to companies which do not participate in VAN

9.8 FINANCIAL EDI

Financial EDI (FEDI) is the computer-to-computer exchange of payments and payment-related information between companies using a standard format. Financial EDI works much like non-financial EDI - which involves the electronic exchange of business data such as price quotes, purchase orders, and shipping information - but is also significantly different in that, to move a payment, a bank must be involved. Because of this difference, the buyer and seller must work closely with their respective banks to effect a financial EDI transaction. The sequence of events is as follows:

1. The buyer, or originator, electronically extracts payment information from the company's accounts payable system.
2. The buyer formats the data into an EDI ANSI standard, the ANSI 820 transaction set, or the ANSI 835 transaction set for health care. (This is usually done by sending the file through an EDI translation software package.)
3. The buyer then transmits an ANSI 820 format to its bank for processing.
4. The bank then takes the 820 data and puts it into a format so that it can be sent through the Automated Clearinghouse network as an ACH transaction.
5. The ACH network then delivers the payment data to the seller's, or receiver's, bank.
6. The receiving bank credits the seller's account with the proceeds and delivers the remittance information to the seller for automatic accounts receivable posting. The remittance data can be delivered electronically in a variety of formats: ANSI 820, 835 or 823 format (true EDI formats) or BAI format. (Information can also be sent in other ways that cannot generally result in automatic cash application for the seller: through a bank's on-line balance reporting system, or in a paper report via fax or mail.)

9.8.1 The Benefits of Financial EDI

To be successful in any business practice usually means that all the participants affected by the process share in the benefits. In financial EDI, there are ample advantages for both the buyer and the seller.

The buyer enjoys a number of benefits, such as increased productivity, the ability to use a less expensive payment method (electronic vs. paper check) that does not require reconciliation, a reduction in the risk of fraud, and the ability to invoice electronically. The seller benefits because it can reduce the average age of its receivables, lower processing costs by automatic A/R posting, improve quality by minimizing errors, and generate predictable cash flows. The result of these benefits is that both buyer and seller become more valued trading partners to each other.

9.8.2 Expanding the Use of Financial EDI

Financial EDI has been actively used by corporations for the last five or six years and has increasingly become the payment method of choice as more and more trading partners have seen the benefits provided to their competitors and have consequently adopted an EDI platform for their own company.

As corporations reengineer their current business practices, many are looking to outsource their payments processing, which results in a single file of all payment instructions being sent to the bank in an EDI format. The bank will then execute all payment orders, including ACH and wire transfers, and will also print and mail the payable checks. In this way, a company can deal electronically with all of its payments even though some are being converted to paper checks by the bank for those trading partners who still want the paper.

On the collection side, companies are also streamlining the receivables process by having remittance information collected by their bank - whether through the ACH, lockbox, or wire transfer payments - and then sent electronically to the companies' accounts receivable system for automatic cash application. Here again, the company is deriving the benefit of streamlined, automated posting for all of its collections, even though some or perhaps most of its payments received are paper based.

9.8.3 Another Kind of Receivables Application

Several financial institutions are going one step beyond this and are beginning to provide true matching of accounts receivable. Suppose a company has outsourced a good portion of its A/R processing to its bank, then the process works in the following manner:

- The company electronically sends its receivables file to the bank on either a daily or weekly basis.
- The bank stores these data in a data base.
- As lockbox receipts or ACH collections are received, the database is queried to determine if there is a match between an open receivable item and a remittance.
- If there is a match, then the database is appended with the remittance information and a file of the matched items is created.
- Unmatched items are separately batched.
- Optionally, a bank might display the unmatched remittance information on its balance reporting systems.
- Also optionally, the company can then view these data and, based on the information it has, now match the previously unmatched items.
- Matched items and the remaining unmatched items are electronically sent to the customer in any desired format, EDI or proprietary.
- The customer automatically updates its accounts receivable system.

9.8.4 Financial EDI for Consumer Payments

Although financial EDI has been confined to business-to-business transactions, it can also be successfully deployed in the handling of consumer payments and associated remittance data. As an example, consumer payments initiated through a bill payment service or a home banking system can be directed through Visa's ePay network by having this data handled by a bank's Financial EDI system. The bank can reformat the remittance data and deliver it electronically to the billing party (for example, a utility company) for automated posting. This new way of using financial EDI benefits parties who send large bills by eliminating the expense and operating inefficiency of receiving a check and a list and having the billet manually key in the remittance data for cash application.

Financial EDI comprises the electronic transmission of payments and remittance information between a payer, payee and their respective banks. Financial EDI allows businesses to replace the labour-intensive activities associated with issuing, mailing and collecting cheques through the banking system with automated initiation, transmission and processing of payment systems. Thus it eliminates the delays inherent in processing cheques.

9.8.5 Types of Financial EDI

Business to business payment is accomplished using cheques, EFT and automated clearing houses (ACH) for domestic and international funds transfer.

1. **Bank cheques**

   Cheques are instruments for debit transfers, where payees collect funds from payers. Businesses use cheques to make payments for two reasons:

   - They are a familiar and readily accepted form of payment despite some uncertainty about receiving final payments.
   - Businesses benefit from the float created by the delays in the cheque collection processes.

Businesses find float valuable because they continue to use or invest funds for several days after they have issued a cheque. Float is created when there is a delay between the initiation of a payment and the availability of the funds to the recipient.

2. **Electronic funds transfer**

   - Electronic funds transfers are credit transfers between banks where funds flow directly from the payer's bank to the payee's bank.
   - EFT is one of the earliest examples of payment systems that use on-line transactions although these transactions are carried out on private networks.

3. **Automated clearing house**

   Two types of ACH transfers are used:

   - Credit transfers
   - Debit transfers

Credit transfers are similar to transfer of large funds in that funds flow directly from the payer's bank to the payee's bank, whereas ACH debit transfers are used when the payee's bank initiates the transfer and receives funds immediately from payers.

An ACH provides the following services:

- Preauthorized debits – such as repetitive bill payments and consumer initiated payments.
- Preauthorized credits – such as the direct deposit of payrolls.

To provide these and other services, banks have not only set up their own systems but have also shared ACH systems with other banks.

Note :

CHIPS => Clearing house inter-bank payments systems.
SWIFT=> Society for world wide inter-bank financial telecommunications.

9.9 CUSTOMER RELATIONSHIP MANAGEMENT (CRM)

9.9.1 What is CRM?

CRM stands for customer relationship management. It is a process or methodology used to learn more about customers' needs and behaviour in order to develop stronger relationships with them. There are many technological components to CRM, but thinking about CRM in primarily technological terms is a mistake. A more useful way to think about CRM is as a process that will help bring together lots of pieces of information about customers, sales, marketing effectiveness, responsiveness and market trends. CRM helps businesses use technology and human resources to gain an insight into the behaviour of customers and the value of those customers.

CRM is a combination of business processes and IT, with which an organization can attain a competitive edge. Customer relationship management, is a concept that evolved from sales automation, sales automation evolved into customer assets management and then into CRM. CRM implies an organizational focus on the customer, with an emphasis on building a long term relationship. The new economy mandate for business success is clear; companies must exceed their customers' expectations at all times.

Most of the companies believe that the way to achieve this goal is to put their basic business activities like marketing, sales and financial transactions on the Web and let the customers serve themselves. The idea behind customer relationship management is for the whole enterprise to have a single view of the customer for the purpose of cultivating a high quality relationship that leads to improved profits. This means that being able to identify all the products, services and intermediary relationships that a customer has with the organization, as well as knowing all the interactions that have taken place between the customer and the company since the start of the relationship. The distinguishing feature of modern CRM is the emphasis on a complete view of the customer.

9.9.2 CRM Software

Sales force automation

- **Contact management:** Contact management software stores, tracks and manages contacts, leads of an enterprise.
- **Lead management:** Enterprise lead management software enables an organization to manage, track and forecast sales leads. It also helps the organization to understand and improve conversion rates.

e-CRM or Web based CRM

- **Self service CRM:** Self service CRM (eCRM) software enables Web based customer interaction, automation of e-mail, call logs, web site analytics, campaign management.

- **Survey management software:** Survey software automates an enterprise's electronic surveys, polls, questionnaires and enables the firm to understand customer preferences.

Customer service

- Call centre software
- Help desk software

Partner relationship management

- **Contract management software:** Contract management software enables an enterprise to create, track and manage partnerships, contracts, agreements.
- **Distribution management software**

9.9.3 Advantages of CRM

Using CRM, a business can:

- Provide better customer service
- Increase customer revenues
- Discover new customers
- Cross sell/Up sell products more effectively
- Help sales staff close deals faster
- Make call centres more efficient
- Simplify marketing and sales processes

The types of data CRM projects collect are as follows:

- Responses to campaigns
- Shipping and fulfilment dates
- Sales and purchase data
- Account information
- Web registration data
- Service and support records
- Demographic data
- Web sales data

9.9.4 CRM and e-CRM

CRM is the philosophy of interaction with the customer and e-CRM is electronic CRM, which is conceptually the same as CRM, the only difference being that it is a new term where integration of the customer takes place with the help of an electronic media.

This 'e' in e-CRM enables an organization to extend its infrastructure to customers and partners in ways that offer new opportunity to learn about customer needs, add value, gain new economies, and reach new customers.

E-commerce provides businesses with a growing dynamic channel for efficient delivery of goods and services to consumers through the supply chain. E-commerce helps an organization in serving their customers better in the following ways:

1. Increased speed and accuracy of sharing information between the organization and their customers.
2. Improved relationships with customers.
3. Better management of customer relationship using e-mail, on line frequently asked questions (FAQ), lists, and automated problem resolution systems.
4. Faster response to customer orders, requests and problems, which ultimately helps to increase customer satisfaction.

9.9.5 Goals of CRM

1. To use existing relationship to increase revenue.
2. To use integrated information for the service excellence.
3. To introduce more repeatable sales processes and procedures.
4. To create new values and improve loyalty.
5. To implement a more proactive strategy.

9.9.6 Core Process (Components) of CRM

1. Cross selling and up-selling:
   Cross selling - Similar products are recommended
   Up selling - Purchasing better quality products
2. Direct marketing and fulfilment: - Direct marketing identifies the needs of customers and satisfies these needs.
3. Customer services and supports - Call centres.
4. Field services - Depending on the nature of the customers' requests field services are given. If it is not possible for a call centre to solve the problem then field services come in.
5. Retention marketing - Retention marketing is knowing the customer fully because some require quality and some require quantity.

9.9.7 The Four Principles of E-CRM

1. E-business offers its customers multiple channels for communication.
2. E-business delivers real value to the customer with every interaction.
3. Knowledge regarding e-business is captured and given context during the customer interaction.
4. E-business systems are integrated throughout the value chain, not just at the level of the financial transaction.

9.9.8 Example of CRM Product – CRI or Functions of CRM

CRM implies customer relationship intelligence.

1. Identification and collection of inputs
2. Input standardization
3. Analysis
4. Generation of reports

9.9.9 Legal Issues in E-commerce

The world of e-commerce has exposed various issues which till date were unknown. Trading partners exchange documents electronically. They need to convince themselves that such documents are authentic when received over networks and that they can be authenticated in case of a dispute.

There must be a way to prove that a message existed, that it was sent and received and was not changed between the sending and receiving, i.e. it could not be read and interpreted by any third party. The security of an electronic message, a legal requirement is thus directly linked to the technical methods for security of computers and networks.

In addition to all the general legal issues that affect every business, there are a number of areas that are of particular importance in online trading. Internet related legal actions are growing exponentially and new legislation is coming on stream all over the world to further protect customers' interests.

The areas of law include:

- EDI
- Marketing
- Confidentiality
- Electronic contracts
- Copyright and intellectual property
- Directives

9.9.10 Tax Issues in E-commerce

Issues surrounding sales tax are particularly problematic for lawmakers. For example if an Indian company is using a web server located in the USA, and an Internet service provider is at Delhi, then which country, if any is entitled to taxes on goods and services sold? So far this issue remains unanswered.

In virtually all countries, the tax policy on web commerce is best described as 'tax neutral' with few attempts being made to collect new duties on e-business. However, the very nature of the Web is making it difficult for governments to collect tax revenue. Encryption and digital cash make transactions more difficult to tax, even within a single jurisdiction.

As e-commerce represents an increasing proportion of all taxable transactions, one thing is becoming clear, governments will have to find a way to collect the appropriate level of tax revenue from e-commerce.

Short Notes

1. **EDI: Electronic data interchange:** Electronic data interchange covers the legal aspects of the automatic exchange and processing of information between computers, for example, where payments are made using online internet banking systems.
2. **Marketing:** Internet marketing is also governed by legislations to protect consumer rights and trade related mail practices. For example, the practice of inserting neta tags in hidden text in the first pages of a competitor's website, a technique for diverting traffic from a rival is site.
3. **Confidentiality:** Non-disclosure agreements and confidentially agreements are also required to ensure confidentially of discussions regarding commercially sensitive information with internet partners, affiliates, advisors and suppliers of software and hardware.
4. **Electronic contracts:** Electronic contracts, just like paper based contractual agreements, must contain the elements of an offer, an acceptance and a consideration, along with mention of the governing laws, digital signature schemes to be used and written evidence procedures.
5. **Copyright and intellectual property:** Copyright applies to everything published on the internet as it does elsewhere. Intellectual property rights apply to internet business models, website designs, site navigation tools, ordering systems and domain names, so one cannot just copy an interesting website and add it to his/her products and services.
6. **Directives:** Directives relevant to online trading are for example:
   - Data protection deals with the holding of personal data on living individuals.
   - Distance selling provides protection for consumers of direct internet selling.

   The World Trade Organization (WTO) has come up with an exhaustive set of regulations to govern electronic transactions uniformly across the globe.
7. **Improving market access for e-commerce services:**
   - Refining the classification system
   - Finalizing the methods to be used in negotiations
   - Drafting preliminary positions
8. **Regulating the provision of e-commerce services:**
   - Domestic regulation of services
   - Subsidies
   - Government procurement
   - Safeguards

These rules would likely apply to all services and could have a significant effect on domestic laws, regulations and practices applicable in domestic markets to services that are essential for e-commerce.

If a member makes a commitment to grant market access for a particular services, it must not limit:

- The number of services suppliers
- The value of service transactions or assets
- The quantity of service output
- The number of natural persons employed
- The type of legal entity or joint venture

General issues concerning e-commerce laws are:

- Functional equivalence of traditional trade practices and commercial transactions laws and electronic transactions.
- Undisputable, valid and enforceable sources of law regarding trade agreements, dealing with civil codes of jurisdiction etc.
- Validity and enforceability of agreements like offer, acceptance and contracts.
- Various contrast parameters to ensure detection and prevention of fraudulent activities
- The structure and format of the evidence required to enforce laws
- Conspicuousness
- Consumer protection related issues
- Negotiability
- New regulations and legislations

Out of these issues, some are exclusively commercial, for example:

- Consumer protection related issues
- Market competition and fair trade practices related issues
- Financial services and payment systems
- Intellectual property rights

Other resources are more technology oriented like:

- System performance
- Resource allocation
- Information security
- Encryption

SUMMARY

- EDI is the transfer of data between different companies using networks, such as VANs or the Internet. As more and more companies are connected to the Internet, EDI is becoming increasingly important as an easy mechanism for companies to buy, sell, and trade information.
- EDI is the computer-to-computer exchange of structured information, by agreed message standards, from one computer application to another by electronic means and with a minimum of human intervention.

- In common usage, EDI is understood to mean specific interchange methods agreed upon by national or international standards bodies for the transfer of business transaction data, with one typical application being the automated purchase of goods and services.
- The EDI semantic layer describes the business application that is driving EDI. This layer is specific to a company and the software it uses. In other words, the user interface and content visible on the screen are tailored or customized to local environments.
- EDI standards specify business form structure and to some extent influence the content seen at the application layer. For instance, a purchase order name field in an X12 standard might be specified to hold a maximum of 50 characters.
- The EDI transport layer corresponds closely to the non-electronic activity of sending a business form from company A to company B. The business form could be sent via regular postal service, registered mail, certified mail or private carrier or simply faxed between the companies.
- A value-added network (VAN) is a private network provider (sometimes called a turnkey communications line) that is hired by a company to facilitate electronic data interchange (EDI) or provide other network services.
- Financial EDI (FEDI) is the computer-to-computer exchange of payment and payment-related information between companies using a standard format. Financial EDI works much like non-financial EDI, which involves the electronic exchange of business data such as price quotes, purchase orders, and shipping information. However, is also significantly different in that, to move a payment, a bank must be involved. Because of this difference, the buyer and seller must work closely with their respective banks to effect a financial EDI transaction.
- CRM stands for customer relationship management. It is a process or methodology used to learn more about customers' needs and behaviour in order to develop stronger relationships with them.
- CRM is the philosophy of interaction with the customer and e-CRM is electronic CRM, which is conceptually the same as CRM, the only difference being that it is a new term where all integration of the customer takes place with the help of an electronic media.

REVIEW QUESTIONS

1. Define EDI. Discuss EDI applications in business.
2. (a) What do you mean by internal commerce. How does SCM help in customization of services?

   (b) Write short notes on:

      (i) JIT manufacturing

      (ii) The importance of CRM

CHAPTER 10

E-Business

Many people use the term e-business and e-commerce interchangeably. However, e-commerce is often interpreted as a narrower concept describing only transactions conducted between business partners via computer networks. E-business has a broader definition of electronic commerce, not just the buying and selling of goods and services, but also servicing customers, collaboration with business partners, and conducting electronic transactions within an organization. Basically, the term e-commerce is used as an equivalent to the definition of e-business.

10.1 E-BUSINESS FIRM

If a company has a web-site on the Internet, it does not make it an e-commerce company. Some researchers define an e-business firm as one that derives a significant proportion (at least 10%) of its revenues from transactions conducted over the Internet. A model that helps to comprehend the different forms of electronic commerce is as shown in Fig. 10.1. There are three dimensions in the model which present the degree of digitization of:

1. The *product* sold
2. The *process*
3. The *delivery agent*

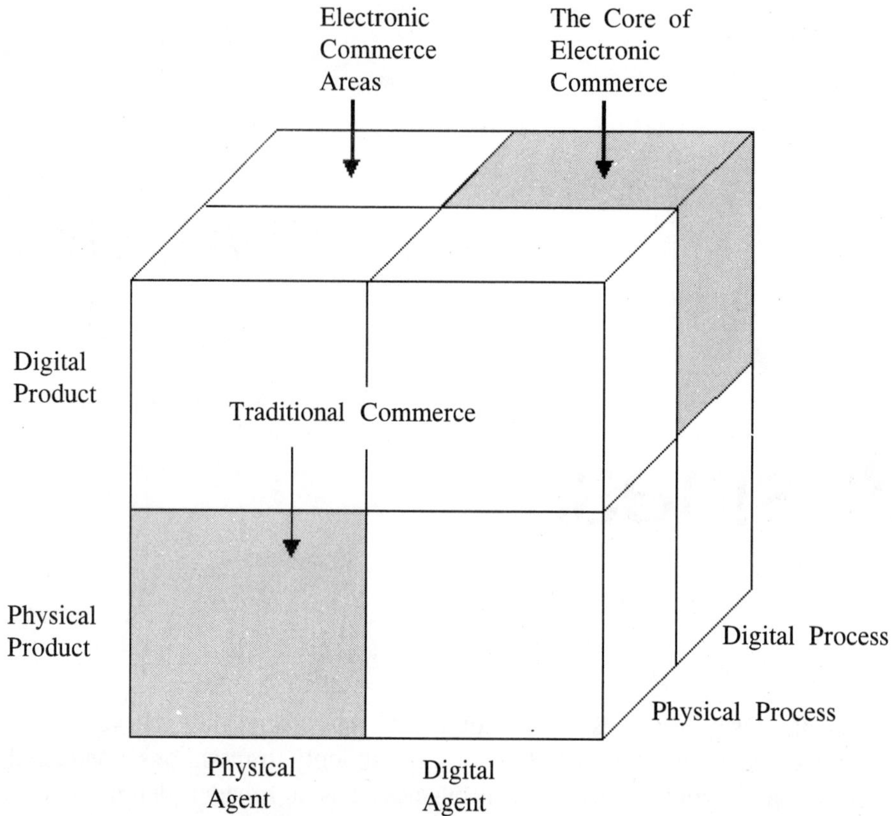

Fig. 10.1: ***The dimensions of electronic commerce***

In traditional commerce all dimensions, product, process and agent, are physical (lower-left cube), whereas in pure electronic commerce organizations all dimensions are digital (upper-right cube). A pure e-commerce company would have a digitized product, e.g. a music album, which would be sold over the Internet and delivered through the Internet. Turban *et al*. (2002: 6) claim that if there is at least one digital dimension the situation is considered electronic commerce, but not pure electronic commerce. An exception to this could be when only the product is digital, e.g. companies that sell CDs only through physical stores are not electronic commerce companies.

The retail business has its own definitions for different retailers. Traditional retailers with physical retail stores arc called *"brick-and-mortar"* companies or *incumbents*. Electronic retailers are called *e-tailers*. Companies who have both a physical and online presence in the market are called *"click-and-mortar"* companies. (Turban *et al*. 2002: 85-86). The firms that sell directly to consumers over the Internet and do not have any physical sales channel are *"pure-play"* e-tailers.

10.2 IMPACTS OF E-BUSINESS

E-business has influenced the whole economy. It has had an impact on industry structures, intermediaries, business processes, organizations, and competition. Moreover, it has created new ways to conduct business and even totally new business models.

In this chapter, the impacts of e-business on industry structures, business models, competition, and the value creation of organizations are examined. The chapter is concluded by presenting the benefits of e-commerce to consumers, organizations and society. The limitations of e-commerce are also discussed.

10.3 STRUCTURE OF THE INDUSTRY

Electronic markets can change the industry structures and the way the value is created in the industry. In traditional distribution channels, there are intermediaries between the consumer and manufacturer, such as wholesalers, distributors and retailers. The Internet has shortened the traditional value chain so that manufacturers can sell directly to customers and provide customer support online, as shown in Fig. 10.2. Consequently, the traditional intermediaries are eliminated from the value chain. This phenomenon is called *disintermediation*, which more accurately means "the removal of organizations or business process layers responsible for certain intermediary steps in a given value chain".

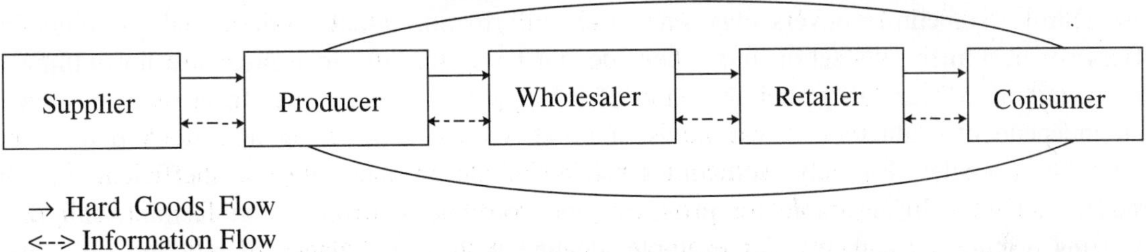

→ Hard Goods Flow
<--> Information Flow

Fig. 10.2: *Disintermediation*

Much inefficiency can be eliminated when manufacturers sell directly to the consumers. Intermediaries do not add the product price, product delivery times can be reduced, and manufacturers can build a closer relationship with their customers. Forecasting the demand also becomes easier for the manufactures if they are closer to their customers and get an immediate signal of the order. Computer manufacturer Dell Computers is a good example of a successful e-tailing manufacturer. Dell has managed to profitably sell computers over the Internet to millions of consumers.

However, selling products over the Internet is not an easy task. One of the difficulties is to attract consumers' attention and to get them to visit the Web site. At the same time, it is hard for consumers to find the right products and manufactures on the Internet. To fill this need, new intermediaries like online shopping assistants are emerging and replacing the role of traditional intermediaries. This phenomenon is known as *reintermediation*, and it is illustrated in Fig. 10.3. This is a new way of bringing value to the customer and maybe generating revenues. Some of the reintermediaries are competitors to the traditional retail stores, such as pure-play e-tailers, and some of the reintermediaries are traditional retailers with online businesses. Other intermediaries include shopping portals, directories, and comparison-shopping agents.

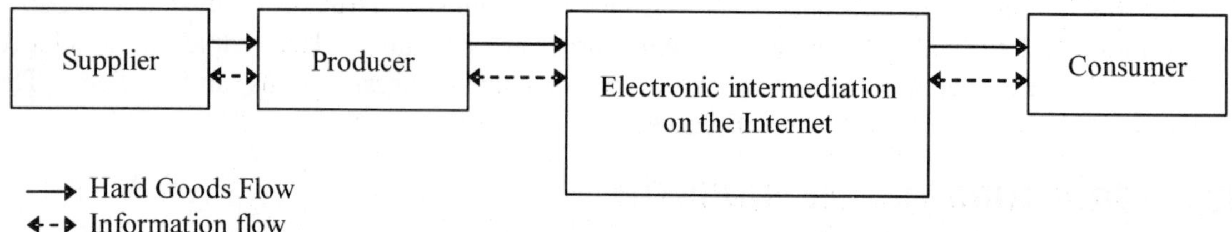

Fig.10.3: ***Reintermediation***

Electronic reintermediaries create value in many ways in the supply chain. First of all, they can reduce the search cost of products and services. It may be hard for sellers and buyers to find each other. Brokers can reduce the search costs by matching customers with products by maintaining databases of customer preferences. Secondly, brokers may protect the privacy of the buyer or seller if they wish to remain anonymous or protect some information relevant to a trade.

Thirdly, sometimes buyers may want more information about product quality, competing offers, or customer satisfaction but sellers do not have this information or are not willing to give it out. A broker can gather this kind of information, for example, from other customers and independent evaluators. These kinds of brokers include travel agents, stockbrokers, and real estate agencies. Fourthly, sometimes pricing of the products may be inefficient, i.e. the trade is not mutually desirable for providers and consumers. Brokers can facilitate fair deals by using pricing mechanisms, for example, dealing with an imbalance of buy and sell orders in the stock market. Fifthly, reintermediary can decrease the risk of the buyer and seller participating in the trade. For example, a consumer may refuse to pay after receiving a product, or a buyer may provide a product of bad quality. The broker can provide an insurance against this kind of behaviour.

Electronic intermediaries are one kind of a new business model that e-commerce has created. In the next section, some business models are examined in more detail.

10.4 NEW BUSINESS MODELS

The term business model can be defined in many different ways. A simple definition is to call it a method of doing business by which a company generates revenue. In other words, a business model specifies where a company is in the value chain and how it makes money. Electronic commerce has given rise to new kinds of business models. Some of these, such as Internet auctions, are completely novel, while some are reinvented traditional models that are modified to suit the digital world.

In addition to definitions, business models can be categorized in many ways. Companies may also combine different models as part of their business strategy and create new variations. New business models for electronic commerce are emerging constantly. Michael Rappa (2001) has presented an extensive categorization of business models for the Web.

10.4.1 Brokerage Model

Brokerage model is practiced by brokers, market-makers who bring buyers and sellers together and facilitate transactions. Brokers make money by charging a fee or commission for each transaction they enable. There are several forms of brokerage models, a few examples of which are presented below.

Auction broker: Conducts Internet auctions for sellers and charges the seller a listing fee and a commission, which is typically scaled with the value of the transaction. There are different variations of auctions in terms of the offering and bidding rules, including reverse auctions.

Buy/Sell fulfilment: The customer specifies buying or selling orders for a specific product or service, including price, delivery etc, and the broker charges the buyer and/or seller a transaction fee.

Virtual mall: Hosts several online merchants and typically charges setup, monthly listing and/or transaction fees. A mall may provide automated transaction services and relationship marketing opportunities.

An example of a company that uses a brokerage model as a dominant business model is eBay.com. It is the world's largest online auction site having more than 20 million registered users in 2001. In 2000 its sales transactions were $5 billion. E-Bay has global sites, country specific sites in e.g. US, Canada, France, the UK, Australia and Japan, and also 53 local sites in the US. The site primarily serves individuals, but also offers a business exchange.

10.4.2 Advertising Model

The Web advertising model can be seen as an extension of the traditional media broadcasting model. In this model, a Web site serves as a broadcaster and provides content and services, usually free of charge. The Web page contains advertising messages in the form of banner advertisements, which are the major or sole source of revenue for the broadcaster. The broadcaster may be a content creator or distribute content that is created elsewhere. This business model only works when the volume of visitors to the site is large. There are several forms of the model, including the following:

Portal: High-volume traffic page, a point of entry to the Web. A portal may contain search engines, directories, and other diversified content or services.

Personalized portal: Allows users to customize the interface and content of the portal in order to increase loyalty as a result of the user's time invested in personalizing the site.

Query-based paid placement: The selling of favourable link positioning (sponsored links) or advertising, keyed to particular search terms of the user's query.

10.4.3 Infomediary Model

Data about consumers and their consumption habits are very valuable, especially after the information is categorized and analyzed in a proper way. On the other hand, data about producers and their products can be useful to consumers when they are considering a purchase. Some companies function as information intermediaries, infomediaries who collect and sell information to sellers and buyers on the Web. Some forms of infomediary models are presented below.

Incentive marketing: Provides incentives to customers in the form of redeemable points, coupons etc. for making purchases from specific retailers. Data about users are collected and sold for targeted advertising.

Metamediary: Facilitates transactions between buyers and sellers by providing information services without getting involved in the actual process of exchanging goods or services between parties.

10.4.4 Merchant Model

Merchants are wholesalers or retailers of goods and services. Sales can be based on fixed list prices or the price can be determined through auction.

Virtual merchant: So-called pure-play e-tailer, a merchant that operates only over the Web.

Catalog merchant: Mail-order business that has a web-based catalogue of its products and services. Often combines mail, telephone and web ordering mechanisms.

Click-and-mortar: Traditional brick-and-mortar retail establishment that also has a Web storefront.

Bit vendor: A merchant that only deals with digital products and services and conducts both sales and distribution over the Web. One of the best known e-business merchants is Amazon.com. Amazon is the largest online bookstore in the world and unlike its competitors it does not operate only in the book sector but also sells music, toys and cars. Most of Amazon's customers are individual buyers. More about Amazon's business strategy is discussed in a case example at the end of the chapter.

10.4.5 Manufacturer Model

The manufacturer model is based on the power of the Web to allow manufactures to reach buyers directly. This compression of the distribution channel aims at efficiency, improved customer service, or better understanding of customer preferences. As mentioned previously, one of the most successful manufacturers that sell directly to the consumers is the computer manufacturer Dell Computers. Dell receives customer orders online, which are then automatically transferred to production and the computer is configured according to the customer's wants. Dell's success factors are superb logistics and order fulfilment system.

10.4.6 Affiliate Model

The affiliate model is the opposite of the generalized portal, which seeks to drive a high volume of traffic to one specific site. The affiliate model provides purchase opportunities wherever people may be surfing by offering financial incentives to affiliated partner sites in the form of a percentage of revenue. It is a pay-for-performance model, because it represents no cost to the merchant, if the affiliate does not generate sales. There are many variations of the model, including banner exchange, pay-per-click and revenue sharing programs.

The simple example of an affiliate model is that affiliates are invited to put a banner of a vendor, such as Amazon.com, on their sites. Whenever a consumer clicks on Amazon's banner at a vendor's site, a commission is paid to the vendor, if the customer makes a purchase.

10.4.7 Community Model

The community model is based on user loyalty. Users are supposed to have high investments in the Web site in both time and emotion and they may be regular contributors of content or money. Users who visit the site continually offer advertising, infomediary and specialized portal opportunities. The model may also run on subscription fees for premium service. There are several forms of the model, including the following:

Voluntary contributor model: Similar to the traditional listener or viewer contributor method used in not-for-profit radio and television broadcasting. This model is based on the creation of a community of users who support the site through voluntary donations or funding from foundations and corporate sponsors that support the organization's mission.

Knowledge networks: Expert sites that provide information based on professional expertise or experience of other users of the site. There is typically a forum where people may pose questions and receive answers from other users or from employed staff. GeoCites is an example of a community model, in which 40 million members are organized into dozens of communities such as car lovers. The members of GeoCites also have a marketplace for buying and selling goods and services. (Turban *et al.* 2002: 789)

10.4.8 Subscription Model

In the subscription model, users are charged a periodic fee to subscribe to a service every day, month or year. Sites may combine free content with premium, member-only content. The model is often combined with the advertising model. Some possible forms of the subscription model are presented below.

Content services: The possible content that is offered includes, for example, news, magazines, music and video.

Trust services: An independent trusted third party engenders trust between parties of transaction through, for example, certificate services, and charges a subscription fee from its members.

10.4.9 Utility Model

The utility model is based on metering usage and charging the users by actual usage rates in an on-demand manner. The most common form of the model is metered subscription, where subscribers purchase access to content in metered portions, such as numbers of pages viewed by the user.

10.5 COMPETITION IN THE MARKETPLACE

E-business has also influenced the competition in the marketplace. The basic theories of competition still remained unchanged, but the rules of the competition are now different. Competition in e-markets is often more intense than in traditional business. This is partly because e-markets tend to function more efficiently and are closer to perfect competition. Turban *et al.* (2002: 51-52) have discussed some factors that make the competition more equal but at the same time fiercer in e-markets:

Low entry barriers. As the costs of market entry are almost nonexistent, many buyers and sellers can enter the market. Also as there is no need for expensive physical stores, also small businesses are able to take part in the competition. Thus, the size of the company is no longer necessarily a significant competitive advantage. Companies in the market cannot charge too much excess over the costs of the service or otherwise new competitors will enter the market.

More comprehensive information: Both buyers and sellers benefit from the more comprehensive information that the Internet enables. Sellers get information about customer demand and customer needs. Consumers, on the other hand, can search for information of products cost-effectively and quickly and compare the competing offers. Thus, sellers may be forced to reduce prices as customers can easily find cheaper products.

There are also other factors that have influenced the competition. Differentiation and personalization have become important competitive factors, which enable small niche markets and better customer service. Due to the Internet, competition is becoming global. This brings great opportunities for many companies, but it is a threat to others. Internationalization is not easy, nor fast in most cases. There are many barriers that limit global electronic commerce, such as legal, financial, and cultural issues, (Turban *et al.* 2002: 51-52).

It is probable that as the technology evolves and the Internet becomes available to more consumers, more companies will participate in e-commerce. Considering the intense competition, it is evident that the law of natural selection will also apply over the Internet, and thus all businesses will not survive the competition.

10.6 VALUE CREATION OF ORGANIZATIONS

E-commerce is not only changing the way the value is created in industries, but also value created within an organization. Value creation is a requirement for every profitable business. A company must add value to their customers in some way that makes them willing to pay. Companies create value for their customers in many different ways, and different business models have different value configurations. However, Norwegian researchers Stabell and Fjeldstat (1998, cit. Afuah & Tucci 2001: 87) have found that there are three fundamental "value creation configurations" in the economy. These three value configurations are called: the value chain, value shop, and value network.

The value chain configuration created by Michael Porter is well known in the strategic management field and has been the dominant value creation logic in the economy for the last century. The model was developed for the needs of manufacturing economy and that is why the model poorly meets the requirements of the Internet and service economy. Still, many books about e-commerce only introduce the value chain as a framework for the Internet value creation (e.g. Turban 2002; Awad 2002). Likewise, many e-businesses offering e-commerce services use the values chain as a framework for value creation, which can lead to building of the wrong kind of capabilities.

Companies should understand all three value configurations and the impact of the Internet and e-business on the current value configuration so that they can choose the most appropriate value configuration. The next section gives the primary activities associated with each value configuration and discusses how the Internet has affected the configurations.

10.6.1 Value Chain

The value chain popularized by Michael Porter involves the production and sale of manufactured goods. In this model, value adding comes from transforming the raw materials into tangible products. There are several primary and support activities in which a manufacturer can add value. Primary activities are closely associated with transforming inputs into outputs. These activities are illustrated in Fig. 10.4. The first activity in the chain is inbound logistics which involves moving the raw materials into the plant in an efficient way. The second activity is the operation of transforming raw materials into a more finished product. The outbound logistics stage involves order processing and shipping and the marketing and sales stage is about advertising, pricing, promotion and management of the sales force. The final stage, service, involves managing technical support and other after sales services. The primary activities are supported by support activities of the firm's infrastructure, human resource management, technology development, and procurement, (Afuah & Tucci 2001: 89-93).

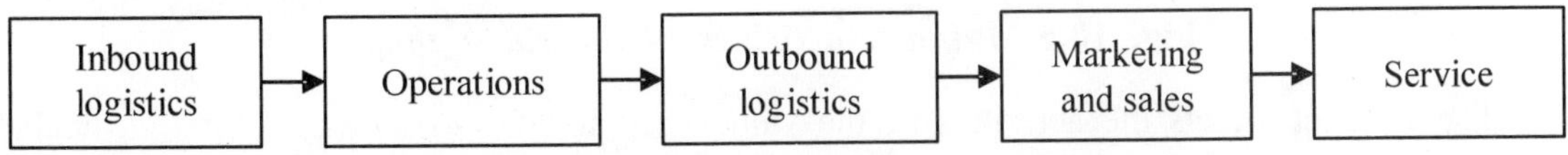

Fig. 10.4: ***Primary activities of the value chain***

The Internet affects the activities of the value chain in many ways. First, the connected activities of the value chain allow a firm to learn more about end users. This means that the connections enabled by the Internet make a denser social web which, in turn, allows marketing and sales functions to be in more direct contact with end users and intermediaries that operate in the chain before the end user. Thus, companies can assess market needs better and also stimulate demand more easily. Second, it widens the geographic scope of the company. The companies can sell outside their geographic area. Third, it enables a new delivery mechanism. Information, software and content can be delivered instantaneously over the Web. The company can also cut transaction costs by receiving and sending orders through the Internet. This new ordering mechanism also affects the operation activity of the value chain as products can now be manufactured to order. Thus, production is changing from push type to pull type. Fourth, it enables larger scale of operation with a larger customer base provided through the Internet.

10.6.2 Value Shop

Stabell and Fjeldstad (1998, cit. Afuah & Tucci 2001: 93) stressed that focusing on the primary activities of the value chain was forcing the company into a business model around manufactured goods. They argued that service provisioning has different value creation logic. The major difference between service provisioning and manufacturing is that service providers normally customize their service to the needs of their customers in real time, rather that developing one solution and mass-producing it time and again. In the value chain, the time from searching for a solution and commercializing one may take years, while in a value shop it is a matter of hours. An example of value shop logic is a travel agent who must first determine what the customer wants and needs and then propose a method of filling that need.

In value shop, a company focuses on discovering what the customer wants, figuring out a way to develop value, determining whether the customer's needs were fulfilled, and, if necessary, repeating the process again. The value shop includes the primary activities, as shown in Fig. 10.5. The first activity is problem finding, this involves finding together with the customer the problem and the need. The second stage, problem solving, is about the generation of ideas and making an action plan. In the choice phase the decision between alternatives is made. The execution stage includes communication, organizing, and implementing the decision. Finally, in the control and evaluation stage, how well the solution solved the original problem is monitored and measured.

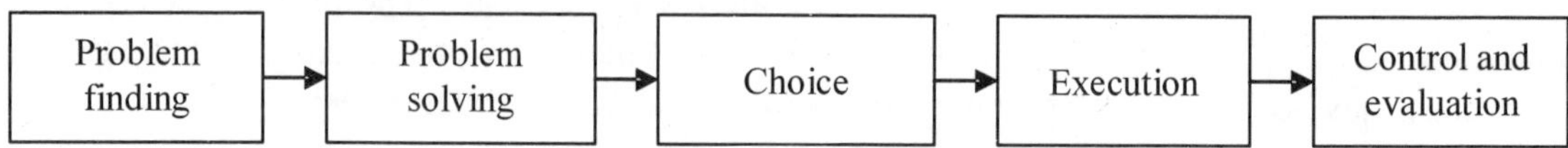

Fig. 10.5: ***Primary activities of the value shop***

The Internet affects the activities of the value shop in four main ways. First, it enables a larger scale of operations. The company can serve more customers at once. Previously a travel agent was limited to sell flights by the number of people performing customer service. Now a customer can buy a ticket over the Internet without the intervention of customer service agents. Second, it widens the geographic scope of the area the firm presents. The companies can deliver service in distant regions. Some services like a haircut cannot be delivered over the Internet, but services like travel agencies, real estate agencies, and engineering can widen their geographical scope of the company. Third, it allows more information to be collected and processed by the service provider. This enables better problem solving in two ways. The first way is group decision making and the second way is the option of researching information available on the Web to aid in the decision making process. On the other hand, information provided on the Internet may also be a disadvantage for some of the information-based value shop businesses, as they may face competition from the general knowledge base available on the Internet. Fourth, it enables a new delivery medium or mechanism. For examples, stock quotations and architectural designs can be sent over the Internet.

10.6.3 Value Network

The third value configuration, the value network is the case when a firm is an intermediary such as a broker. The broker makes money by bringing buyers and sellers together. This is one of the common business models of e-business. For instance, many of the Internet e-tailers are intermediaries. The intermediary makes money only if both buyers and sellers perceive value from it. For example, travel agencies want to sell more tickets through an intermediary, and customers who want to find the lowest possible fare.

Rather than focusing on transforming raw materials into finished goods, the intermediary should focus on the following primary activities: network promotion and contract management, service provisioning and infrastructure operations. Network promotion and contract management involves promoting and building the network, acquiring customers, and managing contracts for service provision. Service provisioning connects people in the network and then charges a payment from them for making the connection. First, it involves setting up contacts, seeing that the contacts are maintained, and finally, ending the contact at the appropriate moment. Infrastructure operations guarantee that infrastructure operates efficiently and is ready to provide service to the next customer.

The Internet affects the activities of the value network in three main ways. First, it compounds network externalities. This means that the value network becomes more valuable to users if more people take advantage of it. For example, a collector wants to auction off a valuable piece of art. The auction firm that she uses is more valuable to her if there are more bidders for her work. Since a network is more attractive the more members it has, one can expect larger networks to gain new members at a faster rate than smaller ones. This often means that large networks grow larger and smaller ones become smaller. Thus, it is extremely important for intermediaries to pay attention to the developing the size of their network. Second, it widens the geographic scope of the network. Just like all the previous value configurations, e-business widens the geographic scope of the network. This is particularly important for value networks, as a larger geographic base of users allows the network to grow more quickly. Thus, the size of the network grows and it is more useful for the users. Third, it enables a larger scale of the network. Expansion of the network of value network business is a primary way the business can add value. This also makes it possible to serve many more customers.

The companies should be aware of how the Internet and e-commerce have changed their value configurations in order to build the right competencies. The traditional companies use the value chain as their framework for value creation. However, if they start conducting e-business, the value chain may not be an adequate model for value creation.

10.7 BENEFITS OF ELECTRONIC COMMERCE

Electronic commerce has many potential benefits over traditional commerce. Some of the benefits are just starting to appear and some will be reached in the future as the electronic commerce expands. Next, the benefits of e-commerce to organizations, consumers and society are presented. Some of the situations are win-win propositions, meaning that both the consumer and organization gain from e-commerce. The benefits are taken from the extensive lists of benefits of e-commerce introduced by Awad (2002: 13-16) and Turban *et al.* (2002: 25-27). The benefits presented below are not the complete list, but includes the most important or visible benefits of B2C e-commerce.

10.7.1 Benefits to Organizations

- **Lower costs:** First, electronic commerce cuts the cost of creating, processing, distributing, storing and retrieving paper-based information. Second, huge savings can be made in supply chain problems, such as excessive inventories and delivery delays. For example, it is believed that the auto industry saves tens of billions of dollars annually only from inventory reduction, as electronic commerce enables building cars to order (Turban *et al.* 2002: 25). Third, electronic commerce reduces the transaction costs. Every financial transaction must be put into electronic form. The sooner the conversion, the cheaper the transaction becomes. For example, the cost of processing an air line ticket is $8 whereas processing the same ticket over the Internet costs $1 (Turban *et al.* 2002: 26). Another cost saving comes from the lower cost of office premises. As virtual companies do not have physical stores and infrastructure, there can be huge savings.
- **Bigger marketplace**: A company can easily and quickly serve more customers and locate the best suppliers and business partners in international markets. For example, small vendors may have better business opportunities as they can answer the requests for a proposal of international companies posted on the Web, and win the electronic bid.
- **Better customer service:** An e-commerce company can gain competitive advantage over the traditional companies by providing better and quicker customer service over the Internet. The customer can get immediate service by purchasing a product or service online. The company can sell their products 24 hours a day and 7 days a week. Electronic commerce also enables companies to interact more closely with customers, which in turn, enables better customer relationship management and customer loyalty.
- **Customization:** Digital products are easily customizable. Products can be differentiated and matched to individual needs easily if the information regarding consumer tastes and preferences is available. For example, an Internet book store can inform the customer when a new book from his or her favourite author is published and is on sale. Electronic commerce also enables products to be made to order which allows inexpensive customization of products.

10.7.2 Benefits to Consumers

- **Lower price:** Electronic commerce increases the competition among the sellers which often results in lower prices. Moreover, virtual auctions are good places for consumers to find good bargains. Often reduced transaction costs for a seller can be seen in lower prices of products or services. For example, the cost of paying an invoice through a branch of a bank is often included in a service packet on the Internet
- **Better service:** As companies can sell their products 24 hours a day and 7 days a week, customers can do their shopping whenever they want to. Customers can shop from almost any location. Instead of travelling to the travel agency and standing in the queue to buy a flight ticket, a customer can book the flight online and, as a result, save time and money. In addition, in the case of digitized products and services electronic commerce allows quick delivery.
- **Quick comparison shopping:** Electronic commerce not only provides consumers with more vendors and more products but also helps consumers conduct quick comparisons. Automated online shopping assistants called hopbots search the Internet stores and find deals on everything from groceries to computers. Thus, consumers can save a lot of money by finding the best available offers easily.
- **Information sharing and control:** Electronic commerce improves information sharing between customers and merchants. Nowadays, many companies provide customers with an opportunity to follow the shipping process of the products on the Web. If there are any delays, a customer will get the information immediately, for example via e-mail. Customers can also communicate with other customers in electronic communities where they can compare the products and services and exchange ideas.

  Electronic commerce often gives customers more control of their services. For example, banks alone do not control the relationship with the customer. Customers can have more control of their banking needs via Web sites.

10.7.3 Benefits to Society

- **Reduced air pollution:** There is less traffic on the road as more individuals can now work and shop at home.
- **Better services in rural areas:** People in rural areas now have access to services and products that earlier where unavailable.
- **Cheaper public services:** It is believed that in the future, some of the public services, such as health care, education, and distribution of government social services can be delivered cheaper and with better quality over the Internet.

10.8 LIMITATIONS OF ELECTRONIC COMMERCE

Although electronic commerce has a number of benefits to consumers, organizations and society, there are still problems and limitations that should be taken into account when conducting commerce on the Internet. Some of the technical and non-technical limitations of electronic commerce that Awad (2002: 17-20) and Turban *et al.* (2002: 27-28) have presented, are given below.

9.8.1 Technical limitations

- **Security, reliability and standards:** System security, reliability, standards, and some communication protocols are still evolving. Many of the consumers are still wary of giving their credit card numbers on the Internet. In fact, the security issues are perceived to be more serious than they actually are, and companies are able to convince their customers that online transactions and privacy are secured. For example, viruses cause unnecessary delays, file backups, and storage problems. Moreover, there is always a fear of hackers accessing files and violating customer accounts.
- **System scalability:** A company that sells its products over the Internet needs to develop an interactive interface with customers via a Web site. A web site must be scalable or upgradable, as the number of customers visiting the Web site daily might change dramatically within a short period of time. For example, if a company has built its web site to serve 2 million customers a day and 6 million customers show up, the Web site becomes slower or may crash totally, and this will eventually result in a loss of customers.
- **Insufficient technology or tools:** Some e-commerce applications require more bandwidth than is available. Also some of the software development tools are still evolving and changing.
- **Integration:** Some electronic commerce software might not fit with some hardware. It might also be difficult to integrate the Internet and electronic commerce software with existing applications and databases.
- These limitations will lessen or will be overcome in the future as technology evolves. The impacts of these limitations can be reduced by careful planning.

10.8.2 Non-technical limitations

- **E-commerce is not free:** Setting up a web site is not an easy task. The development of an electronic commerce-system in-house can be very expensive and time consuming. This is one reason why large companies that have more money have been more successful than small retailers. The electronic commerce infrastructure can be outsourced but it has also its own problems. Just the baseline technology of an e-commerce system may cost a larger organization an average of US $750 000. A major licensing deal on a high traffic portal per year is normally even more expensive, (Awad 2002, 9).
- **Inefficient consumer search:** Acquiring new customers is difficult and expensive for Internet retailers. Some studies suggest that online retailers spend five times more than store and catalogue retailers on customer acquisition. In addition, e-commerce needs new types of intermediaries between sellers and buyers which all increase the

transaction costs, for example, electronic malls that guarantee a product quality, and certification authorities to assure the legitimacy of a transaction.

- **Fulfilment problems:** E-tailing brings out new problems that were nonexistent in traditional retailing, such as shipping delays, product mix-ups, and crashing web sites. These are especially big problems during holiday seasons when the number of customers is far more than that on an average shopping day.
- **Customer relations problems:** Whereas quick comparison shopping is an advantage to customers, it is a disadvantage to sellers. Just like traditional retailers e-businesses need loyal customers. Now it is very easy to click on the competitor's site, who offers the same product at a lower price. Trust is also an issue in online shopping. Some customers do not trust an unknown, faceless seller, paperless transaction and electronic money.

Products: Some products, such as heavy products and products that consumers want to touch and test, do not sell online. Heavy products such as sofas become expensive to deliver and the retailer may also incur costly returns. Some customers like to try on items such as clothes to know exactly what they are buying.

Legal and support services: Many legal issues are yet unresolved. For example, qualified electronic commerce tax experts and copyright clearance centres are just coming into being.

Lack of actors: In many cases, there are not yet enough sellers and buyers for profitable electronic commerce. Many people do not want to enter the e-business until it is stabilized.

In spite of these limitations, electronic commerce is rapidly expanding. As technology and services evolve and experience and knowledge accumulate, electronic commerce will become more efficient, and thus more widely used.

10.9 REASONS FOR FAILURE OF E-COMMERCE COMPANIES

From the middle to the late 1990s the media were full of success stories about Internet start-ups. At the height of the boom, it seemed that everyone wanted to be part of the dotcom boom, including the venture capitalists and other investors. Many dotcoms aimed at early IPOs and stock prices of publicly traded Internet companies exploded to unbelievable highs. The dotcom bubble finally burst in April 2000 and venture capital money dried up. Several dotcoms closed their doors and survivors were often forced to lay off staff and to redirect their businesses. Few Internet companies were actually showing profit.

In 2000, at least 210 Internet companies went out of business. About 125 of these failures occurred in the fourth quarter of the year and about 40 in December alone. About 75% of the failed companies were in the B2C sector, (Nwachukwu 2002). The dotcom bubble, reinforced by unrealistic investor expectations, happened because the stock market was in a new and unfamiliar situation. As the Internet was clearly going to be the major driver and business mechanism of the new world economy, everything connected with it had seemed worth investing in. However, it was forgotten that business over the Internet was just a new form of business and thus the basic rules of doing business should also apply to it, (Starling 2000).

Many traditional brick-and-mortar enterprises have not been very successful in their online ventures either and also their revenues have remained low. Nevertheless, for traditional brick-and-mortar enterprises, online presence has considerable value beyond revenues from online transactions. The value is derived from marketing and brand promotion, reduced overheads and lowered costs of customer acquisition and retention. Thus, the return on investment and the success of an online venture of a traditional bricks-and-mortar company should not be measured by transaction value alone, (Gambhir *et al.* 2001).

In the following section failures are focused mainly on pure play e-commerce companies. However, many reasons for failure are also common to online ventures of bricks-and-mortar enterprises. It is impossible to name one single reason for dotcom failures and low profitability of Internet business. From a single dotcom's point of view, some of the factors that have led to failures and low profitability are internal and others external to the company.

External Reasons

External reasons for failure are common to all the players on the field, although they may affect some companies more than the others.

Competition: Free competition is clearly one factor that has led to the low profitability. As consumers can easily compare the prices and find the lowest one, e-commerce companies have not been able to put their prices to the level where they could make a profit, (Starling 2000), especially in the B2C sector. As the entry barriers have been very low and setting up an Internet business has been relatively easy, inexpensive and quick, competition has become very severe in most modes of online business.

Consumer resistance: Consumer resistance to shopping online proved greater than expected, which was another important market reason for the modest success of B2C e-commerce. As mentioned previously, many people are still worried about frauds and other security risks of buying over the Internet.

In addition, especially in online retail that focuses on necessities such as groceries, many people have the habit of purchasing at the same store, approximately at the same time every week. People want to see and touch the selections before making buying decisions. These preferences are hard to overcome, (Silverstein *et al.* 2001: 9)

General economic situation: It is clear that the general economic situation has an effect on the volume of e-commerce sales. Consumers are more cautious about spending than in the end of 1990s and this applies also to online shopping.

Availability of capital: As long as the e-business boom continued, it was easy to get venture capital. Many companies spent all the money before they had acquired a large enough customer base. Suddenly, after the spring of 2000, the investors were not willing to wait a long time for profits, as the risks were considered too high. If the companies could not demonstrate success and measurable results during the early start-up phase they could not get funded. Thus, many companies reached bankruptcy due to lack of additional funding. Boo.com is a famous example of a company that went bankrupt for this reason, (Turban *et al.* 2002: 717, Fleming 2002).

Internal Reasons

Internal reasons for failures are the ones that are more firm-specific. However, they have been very common in the industry and many start-ups have suffered from nearly all of them.

10.10 BUSINESS/REVENUE MODEL AND FINANCIAL MANAGEMENT

As it was very easy to raise financing, lots of investment capital was spent on companies with poor business plans that clearly could not reach profitability (Bazac 2002). During the e-business boom, many companies had forgotten the rule that marginal sales should lead to marginal profits. Most pure e-tailers had been losing money on every sale as they tried to become profitable in size and scale, and thus many never reached the goal. The revenue model of many companies was incorrect: companies spent as much money as they could on customer acquisition, hoping to attract millions of visitors per month and thus attracting advertisement money. However, with little revenue and huge expenses many of these companies reached bankruptcy quickly, (Turban *et al.* 2002: 107, 717). For example, many of the smaller Internet companies using the advertising model could not succeed since they did not have sufficiently large audiences or did not have enough capital to be able to stay in business long enough to attract and build a sufficiently large audience. It is doubtful whether online advertising will ever grow large enough to support all the dotcom companies that would like to rely on the model, as very few have the financial resources and time necessary to develop to the size large enough to attract substantial advertising revenue, (Fleming 2002).

One common problem for Internet start-ups has been poor financial management. Initially, as it was easy to raise financing, many dotcoms used enormous amounts of money for fancy offices, free food etc. with little consideration for earning profits and keeping the cash flow sustainable (Bazac 2002, Walters 2002). In addition, as with any business, Internet start-ups should be given time to succeed. Daugherty (2002) states that many online entrepreneurs have simply been too impatient and they have not given their ventures enough time to grow. True commitment and perseverance are needed in order to create success.

10.10.1 Technology, Design and Usability

Internet users expect web sites to offer superior technical performance, including fast page loading, quick database searches and streamlined graphics, and thus errors in a company's site frustrates potential customers and results as abandoned purchases (Turban *et al.* 2002: 108). Daugherty (2001) defines a dysfunctional web site as any site with design flaws or chronic technical problems that make it either difficult or impossible to use. Technical problems include long downloading times and sites that suffer from a lot of downtime. Design flaws are often related to usability and they can, for example, make the site difficult to navigate. It is obvious that both kinds of problems hurt the business. However, sometimes even hundreds of errors can be found on one single web page (Bazac 2002).

Many shopping attempts fail and consumers could not purchase the items they wished for, mainly due to problems in searching the desired products or in finalizing the purchasing process and other kinds of usability problems. For example, in Akateeminen.com bookstore, novels by Stephen King could only be searched by words "King" or "King S", not by the author's full name.

According to the study, among the biggest problems in purchasing process were failing in adding products to the shopping basket and in confirming the purchase. Also obligatory registration caused problems, as consumers are unwilling to give out their personal information before they can make a purchase. The study recommends that user interfaces should be made simpler and that users should all the time be aware of what is happening during the buying process. The service should be designed according to user wants and needs. For example, complicated graphical solutions can confuse the potential customers and thus only make the purchasing more difficult.

10.10.2 Marketing

Poor promotion is one of the major reasons for dotcom failures (Bazac 2002). It is a common mistake to try to market e-business as if it was a local brick and mortar business. However, the traditional marketing approach is not applicable to an Internet business. For example, Internet marketing should be directed to a global consumer base and it should be designed to catch potential customers' attention as they move quickly from site to site. Online business is faster paced than traditional business and marketing plans should match this pace. Thus, e-commerce requires a totally new marketing mindset, (Daugherty 2001).

Branding is considered as the key to success for e-tailers. However, for some companies the drive to establish a brand has led to excessive spending. One often-cited example is a start-up e-tailer that spent over 50% of its venture capital funding on just one 30-second television advertisement. It should be realized that most customers come to the website from search engines, affiliate links and personal recommendations, than due to a single television advertisement, (Turban *et al.* 2002: 107-108).

10.10.3 Customer Service and Reputation

Poor customer service is one reason for dotcom failures. Unanswered customer emails and delivery delays are some symptoms of inadequate attention to customer service, (Plant 2001). During the old economy, the unhappy customer may have told 50 friends and co-workers about the poor service and it could have resulted in a few lost sales. However, with the Internet he or she can reach even millions of potential customers, (Turban *et al.* 2002: 110). Thus, the companies cannot afford to neglect any of their customers or to betray their trust.

10.10.4 Organizational and Management Issues

In many cases, problems have occurred as the management team has been inexperienced. The enthusiasm cannot compensate for the lack of basic management skills.

Human resources management issues, is one area that often is forgotten when analysing Internet start-up failures. Dazzled with the investor money, many start-up companies hired too many employees and even unqualified staff. Many companies started by hiring friends and relatives of founders instead of analysing recruitment needs and hiring professionals, (Bazac 2002).

10.10.5 Speed

In a high-tech world, speed has been seen as a competitive advantage. However, moving too fast has resulted in severe mistakes, such as poor customer service, diversions from the original vision and mission and ignoring signs of employee burnout, (Walters 2002).

10.11 OWNERS' EVALUATION OF FAILURES

Table 10.1 presents the main reasons for dotcom failures according to company owners, gathered by dotcomfailures.com (*Entrepreneur Resource Center*). It can be seen that only 3% state that the main reason for failure was immature market, i.e. that the users were not ready for this kind of business. Thus, it seems that internal reasons for failures have been more severe.

Table 10.1 Reasons for dotcom failures according to the owners

Reason for Failure According to Owners	% of Business Failures
Faulty Business Model	47
Technology	17
Poor Management	15
Too Many Parties	9
Advertising Waste	7
User Not Ready	3

Source : (www.dotcomfailures.com, cit. *Entrepreneur Resource Center*)

10.12 EVALUATION OF THE SITUATION

The number of failed dotcoms may seem impressive. However, it should be realized that during the first five years of existence, 68-80% of all businesses fail. The reasons for failures are numerous. Mason lists the following: wrong basic idea; inadequate start-up capital; wasteful use of capital, a lack of stubborn staying power; a lack of financial know-how; inability to deal with a variety of people including suppliers, customers and employees; bad pricing; ignorance of government restraints; and taking the competition too lightly. Clark states that the four most common reasons for business failures are poor management; unbalanced managerial experience; a lack of managerial ability; and a lack of market-specific experience.

It can be seen that most of the reasons for failures of Internet businesses presented earlier in this chapter are the same as the general reasons for business failures listed above. When examining the failure rates of all new businesses, e-business failures can be seen as a normal consolidation of a new industry.

In the next section, we present a case example of how both traditional retailer, Toys R Us with a new Web site, and pure-play e-tailer Amazon.com failed to sell toys profitably over the Internet.

10.13 CASE STUDY: ONLINE TOY COMMERCE FAILURES (TOYS R US/AMAZON)

Toys R Us is a traditional toy retailer with broad product selection and 40 years of experience in the industry. The company is famous for strong B2B supplier relationships and a well developed inventory system. However, Toys R Us faced several problems in selling toys on the Web. It failed to effectively manage a direct-to-consumer distribution centre and balance its retail store business with its online business, (Turban *et al.* 2002: 105-106).

The problems occurred especially during the Christmas seasons. Toys R Us' web site could not handle large amounts of traffic and shipping orders. The ineffective web business was a consequence of lack of experience with both the front-end design and the back-end order fulfilment process. As a consequence, during the Christmas season of 1999, Toys R Us failed to profitably deliver toys on time for Christmas. In fact, 1 in 20 children did not receive their presents in time, (Turban *et al.* 2002: 105-106).

Amazon.com, a pure-play e-tailer, is famous for a premier site for creating customer loyalty and for efficient back-office order fulfilment system. In spite of its competence on e-business, it failed in the toy business on the Internet. One reason for this was that it did not have the strong supplier relationships with toy manufacturers. It did not manage to get the best toys and was not able to manage inventory against the demand. The same thing what happened to Toys R Us in Christmas 1999 happened to Amazon: it failed to profitably deliver toys on time. Amazon.com did not manage its inventory calculations, and after Christmas it has millions of toys to write off.

As the case demonstrates, Toys R Us had very typical problems that many manufactures face when starting to sell directly to consumers over the Internet. The company did not have enough expertise in the front end Web business. The Web site could not handle the large amount of shipping orders. The company also realized that its old delivery system which was designed for delivering to businesses did not work in delivering directly to consumers. Amazon's weakness in the toy business turned out to be weak supplier relationships and the lack of expertise in prediction of demand of toy markets and inventory management.

The consequences of the failures of the companies were severe. They both got bad reputation, fines, and the result was lost business. The companies decided to combine their expertise and formed a single online toy store. The alliance enables both parties to leverage their core strengths. The agreement is that Toys R Us will manage inventory and supplier relationships and Amazon.com distribution and customer service. This is an innovative model, but it also has it own problems which mainly come from integration of operational, technological, financial and cultural systems. The following years will show whether this will be success and whether this kind of alliance model works in e-tailing.

10.14 WINNERS OF THE FUTURE MARKETS

During the past years, the markets have undergone great changes and the pace of change is still extremely fast. The industry is still very young, but it is maturing. It is very hard to predict how the markets will look in five years and who will be the winning players then.

10.14.1 Winning Players in Future E-tailing

Silverstein *et al*. (2001:14), from the Boston Consulting Group, predict that there will be three kinds of winning players in the future of online retailing: attackers, niche players and, most promising of all, incumbents.

Attackers

Attackers are pure-play online retailers, who have achieved the scale that is needed to reduce their total costs. In addition, they have been able to build competitive advantages in key areas, such as brand strength, procurement, order fulfilment, customer acquisition and customer service. Amazon is the best example of an attacker. However, even it has not proven its long-term success. To date, the success of Amazon has been unique, driven by entrepreneurial vibrancy and access to abundant capital. It is predicted that such successes will be rare, even though some other online categories are still young enough for an aggressive player to turn its business into a success story, (Silverstein *et al*. 2001: 14-15).

Niche players

Niche players can either be pure-play start-ups or small offline retailers that have been able to build a strong and loyal franchise with limited target population. Their loyal customer base ensures a constant stream of revenues and also eliminates the need for spending a fortune on acquisition of new customers. However, as both the scope and size of niche players is small, they will probably only have limited influence on the evolution of their categories of e-commerce markets, (Silverstein *et al*. 2001: 15).

Incumbents

Silverstein *et al*. label incumbents as the most promising type of future online players. Many other experts share their opinion (e.g. Deluria 2001; Cronin 2000: 107). The incumbents most likely to excel are major offline players that are able to effectively leverage their existing assets in their online ventures. These assets include a recognized brand, an established infrastructure and strong operating capabilities. The brand advantage can be used to generate traffic and online relationships with their existing customers. Established retail and distribution sources can be used to serve online customers profitably and efficiently. Other kinds of incumbents can establish multichannel relationships with their customers. They can design and continually improve their offerings by using their knowledge about offline customers to better understand and anticipate their online customers' needs and preferences, (Silverstein et al. 2001:16).

To date, most incumbents have been cautious in moving to online business. For example, listening too often to those existing customers that are not ready to move to the Internet may have delayed the online efforts (Afuah & Tucci 2001: 77). However, as more and more consumers are going online, incumbents risk losing their customers to dotcoms if they prefer to wait and see for too long.

Incumbents vs. pure-plays

According to Afuah and Tucci, an incumbent's ability to develop and execute a profitable Internet business model depends on the company's incentives to invest in the new technology, and on the company's traditional brick-and-mortar capabilities. In the best case, the capabilities required to exploit the new technology build on the company's existing capabilities. On the other hand, old capabilities can also be a handicap to incumbents, as they may try to hold onto obsolete competitive advantages. Compared to new entrants, the incumbents may not have the ability to perform well with the new technology. Unlike incumbents, new entrants do not have old knowledge that needs to be unlearnt (Afuah & Tucci 2001: 76-77).

Due to different starting points, incumbents and pure-plays face different kinds of challenges when managing an electronic business. Recommendations and managerial issues for both kinds of companies are discussed in the next section.

10.15 MANAGING E-BUSINESSES

In this final section, issues that are central in managing different kinds of e-businesses are discussed. The discussion is concentrated on managing e-tailers, although many principles also apply to other kinds of e-businesses.

10.15.1 Managing Incumbents

Incumbents have several assets that can be translated into online advantages. Silverstein *et al.* have listed ten recommendations for incumbents about strategic and operational challenges of the online marketplace, (Silverstein *et al.* 2001: 19-21). Some of these recommendations are regarding the way in which incumbents should use their advantages and others about how they should handle the potential disadvantages. These recommendations are presented below.

Leverage the brand: Incumbents have clear brand advantage over dotcoms that have spent huge sums in their brand building efforts. In the Internet business, trust is essential, and due to well-developed brand recognition and trust, incumbents should have lower customer acquisition costs than pure-plays.

Create incentives to entice customers online: As the cost to serve a customer online can be lower than it is offline, customers of multi-channel players should be actively encouraged to use the Internet.

Make the most of customer information and relationships: Compared to pure plays, many incumbents already have a lot of information about their customers and strong customer relationships. Incumbents should leverage these to provide superior service to their online customers.

Integrate online and offline channels: Incumbents are well positioned to move into a multi-channel format that an increasing number of customers are looking to as their retailers of choice, but the incumbents should not simply manage several channels at the same time. Instead, they should manage across the channels, integrating all aspects of online and offline retailing, including branding, inventory forecasting and product returns. For example, customers may be given an option of picking up an online order at a nearby store rather than having it delivered to their home (Cronin 2000: 107).

Leverage offline scale: As size is one of the incumbents' greatest assets, their marketing and purchasing power gives them a significant cost advantage. These savings can be spent on customer acquisition, innovation, development and improving the overall offering.

Use distribution infrastructure to advantage: Compared to pure plays, incumbents already have established systems and networks that may also be appropriate for the new online channel. Especially catalogue retailers have distribution networks that are ideal for online sales, since the distribution process is virtually the same.

Manage channel conflict: The incumbents should be aware that moving online may trigger conflict between the channels. Problems can arise either within a company or within a supply chain and they can lead to damaged relationships on many levels, as different channels step on each others' toes. For example, existing sales force and distributors may fight hard against the new channel rather than see their revenues go to the new channel (Afuah & Tucci 2001: 142). Offering new products and services may be seen to cannibalize the existing ones since fewer customers may buy the old product (Afuah & Tucci 2001: 141). Thus, the companies should try to carefully anticipate and avoid these kinds of conflicts and solve the problems as quickly as possible if they emerge.

Exploit opportunities for partnering: It is not necessary to do everything in-house. Partnering can give access to critical skills that the company lacks, which may speed up the execution of online ventures. Incumbents have assets that are attractive to start-ups. Thus, incumbents have plenty of partnering opportunities. They need to identify and value physical and information-based assets of each potential partner to find the deal that is most beneficial to them.

Target total customer wallet: Retailers should aim at capturing 100 percent of the total category spending from each customer household in their product categories. To get closer to this goal, they should establish mechanisms for measuring customer satisfaction, repurchase rates and the effectiveness of customer service.

Use your best customers to model future improvements: Market understanding should not be gained based on averages but on in-depth dialogue with the best customers. This feedback should be used to continually improve the whole purchase experience. Customers' experiences of dissatisfactions are valuable as they can be used to develop offerings, pricing options, communications, and delivery and return alternatives.

Separate entity vs. a unit within: If an incumbent decides to go online, it must decide whether it will create a separate legal entity or develop the technology within the existing brick-and-mortar organization. There are several arguments for creating a separate entity. First of all, it prevents the dominant managerial logic and political power related to the old brick-and-mortar organization from interfering with the new venture. Doing so also avoids the competency trap – the inability to shed old successful ways of doing business and to adopt new ones. In addition, it may attract more talent that would prefer to work in an entrepreneurial environment, possibly seeking a payoff through an IPO. On the other hand, most incumbents have complementary assets and capabilities that could be very valuable for the new venture. In addition, if the company chooses to develop the new technology within, the brick-and-mortar personnel could learn from it and the company does not have to worry about the difficult process of integrating the entity to the organization later. The option that is best for the company depends on the company, its business model, and industry (Afuah & Tucci 2001: 79, 144).

10.15.2 Managing Pure-plays

Afuah and Tucci state that new entrants can adopt the new technology more easily than brick-and-mortar companies, as they do not have many of the handicaps faced by the latter, such as channel conflicts, dominant managerial logic, competency traps and potential cannibalization. In addition, they may attract new talent that would rather work for a pure play start-up than for an established brick-and-mortar company, (Afuah & Tucci 2001: 144-145). However, after the dotcom bubble burst this may no longer be the case as employees may have started to appreciate the stability of working in a well-established company more than before.

The major disadvantage for pure-play start-ups is that they lack the requisite complementary assets such as brand, client base and distribution channels, and they must develop them from scratch, which is often very expensive. Another disadvantage is the fact that the technology could be easy to imitate and thus any lead that the pure-plays could have over the incumbents can be difficult to protect. In order to overcome disadvantages, a new entrant may want to build capabilities that are extendable so that different or better values are offered to the same or different customers in order to generate revenues and profit. For example, Amazon has continually extended its capabilities from selling books, music and videos. Amazon's marginal cost of adding toys to its offering was lower than the cost to a new entrant of entering the toy retail market with the same scale, (Afuah & Tucci 2001: 145).

Branding and advertising: These are among the most crucial tasks a pure-play start-up has to take over. The mixture of traditional media and online marketing is usually the solution. However, successful e-commerce companies tend to rely heavily on non-traditional marketing channels rather than on traditional advertising. In addition to banner advertisements and affiliate programs, community building is a method that has proven successful for many. Having a simple but catchy universal resource locator punchy (URL) address and getting good search engine rankings are also fundamental (Fox 2000:13).

First-mover advantage vs. wait and learn: Since the new pure-play entrants are free from the burden of old ways of doing business and they have the technological capabilities that are required, they may have a better chance at first-mover advantages. If the firm is able to enter a market first, it can build a large network before its competitors come on the market. First-mover companies can also advertise and build brand loyalty before incumbents recover from dominant managerial logic and other problems related to incumbents, (Afuah & Tucci 2001: 145).

However, it must be kept in mind that the first-mover advantage depends on getting the fundamentals right (Silverstein *et al.* 2001: 7). In many cases, the first-mover companies make severe mistakes, and if they cannot adapt to the market or other conditions, they may fail, leaving the market for the second-mover companies to attract the former customers of the first-mover. Often, the second-movers can learn from the initial company's mistakes and avoid them. If the first mover makes a strategic mistake that upsets buyers, e.g. fails to deliver items on time or violates personal information privacy, the buyers will start to actively look for another e-tailer, (Turban et al. 2002: 109). Thus, companies should not aim to be the first mover at any cost.

The new entrant's manager's responsibility is to decide, when and how the company will create the complementary assets that are needed. The company may choose to develop its own assets or it may want to team up with an incumbent that already has them. If it chooses to develop its own assets, it should start early, since with assets such as brand reputation and network size the first-mover advantage is important, (Afuah & Tucci 2001: 146).

10.16 GENERAL MANAGERIAL ISSUES

Regardless of the business model, there are several managerial issues that an e-business has to consider. For instance, it is clear that all the factors that may have lead to failures should be taken into account. There are many issues to consider. For example, the overall business and revenue model including the product offering and pricing strategy should be well designed. In addition, issues such as logistics, order fulfilment, customer service and advertising strategies must also be carefully planned. Moreover, changes in technology, the regulatory environment, and the market environment must be constantly observed. The market considerations include, for example, general economic conditions, demographics and consumer preferences, (Turban et al. 2002: 108).

Creating a successful online business requires a lot of planning and effort. In addition to getting the fundamentals right, right timing and maybe even some luck is needed in order to convert an online start-up into a success.

Amazon.com is perhaps the company that is most closely linked with the e-business phenomenon. In its early years, investors believed that Amazon would be the success story of the decade and it was valued at more than $30 billion. However, quite soon it was realized that the initial expectations were over-optimistic. The purpose of the following case example is to briefly present the company, the company's two underlying business models and also company's value configuration.

10.17 CASE STUDY: BEST KNOWN E-COMMERCE COMPANY (AMAZON)

Amazon.com is the best known e-commerce site and the largest online bookstore in the world. It serves over 17 million customers in over 150 countries, and offers millions of items in categories such as books, music, DVDs, videos, toys, electronics, software, video games, and home improvement products. (Turban et al. 2002, 84-85). The company has grown at a tremendous rate with revenues rising from about $150 million in 1997 to $3.1 billion in 2001. The company began its operation in 1995 by selling books online. However, the rise in revenues has led to a commensurate increase in operating losses leaving the company with large deficit. The company made its first quarterly profit of $5.8 million in the fourth quarter of 2001. (BusinessWeek, 2002)

Amazon.com's greatest strengths may be that it was the first online bookseller backed up with substantial capital from its IPO, impressive customer service and a large selection of books. The key features of the Amzon.com according to Turban et al. (2002, 84-85) are easy browsing and searching, useful product information, reviews, recommendations and personalization, broad selection, low prices, 1-click order technology, secure payment systems, and efficient order fulfillment.

Three years after the establishment, the company started to diversify its product offering from books to CDs, videotapes etc., but the company still remained within a pure retailer model. The auction site introduced in the beginning of 1999 was the only product which did not fit to the pure retail model. In September 1999 Amazon added another new category to its business, the zShops, which offers an unlimited number of independent shops and products to its customers. This business model is different from retail model in which Amazon sells and controls the service to the customers. In zShops, Amazon acts as an intermediary where shops can sell their products to customers. Amazon charges merchants a $9.99 monthly fee and commissions of 1 percent to 5 percent in return for access to Amazon's large customer base. (Afuah & Tucci 2002: 158-175)

Afuah and Tucci (2002: 169) argue that Amazon.com appears unfocused in its value configuration, simultaneously pursuing both a value chain and a value network approach (these value configurations were discussed in chapter 0). The company has focused on value chain activities despite its apparent customer value as an intermediary. Amazon should be aware that network externalities that were not part of the pure retailer model are important aspects of the market-maker model. In market-maker model, the network size and quality and the size of the customer base are important for the success. Small network will lead to a vicious circle of customers and zShop participants, ie. merchants. If the zShop network is small, customers are not attracted, resulting in smaller customer network. Small customer network, in turn, does not attract merchants to participate in zShop, resulting in smaller zShop network.

The question is, will Amazon make money out of electronic retailer or intermediary business models. In late 2000, CEO Jeff Bezos announced that Amazon.com's oldest business, the US-based stores for books, music, and DVD/video titles was profitable (Turban et al. 2002:85). Revenues from the zShop services, which hit $225 million in the fourth quarter, carry gross margins of at least 45%, nearly twice Amazon's retail margins. The future will show how Amazon will succeed. The company's CEO Jeff Bezos admits that Amazon must continue to get many more small things right before he can build the huge, lasting company he's aiming for. (BusinessWeek, 2002)

SUMMARY

- The field of electronic commerce is fairly new, and thus the terminology used to describe the phenomenon is still developing. That is probably the reason why there are many different definitions for e-commerce in the literature.
- During the past five years, e-commerce markets have grown substantially. The growth rate has been even higher that expected. Estimates about future market size and value of B2C e-commerce still vary a lot. One estimate is that global B2C e-commerce transaction revenues will grow from EUR 88 in 2002 billion to EUR 361 billion until 2007.
- E-business has changed the way of conducting business and influenced the whole economy. It has had an impact on industry structures, competition, business processes, and value creation of the companies. Moreover, it has even created totally new business models. E-business has also shortened the traditional value chain of industries. Now, manufactures are able to sell directly to consumers and provide customer support online. Thus, the traditional intermediaries such as wholesalers and retailers can be eliminated from the value chain. However, new kinds of intermediaries are emerging and replacing the role of the traditional ones.
- E-commerce has given rise to new kinds of business models. In other words, it has created new ways to generate revenue for a company. The way value is created within organizations is also changing. However, many e-businesses use the traditional value chain, which was developed for the need of the manufacturing economy, as their primary value configuration. Nevertheless, the value network model, which is a model of the Internet economy, would be more suitable for their needs.
- The basic theories of competition in electronic business still remained unchanged but the rules of the competition are different from the traditional ones. E-markets tend to function more efficiently, and are closer to the situation of perfect competition. Some reasons for this are that in e-markets entry barriers are lower, and both buyers and sellers have more comprehensive information about each other and the merchandise. Also, since competition is now global, the competition in e-markets if often more intense than in traditional markets.
- There are several reasons for e-business failures. Some of these, such as fierce competition, consumer resistance and general economic conditions affect all the players. Other reasons are more company specific. In many cases, faulty business and revenue models have been identified as the main reason for failure. There have also been significant problems in, for example, usability of web sites, customer service, marketing, order fulfilment and financial management.

  Most of the identified reasons for e-business failures are the same as the general reasons for failure of any new businesses. When examining the general failure rates of all new businesses, e-business failures can be seen as a normal consolidation of a new industry. Nevertheless, in the beginning of the Internet business era the whole field was totally new for everyone and there were no established rules for doing business. Hundreds, even thousands of enthusiastic entrepreneurs were attracted to the field due to unrealistically high investor predictions and expectations. Everything happened very fast. In this light, the burst of the dotcom bubble was not surprising.

- Since the dotcom bubble burst, there has been a lot of discussion in the media about the future of e-commerce. It seems to be agreed upon that the era of e-commerce is by no means over. However, the Internet is no longer a fad: The online consumer population looks more and more like the mass market and online success will depend on all the same factors that have always driven business success, in addition to the ability to effectively use the new channel.
- It is hard to predict which Internet business models will be the most successful in the future and how they should be managed. For example, advertising cannot support all the businesses and thus many sites that provide content or services consider moving to pay-per-view model. However, the success depends on consumers' readiness to start paying for content and services that many consider free by nature. New business model variations and combinations are constantly emerging, as many are seeking new and more sustainable ways to make money on the Internet.
- Electronic retailing markets will evidently continue to grow. It is expected that in the future consumers are most likely to buy standard products, such as books and CDs, online. In our opinion, especially in these categories, only the products and services which are clearly cheaper for the consumer when bought online are the ones that will succeed. These already include, for example, leisure travel and internet banking services. However, the huge overall volume of necessities categories such as grocery and clothing will also make their online sales volume significant in the near future even though their online sales will still only represent a marginal percentage of the total amount spend on those products.
- Especially in physical product groups traditional brick-and-mortar companies who already possess valuable assets such as established supplier networks, well-known brands, and large customer bases have a clear advantage over new entrants. Pure-play online retailers have potential to succeed if they can build a strong brand and acquire a large enough customer base to become profitable. They may also succeed by concentrating on a certain small, niche market.
- Whatever the business model is, in order to succeed online the company needs to get the fundamentals right. The basic managerial issues cannot be forgotten. In addition, it must be kept in mind that the markets are still evolving and thus constant monitoring is needed to keep up with the evolvement of competition environment and consumer preferences.

REVIEW QUESTIONS

1. Discuss the use of digital signature in e-business transactions with the help of suitable examples.
2. What is environmental scanning? Explain the purpose of network security and fire-walls in e-business.

CHAPTER 11

Legal Issues for E-Business

11.1 E-BUSINESS

Broadly speaking, the term "e-business" refers to using the Internet for doing business.

11.1.1 How to Determine if a Company is Engaged in E-business

If a company carries out any of the points given below, then it can be said to be engaged in e-business.

- Communication with customers, clients or suppliers is via email.
- E-mails are sent to other businesses to order products and services.
- Products or services are sold via a website.
- The Web is used to find information, such as prices, phone numbers, reviews of products.
- The Web is used for research, such as the latest industry trends.
- Information about products and services are provided over a website.
- The website is used as a means of managing information in the business.
- The Internet is used for online banking and paying bills.

No level of e-business is necessarily better than any other level. Some businesses do not need a website but deal all day with other businesses and customers online via email and an e-marketplace. Other businesses have a website that helps them sell their products all around the world. It is up to each business to determine what level of e-business is right for them.

11.1.2 The Difference between E-business and E-commerce

The term e-commerce has a narrower meaning than e-business. It refers to using the Internet to order and pay for products or services. So e-commerce is a sub-set of e-business. E-commerce is when consumers order a product from a business and pay for it either when they receive the product or directly online at the time of ordering or when a business pays another business via its website for supplies.

E-commerce refers specifically to paying for goods and services, whereas e-business covers the full range of business activities that can take place or be assisted via e-mail or the Web.

11.1.3 Benefits of E-business

1. **Creates cost-savings and operati**onal efficiencies: Some businesses make a great deal 'of money from their websites through greatly increased sales and uptake of services. Many more benefit from the ability of an e-business plan, properly thought out and implemented, to minimize day-to-day costs and save staff time. Many companies still rely on purchasing and back-office systems that revolve around the fax machine, telephone, or even handwritten forms. Companies that have adopted e-business are reaping the advantages that come from replacing manual processes with automated, digital systems that provide fast, accurate, customer-centric experiences. This can lead to a range of efficiencies such as getting paid faster.
2. **Cost saving checklist:** The checklist given below can be used to identify the cost-saving centres and areas of efficiency gains that effective use of e-mail and a carefully planned website can offer.
    - **Providing information** - reduce staff time on the telephone with customers and suppliers by referring them to the website - also some telephone enquirers will be better informed as a result of referring to the site and therefore will take less time.
    - **Bookings and orders** - data entered into an online form with appropriate links into the organisation's database accounting system bypasses staff, freeing them to market and sell more tickets, memberships etc.
    - **Publishing/Printing** - reduce cost of outsourcing to printers and graphic designers for brochures, research, concert programmes.
    - **Photocopying** - reduce through-put and need for more and/or larger photocopiers.
    - **Faxing** - reduce cost and time involved in re-keying data and reduce errors in interpretation of poor quality originals, e.g. handwritten forms and poor quality faxes.
    - **Postage and handling** - reduce expense and time.
    - **Paper** - reduce the overall paper consumption and therefore cost.

- **Processing time** - streamline processing of forms, e.g. online membership applications and orders.
- **Account management** - an e-commerce solution reduces processing of accounts, reconciliation, banking and can improve cash-flow.
- **Communication and meeting costs** - using email groups can reduce phone calls, time consumed in arranging meetings, number of face-to-face meetings, cost of getting people to meetings

3. **Create additional revenue:** In the early days of the Web, some people sold websites to businesses promising they would generate large revenues from online sales. However, this actually, sometimes leading to extreme scepticism and unwillingness to use the Internet for business at all. Of course, the reality of the potential of websites is to provide another source of revenue, and this lies somewhere in the middle of these two extremes. For some, a website will not generate income directly; rather it supports their offline activities and contributes to meeting business goals and financial targets. Others reap considerable additional revenue from their website via selling information, products or services online.

   Some businesses are fortunate because they provide information, goods and services that users seem very willing to purchase online, such as travel, financial services, books, CDs, entertainment, and many items traditionally bought through mail-order catalogues. The Internet has provided many businesses with a whole new revenue stream at a relatively low cost.

4. **Reach more customers and markets:** One of the great benefits of the Web is that it can help broaden a firm's customer base at a relatively low cost. As more and more people gain access to the Internet and become confident Web users, the potential to expand customer-bases will increase proportionally.

   Effective use of e-mail and an appropriately designed and promoted website can attract new customers and open new markets for products and services by providing:

   - Affordable access to customers all over the world.
   - A means by which to communicate with people for who English is not their native language.
   - Access to products and services for people with a disability who may not have had access to them when distributed by traditional means – e.g. a shop-front.

   A number of online market places have been created that match suppliers and buyers. They work by creating a website featuring a common catalogue to which suppliers add their products, and from which buyers can search and select the best product. Joining an appropriate market place (often called e-marketplaces) as a supplier can provide cheap access to many more buyers than an average small business could hope to reach on its own.

5. **Improve marketing and promotions:** A well-designed and maintained website can be a highly effective promotional tool. This is not to say that promoting a business on the Web

is better or more effective than traditional forms of promotion. It is simply another promotional tool that should complement other forms of promotion.

A website provides some unique promotional potential because:

- It is visible to potential customers and suppliers 24 hours a day, seven days a week.
- There are no borders, so it is visible to potential customers wherever they are in the world.
- A great deal more information can be provided on a website than in a brochure.
- Products can be illustrated from multiple angles and animations can be used, allowing the user to turn an image of the product around, up and down, giving a better understanding of its advantages.
- It is very easy to collate and analyze information about those visiting and buying from the site and equally easy to change the promotional aspects to maximize their impact on sales.

6. **Meet the needs and expectations of customers and suppliers:** Increasingly today, the terms "available" and "accessible" to a business mean twenty-four hours a day, seven days a week access to information, products and services. Customers, suppliers and interested parties are not satisfied if they are restricted to the traditional opening hours of a business and will not be impressed if they cannot do such things as order items, book tickets or discover information for themselves in the comfort of their own homes and offices when it suits them.

   The expectations of online audiences will not diminish over time - they will only increase. For example, the increasing ability to provide video and sound online at premium quality and speed is likely to force many businesses into presenting information in multimedia format on their websites. This will raise the bar in terms of delivery methodology, content, structure and quality of online material. To fail to be online or to fail to provide a website that is user-friendly, informative, and up-to-date in every respect is to risk alienating web-enabled customers and suppliers and thereby lose their confidence and business.

7. **Concentrate on the things that matter:** One of the most important consequences of using the Internet in a business is that it can reduce the time staff spends carrying out administrative tasks, freeing them to concentrate on the things that really matter - servicing customers and increasing sales. Whether the things that matter are promoting the business, generating repeat business, managing customers and suppliers, chasing leads, or undertaking professional development, an e-business plan should minimise wasted time doing unproductive tasks.

   By shifting the emphasis of the role of staff from processing data and undertaking routine administrative work, to providing quality of service, seeking new customers and selling more products, a business is likely to make a fundamental improvement in staff satisfaction and sales figures.

8. **Make it easier for people to do business:** A website is an additional and unique tool for facilitating business. An effective use of e-mail and a website can make it easier for

customers, visitors, suppliers, distributors or associates to do business. It will be easier for people to do business with a company if it has a website that:

- Is quick and easy to navigate.
- Is customer-focused.
- Offers abundant relevant information – e.g. contact details.
- Provides numerous opportunities for two-way communication.
- Provides a variety of convenient ways of ordering and paying for information, products and services.

A website and e-mail address form another shop-front, helpdesk, outlet, channel, advertisement and contact point, through which a company can make its information, products and services available twenty four hours a day, seven days a week to the whole world. The success of the website as a business tool will ultimately depend on the appropriateness of its design, promotion and on-going maintenance and the extent to which the business embraces it. It will also rely on the imagination of staff in providing content and features on the site that will entice users and make it easy for them to do business.

9. **The cost of not being there:** The "cost" of **not** having a credible website or using email effectively can be measured in terms of lost opportunities to create more revenue and cut costs. Some of the costs of not being there (online) include:

   - Loss of customers to competitors who do have a good website and e-mail contact with customers.
   - Loss of potential revenue from online sales or uptake of services.
   - Mounting costs associated with existing inefficient office practices that an effective e-business plan could minimise.
   - Mounting costs associated with existing inefficient supply-chain management.
   - Loss of credibility as an innovative, forward-thinking business.

10. **Play on a level playing field:** The street location of a business, or the size and design of the building it is in, gives the physical visitor an immediate impression of the stature of the business. For some customers and clients, this first impression of company size is an important factor in determining whether they will even walk in the front door. However, the Web is a great leveller because there is no main shopping street or business address or hierarchy of web addresses on the Internet.

    Even when the Web visitor has entered a company's website, they cannot easily tell how big the business is at first glance. Without being deceptive, a small business can appear to be as large as any of its larger competitors, and large companies can appear to be as small as the corner shop.

    Website front doors are all on the same street and are the same size on the Web. This levelling effect can help neutralize any prejudices potential customers, clients or suppliers might have about the size of the company they prefer to deal with.

11. **Help meet business goals:** Businesses the world over develop business plans to provide direction for their business activities. Business plans generally cover areas such as: sales targets, marketing plans, staffing, competitor analysis, research and development and budgets.

    The Internet can be used to help businesses research their business plans and as a tool for achieving the aims of the plan. The Web provides a relatively cheap means of investigating competitors, testing out the market, entering new markets and seeking new strategic partners. A company's website can contribute to achieving increased sales and can be used to improve the management of relations with customers.

    There are numerous ways in which a website and clever use of email can help a company meet its business goals.

11.1.4 Planning to Meet Business Goals

Most businesses would not adopt a new business strategy, such as opening up a new office or shop, without first doing some very careful planning. Planning helps to ensure that precious time, money and energy invested in any new strategy are not wasted. Without good plans new ventures can easily go wrong, due to such things as poor timing, unreasonable expectations or even adopting the wrong approach in the first place. Good planning maximizes the benefits to a business of a new or expanded business venture and reduces the risk of things going wrong.

11.1.4.1 How to plan

The planning process needs to be managed well and involve the people who hold important roles in the business - or who provide important business advice to the business. For some very small businesses, the owner/operator may be the sole person to develop the e-business plan. But whether it is developed by one person or a team, the goal is to produce an e-business plan document and to implement a practical schedule for reviewing and updating it.

Managing the planning process is not difficult, but it does require a disciplined approach.

11.1.4.2 What to do

The person responsible for delivering the plan should establish:

- Who should be involved in the process – e.g. micro-businesses might have the owner and the accountant; larger organizations may have people from management, accounts, marketing, sales, technical, operations and possibly external advisors.
- The responsibilities of the planning team.
- What the plan is to include.
- What background research is required in order to produce the plan?
- The time-frame for delivering the plan.
- An internal communications plan to keep everyone informed about the plan.
- When and how the plan will be reviewed and updated.

11.1.4.3 Researching the opportunities

There are many ways the Internet can be used to help a business conduct its day-to-day business. When developing an e-business plan one must be sure to know what the possibilities are for a particular business so they can be incorporated into the planning.

11.1.4.4 Key planning issues to consider

Whoever is developing the e-business plan needs to consider the key issues in parallel because decisions made on one issue will often impact on other issues. The issues involved in planning are:

- Innovation and imagination
- Integration with existing office systems
- Developing a healthy e-business culture
- Security
- Knowledge management
- Estimating the budget

11.1.5 What level of e-business is right?

In the planning stage a firm should ask the question: 'What is the optimum level of e-business for us'? For one business there maybe nothing to be gained by doing anything more than simply using e-mail and banking online, whereas, for another business, the optimum level of e-business may be having a website with e-commerce facilities.

- Identify the aims of the e-business
- Identify the target audience
- Select the appropriate level of e-business

11.1.6 Writing an e-business plan

The e-business plan is a document that states the type and level of e-business that a business will engage in. There are e-business advisors who can help with it.

11.1.6.1 Building

This section explains how an organisation might approach the building of a website that will meet its needs. It raises and explains key technical content and design issues so that business owners, their staff and advisors can confidently brief technical experts about their e-business needs and manage those experts.

The main areas of this section are:

- Technical issues
- Choosing and preparing contents
- What is expected from the users
- Marketing your website

- Designing a website
- E-commerce - selling via a website
- Maintenance considerations
- Developing the website

11.1.6.2 Protection

As the Internet becomes an increasingly important tool for businesses, electronic security (e-security) has emerged as a major issue. Many businesses want to expand their use of the Internet but are not sure how to do so in a secure way. It is necessary to decide which strategies and processes are appropriate for a business's e-security needs.

- If a business is connected to the Internet, it is essential to ensure that business data, including customer information, is safe and that transactions are carried out securely. Otherwise, there is a risk of transactions being intercepted, privacy codes being breached, confidential information being taken or money being stolen.

11.1.6.3 Management

Like key aspects of any business, an e-business requires good management if it is to succeed. Just as people require managing, systems need to be maintained and budgets have to be monitored, any strategic use of the Internet by a business needs to be closely controlled. The major aspects of managing are:

- Who does the managing?
- Maintaining e-business systems
- Internal policies and guidelines
- Promoting the website
- Budgeting for maintenance
- Controlling the risks
- Legal issues
- Spam and ethical e-marketing

11.1.6.4 Improvement

Most businesses using the Internet as a business tool know that the technology and use of e-mail, e-commerce and just about everything to do with the Internet is always changing. So looking for ways to improve current uses of the Internet is necessary and makes sense.

This section provides suggestions for ways in which a business that already has a website and uses e-mail, can make even better use of the Internet. It contains:

- Information and resources on how to identify improvements in the way the Internet is used in a business.
- Information about some advanced uses of the Internet.

The major aspects of improving a business that already has a website and uses e-mail are the following:

- Evaluating the e-business
- Doing business with government online
- Procurement over the Internet
- Managing the supply-chain and logistics
- Putting the firm's catalogue online
- E-marketplaces
- Exporting

11.2 LEGAL ISSUES FOR E-BUSINESS

The legal aspect of e-business is all about managing risks. It is important to ensure that the content of a website is accurate and complies with current laws. It is also important to regularly review the website once it is up and running to ensure that it continues to comply. Some of the important general legal issues affecting e-business are listed below:

- Privacy laws
- Defamation
- Taxation and GST
- Contracts
- Terms and conditions
- Trade practices
- Intellectual property
- Copyright
- Trade marks
- Confidential information
- Digital signatures
- Security
- Jurisdiction
- Disability discrimination

Legal problems affect all parts of electronic transactions in e-commerce. The main importance is given to issues related to electronic signatures, security of payments and the validity of a contract concluded by electronic means. Other issues, such as those related to e-invoices, taxation/customs and the obligation to register authorisation to provide cross-border on-line services are also considered.

As the main important issues relate to new e-commerce initiatives (electronic signature, security of payments, and validity of contracts), companies might have to modify their commercial policy in order to comply with legal provisions. These issues relate to the fact that enterprises admit that they might not be familiar with online payment systems and contracts or that consumers do not trust the use of electronic payments over the Internet. Also, companies complain about the lack of common standards for the implementation of e-signatures and e-invoices.

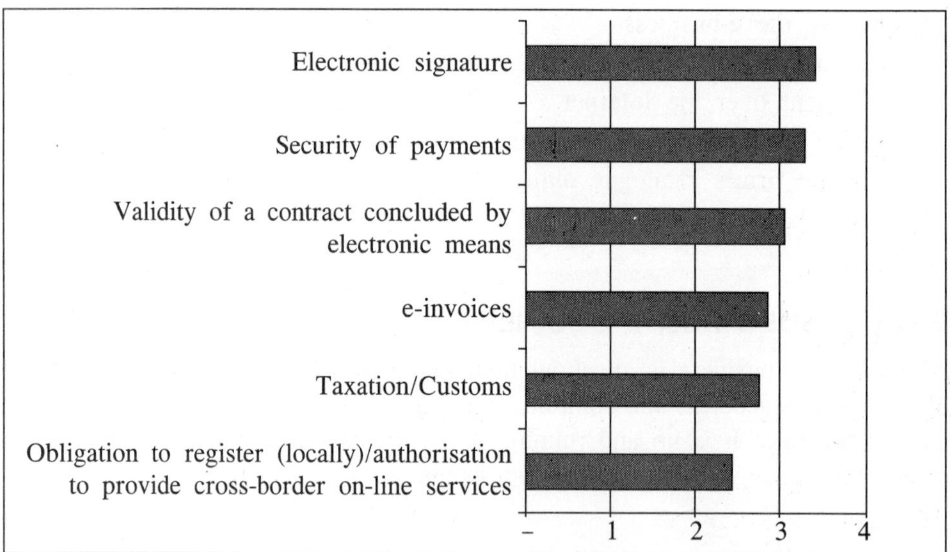

Fig. 11.1: ***Legal issues regarding e-commerce transactions***

11.2.1 Importance of Ethics on the Internet

In a society where legal and ethical limits are pushed to the maximum one may wonder why we even ask about ethics and values on the Web. The answer is that they have a considerable effect on a business.

11.2.2 Business Ethics

The Internet is growing and continually evolving. As such, it is necessary to consider legal and Internet marketing ethical issues of B2B & B2C. Whatever is written and published online will be there forever. Imagine the billions upon billions of text information pages that are and will be stored for a long time. There is even a site where you can check out archives of other websites and view pages that were created at their inception. Additionally, video, films, movies, and audio in various application formats are also viewable.

Now, with the new wireless web mail from cell phones and other PDA communication devices, the Internet will affect more lives than ever before. Security and privacy concerns along with e-business regulatory issues will become more prevalent. It will become more difficult to determine who one can trust online, with all the unethical, illegal, and Internet marketing and online advertising frauds and E-business e-mail scams.

11.3 IMPORTANT ETHICAL E-BUSINESS LEGAL ISSUES

A person writing copy and maintaining a client's e-business or e-commerce website should consider the following consumer privacy and legal matters.

What is said when copywriting and publishing for a client is a reflection of how they are viewed by the rest of the world. Negative or defamatory articles published about various people and companies on other websites, if not properly researched, could possibly have legal consequences of libel that can stretch across countries. Additionally, one should consider carefully what is published on Web logs or Blogs for short. A blog is simply a website where daily, weekly, or monthly personal or corporate thoughts, ideas, and happenings can be published and shared with others. Interaction with readers can be set up in the form of comments from visitors.

If webmasters perform unethical optimization of a client's website, it could have long lasting negative business consequences, which initially may seem insignificant, for that client and which cannot be easily repaired. People are getting savvier online and are able to see through the e-business false advertising. It is just a matter of time until legal action is taken.

11.3.1 Intellectual Property

When dealing with ethics in a B2B company and with B2C clients there is a major degree of trust and responsibility that is imparted to a person or group that maintains the web site. It is very important from both an ethical values based e-business and legal B2B and B2C perspective to make sure that the written words and what is portrayed about a company are factual. Because issues arise that involve marketing ethics and the importance of understanding a business for Internet marketing issues and advertising purposes, there are potential areas for revealing trade secrets or intellectual property if proper B2B ethical behaviour is not followed.

E-mail correspondence should be private and confidential. While certain individuals might not see any harm quoting on the Web from an e-mail sent, it is always advisable to get a person's consent prior to publishing anything. While the person might give consent, they might not realize the full implications, online privacy issues, or impact of having it published online. Therefore, it would be wise to consider it very carefully before even asking for their approval.

11.3.2 Ethical Issues in e-Business and Challenges for Implementing e-Commerce

There are many legal and web site regulatory issues involved. Electronic copyright, e-commerce, credit/cash policies, international trade, tariffs, privacy, digital media offers, and security are a few of the items to be considered.

11.3.3 Trust, Importance of Ethics

- The ethics of Internet marketing
- E-business legal, ethical, and regulatory issues with B2B and B2C
- Marketing on B2B website
- Ethics B2B copyright law
- Ethical B2B practices
- Marketing ethics issues
- B2B vs. B2C legal

- E-commerce Ethical Facts site:.gov
- Ethics In Advertising site:.gov
- Advertising And Marketing On The Internet - Honesty

11.3.4 E-mail Marketing

E-mail has a number of regulations implemented by the government. Email marketing View IAB, Interactive Advertising Bureau Standards and Guidelines – e-Mail Guidelines. Share your comments at unsolicited b2b and b2c emails "The Email Junk Mail Trash Heap" Pop up ads, email, instant messengers, consumer privacy information, and online security threats. Ads that make you double click at a wrong location and the very click installs some sort of ad ware, spy ware, or mal ware on your computer.

11.3.5 Consumers Survey Scams and Hoaxes

One should beware of Phone "survey" scams, "charity" appeals for chain mail, online security, and spam. Another area that can be dangerous is "The Never-Ending Hoax Viruses".

11.3.6 Copyright Infringement

There are sites that copy a website's text (legal issues) or name while trying to advertise some other item they are selling.

11.3.7 Website Issues

There can be unethical redirects to other pages with completely different information than what was shown in the search results. For example a site may no longer be available because of this type of spamming ethical issues in a B2C website.

11.3.8 Advertising and Keywords Scams

Unethical spyware/adware companies are promoting themselves as: "get to the top of Google, Yahoo, and MSN search guaranteed for your keywords." These companies are using the term "Search Engine Data Merging." Spy ware and ad ware is installed on some users' computers, then they sell keywords to professionals for thousands of dollars a year. This is a huge money making scam. The company is using various names: Search Elevators, Link Positions, Window Billboards Network, Win speed Network, Real Positions Network, Keywords Guru, and even a new search engine labeled Red Zee Search.

11.3.9 Identity Theft and Internet Fraud

Identity theft is a major problem; this issue is related to online B2C ethical business issues and legal issues.

11.3.10 Domain Name Registration Issues and Scams

Domain name registration is another area online where ethics have been thrown out. Certainly there are some grey areas for someone to be registering a domain name that is close to some other corporate identity's name. But, many of these individuals and corporations that register domain names, in the same country and other countries, that are near to, or similar to the spellings of others, are registering the names to infringe upon the trademarks and brands of other corporations and organizations.

11.3.11 Domain Name Disputes

The use of a name can be legal for many parties whether they have a trademark or not. Two or more parties may have the same trademark in different jurisdictions, may have the same trademark in the same jurisdiction but in different industries, or may legally use a name without owning a trademark to it. It is not necessary to own a trademark, to use a particular name. This being the case, domain name registration on a first-come, first-serve basis is the most logical. If two (or more) parties have the right to use a name (even if one has a trademark and the other does not), neither party should be given preference in using that name.

With the proliferation of world wide domains, name registrars from all countries around the globe, in which many of these countries, such as China do not even maintain the same social/ethical value systems, makes it even more difficult to protect corporate trademarks, copyrights, and intellectual property rights. Additionally, because many of these countries have their own rules and regulations for bringing domain disputes in which the complainant bears the legal burden of proof for their own claims in the native language of the country (as opposed to English), and differs greatly from that of the ICANN, Internet Corporation for Assigned Names and Numbers, registration and domain dispute resolution policies, it will become increasingly difficult to protect corporate identities on the Internet.

11.4 DEFINITION OF ETHICAL ISSUES IN B2B

Ethics in B2B and B2C is defined as "A set of principles of right conduct" and "The rules or standards governing the conduct of a person or the conduct of the members of a profession."

11.4.1 Honesty, Integrity and Trust

"Honesty is the best policy," when dealing with customers and clients. Not following this policy rebounds time and time again.

One should not be short sighted. If a company sees a way o make fast money it should ask whether this is really the proper way to go about doing something. Businesses have been guilty of short sightedness and have made easy money at the expense of their integrity and consumers' wallets, which has led to loss of customers in the long run.

One should remember that when working with clients, that they trust the website. This should not be valued lightly. They are placing their trust in the firm and relying on the website to help them out on the Net. Customers will appreciate the truth.

11.4.2 Personal and Consumer Rights

Companies consider data protection a very important issue, followed by privacy and data retention. It is important that personal and consumer rights are consistent, with better and harmonized information on the regulatory framework for these issues in e-business. Legal information for commercial and technological advice is needed.

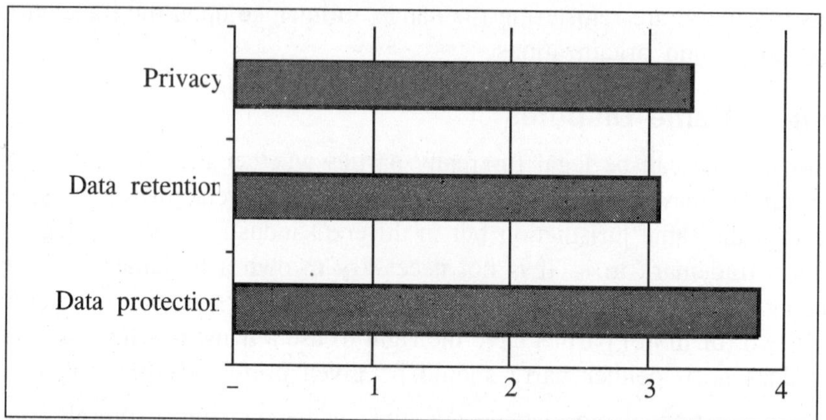

Fig. 11.2: ***Legal issues regarding personal and consumer rights***

11.4.3 Liabilities

Differences in the legal validity of electronic contracts, registration requirements, appropriate action towards conflict resolution and appropriate actions towards consumer protection and complaints all have the same degree of importance.

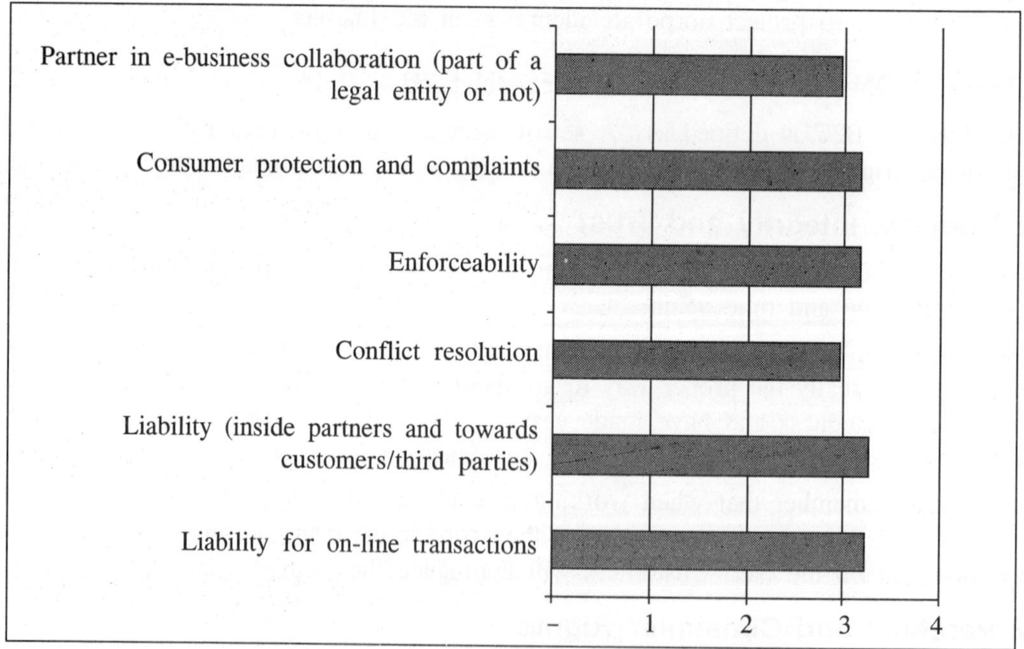

Fig. 11.3: ***Legal issues regarding liabilities***

11.4.5 Intellectual Property Rights (IPR)

In this area, importance is given to issues related to the protection of copyrights and the usage of licenses. In order to exploit the potential of e-business and market opportunities, a business needs to count on a long term strategy, which currently it cannot.

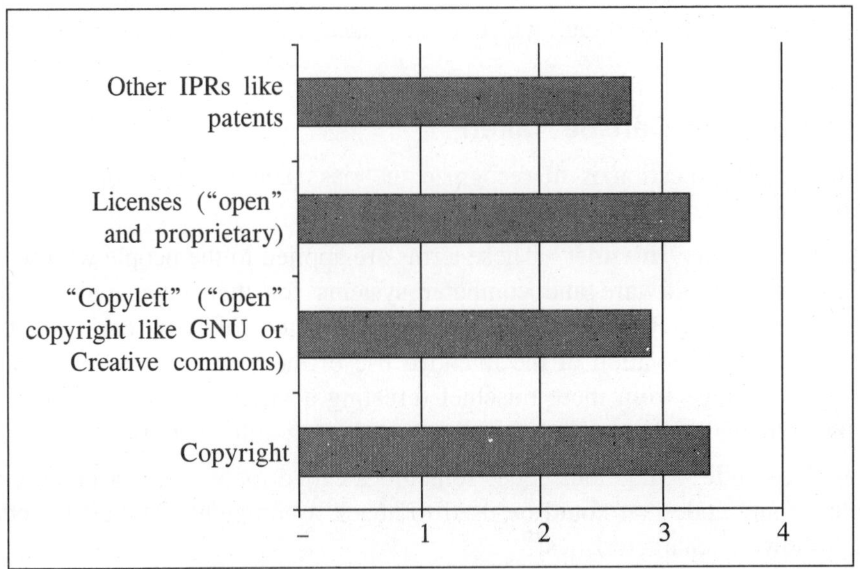

Fig. 11.4: ***Legal issues regarding IPR***

11.5 CYBER SECURITY

Cyber security standards are security standards which enable organizations to practice safe security techniques in order to minimize the number of successful cyber security attacks. These guides provide general outlines as well as specific techniques for implementing cyber security. For certain specific standards, **cyber security certification** by an accredited body can be obtained. There are many advantages to obtaining certification including the ability to get cyber security insurance.

11.5.1 What is Cyber Security?

Today it seems that everything relies on computers and the Internet - communication (e-mail, cell phones), entertainment (digital cable, mp3s), transportation (car engine systems, airplane navigation), shopping (online stores, credit cards), medicine (equipment, medical records), and the list goes on. A lot in person's daily life relies on computers and their personal information is stored either on their own computer or on someone else's system.

Cyber security involves protecting that information by preventing, detecting, and responding to attacks.

11.5.2 The Risks

There are many risks, some more serious than others. Among these dangers are viruses erasing the entire system, someone breaking into a system and altering files, someone using another person's computer to attack others, or someone stealing credit card information and making unauthorized purchases. Unfortunately, there is no 100% guarantee that even with the best precautions some of these things will not take place, but there are steps that can be taken to minimize the chances.

11.5.3 Measures that Can be Taken

The first step in protection is to recognize the risks and become familiar with some of the terminology associated with them.

- **Hacker/Attacker/Intruder** - These terms are applied to the people who seek to exploit weaknesses in software and computer systems for their own gain. Although their intentions are sometimes fairly benign and motivated solely by curiosity, their actions are typically in violation of the intended use of the systems they are exploiting. The results can range from mere mischief (creating a virus with no intentionally negative impact) to malicious activity (stealing or altering information).
- **Malicious code** - Malicious code, sometimes called malware, is a broad category that includes any code that could be used to attack a computer. Malicious code can have the following characteristics:
  - It might require the user to actually do something before it infects the computer. This action could be opening an e-mail attachment or going to a particular web page.
  - Some forms propagate without user intervention and typically start by exploiting software vulnerability. Once the victim's computer has been infected, the malicious code will attempt to find and infect other computers. This code can also propagate via e-mail, websites, or network-based software.
  - Some malicious code claims to be one thing while in fact doing something different behind the scenes. For example, a program that claims it will speed up your computer may actually be sending confidential information to a remote intruder. Viruses and worms are examples of malicious code.
- **Vulnerability** - In most cases, vulnerabilities are caused by programming errors in software. Attackers might be able to take advantage of these errors to infect a computer, so it is important to apply updates or patches that address known vulnerabilities.

11.6 CYBER CRIME

- The main issue is to build trust for consumers so that there are better e-market perspectives and wider opportunities. The importance of showing and ensuring consumers a high level of consumer protection cannot be underestimated. However, constant threats, such as unsolicited commercial e-mails, do not reassure customers. The issue of fighting cyber crime also constrains the practical aspects for advertising and commercial practices in e-commerce. There is a need to balance consumer rights and practical lawful advertisement for companies.

11.7 CONVENTIONAL CRIME

Crime is a social and economic phenomenon and is as old as human society. Crime is a legal concept and is punishable by law. Crime or an offence is "a legal wrong that can be followed by criminal proceedings which may result into punishment." The hallmark of criminality is that, it is breach of the criminal law. According to Lord Atkin "the criminal quality of an act cannot be discovered by reference to any standard but one: is the act prohibited with penal consequences".

A crime may be said to be any conduct accompanied by act or omission prohibited by law and consequential breach of which is visited by penal consequences.

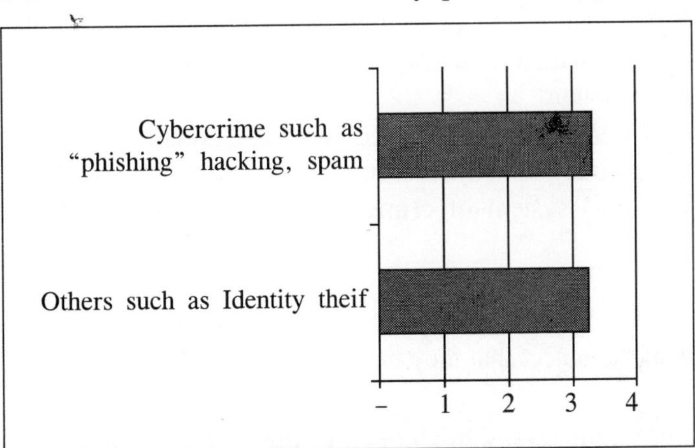

Fig. 11.5: ***Legal issues regarding cyber crime***

11.8 DISTINCTION BETWEEN CONVENTIONAL AND CYBER CRIME

There is apparently no distinction between cyber and conventional crime. However on introspection we may say that there exists a fine line of demarcation between them. The demarcation lies in the involvement of the medium in cases of cyber crime. The *sine qua non* for cyber crime is that there should be an involvement, at any stage, of the virtual cyber medium.

11.8.1 Reasons for Cyber Crime

The Concept of Law has said 'human beings are vulnerable so rule of law is required to protect them'. Applying this to the cyberspace we may say that computers are vulnerable so rule of law is required to protect and safeguard them against cyber crime. The reasons for the vulnerability of computers may be said to be:

1. **Capacity to store data in a comparatively small space:** The computer has the unique characteristic of being able to store data in a very small space. This makes it much easier for a person to remove or derive information either through physical or virtual medium.
2. **Easy to access:** The problem encountered in guarding a computer system from unauthorised access is that there is every possibility of a breach, not due to human error, but due to the complex technology. By secretly implanting logic bombs, key loggers that can steal access codes, advanced voice recorders; retina imagers etc. that can fool biometric systems and bypass firewalls an unauthorised user can get past many a security system.
3. **Complex:** Computers work on operating systems and these operating systems in turn are composed of millions of codes. The human mind is fallible and it is not possible that there might not be a lapse at any stage. The cyber criminals take advantage of these lacunae and penetrate into the computer system.
4. **Negligence:** Negligence is very closely connected with human conduct. It is therefore very probable that while protecting the computer system there might be some negligence, which in turn allows a cyber criminal to gain access and control over the computer system.
5. **Loss of evidence:** Loss of evidence is a very common and obvious problem as all the data are routinely destroyed. Further collection of data outside the territorial extent also paralyses this system of crime investigation.

11.8.2 Cyber Criminals

Cyber criminals can be considered in various groups/categories. This division may be justified on the basis of the object that they have in their mind. The categories of cyber criminals are given below:

1. **Children and adolescents in the age group of 6 – 18 years:** The simple reason for this type of delinquent behaviour pattern in children is mostly due to the inquisitiveness to know and explore the things. Another cognate reason may be to prove that they are outstanding compared to other children in their group. The he reasons may even be psychological, e.g. the Bal Bharati (Delhi) case was the outcome of harassment of the delinquent by his friends.
2. **Organised hackers:** These kinds of hackers mostly come together to fulfil certain objectives. The reason may be to fulfil their political bias, fundamentalism, etc. Pakistan is said to have some of the best quality hackers in the world. They mainly target the Indian government sites with the purpose of fulfilling their political objectives.
3. **Professional hackers/crackers:** Their work is motivated by the colour of money. These kinds of hackers are mostly employed to hack the sites of a company's rivals and get credible, reliable and valuable information. Further they are even employed

to crack the system of the employer basically as a measure to make it safer by detecting the loopholes.

4. **Discontented employees:** This group includes those people who have been either sacked by their employer or are dissatisfied with their employer. To avenge themselves, they normally hack the system of their employer.

11.8.3 Mode and Manner of Committing a Cyber Crime

1. **Unauthorized access to computer systems or networks - Hacking:** This kind of offence is normally referred as hacking in the generic sense. However, to avoid any confusion we will not interchangeably use the word hacking for 'unauthorized access' as the latter has wide connotations.
2. **Theft of information contained in electronic form:** This includes information stored in computer hard disks, removable storage media etc. Theft may be either by appropriating the data physically or by tampering with them through the virtual medium.
3. **Email bombing:** This kind of activity refers to sending large numbers of e-mails to the victim, who may be an individual or a company or even mail servers, thereby ultimately resulting in the victim's system crashing.
5. **Data diddling:** This kind of an attack involves altering raw data just before a computer processes it and then changing it back after the processing is completed. **Salami attacks:** This kind of crime is normally prevalent in financial institutions or is used for the purpose of committing financial crimes. An important feature of this type of offence is that the alteration is so small that it would normally go unnoticed, e.g. in the Ziegler case, wherein a logic bomb was introduced in the bank's system, which deducted 10 cents from every account and deposited it in a particular account.
6. **Denial of service attack:** The computer of the victim is flooded with more requests than it can handle which causes it to crash. Distributed denial of service (DDoS) attack is also a type of denial of service attack, in which the offenders are large in number and widespread, e.g. Amazon, Yahoo.
7. **Virus/Worm attacks:** Viruses are programs that attach themselves to a computer or a file and then circulate themselves to other files and to other computers on a network. They usually affect data on a computer, either by altering or deleting them. Worms, unlike viruses do not need the host to attach themselves to. They merely make functional copies of themselves and do this repeatedly till they eat up all the available space on a computer's memory. E.g. love bug virus, which affected at least 5% of the computers in the world. The losses were accounted to be $10 million. The world's most famous worm was the Internet worm let loose on the Internet by Robert Morris sometime in 1988. It almost brought development of the Internet to a complete halt.
8. **Logic bombs:** These are event dependent programs. This implies that these programs are created to do something only when a certain event (known as a trigger event)

occurs. E.g. some viruses may be termed as logic bombs because they lie dormant all through the year and become active only on a particular date (like the *Chernobyl virus*).

9. **Trojan attacks:** This term has its origin in the word 'Trojan horse'. In the software field this means an unauthorized program, which passively gains control over another's system by representing itself as an authorised program. The most common form of installing a Trojan is through e-mail. E.g. a Trojan was installed in the computer of a *lady film director* in the U.S. while chatting. The cyber criminal through the web cam installed in the computer obtained her nude photographs and further harassed the lady.
10. **Internet time thefts:** Normally in these kinds of thefts the Internet surfing hours of the victim are used up by another person. This is done by gaining access to the login ID and the password, e.g. *Colonel Bajwa's case*- the Internet hours were used up by another person. This was perhaps one of the first reported cases related to cyber crime in India. However this case made the police infamous as to their lack of understanding of the nature of cyber crime.
11. **Web jacking:** This term is derived from the term hi jacking. In these kinds of offences the hacker gains access and control over the website of another person. He may even mutilate or change the information on the site. This may be done for fulfilling political objectives or for money. E.g. recently the site of the Ministry of Information Technology (MIT) was hacked by Pakistani hackers and some obscene matter was placed therein. Further the site of the Mumbai crime branch was also web jacked. Another case of web jacking is that of the *'gold fish'* case. In this case the site was hacked and the information pertaining to gold fish was changed. Further a sum of US $1 million was demanded as ransom. Thus web jacking is a process whereby control over the site of another is made backed by some consideration for it.

11.8.4 Classification

The subject of cyber crime may be broadly classified under the following three groups:

1. Against individuals
   - their person
   - the property of an individual
2. Against an organization
   - The government
   - A firm, company, group of individuals
3. Against society at large

The following are the crimes, which can be committed against the above groups:

Against individuals

- Harassment via e-mails
- Cyber-stalking
- Dissemination of obscene material
- Defamation
- Unauthorized control/access over a computer system
- Indecent exposure
- E-mail spoofing
- Cheating and fraud

Against individual property

- Computer vandalism
- Transmitting a virus
- Netrespass
- Unauthorized control/access over a computer system
- Intellectual property crimes
- Internet time thefts

Against an organization

- Unauthorized control/access over a computer system
- Possession of unauthorized information
- Cyber terrorism against a government organization
- Distribution of pirated software etc.

Against society at large

- Pornography (basically child pornography)
- Polluting the youth through indecent exposure
- Trafficking
- Financial crimes
- Sale of illegal articles
- Online gambling
- Forgery

The above mentioned offences are discussed in brief below.

1. **Harassment via e-mails:** Harassment through e-mails is not a new concept. It is very similar to harassment through letters. Former boy/girl friends constantly sending e-mails, often emotionally blackmailing or threatening the other person is a very common type of harassment.
2. **Cyber-stalking:** The Oxford dictionary defines stalking as "pursuing stealthily". Cyber stalking involves following a person's movements across the Internet by

posting messages (sometimes threatening) on the bulletin boards frequented by the victim, entering the chat-rooms frequented by the victim, constantly bombarding the victim with e-mails etc.

3. **Dissemination of obscene material/indecent exposure/pornography (often child pornography):** Pornography on the net can take various forms. It may include the hosting of a web site containing these prohibited materials, use of computers for producing these obscene materials, downloading obscene materials through the Internet. These obscene matters may cause harm to the mind of the adolescents and tend to deprave or corrupt their minds. Two known cases of pornography are the *Delhi Bal Bharati case* and the *Bombay case* wherein a Swiss couple used to force slum children into posing for obscene photographs. The Mumbai police later arrested them.
4. **Defamation:** This is an act of imputing any person with intent to lower the person in the estimation of the right-thinking members of society generally, or to cause him to be shunned or avoided or to expose him to hatred, contempt or ridicule. Cyber defamation is not different from conventional defamation except for the involvement of a virtual medium. The mail account of the victim can be hacked and mails sent from his/her account to other persons regarding his/her personal affairs, with intent to defame him.
5. **Unauthorized control/access over a computer system:** This activity is commonly referred to as hacking. The Indian law has however given a different connotation to the term hacking, so we will not use the term "unauthorized access" interchangeably with the term "hacking" to prevent confusion as the term used in the Act of 2000 is much wider than hacking.
6. **E-mail spoofing:** A spoofed e-mail is one, which misrepresents its origin. It shows its origin to be different from which actually it originates and they can often contain a virus. An example is that of a graduate student at Purdue University in Indiana, who was arrested for threatening to detonate a nuclear device in the college campus. The alleged e-mail was sent from the account of another student to the vice president for student services. However the mail was traced to be sent from the account of the spoofer.
7. **Computer vandalism:** Vandalism means deliberately destroying or damaging the property of another. Thus computer vandalism may include any kind of physical harm done to the computer of any person. These acts may take the form of the theft of a computer, some part of a computer or a peripheral attached to the computer or causing physical damage to a computer or its peripherals.
8. **Transmitting virus/worms:** This topic has been adequately dealt with above.
9. **Intellectual property crimes/Distribution of pirated software:** Intellectual property consists of a number of rights. Any unlawful act by which the owner is deprived completely or partially of his rights is an offence. The common forms of IPR violation are software piracy, copyright infringement, trademark and service mark violation, theft of computer source code, etc.

The Hyderabad Court in a land mark judgement has convicted three people and sentenced them to six months imprisonment and a fine of Rs. 50,000 each for unauthorized copying and selling of pirated software.

10. **Cyber terrorism against government organizations:** At this juncture it is necessary to distinguish between cyber terrorism and cyber crime. Despite the fact that both are criminal acts, a cyber crime is generally a domestic issue, which may have international consequences, however cyber terrorism is a global concern, which has domestic as well as international consequences. The common form of these terrorist attacks on the Internet is by distributed denial of service attacks, hate websites and hate e-mails, attacks on sensitive computer networks, etc. Technology savvy terrorists are using 512-bit encryption, which is next to impossible to decrypt. Recent examples are: *Osama Bin Laden*, the *LTTE*, the attack on *America's army deployment system* during the Iraq war.

    Cyber terrorism may be defined as: "*the premeditated use of disruptive activities, or the threat thereof, in cyber space, with the intention to further social, ideological, religious, political or similar objectives or to intimidate any person in furtherance of such objectives*"

    Another definition to cover every act of cyber terrorism is given below.

    A terrorist is a person who indulges in wanton killing of persons or in violence or in disruption of services or means of communications essential to the community or in damaging property with the view to:

    1. *Instilling fear in the public or any section of the public*
    2. *Adversely affecting the harmony between different religious, racial, lingual or regional groups, castes or communities*
    3. *Coercing or overawing the government established by law*
    4. *Endangering the sovereignty and integrity of the nation*

    A cyber terrorist is a person who uses the computer system as a means or ends to achieve the above objectives. Every act done in pursuance thereof is an act of cyber terrorism.

11. **Trafficking:** Trafficking may assume different forms. It may be trafficking in drugs, human beings, arms weapons etc. These forms of trafficking are going unchecked because they are carried on under pseudonyms. A racket was busted in Chennai where drugs were being sold under the pseudonym of honey.

12. **Fraud and cheating:** Online fraud and cheating is one of the most lucrative business that is growing today in cyber space. It may assume different forms. Some of the cases of online fraud and cheating that have come to light are those pertaining to credit card crimes, contractual crimes, offering jobs, etc.

    Recently the *Court of Metropolitan Magistrate Delhi* found a 24-year-old engineer working in a call centre guilty of fraudulently gaining the details of Campa's credit card and buying a television and a cordless phone from the Sony website. Metropolitan magistrate Gulshan Kumar convicted one Azim for cheating under IPC, but did not send him to jail. Instead, Azim was asked to furnish a personal bond of Rs 20,000, and was released on a year's probation.

11.8.5 Statutory Provisions

The Indian parliament considered it necessary to give effect to the resolution by which the General Assembly adopted the Model Law on Electronic Commerce adopted by the United Nations Commission on Trade Law. As a consequence of which the Information Technology Act 2000 was passed and enforced on 17th May 2000. The preamble of this Act states its objective to legalise e-commerce and further amend the Indian Penal Code of 1860, the Indian Evidence Act of 1872, the Banker's Book Evidence Act of 1891 and the Reserve Bank of India Act of 1934. The basic purpose to incorporate the changes in these Acts is to make them compatible with the Act of 2000, so that they may regulate and control the affairs of the cyber world in an effective manner.

The Information Technology Act deals with the various cyber crimes dealt with above. The important sections are Ss. 43,65,66,67. Section 43 in particular deals with the unauthorised access, unauthorised downloading, virus attacks or any contaminant that causes damage, disruption, denial of access, interference with the service availed by a person. This section provides for a fine up to Rs. 1 Crore by way of remedy. Section 65 deals with '*tampering with computer source documents*' and provides for imprisonment up to 3 years or a fine, which may extend up to 2 years or both. Section 66 deals with '*hacking with computer system*' and provides for imprisonment up to 3 years or fine, which may extend up to 2 years or both. Further section 67 deals with publication of obscene material and provides for imprisonment up to a term of 10 years and also with fine up to Rs. 2 lakhs.

11.9 PREVENTION OF CYBER CRIME

Prevention is always better than the cure. It is always better to take certain precautions while operating on the net. A person should make them part of their cyber life. Sailesh Kumar Zarkar, technical advisor and network security consultant to the Mumbai Police Cyber crime Cell advocates the 5P mantra for online security: *Precaution, Prevention, Protection, Preservation and Perseverance.* A netizen should keep in mind the following:

1. To prevent cyber stalking one should avoid disclosing any personal information. This is as good as disclosing one's identity to strangers in a public place.
2. One should always avoid sending any photograph online particularly to strangers and chat friends as there have been incidents of misuse of the photographs.
3. The latest and most up date anti virus software should be installed to guard against virus attacks.
4. Back up volumes should always be maintained so that one does not suffer data loss in case of virus contamination.

5. Credit card numbers should not be sent to any site that is not secured, to guard against frauds.
6. Parents should always keep a watch on the sites that their children are accessing to prevent any kind of harassment or depravation in children.
7. It is better to use a security programme that gives control over the cookies and send information back to the site as leaving the cookies unguarded might prove fatal.
8. Web site owners should watch traffic and check any irregularity on the site. Putting host-based intrusion detection devices on servers may do this.
9. Use of firewalls may be beneficial.
10. Web servers running public sites must be physically separate protected from internal corporate network.

Adjudication of a cyber crime: On the directions of the Bombay High Court the Central Government has by a notification dated 25.03.03 decided that the Secretary to the Information Technology Department in each state by designation would be appointed as the AO for each state.

11.10 LEGAL PROBLEMS OR LEGAL INSECURITIES DRIVERS

Basically, legal problems and legal insecurities result from:

- **Not enough legal advice in many contracts:** No legal practices have been established, for the kind of administrative or court practices. Also, there is lack of legal information for legal aspects related to workers. To overcome this barrier some companies contract a professional legal advisor. There is also a lack of professionals specialized in e-business/e-commerce law.
- **Fear due to ignorance, and fear to give out prices openly:** To overcome this kind of problem, some companies create a package of supply services, so consumers can choose between a selective set of options.
- **Lack of awareness of the legal framework:** This is a recurrent problem and evolves into the fact that most of the mentioned legal issues are perceived as legal business barriers, although in reality they are "practical logistics" e-business barriers. The lack of awareness of these legal practices, in addition to the lack of trust that consumers have, has created a wider perception of "distrust", consequently raising a direct barrier to e-business. There are still many legal gaps and grey areas. Some concerns are related to taxes, VAT, domain registration, brands, copyright and data confidentiality abroad.

To overcome these gaps, companies prefer to compensate the client/consumer when something goes wrong and solve the problem once the customer is satisfied. They absorb the costs when a problem occurs and they base adjust logistics or sales management in order to remedy the procedures and avoid further similar problems. To avoid further problems, contracting legal advisors or training an employee or the owner with reference to legal matters is advisable. In addition, the impact of consumer mismanagement is high, because having problems with consumers might evolve into a big issue regarding the company's image, affecting future sales. This could cause a lot of damage. Information over the Internet spreads very fast.

Figure 11.6 lists the sources currently used for being informed about relevant legal issues for e-businesses.

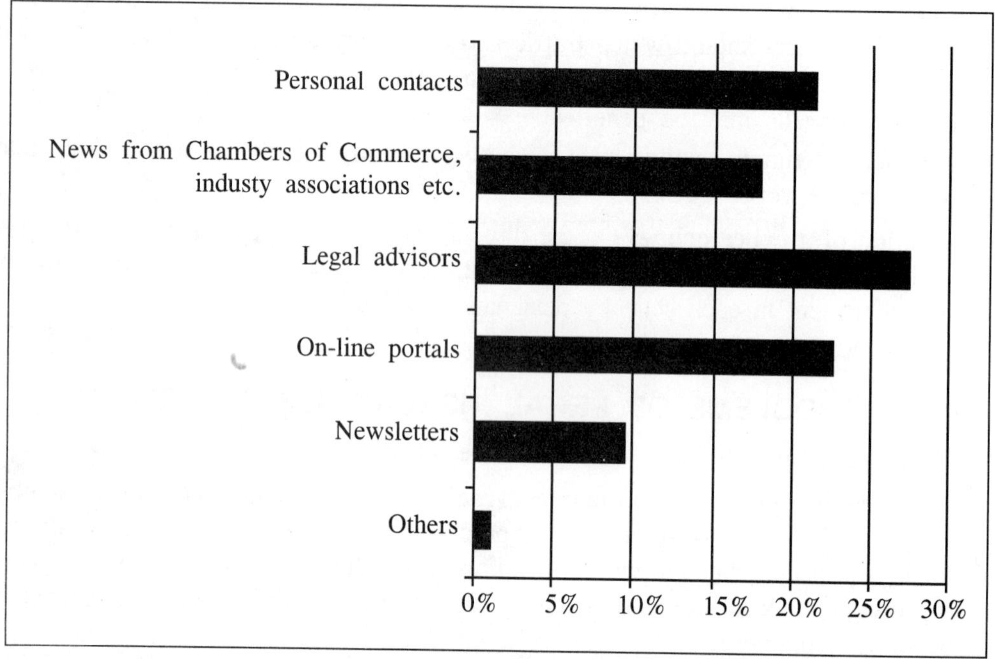

Fig. 11.6: ***Sources of legal information for e-businesses***

About 84% currently use on-line tools for getting information about relevant legal issues for e-businesses. Others prefer to contract a legal advisor, as they felt the need to have the information interpreted by a professional in the field.

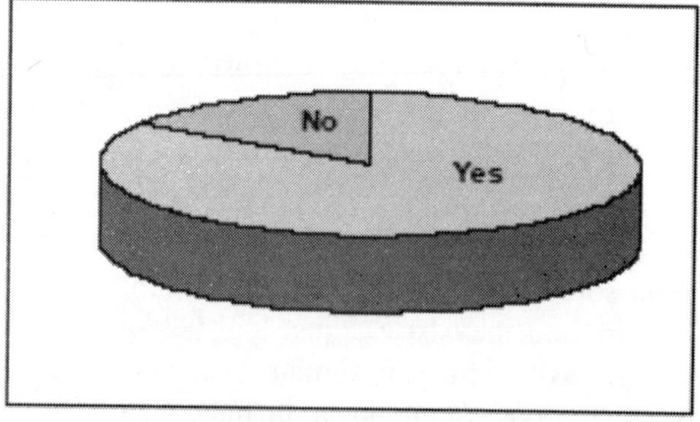

Fig. 11.7: ***Use of on-line tools***

Figure 11.8 gives the methods for companies to remain informed about legal aspects that could be important for their business.

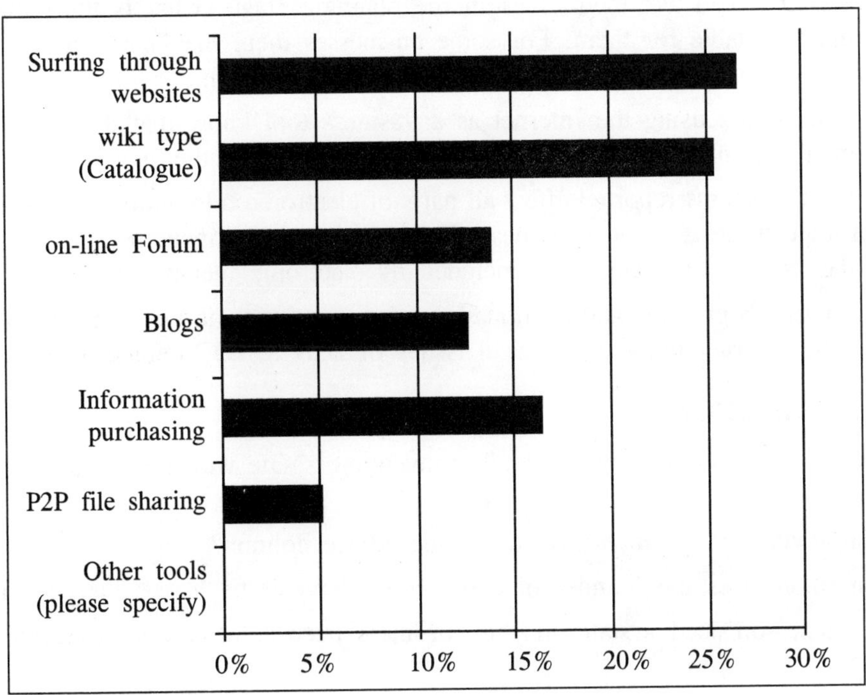

Fig. 11.8: ***Sources of information for legal issues***

SUMMARY

- The term e-commerce has a narrower meaning than e-business. It refers to using the Internet to order and pay for products or services. So e-commerce is a sub-set of e-business.
- E-commerce is said to be carried out when a consumer orders a product from a business and pays for it either when they receive the product or directly online at the time of ordering.
- Most businesses would not adopt a new business strategy, such as opening up a new office or shop, without first doing some very careful planning. Planning helps to ensure that precious time, money and energy invested in any new strategy are not wasted.
- Without good plans new ventures can easily go wrong, due to poor timing, unreasonable expectations or even adopting the wrong approach in the first place.
- Good planning maximizes the benefits to a business of a new or expanded business venture and reduces the risk of things going wrong.
- The planning process needs to be managed well and involve the people who hold important roles in the business - or who provide important business advice to the business.

- The key issues need to be considered by whoever is developing the e-business plan in parallel because decisions made on one issue will often impact on other issues.
- Businesses should ask themselves in the planning stage, what is the optimum level of e-business suitable for them. For some businesses there maybe nothing to be gained by doing anything more than simply using e-mail and banking online.
- Most businesses using the Internet as a business tool know that the technology and use of e-mail, e-commerce and just about everything to do with the Internet is always changing.
- The legal problems reported affect all parts of electronic transactions for e-commerce. The main importance is given to issues related to electronic signatures, security of payments and the validity of a contract concluded by electronic means.
- The Internet is growing and continually evolving, as such, it would be wise to think about legal and Internet marketing ethical issues of B2B & B2C related to e-business.

REVIEW QUESTIONS

1. How does a person ensure that his/her invention is safe with the company they submitted it to?
2. What should one do to protect an online advice column?
3. What rights does the founder of a non-profit have if he leaves the organization?
4. Does a person need a state and city business license for a web-based company?

Case Studies

NATIONWIDE PROJECT: APTECH'S VIDYA (COMPUTER LITERACY PROGRAMME)

Aptech Ltd., is a well known computer education company, with branches all over India. Aptech plans to cater to computer education for school students and professionals for economic development and computer education. However, the fees for computer education may not be viable for economical challenged students and those who have had little or no contact with computers, such as retirees. It is towards these people that Aptech's Vidya, a project based on the e-governance system, is targeted.

Vidya is a corporate citizenship effort to expand Aptech's course catalogue beyond the company's core offerings targeted at computer professionals and corporate markets. Vidya's instruction begins with introducing users to the computer's power switch and progressing through skills and training for the Internet and other useful software.

Vidya is offered both as a stand-alone course and as "Module 0" of the company's more advanced programming and multi-media courses. Vidya has opened new markets, particularly in state and national governments and schools, and helped to pave the way for increased international expansion by providing training that is not typically available in most public schools, charging a low price and accepting a lower margin. In this process, Aptech made Vidya accessible to a wider segment of the population.

GOVERNMENT OF INDIA

E-Governance Project: Wireless Internet Post Office (WIPO)

The Government of India proposed an e-governance project to modernize the communication services. The objective of the project, Wireless Internet Post Office, is to couple advances in consumer electronics with an entrepreneur model and to foster the deployment of text-based digital communication. Wireless Internet Post Office (WIPO) provides complete specification documents for system design, and serves as a focal point of discussion and provides links to similar work to the end-users. Villagers who want to contact relatives in distant locations, farmers who want information on prices, access to markets, and advice on disease and pest control, small businesses who want access to trade information, educators who want teaching materials, and medical and aid workers who require information in their respective fields should use the WIPO services.

Design of the WIPO system was completed and a working prototype has been set up at the Government Educational Agency. The WIPO creates an entrepreneurial opportunity for PDA owners to become micro-businesses by providing services such as scribing, data collection, crop pricing, and matching buyers with sellers. WIPO brought the digital divide and low-cost communication to the neediest areas, like villages.

E-Governance Project: Health Inter Network (HIN) (4 Metropolitan Cities)

India Pilot: Bringing Digital Divide in Health Information

The Government of India planned the project with more than 40 national as well as international organizations with the objective of improving public health using internet technologies. The project was implemented in four metropolitan cities of India:

1. Mumbai
2. Chennai
3. Bangalore
4. Delhi

The Health Inter Network (HIN) a part of the millennium action plan, has four focus areas:

- Connectivity
- Content
- Capacity building
- Policy

The pilot focused on two national priority health programs in India

- Tuberculosis control
- Tobacco control

It emphasized strengthening the ICT capacity at medical colleges. The initiative brings together the international development community, governments, the private sector, foundations and non-governmental organisations in a global partnership to improve public health using Internet technologies.

The project introduced ICT into seven primary health centres and three community health centres, and upgraded computers, internet connections and networks in four research institutions and two medical colleges. Through local firms, the project provided training in basic computer and Internet skills for more than 300 staff and students at pilot sites. This was a catalyst to networking among professionals and supported local business.

E-Governance Project: Vote Smart For India (VSFI)

To Encourage citizens to vote, the Government of India proposed the Vote Smart For India (VSFI) project, which is a citizen's organization dedicated to giving all citizens accurate and unbiased information to make electoral decisions and about the electoral process.

Vote Smart For India (VSFI) provides a comprehensive database of thousands of candidates and elected officials at the centre and state level using Information Communication Technology. At VSFI, every candidate is treated with equal deference and only relevant and unbiased facts are presented. Various interactive programs like One to One Contact and biographical information have been attempted to procure information from the candidates.

The VSFI website is provided for voter declaration and nomination forms for all candidates. The PVS (Specification and Verification System) website includes an education program for schools and colleges. Vote Smart Classroom, a program which is conducted, includes classroom activities, suggestions for teachers by fellow educators, an index of advocacy groups and other resources for issue research. Specific lesson plans include campaign promises, types of advertising, how people make voting decisions, political parties and a way to track candidates.

E-Governance Project: e-Lens (IT enabled Braille)

The Government of India is trying to enhance the life of each and every citizen of the country with various E-Government initiatives. A special effort is being made to help visually challenged persons with a project named e-Lens: IT enabled Braille. The aim of the government is to provide education through computers to the visually impaired so that they become independent.

The 'Golden Icon' award winner e-Lens (electronic lens) developed in local languages, a Braille text, that could be read through a computer for visually impaired people. The software Shruti Drishti developed by WML enables access to websites and opens a new world to these persons by providing elements including links, buttons, check boxes, text and so on. Using Vachantar technology prepared by a government agency. Shruti Drishti is keyboard event driven and provides 'keyboard only' accessibility using a minimal set of keys. It offers a verbal mode using a speech synthesizer with different computer utilities like text editing, calculating spreadsheets, storing databases, reading or writing e-mails etc. and also maths and science Braille software. The project provides the infrastructure at 27 institutes for the visually impaired and 2 libraries and developed a computerized Braille transcription system, Braille conversion software and an automatic Braille embosser.

WML has so far installed IT based Braille systems at 70 special schools.

The website for the project is www.webel-india.com, www.webelmediatronics.in

E-Governance Project: Envision Project

The Government of India promotes an e-government project named "Envision Project" with the aim to promote conservation of natural resources, protection of the environment and to create awareness of these issues.

This project is targeted at citizens of all India but the primary task is to apply the principles of good governance to the management and regulation of use of environmental resources. So the project works to monitor natural resources as well as to moderate government agencies for regulation and management regarding use of environment resources.

E-Governance Project: Technology and Action for Rural Advancement (TARAhaat) – (3 States)

TARAhaat is an e-governance project proposed by the Government of India for rural advancement, specially focused on northern India's rural population. The aim of the project is to deliver its services through a network of franchised community and business centres owned by individual entrepreneurs. These village knowledge centres are equipped with computers and Internet connections.

The TARAhaat project was implemented in three locations in northern India, namely:

- Bundelkhand in Uttar Pradesh
- Madhya Pradesh
- Bathinda in Punjab

TARA stands for Technology and Action for Rural Advancement. TARAhaat uses a franchise-based business model to bring computer and Internet technology to rural regions and plans to use these technologies to create revenue streams leading to financial viability for itself and its franchisees.

TARAhaat will deliver various services at its kendras like:

- Education
- Information
- Services
- Online market opportunities to rural consumers via the internet

It also provides a cost-effective gateway by which larger corporations can reach rural customers. It will offer information, email and web services, and eventually e-commerce and fulfilment services, earning revenues through membership fees and commissions.

E-Governance Project: Financial Accounting Information System (7- States)

Jute is a wide spectrum industry in India. The Indian Government's agency, the Jute Corporation of India implements a project named

"Financial Accounting Information System", to provide ICT enabled services to jute growers. Jute is produced in the eastern states of India. So the project impacts on the following states' jute grower communities.

1. Andhra Pradesh
2. Assam
3. Bihar

4. Meghalaya
5. Orissa
6. Tripura
7. West Bengal

The aim of the Financial Accounting Information System is to establish account code structures for the Jute Corporation of India on the following aspects:

- Accounting policies
- Promotion of widespread understanding of basic accounting activities
- Track depreciation/write-down value of individual assets
- Automation of manual tasks
- Keeping the accounts accurate and secure

JCI initiated the project 'Financial Accounting Information System' in order to improve the efficiency by automating common accounting activities by using a DBMS system.

E-Governance Project: Community Information Centre (CIC) (North East Regions – 8 States)

The National Information Centre, a Government of India body, and Arunachal Pradesh Government plan to deploy community information centres state wide. This project started in 2002 with the aim of linking the blocks in the north eastern states through Very Small Aperture Terminals (VSATs), and providing Community Information Centres (CICs). Along with various government agencies and Arunachal Pradesh this project covers 8 north eastern states:

1. Arunachal Pradesh
2. Assam
3. Manipur
4. Meghalaya
5. Mizoram
6. Nagaland
7. Tripura
8. Sikkim

The objective of the Government of India for this CIC project is to provide Internet connectivity and citizen services delivery. The overall aim is to speed up economic development in the north east. Across Arunachal Pradesh and the north eastern states, 487 community information centres were implemented within 2 years. Each centre is well- equipped with the following infrastructure:

- One server machine
- Five client systems
- One each of a VSAT
- Laser printer

- Dot matrix printer
- Modem
- LAN hub
- TV, WEBCAM
- Two UPS (1KVA, 2 KVA)

Each centre has two operators to manage the centre and provide services to the public. Basic services to be provided by CICs include:

- Internet access
- e-mail
- Printing
- Data entry
- Word processing training for the local populace

Operational CICs may charge nominal amounts for services to uses, so that they can meet office expenses. G2C based services are provided at each CICs include:

- Copies of certificates that are issued by block/district offices
- Market information
- Educational opportunities
- Connectivity to major job portals
- Schools, hospitals

Website: www.cic.nic.in

E-Governance Project: CBI Website

Security and alertness is must for all citizens. With this aim, the Government of India enabled a channel for citizens to register their complaints, alerts, and supplement various information, warn about threats and pass on information online. The Central Bureau of Investigation (CBI) an investigation wing of the Government of India, launched its website http://cbi.nic.in, which is an interactive website that allows people to register complaints and pass on information online.

The website contains information on:

- Interpol
- Red corner notices
- Fraud alerts
- Central Forensic Science Laboratory
- CBI academy
- Important judicial rulings

The site will also enable people to pass on information regarding various crimes and criminals. A variety of projects for e-government have been implemented and many others are under development. A major issue of crime and e-government are covered under this project.

Website: http://cbi.nic.in

E-Governance Project: Rural Knowledge Centre (9-States)

The Indian Government along with national and international organisations proposed an e-governance project focusing on villagers and people of remote areas. The aim of the project named "Rural Knowledge Centre" is to provide information and knowledge systems, health, e-governance and other services with the emphasis on youth, children and women.

The areas covered under this project are nine coastal states of India, namely:

1. West Bengal
2. Orissa
3. Andhra Pradesh
4. Tamilnadu
5. Kerala
6. Karnataka
7. Goa
8. Maharashtra
9. Gujarat

The Rural Knowledge Centre (RKC) is envisaged as a centre for the delivery of ICT skills and income-generating vocational training programs, which besides providing facilities encourage entrepreneurship at the grass root level such as:

- E-governance services
- E-learning programs
- Community based disaster preparedness initiatives
- Information related to ecological security
- Health and agriculture

The content of the presented at Rural Knowledge Centre is being translated to Hindi, Tamil, Gujarati and Malayalam languages.

E-Governance Project: Content Development and IT Localization Network (Coil-Net): (9-States)

The Rajasthan Government plans to offer socio-economic developments in the areas of culture and art with the use of ICT in the Hindi speaking states, with the project Content Development and IT Localization Network (Coil-Net). The Rajasthan Government plans to create a cultural heritage digital library, especially to support and serve the Hindi speaking states' cultural aspects.

This project covers many Hindi speaking states like:

1. Rajasthan
2. Haryana
3. Delhi
4. Uttaranchal

5. Uttar Pradesh
6. Madhya Pradesh
7. Chattisgarh
8. Jharkhand
9. Bihar

Government agencies planned this project by developing a website, Coil-Net which has the following components for the sustainable development in the Hindi speaking belts of India:

- Language tools
- Customized software
- Information appliances
- Internet
- Other access mechanisms
- OCR
- Text-to-Speech

This e-government project work on localization of e-government is a regional language project. It covers all possible branches of development, namely, social, economic, historical, cultural and scientific.

This digital library has promoted preparation and publication of following:

- IT learning material in Hindi
- Content development,
- Research and its production through various existing mechanisms and methodologies in selected areas of application to maximize the usage of IT and its benefits.

IT has catered to the areas of education and training, health, governance, agriculture, tourism and small-scale businesses.

Website: www.itinhindi.org, www.tdil.mit.gov.in/coilnet/ignca

E-Governance Project: Bhurekha (Computerization of Land Records (CLR))

The Kerala Government's project Bhurekha, was a milestone towards implementation of ICT in maintaining land records. The primary objective of the project as envisaged by the Government of India was to issue records of rights to needy land holders without delay. This prcject is based on G2C transition with the sector maintaining land records.

Under the project a comprehensive data bank of all land holdings in the state is made available, which facilitates easy querying and report generation.

Data related is to various activities namely:

- Transfer of registry
- Land assignment
- Land acquisition
- Land relinquishment

These are all captured with the help of the software to form a centralized database for land records. The projects focused on rural farmers, and could cater to their needs regarding land records instantly with this project. The system implemented various centres with a state-wide central server to store all the information.

E-Governance Project: Computerized Rural Information Systems Project (CRISP)

The Government of India plans to set up a Computer Based Information System (CBIS) with the aim of monitoring poverty alleviation schemes of the District Rural Development Agencies (DRDAs).

The Computerized Rural Information Systems Project (CRISP) was initiated to design and develop software solutions to cater to and process the poverty alleviation schemes at the DRDA level and generate output report monitoring of the schemes, to provide training to the DRDA staff on the operational aspects and to facilitate data entry and report generation on line.

Its services are geared to people living in rural areas and remote locations of India, for which it developed some initiatives like:

Rural bazaar - introducing the fine creations of the Indian rural population to the Internet world

Rural soft - software for capturing and processing data related to poverty alleviation schemes

Priya Soft (Panchayati Raj Institution Accounting Software) - software package, designed for Tamil Nadu to monitor :

- Allocated funds
- Expenditure pattern
- Local revenue generation
- Transmission of intended reports to various monitoring agencies

Enrich - a customizable browser for a community to increase its own knowledge and communication and for its empowerment.

E-Governance Project: CORE

The only Indian Consumer Resource and Grievance Redressal System

To protect consumers across India, the Government of India planned the CORE project, which is the only Indian consumer resource and grievance redressal system.

The CORE works to:

- Generate awareness
- Develop consumer rights
- Orient government functioning
- Enforce citizen charters with the effective use of ICT

Since it is the only consumer resource and grievance redressal system, CORE has become a nodal agency to protect the interests of Indian consumers. The project is available online at www.core.nic.in, where any consumer can access and submit a grievance form.

The consumers register themselves and lodge their grievance online through the CORE website, which is forwarded to the complaint manager, and then an alert is sent to the brand for resolution and published on the CORE website. After bringing the complaint to the notice of the brand involved and redressing it, if the complainant is satisfied then the case is treated as closed. This way consumers can follow their case proceedings as well.

E-Governance Project: Drishtee

The Government of India implemented Drishtee in 1999, with the aim of replicating the Gyandoot model throughout India. Drishtee is a software platform having the following aspects:

- Enabling governance
- Commerce
- Education
- Health services

It facilitates communication and exchange of information within a localised intranet between villages and a district centre. Technology-assisted strategies represent the only realistic hope of improving government service delivery to the villages in India. Drishtee Ltd was established following the success of of the Gyandoot project in Dhar, Madhya Pradesh. This project is now successfully active in 5 districts of Punjab, Haryana, Rajasthan, M.P. and Bihar. Its focus is on providing knowledge based service to poor communities residing in villages.

Website: www.drishtee.com

E-Governance Project: India.gov.in—The National Portal of India

The Government of India planned the project with the aim of providing a single window access of information and services by the Indian Government for the citizens and other stakeholders. This is the official portal of the Indian Government - India.gov.in, was developed as a mission mode project under the National e-Governance Plan (NeGP) and designed, developed and hosted by NIC, DIT and MoCIT.

Through this portal comprehensive, accurate, reliable and one stop source of information about India and its various facets are provided to the citizens and stakeholders. The portal provides information related to health, education, employment, housing, law and order, travel and tourism, banking and insurance and more.

A web based secured Content Management System (CMS) has been developed to facilitate contribution of content. It is aimed to continue the enhancement and enrichment of this portal in terms of content coverage, design and technology on a regular basis.

Website: www.india.gov.in , www.portalcontent.nic.in

E-Governance Project: Indian Computer Emergency Response Team (CERT-In)

Security is a key factor for any information system. The Government of India plans to create awareness on security issues through dissemination of information and to conduct various training programs for best practices to secure their systems. The project named "Indian Computer Emergency Response Team" (CERT) was set up to ensure information assets of India, such as:

- Strategic
- Commercial
- Financial
- Government

It recommends necessary protection, and India's IT infrastructure is appropriately and adequately protected to counter threats to its resources and stable operation. CERT-IN provides various kinds of services to minimize damage and services in the form of:

- Advisories
- Security alerts
- Vulnerability notes
- Incident notes
- Security guidelines

It aims to help organisations secure their systems and networks. CERT-In is also tracking defacement of India websites and has issued guidelines on security to prevent hacking/ defacement of websites. It operates an independent desk to provide support on a 24x7 basis, which helps in responding to computer security incidents which are reported through e-mail.

Website: www.cert-in.org.in/

E-Governance Project: Common Service Centres (CSC)

The Government of India has already planned many other future e-government projects, but the rural population of India is disconnected from communication networks. There are many locations where the local community is not even able to connect to any kind of permanent network. The Government of India plans to use Wimax Technology based common service centres across India. The aim of this project is to connect rural India to the common service centres, as part of the National e-Governance Plan (NeGP) in India.

The government will invest crores of rupees in this project, to connect more than a thousand blocks in the country. In the first phase, the government will provide an over the air point-to-point connectivity to common services centres. The government will set up one-base station in each block to provide P2P access.

After completion of the first phase the base-station was established, more than about another five thousand blocks will also be connected using WiMax technology. The government owned telecom operator BSNL will implement the project, which will be funded by the Department of Information Technology.

After the implementation of the WiMax project, the government is looking at taking in the areas of education and health to the grassroots levels.

E-Governance Project: Information and Communications Technologies for Development (ICTD)

The Government of India along with the government agency, the National Institute of Smart Governance and International agency planned the project called Information and Communications Technologies for Development (ICTD), with the motto of "Making ICT work for people". The project was set up for rural and urban areas with the objective of improving the social, economical and political condition of rural and urban areas with the implementation of ICT.

Information and Communications Technologies for Development (ICTD) generates new jobs, income opportunities, public service and governance system with ICT tools. ICT focuses on the social, economical and political development of common people.

This works as a catalyst and engine for social growth. Use of ICT brings transparency, accountability and empowerment to the government as well as the citizens. ICTD pilot projects were implemented by state governments and non-government organizations on a public-private partnership basis.

The various projects are categorized under four categories:

- Integrated citizen services
- ICTs for enhancing rural livelihoods
- ICTs for transforming rural governance
- ICTs for women's empowerment

Information and Communications Technologies for Development is running more than 150 pilots projects.

E-Governance Project: Empowers Indian Farmers (Project by Infosys)

In India a majority of the population resides in villages and work in the agriculture sector. Infosys a major IT company initiated the project "Empowers Indian Farmers" with the aim of managing the supply chain for farmers. The supply varies in various stages and for each stage Infosys applies ICT enabled systems to provide technical support to farmers. The application manages the supply chain from:

- Level of profiling of farmer clusters
- Crop planning
- Scheduling
- Tracking
- Forecasting

The information and communication technology-enabled application minimises inventory requirements, reduces waste and facilitates better integration between retailers and farmers. It also enables farmers to access technical information like:

- Data and images
- Access to region-specific weather updates
- Market information - daily sales volumes
- Market information - average prices

The usage is expected to increase to a million farmers. This solution gives the organised retail sector access to a reliable small holder production base.

E-Governance Project: Instant Money Order (iMO)

The Government of India planned a key project based only on money transfer. However, unlike conventional systems of money transfer like demand drafts, money orders etc, this system works instantly with the use of ICT. The project was thus named Instant Money Order (iMO) and was implemented by the Department of Post in 2006. The aim of the project is to provide speed, mobility, safety and reliability for transfer of money through post offices (iMO centres) in India between two resident individuals in Indian territory.

In this age of instant fund transfers from one part of the globe to another, it is but natural that money orders too graduate to the efficiency level of digital communication. Within minutes of booking an amount ranging from Rs. 1,000 to Rs. 50,000, the recipient receives the money at a nominal cost to the sender using ICT infrastructure.

Instant Money Order facility is now available at various main post offices across the country. Plans are afoot to expand it to more post offices in the future using the existing human resources and ICT infrastructure. A digital signature has been used for the first time in the Department of Posts for accessing the application.

E-Governance Project: Janmitra

The Government of India along with national and international agencies enabled the project called Janmitra, which means "a friend of the public". This project was not implemented over a state or part of the country, but over a selected district, which was chosen. The sites are mainly remote villages of the following districts:

- Jhalawar in Rajasthan
- Madhya in Karnataka
- Bhuj and Panchmal in Gujarat
- Bhopal in Madhya Pradesh
- Kalahandi in Orrisa

Jan-mitra provides e-services to the villagers such as:

- Registration of births
- Registration of deaths
- Land records
- Grievance redressal
- Submission of on-line applications
- Examination results

With these services the project aims to improve citizens' access to information by empowering them, making administration more participatory, ensuring greater transparency, and deterring the arbitrary exercise of official power.

Kiosk operators are mandated to provide certain services of public interest to BPL families, development schemes free of cost. For other services there is a nominal charge, determined by society, for expenses incurred on electricity, internet connectivity, print outs plus a small profit for the kiosk operator.

The villagers are paying happily, and counting their savings in terms of time and effort. Issues such as health and hygiene, family planning are provided free of cost to encourage women. The kiosk owners are trained to operate the customized Jan Mitra software as well as in the functioning of government departments.

E-Governance Project: Kuppam i-community

The Government of India, enables private companies like HP to work out several e-government project. The Kuppam i-community project was proposed by HP in 2002. It focuses on communities around:

- Kuppam constituency
- Madanapally division
- Chittoor district

The special focus group is rural communities with the aim to turn the region into a thriving, self-sustaining economic community, where technology helps literacy, job creation, income, government services, education and health care. The services the i-Community expects to provide include automated government services for:

- Land records,
- Birth registration
- Death registration
- Bill payments
- Connectivity to local schools
- Colleges
- Hospitals
- Youth educational services
- Vocational training through direct and distance learning
- Agriculture services
- Health services

E-Governance Project: n-Logue's Rural Connectivity Model

The Government of India plans to connect all villages with the Internet. With this aim the project n-Logue's Rural Connectivity Model was initiated. The project's objectives are to deploy wirelessly connected internet kiosks in villages throughout India to enhance the quality of the life of rural Indians. n-Logue Communications Ltd. has developed a non-profit business model for establishing rural connectivity based on demand. It has a three-tiered business model where:

- The top tier, n-Logue is responsible for managing overall operations.
- The second tier, consisting of local service providers (lsps), sets up the infrastructure providing connectivity.
- The third tier is the village, where local kiosk owners supply the rural population with information-based services.

To provide its internet protocol (IP) network backbone, it uses a cost-effective fixed Wireless Local Loop (WLL) technology called corDECT, developed by the Telecommunications and Computer Networks (TeNeT) Group at the IIT- Madras. Supporting simultaneous data and voice channels to subscribers within 10 kilometres of the broadcast location, the range of this point-to-multipoint wireless radio frequency technology can be extended to 25 kilometres by using a repeater.

E-Governance Project: Open Source GIS/Mapping Solution for the Indian Tsunami Information Resource Centre.

The Indian Government along with national and international organisations planned a Tsunami Information System for coastal areas of the country. The project was initially implemented in Kerala in 2005/06 after the tsunami that struck the coastal areas of India.

The project aims to develop a free and open source Geographic Information System (GIS) mapping solution for the existing Indian Tsunami Information Resource Centre. The project, created using the free and open source technology (named Janatsu), will apply a powerful GIS/ mapping solution to the Indian Tsunami Information Resource Centre making it more effective for the people and organisations.

The GIS/mapping solution will train organizations on how to collect GIS data, how to enter data into the system and how to use the system to visualize the data. The Janastu (the Pantoto toolkit), a free and open source technology allows users greater access to the significant benefits of powerful Geographic Information Scheme (GIS) applications. Activists go out and collect the geo-referenced data using Geographic Positioning System (GPS) and other tools.

In future the project will be useful to prevent deaths and damages along coastal India, which was impacted in the year 2005. The project hopes that visual documentation of environmental and/or human impact on the surroundings will empower villagers to make claims with support of visual evidence.

E-Governance Project: Online Pathology Report Facility by Patna Medical College and Hospital

With the aim of using ICT to improve medical facilities in the state, the Government of Bihar has launched online reporting facility for the pathology department of its premier medical institute — Patna Medical College and Hospital (PMCH). The online project was implemented with the objectives of:

1. Enabling citizens to download test reports of their pathological investigations directly from the PMCH website
2. Printing them from the comfort of their homes
3. Freeing patients and/or their attendants from coming to the hospital to collect reports

To avail of the facility, patients or their attendants need to enter the registration number as login and the patient lab bill number as password. The system is just a start to make the hospital hi-tech. Patients can access this online on a 24×7 basis, which saves time. With PMCH, the administration is planning to make the outpatient roster and emergency roster available online as well.

E-Governance Project: Tender Notice Information System (TNIS)

Website for tender notices

The Government of India, planned a portal to provide easy access and online availability of tender details. This project is named "TNIS", which stands for Tender Notice Information System. The government agency for information and publicity accepts advertisements for publication of tenders, with a letter containing a unique number obtained under the Tender Notice Information System (TNIS) which will be available on the Delhi government website.

TNIS will publish tender notice details, provide free registration of vendors and category wise email notification on the internet. Tender documents will be uploaded in a government format. Each department will have to obtain a user ID and password to operate the TNIS. The details may be sent to a user manual containing the procedure for operating the website, which can be obtained from the IT department. TNIS will serve government departments and government bodies as well as suppliers/vendors.

E-Governance Project: The India's Energy and Resources Institute (TERI)

The Government of India planned an e-government project named "TERI" with the aim of providing knowledge and information on clean energy, energy efficiency and issues related to mitigation and adaptation of climate change. Citizens should be aware about the tasks performed by the government on energy issues.

TERI (The India's Energy and Resources Institute: Clean energy knowledge hub) is an internationally recognized centre of excellence, with an existing network of academicians, researchers, resident experts and similar institutions involved in science and technology.

A clean energy knowledge hub set up at Delhi provided information on clean energy as well as collection, structuring and dissemination of knowledge through various resources. The TERI had set up four to six hubs throughout the region providing information related to environment, software tools, databases, research and development, rules and regulations of law and other information. TERI has provided a dynamic and inspiring environment that enables development of solutions to global problems in the fields of energy, environment and current patterns of development, which are largely unsustainable.

E-Governance Project: VoGRAM

The Government of India implemented a special project focused on the illiterate masses of rural communities, named VoGRAM. The aim of the project was to connect the rural and illiterate masses through the facility of a voice telegram. The VoGRAM application, developed by an educational agency of the Government of India, is a combination of speech compression and transmission over the Internet. All a person needs to do is to call up the VoGram call centre and record a voice message using a simple card that compresses the voice message.

The compressed file is sent through the Internet to a post-office close to the recipient's address. The post-office could either print the message out or deliver the message to the recipient or the receiver could call up a local number free of charge, use an access code given by the postman and hear the VoGram. Alternatively, if the postman has a device like a Simputer or PDA, he can play the voice message to the recipient at home.

GOVERNMENT OF ANDHRA PRADESH

E-Governance Project: Vijayawada Online Information Centre (VOICE)

The Vijayawada Online Information Centre (VOICE) has been established to provide computing infrastructure at Vijayawada Municipal Corporation of Andhra Pradesh. The mission, proposed by the municipal corporation, is to set up information kiosks at important public locations in the city of Vijayawada to benefit the local public.

VOICE delivers municipal services to the people of Vijayawada such as:

- Building approvals
- Birth certificates
- Death certificates

It also handles collection of property, water and sewerage taxes. The VOICE system uses five kiosks located close to the citizens. These are linked to the back end processes in municipal offices through a wide area network. The VOICE application has helped reduce corruption, made access to services more convenient, and has improved the finances of the municipal government.

E-Governance Project: Society for Andhra Pradesh Network (SAPNET)

The Andhra Government plans to cover all its citizens by providing distance learning, agriculture extension, rural development, telemedicine and e-governance through five television channels. The project, called SAPNET, which stands for the Society for Andhra Pradesh Network, provides an interactive forum for regular exchange of information and updating knowledge and skills. This project supports:

- Distance education
- Telemedicine
- Agricultural extension

- E-governance
- Human resource development

E-Governance Project: Saukaryam

The Visakhapatnam municipal corporation proposed the project "Saukaryam" so as to deliver all civic services on-line. The Saukaryam project covers all civic services ranging from the facility of online payment of dues to allowing lodging of grievances online or filing building plan applications and getting their status without running from pillar to post. There is also a facility for the hospitals to send birth and death information online, which helps citizens obtain their certificates instantly.

Other services offered include

- Online payment of municipal dues through networked banks
- Payment of property tax
- Payment of water tax
- D & O trade licenses
- Advertisement tax
- Lease rents

E-Governance Project: Rajiv Internet Village

Information Technology has spread rapidly across the world. The Andhra Pradesh Government has made a number of advances in ICT. A milestone in this effort is the "Rajiv Internet Village" project planned for the rural population of the state in 2005.

With this project the Andhra Pradesh Government aims to provide good governance to the citizens of Andhra Pradesh and revitalize the rural economy for integrated and sustained growth, to empower the common man in the rural areas of the state, so that they can access all G2C, G2B, B2C, B2B and C2C services in an integrated manner. This will enable them to create a better means of livelihood and improve the quality of life.

The Rajiv Internet Village project brings the government closer to the people living in rural areas by providing convenient access to information and services covering: agriculture, education, health, market prices, cropping patterns, weather forecasts, agriculture extension, quality inputs, insurance and e-commerce, computer literacy to at least one person in each family in rural areas and connectivity to rural areas with high bandwidth.

E-Governance Project: Parishkruthi

The Government of Andhra Pradesh implemented an e-government initiative named "Parishkruthi" in Khamman District in 2001. The main objectives of Parishkruthi are:

- To provide a caring and responsive governance
- To make the administration transparent
- To make the administration accountable and responsive

- To provide services to rural citizen services on par with those offered by the private sector
- To provide access to the status of information to a petitioner

Parishkruthi is the most important and innovative project of the Khammam District in Andhra Pradesh for grievance redressal in public offices, using both information technology and human resources. The unique feature of Parishkruthi is that is has completed networking between all departmental heads in the government at the district level. At the block and village level the access is through a dial up network.

E-Governance Project: Online Transaction Processing (OLTP)

The Government of Andhra Pradesh planned the one-stop-shop for citizens with the "OLTP", Online Transaction Processing project. This is a system which develops with the help of private organizations with the aim of providing a one-stop-shop for citizen services at the village level through multipurpose kiosks and enabling online updation of core data about land and citizens through the use of PDAs and information kiosks at the village level.

OLTP connects 16 government departments in Andhra Pradesh on a single network. All government records and transaction procedure details at the district level will be centrally stored and managed on a single database. The project will serve the government department users and citizens in villages by efficient service transactions through specially designed internet-enabled kiosks. These transactions can be carried out via English as well as Telugu interfaces. These services include access to information such as:

- Income verification
- Income certificates of citizens
- Land cultivation details
- Agriculture marketing
- Tele-veterinary services
- Registration of small farmers
- Birth and death records
- House numbering, first information reports
- Occupation details of residents
- Drinking water details
- Irrigation sources

Future plans include replication across the state in a phased manner.

E-Governance Project: Multi Purpose Household Survey (MPHS)

The Andhra Pradesh Government initiated an e-governance project with special focus on residents of Andhra Pradesh. The project named Multi Purpose Household Survey (MPHS) aims to create a database of the entire population to facilitate effective governance and development delivery by the state. MPHS was initiated for the basic socio-economic data of all residents of the state and to create a database of land records. This huge database, which covers all districts of Andhra Pradesh, contains the personal, social and economic details of every citizen.

The surveyed data must be accurate, so data are validated through sample verification by independent agencies. Combination of all the data gives the government appropriate vision for future policy. The data warehousing currently organizes a multipurpose survey enabling the decision support system of the government. The MPHS project develops a decision-support system and executive information system on citizen and land data. This will be useful to the state government for accurate forecasts and trend analysis.

E-Governance Project: Fully Automated Services of Transport Department (FAST)

The Andhra Pradesh Government plans to moderate as well as modernize the transport department, for which they implemented an e-government project named FAST, which stands for fully automated services of transport department, in the year 2000. The Andhra Pradesh Government wants to make the transport department citizen-friendly in functioning, improve revenue collections and to centralize information.

A variety of services of the transport department have been covered, such as:

- Issue of driving licenses
- Registration of motor vehicles
- Issue of permits
- Collection of motor vehicle taxes

The government also has plans for the future of this project like:

- Introduction of smart cards
- Integration of FAST systems with police and pollution control systems
- Involving e-seva for rendering services of the transport department

E-Governance Project: E-Seva

The Government of Andhra Pradesh implemented the e-seva project in 1999. The essence of e-seva is integration of all departments of the central and state governments; in their deliveries to the citizen from a single facilitation point, since the integration of services is a major concern. The project will provide real-time utility bill payments for water, electricity, telephones, municipal taxes, birth and death certificates, passport applications, permits and licenses, transport department services and B2C services. Citizens can log on to the e-seva website to avail of these services.

Services offered by e-seva

E-seva offers a wide spectrum of citizen-friendly services that will save citizens the bother of running around to various departments.

Payment of utilities bills
- Electricity bills
- Water and sewerage bills
- Telephone bills (BSNL & TATA Tele services)
- Property tax
- Sales tax

Certificates
- Registration of births/deaths
- Issue of birth/death certificates
- Registration department: Issue of encumbrance certificates
- Issue of caste/nativity certificates

Labour department
- License: New registration
- License renewal

Permits/Licenses
- Medical and health department: Renewal of drug licenses
- Issue/Renewal of trade licenses

Transport department services (available at Banjara Hills Centre (at Hyderabad) only)
- Change of address of a vehicle owner
- Transfer of ownership of a vehicle
- Issue of learners' licenses
- Issue/Renewal of driving licenses (non-transport vehicles)
- Registration of new vehicles

Information
- Transport department procedures
- Registration department: Market value assistance

Reservations
- Reservation of APSRTC bus tickets
- HMWSSB: Reservation of water tankers
- Tourism: Reservation of tickets/accommodation

Other services at E-seva centres
- Sale of passport application forms
- Receipt of passport applications
- Receipt of applications for new telephone connections
- Registration department: Sale of non-judicial stamps
- Registration department: Document writing service
- Collection of small savings

Internet services

- Internet-enabled electronic payments
- Downloading of forms and government orders (GOs)
- Filing of applications on the Web
- Receipt of complaints or requests in connection with citizen services

B2C services

- ATM: Cash withdrawals and deposits
- ATM: Issue of statements of account
- Mutual funds: Collection of applications
- Mutual funds: Transfer of shares
- Cell phone bill payments

Website: www.esevaonline.com

E-Governance Project: E-Justice: Legal Service Portal

The Andhra Pradesh Government planned to implement transparency in legal and judicial services. The project aims to act as a link between rule of law, poverty eradication, human rights and sustainable human development through an electronic platform.

This citizen-centric e-Justice aims to provide access to justice with the use of ICT. e-Justice promotes legal awareness through an electronic interface by presenting the key legislations in a simple manner, simplifying relevant judgments and certain procedural regulations, enlightening citizens on the existence of alternative remedies and making the same available to the general public through information kiosks, rural e-seva centres etc.

Citizens can send online queries to the legal services authorities or the CGG legal experts for legal assistance. The authorities will judge the eligibility and nature of the grievance and refer the same to a court or lok adalat, free of cost. Different sections of society, including the marginalised ones, would be able to access legal information and support just at a click of the mouse. Particularly, women in rural areas can approach the kiosk and get relevant legal information.

The website for this project is www.ejustice.org.in

E-Governance Project: e-Panchayat

The Government of Andhra Pradesh implemented the project "e-Panchayat" with the aim of fully computerizing all activities relating to citizens to government and government to government functions. e-Panchayat is a comprehensive set of Panchayat applications to effectively solve the information management problems at the village level.

It benefits the citizens, the elected representatives, the gram panchayat and other village level officials, the administrators and planners at district and state levels.

The project provides services as following:

- Process related to birth and death registrations
- House tax assessment collections
- Trade licenses
- Old age pensions
- Works monitoring
- Financial accounting
- MIS for Panchayat administration

Website for this project is www.ekpanch.ap.nic.in/

E-Governance Project: Andhra Pradesh State Wide Area Network (APSWAN)

The government of Andhra Pradesh implemented the APSWAN Project in 1999 with the aim of monitoring welfare schemes and providing easy public access to government information. It was an e-government initiative for G2C as well G2G transition; a bridge enhanced by the AP government for the future e-government project with the Andhra Pradesh State Wide Area Network (APSWAN).

- APSWAN is an intranet system carrying voice, data and video traffic, to provide information technology infrastructure network.
- APSWAN connects the secretariat at Hyderabad to all district collectorates and regional divisional offices with 2Mbps optical fibre cables.
- The network provides data linkage by connecting the local-area network of the district headquarters to the local-area network at the secretariat.
- Voice linkages are through interconnecting the PABX exchange at Hyderabad to the exchanges at the district headquarters through a linked numbering system.
- The WAN will provide videoconferencing from the state capital with any of the district-level officers in a broadcast mode. Services to be catered through APSWAN are: e-mail, bulletin board services, data broadcasts, broadcast of various government orders to various government offices, online transactions, processing etc. Internet gateway access will be provided at Hyderabad to make these facilities available to all officers of the government.

  Website: www.apswan.com

E-Governance Project: AP Broadband Project

In the information technology age, the Andhra Pradesh Government plans to offer high speed connectivity for high-ended services for government owned units. The AP Broadband Project was implemented by the Andhra Pradesh Government in 2005.

This project's objective is to offer high speed fibre backbone connectivity to more than 40,000 of the state government owned units like:

- Schools
- Educational institutes
- Hospitals
- Government offices

The government applies the high speed connectivity by offering high-end services to every unit like

- CATV
- Video on demand
- Video conferencing
- Distance education
- Telemedicine
- Micro-banking

The project mainly focused on rural and remote areas and villages in Andhra Pradesh districts, by connecting them with the AP Broadband Project. This project is an infrastructure with broadband access service consisting of customer network equipment, the network connection and broadband access service. The network will have optic fibre connectivity right up to the village level connecting district quarters, mandal quarters, educational institutions and hospitals. This broadband network will enable all government departments to deliver services to citizens through:

- E-seva centres
- Rajiv internet village kiosks
- Web-based online services.

The AP Broadband project seeks to connect all villages across Andhra Pradesh, with a 1-gigabyte pipe up to the mandal level and hopes to make e-governance services available at the doorsteps of people through Internet kiosks.

E-Governance Project: AP Online: One-stop-shop on the Internet

This project was proposed by Andhra Pradesh Government to serve the citizens of Andhra Pradesh with a single window online service through a portal designed to be a one-stop-shop on Internet. The portal seeks to provide information in respect of all services to the citizens and businesses in Andhra Pradesh. A combination of all the information about various services offered by this project are:

- TWINS
- FAST
- CARD
- Basic information regarding all departments of the Government of Andhra Pradesh is available on this portal.

This project has its own web site: www.aponline.gov.in, this website is also available in the Telugu language. So this project is a good example of localization of e-government projects.

E-Governance Project: AP Rural Employment Guarantee Scheme

The Andhra Pradesh Government's project AP Rural Employment Guarantee Scheme proposed to support the state's unemployed population, and see that wage seekers obtain employment under the National Rural Employment Guarantee Scheme (NREGP). The software application for NREGA in Andhra Pradesh is one of the very few examples of an e-governance project in Andhra Pradesh, wherein a scheme itself is launched with the software solutions becoming an integral part of the business processes.

Under the National Rural Employment Guarantee Scheme launched in February 2006, at least 100 days of guaranteed wage employment in every financial year is offered to every household whose adult members are ready to do unskilled manual work.

The works to be taken up under the scheme include

- Water conservation
- Water harvesting
- Drought proofing
- Tree plantation
- Irrigation works
- Irrigation facilities to lands of SCs/STs
- Beneficiaries of land reforms
- Beneficiaries of Indira Aawas Yojana (iay)
- Land development
- Flood control and protection works
- Link roads

In earlier programmes it was observed that all the citizens in need of work were not given work due to lack of works ready for execution. Even those who worked got wages that were far less than their outcome and, in some cases, their names were written down but they were never paid. To ensure transparency in the administrative mechanism, ICT was deployed extensively.

The use of technology begins at the stage of registration of all wage seekers. The Panchayat secretary verifies the applications of wage seekers and enters the details in a register kept in the Gram Panchayat. The information about the wage seeker is entered into the computer placed at the mandal level and the front page of the job card is printed with a unique ID and details of the household. The photo is captured from the database of the civil supplies departments ration cards. All the wage seekers have to open post office/bank accounts and the account numbers are also captured. This way the AP government serve wage seekers. Such projects focused on employment and wage seekers are rare.

E-Governance Project: AP Technology Services Ltd. (APTS)

The Andhra Pradesh government proposed this project with the objective of computerizing the whole state administration. This project mainly focused on government agencies across the state. This project started in 1986 under the name of AP Technology Services Ltd. (APTS). APTS is a frontline organization providing IT solutions to a host of varied governmental, non-governmental, and social organizations. The varied range of quality IT services includes:

- Application development
- Project consultancy
- Web application
- Networking
- Software purchase
- Office automation
- Training in IT related areas
- Hardware procurement etc.

APTS will initially issue digital certificates for users of all e-governance initiatives undertaken by the state government. These applications include:

- E-procurement
- E-seva
- Paperless office
- Smart government initiatives

APTS will provide digital certificates and related services to organizations and individuals interacting with their electronic infrastructure spread across the state.

E-Governance Project: Bhu Bharti, Integrated Land Information System (ILIS)

The government of Andhra Pradesh launched an e-government project with the objective to establish and manage a comprehensive, on-line sustainable land information system for financial self-sustenance, auto-update, transparency and accessibility. The project named Bhu Bharti, an Integrated Land Information System (ILIS), was implemented in 2005-06 with the aim of establishing a land information system across the state. The Integrated Land Information System (ILIS) involves extensive interaction for:

- Revenue
- Survey
- Settlement
- Land records
- Registration departments

Along with the local bodies involved in the administration of land in the state, ILIS works as follows with government agencies:

- Captures
- Stores
- Checks

- Integrates
- Manipulates
- Analyzes
- Displays data about property
- Use of property
- Ownership of property
- Development to the citizen

The system delivers the services to its users through a unified interface, Value-Added Services (VAS). ILIS replaced the manual records with digital records, and created a geographical control network for villages and harmonized the national framework, for the purpose of Geographic Information System (GIS). ILIS involves survey and land records, revenue, stamps and registration and local body departments.

E-Governance Project: E-Seva

Andhra Pradesh initiated an E-government program named e-seva, with the main objective of a single window interface between citizens and the government.

E-Governance Project: Online Grievance Redressal Tracking System (OGRTS)

The Government of Andhra Pradesh proposed a special kind of project for tracking citizens' grievances online. The project named the Online Grievance Redressal Tracking System (OGRTS), aims to provide web and call centre based information efficiently and effectively to the public concerning crimes, accidents, safety and other public issues by the municipality.

OGRTS is an initiative under Mission Mode projects with m-government (multifaced-government) utilization of all wireless devices, like mobile phones, handhelds, PDAs, wearable PCs, Blackberry pagers, etc. taking Urban Local Bodies (ULBs) into consideration. The work of OGRTS goes through different phases like registering a grievance, automatic forwarding of the registered complaints, automatic escalation as per citizen charters, updating action and knowledge status. Reports on OGRTS contain the login part with the username as citizen and the password as guest. Reports on OGRTS are available municipality-wise, location-wise, subsection-wise, status-wise. One can obtain complete details of complaints.

E-Governance Project: Telemedicine

The Andhra Pradesh Government implemented an innovative e-governance project focused on citizens who need medical aid, called "Telemedicine", to create advanced diagnostic facilities throughout the state using equipment that is usually not available to people in district hospitals. The project's plan is to install telemedicine compatible diagnostic medical equipment. Computerization has taken place in the district hospital, Mahboobnagar. The project was developed in partnership with private NGOs.

The state government planned to extend the cath lab facility at the district hospital in collaboration with CARE Hospital. The CARE Foundation will install equipment for medical facilities such as CT scans, ultra sound scanners, colour Doppler, ECG, digital X-rays, cath labs, eco cardiograph (to study the functioning of the heart) and ICCUs. The project is proposed to be extended to district hospitals at various locations in the state.

These kinds of telemedicine services have also been proposed by other state governments, e.g. telemedicine project, Chattisgarh with the support of ISRO, telemedicine services, Pune with the support of Tata.

GOVERNMENT OF ASSAM

E-Governance Project: Dharitee

The Assam State Government enables ICT for maintaining land records, with its project named Dharitee. This project covers 21 district of Assam. The objective of Dharitee is to provide a web-based computerized land records system. Dharitee is the first web-technology based computerized land records system implemented in the country for the revenue department of the Government of Assam.

Besides others, some of the activities undertaken are:

- Online mutation processes
- Up-to-date correction
- Maintenance of land records
- Online access to up-to-date land records for citizens
- Drastic cut down on processing time through process re-engineering
- Linking of cadastral maps with plot data

The project becomes an information system for land, spread all across the state.

E-Governance Project: e-Suvidha

The main objectives of e-Suvidha are to help citizens submit, process and deliver their applications to the local CIC as a delivery point. The status of his/her application can also be viewed on the Internet through the CICs at any point of time. e-Suvidha is a web-based system, through which a land-holder can access his record of right or patta. This system is merely for access and has not been provided with the legal sanctity. The system presently provides five citizen-centric services

1. Certified copy of electoral roll
2. PRC for higher education
3. Land holding certificate
4. Income certificate for service holder
5. Income certificate for cultivators/farmers

Only the usual application fee is charged for these services. The community development centre infrastructure has been used for this purpose.

Website: http://esuvidha.nic.in/

GOVERNMENT OF BIHAR

E-Governance Project: Municipal Corporation towards Digital Revenue Administration (MUDRA)

The Bihar State Government planned the project "MUDRA" in Patna, with the objectives of calculating the assessment value and holding tax, monitoring tax defaulters and daily holding tax collections, and effective planning of tax collection. MUDRA works at the G2G and G2C sectors of e-governance. The system works to computerize the over all functions of the ax collection system of Patna Municipal Corporation. The system has computerized the activities of:

- Holding owners
- Tax collectors
- Bill generation
- Bill dispatch
- Demand note generation
- Online tax collection
- Receipt generation
- Common database etc.

GOVERNMENT OF CHANDIGARH

E-Governance Project: e-Sampark

The Chandigarh Government planned the project to provide multi-service–single window services to the citizen through a one-stop shop by minimizing multiple interaction points, giving a better turnaround time in receipt, processing and issue of services. Its aim is to provide citizen centric services in an efficient, fast, simple and cost effective way. The administration has set up an interactive web portal and electronic citizen service centres across the city which is named e-Sampark. It is a Golden Icon award winner, with extensive use of ICT.

The project e-Sampark offers the following services:

- Payment of utility bills
- Payment of taxes
- Issuing bus passes
- Birth/Death certificates
- Passport applications free of cost

E-Sampark centres are located at various government agencies like:

- Bill collection centres of electricity offices
- Municipal corporations
- Departments of excise and taxation
- Licensing and registering authorities
- Transport offices
- Registries of births and deaths
- Police stations
- Departments of health
- Departments of education
- Departments of food and supplies

The e-Sampark project provides information and services online regarding various government services through its website www.chandigarh.gov.in

E-Governance Project: e-Gram Sampark Centre

Chandigarh, a Union Territory planned the e-gram project in 2007 with the aim to provide e-governance services for empowerment of the rural people. The Chandigarh Administration inaugurated an e-Gram Sampark Centre in several villages of the territory. These Gram Sampark Centres will not only provide various public utility services, but will also act as rural knowledge centres equipped with an IT support structure.

A total pf seven centres across the territory speeded up the renovation of old buildings in a dilapidated condition. The people of the area are advised to actively involve themselves and effectively participate in the developmental process and full opportunities are extended to them to move forward and improve their quality of life.

E-Governance Project: e-Jan Sampark

The Chandigarh Government planned the project with the aim of bridging the digital divide by extending the application of IT for the benefit of the common man. This project provides information about the services of various departments and also information and facilitation to residents regarding private services and other Government of India services from the 70 e-Jan Sampark kiosks which are to be set up in each sector and each village of Chandigarh.

The e-Jan Sampark project enables residents to access information and avail of services from the kiosks with ease, and without any harassment. These centres also enable the citizen to submit their grievances at a common centre and get quick redressal thereafter.

The project aims to provide a single, efficient information dissemination system to the citizens for availing of government services by minimizing multiple interaction points for the citizen and hence save time. These services are provided free of cost except when the citizen needs any print out, the same is available at a nominal cost per page of print out.

GOVERNMENT OF CHATTISGARH

E-Governance Project: e-Gram Suraj

E-Gram Suraj is an MIS based application where the critical information can be stored and passed on through a hand held computer called SIMPUTER. The project has been implemented in Dongargaon and Kurd villages. Some of the features of E-Gram Suraj are as follows:

- The first Hindi based applications to be used by Patwaris/Sarpanches
- The system provides almost all information about a village like its population, families, water resources, human resources, BPL details, land, etc.
- The Patwari/Sarpanch can update grass root level information, which can be transferred to a PC for further compilation to generate various detailed village wise reports
- This application will digitize grass root level information, which was maintained by the Patwari/Sarpanch on paper
- The application has a simple and easy to understand Hindi-interface with touch screens
- This pilot project will make more difficult projects easy and then these can be taken on a Simputer
- Patwari/Sarpanch can take notes by hand

Exclusive features of SIMPUTER

1. Simputer: SIMple inexpensive people's ComPUTER
2. Easy to use: Any layman can use this as there is touch instead of key board
3. Easy portability: Can be carried in the pocket
4. Multi-lingual: Availability of application in local languages
5. Connectivity: With all peripherals through Wi-Fi, BT, IR and Serial, USB ports
6. Last Mile Connectivity: Through the Internet using PSTN or CDMA
7. Global Positioning System: For use by military, police and forest departments.
8. Bridge: Between have and have-nots

It is a totally Indian product: Created by Indian professors and produced by BEL.

E-Governance Project: e-Panchayat

The project was planned by the Government of Chattisgarh for on line monitoring of rural development schemes up to the panchayat level. It involves compilation of basic information of gram panchayats facilitating enhanced decision making using advanced technologies like GIS etc. and panchayat computerization in Chhattisgarh state through use of information and communication technology (ICT). VSAT based e-connectivity of 16 zila panchayats and 146 janpad panchayats is being setup. This project is being carried out with the efforts of the Directorate of Panchayat Chhattisgarh, National Informatics Centre (NIC) and NICSI.

Expected benefits

- On line monitoring of rural development schemes up to the panchayat level.
- Compilation of basic information of gram panchayats facilitating enhanced decision making using advanced technologies like GIS etc.
- Collection and compilation of data regarding gram panchayat resources
- Collection and compilation of data regarding financial resources and income sources of gram panchayats.
- Compilation of gram panchayat funds received through government aid, people's participation and donations.
- Online monitoring of beneficiary schemes.
- Online monitoring of employment generation schemes.
- Better transparency in beneficiary schemes and employment generation schemes.
- Updated information on other government schemes.
- Compilation of data regarding work schemes, administrative management and accounts.

Website: http://epanchayat.cg.nic.in/

E-Governance Project: Chhattisgarh InfoTech Promotion Society (CHIPS)

The Chattisgarh government launched this project with the aim of providing quality and excellence through a single window facility for the district collectorate, municipal corporations, development authorities etc., It is a strategic deployment of information technologies, and a concentrated focus on the opportunities of the information and communication technologies.

ICHiPS is a registered society promoted by the government and the nodal agency. With implication of Information Communication Technology (ICT), CHiPS plans to improve the livelihoods of the overwhelming SC/ST population in forest areas of Chattisgarh, which had largely remained untouched by modern development.

With the implication of ICT the tehsil level offices deal with land records, relief operations etc. All these services have been computerized with the aid of CHiPS. The services of the government reach citizens through centres called the Chhattisgarh Online information System for Citizens Empowerment (CHOiCE). ICT services provide current information related to:

- Monsoon forecasts
- Government schemes
- Information on modern farming practices
- Agriculture and forests which contribute significantly to the state's income.

E-Governance Project: CGnet (Chhattisgarh Net)

The Chhattisgarh government implemented an e-government project for its rural/tribal population in 2004. The project is called CGnet (Chhattisgarh Net), and aims to promote community participation through effective communication for the development of Chhattisgarh.

Chhattisgarh Net is a citizen journalism experiment, whereby CGnet is trying to train citizens in remote tribal Chhattisgarh on how to use new technology to communicate. For this purpose a website www.cgnet.in has been set up, which is a bilingual community portal for Chhattisgarh.

The site is primarily in Hindi and Chhattisgarhi, and runs mainly as an online community through the website and the mailing list, with periodic meetings. The intention is to develop CGNet website as a modern e-Panchayat Ghar, where any Chhattisgarhia, living in any part of the world can visit from time to time, discuss, debate and act when they agree on anything.

Website: www.cgnet.in

E-Governance Project: Chhattisgarh Online Information for Citizen Empowerment (CHOiCE)

A variety of services are provided by the Chhattisgarh government to its citizens. It has implemented a project to provide a one stop solution for anywhere anytime based secured services for all the requirements of citizens. The project called CHOiCE means Chhattisgarh Online Information for Citizen Empowerment.

The Chattisgarh government implemented this project in 2002 for G2C transactions. This project deals with online disbursement of government services to the citizens and it is one of the most comprehensive solutions covering 130 services (G2C, G2B and G2G) which include issuance of:

- Certificates
- Electronic payment
- Information on schemes
- MIS etc.

The project uses state of the art technology with digital signatures and biometric security devices.

Website: www.choice.gov.in

GOVERNMENT OF DELHI

E-Governance Project: (Automatic Vehicle Tracking System Pilot System) (AVTSPS)

The Delhi government proposes this project for tracking and monitoring buses across the city. This is first kind of project which implements Geographic Information System (GIS) & Global Positioning System (GPS) technology as a tool. AVTSPS works by monitoring and moderating Delhi's vehicle tracking system. Automatic Vehicle Tracking System Pilot System (AVTSPS) functions under the Delhi Transport Corporation. AVTSPS is based on Global Positioning System (GPS) and Geographical Information Systems (GIS) technologies with trunk radio-based communication between buses and the control room.

This system will look after fleet management, tracking and monitoring of buses to check operational parameters, speed-limit violations, skipping bus-stops, route adherence, etc. It will also look after two-way emergency communication with drivers. AVTSPS covers the following:

- Reduced the processing time
- More information available on the web
- Checks non-adherence to time-schedules
- Monitors speed-limit violations
- Notes skipping bus-stops

E-Governance Project: Computerized Bus Pass System (CBPS)

The Delhi Government initiated an e-government project to provide computerized bus passes. The CBPS system is not only focused on G2C, but also plans:

- Improve internal efficiency
- Better record management
- Faster processing of application
- Easy availability of information
- Instant booking
- Quick and accurate process for citizens
- Quick preparation of reports

To reduce the time taken to issue passes to bus-commuters, to have their records computerized and to eliminate the possibility of tampering with passes, the Delhi Transport Corporation (DTC) traffic department has initiated the Computerized Bus Pass System (CBPS) project. Data/records, which were not readily available before computerization, are now readily available. Bus passes are issued through computers, photographs of the applicant are taken with a web-camera and fast renewals are made through history data.

The project is the best example of citizen centric e-governance. It will also moderate all government transitions for betterment of the government's transport department.

E-Governance Project: Delhi Slum Computer Kiosks project

Government of Delhi State initiated an e-government project to helping to improve the educational conditions of the Ambedkar Nagar slums as well as to spread computer awareness. The main focus group for this project is girls who reside in slum areas.

In November 2000, the Delhi government initiated a unique project targeted at the urban poor. After using the computer based learning modules, the children's grades in subjects like science, maths and the English language improved remarkably. The community is now lobbying the Delhi government for more content and multimedia based self-paced educational resources.

The project is also exploring the option of providing separate access hours for girls.

E-Governance Project: Hospital Management Information System (HMIS)

The Delhi Government initiated a special kind of e-governance project for hospital management. This works with MIS with the purpose of:

- Improving internal efficiency
- Implementing better record management
- A faster processing of application
- Easy availability of information
- Quick preparation of reports
- Collaboration and sharing of information

HMIS works as an up gradation and patents convenience including telemedicine facility. HMIS has erased the delay/non availability of reports and records, illegible information of out patient department (OPD) cards and lab reports and delay in compilation of statistical reports of post medical record data through the use of computers. Now the patient's demographic details are entered and computerized in the OPD registration, information is fed into the computer and printing of test reports, printing of bar coded sample identifiers and requisition slips is done through the computer. So far HMIS has been successful in improving public health delivery.

E-Governance Project: ICICI Micro-Banking

ICICI Bank is India's second largest financial institution which adopted the franchise model for widening its reach in the rural areas of India by mobilizating the strength of existing microfinance organizations and self-help groups (SHGs). With that aim ICICI along with other private companies like Godrej, Sara Lee and government organizations planned the micro-banking project in 2003. The aim of the project is to serve the poor and rural people, by new partnerships and innovative uses of ICTs to profitably market banking services to the poorest of the poor. This project provides services like:

- Easy loans
- Funds to cattle farmers
- Market research reports for business information
- Corporate training

By formalizing the rural financial services market, ICICI is fulfilling the long unmet demand for rural credit at an interest rate that enables borrowers to uplift themselves.

E-Governance Project: India Calls - Volunteering in the Digital Age

India Calls was implemented by the NGOs MITRA Technology Foundation and 'Swechha-We for Change Foundation'. The aim of the project is to create a world class organization and to fulfil the much needed requirement of professionals. It also aims to service the different volunteer needs of these organizations. The concept of the e-governance project is social development through ICT. A powerful network is created between social and the economic level.

The software here acts as a platform where individuals and organizations register on the site and the organizations post volunteering opportunities. The channel is divided into three major sections:

- Individuals
- Non-profit organizations
- Corporate bodies

A user gets a user name and a password after registration and can log in and use the different features of the site. The organisation can view volunteers who have shown interest in a particular opportunity, search for volunteers based on location, skills and period for which they require the job and then contact them.

GOVERNMENT OF GOA

E-Governance Project: Info Gram

The Goa Government plans to implement a comprehensive IT solution to all the activities in the village panchayats, across twenty village panchayats of Goa. The expected outcome is that the various functions of the panchayat are appropriately automated and maintained.

Info Gram envisages automation of the functions of a village panchayat and maintains on-line records thereby providing efficiency, accountability and transparency in the panchayat administration and also provides vital inputs for decentralized planning.

The information and services provided through Info Gram include:

- Registration of births/deaths
- House Tax
- Licenses
- Caste certificates
- Income certificates
- Accounts
- Panchayat information

GOVERNMENT OF GUJARAT

E-Governance Project: State Wide Attention on Grievances by Application of Technology (SWAGAT)

The Gujarat Government implemented a state-of-the-art project called "SWAGAT", which stands for State Wide Attention on Grievances by Application of Technology. The purpose of the project is to make the public grievance system transparent, accountable and responsive for both the public and the government.

SWAGAT is a unique online grievance redressal system to put the common man in direct touch with the highest office in the administration. The 4th Thursday of every month is a SWAGAT day and citizens can walk in to any district 'Jan Sampark' office and register their complaints. All complaints are registered and sent to the relevant departments for redressal. These departments have to be ready with their responses by 3 pm the same day. SWAGAT relies on the existing ICT infrastructure, particularly the Gujarat State Wide Area Network (GSWAN). Overall, SWAGAT is a very good example of how ICTs could be useful in direct communication and conveying messages from the common man to the government. It is a good example of a citizen centric e-governance system, where citizens can directly present their problem/complaints/grievances.

E-Governance Project: State Wide Information on Financial Transactions (SWIFT)

The Gujarat Government implemented an e-governance initiative for G2G transactions focusing on financial transactions. The project "SWIFT" plans to facilitate the finance department and other government departments, so that they can monitor financial transactions carried out by the department itself and their sub offices at respective District Treasuries and Pay and Account Offices (PAOs).

Financial transactions and their monitoring is a vital part of every government department. The departments mainly collect the inputs from the lower level offices and derive the expenditure incurred and availability of funds. The majority of these transactions are carried out through treasuries and PAOs, which have all computerized their operations and connected to GSWAN.

The project provided the opportunity to disseminate the information to each office and its head office simultaneously. Initially it started with the online status and voucher information for each bill. Now the data from all treasuries and PAOs are compiled at the state data centre on a daily basis and consolidated statements are generated at each level.

E-Governance Project: Smart Card Based Driving Licenses

This smart card based driving license is being issued in the state of Gujarat under the aegis of the transport commissionerate. It is the first of its kind in the world. The aim of the smart card based driving license is to ensure maximum security and eliminate fraud or fake licenses.

The smart card contains details of the person owning it namely, his name, address, date of birth, license number, period of validity of the license, date it was issued, vehicle(s) it is valid for, blood group, photograph and thumb print. The constant personal details, including the thumb impressions, are recorded in the microchip, which is embossed on the card. It is the thumb impression stored on the microchip that makes the smart card unique.

Advantages of the project are:

- With such updated data available, a track can be maintained on accidents violations, and control reports with accurate analysis can be generated.
- All the RTOs in the state will be networked with the central server in Ahemdabad. This, if any license holder obtains a duplicate license it will be known also his/her information can be updated at any RTO office across the state.

E-Governance Project: SICN (Sachivalaya Integrated Communication Network)

The Gujarat Government implemented many e-governance projects to cover citizen-centric services, G2G transitions are also a must for communication of local governments across the state. With this purpose the "SICN" project was implemented by the Government of Gujarat.

The Sachivalaya Integrated Communication Network (SICN) enables excellent connectivity between various government offices with state-of-the-art technology. The electronic telephone system with more than 7000 connections handles around 1,25,000 internal calls and a further 70,000 calls outside the network each day. The system has resulted in tremendous savings for the government on internal calls and also provides enhanced facilities such as voice mailbox, conference calling, CCTV and disaster communication. A state-of-the-art server farm integrated with the network has been commissioned with web servers, DNS servers, mail servers and database servers to enable the government departments to host and manage their websites locally.

E-Governance Project: Sachivalaya Campus Area Network (SCAN)

This is the first state in the country where the residences of secretaries and ministers have direct "fibre to home". The optical fibre (4 core at each termination point) is terminated in each bungalow for data communication and broadband services. Transceivers are used for fibre to UTP conversion. This network enables the officials to have a "virtual office" from home.

SCAN is connected to the Gujarat State Wide Area Network and with broad band connectivity available at home, officers have even the smallest functional unit in the administration at their door step. The interconnection of SCAN has been effected and all nodes at Sachivalaya have total access to the GSWAN resources.

E-Governance Project: Initiative to Nurture a Vibrant Information Technology (INVITE)

The Government of Gujarat initiated an e-governance program INVITE in the education sector. It tied up with the IT service giant IBM, and initiated the project in 2005, INVITE concluded in March-2006. More than 1800 engineering & MCA students of about 31 colleges from 9 universities have participated in this program and they have developed a prototype solution for local e-governance needs at various levels. Under this project, various programs have been conducted in major cities across the state to benefit local IT professionals and college teachers, namely:

- Technical seminars
- Workshops
- Examination on various courses
- Certification courses

E-Governance Project: Gyan Ganga Project

Gyan Ganga is one of the most ambitious initiatives of the Government of Gujarat to ensure wireless internet connectivity to all 18,000 villages. The ultimate objective of the project is to bridge the connectivity gap existing between rural and urban areas in a cost effective manner.

At the heart of the Gyan Ganga project is corDECT - a technology based on Wireless in Local Loop (WLL) - specially developed by the Government of India's education initiatives at IIT-Madras. Under the project an effort will be made to develop services and create local language content relevant to the villagers. These services will initially lay emphasis on the:

- Education sector
- e-governance sector

but will also include

- Agriculture
- Health
- Social welfare

Rural citizens can now access a host of online services such as:

- E-mail
- Internet browsing
- Land records
- Rural job opportunities
- Status of various government projects
- Consult specialists through video conferencing for their queries on
    - Agriculture
    - Veterinary problems
    - Healthcare

E-Governance Project: e-Dhara

The Gujarat Government implemented an e-governance project concentrating on land records system. The e-Dhara project started with the objectives of ensuring an efficient, accurate and transparent delivery mechanism, facilitating conflict resolution in ownership, providing electronic records of rights to land owners at nominal rates and empowering land owners through timely and accurate information. The land owners can get printed copies of their land-holding documents with ease and tampering with revenue records is minimized. From the government side data retrieval is now simpler and detailed reports can be instantly generated regarding:

- Land use
- Crops taken
- Source of water
- Type of electrical equipment fitted
- Trees

This user friendly system with a local language interface benefits citizens as well as the administration.

E-Governance Project: e-City

The Ahmedabad Municipal Corporation, a mega-city of Gujarat State plans to provide a citizen centric service at a one-stop-shop. The project was implemented with the aim to facilitate better performance of the delivery of municipal services like birth and death registration, building plans, primary health and education, city cleanliness, water supply, sewage, road, street-lights, parks and garden through e-governance to the citizens of Ahmedabad city.

Objectives:

- Provide better services to citizens of Ahmedabad
- Provide easy access to information
- Eliminate discretionary human interface
- Reduce files, process data and make the decision making processes faster
- Raise resources for AMC

For this Ahmedabad Municipal Corporation has established six city civic centres located in five zones of Ahmedabad city and also created forty-three ward civic offices, interconnected via intranet/Internet connectivity. At present the following services are offered at each city civic centre:

- Registration of complaints
- Instant issuance of building plan permissions
- Payments of all municipal dues (property tax and vehicle tax etc.)
- Registration and issuance of birth and death certificates
- Issuance of licenses for shops and establishments
- Information on infrastructure projects and tenders
- Issuance of health and hawker's licenses
- Right to information applications received
- Professional tax
- Pro rata charges (PRC connection) water meter

Benefits:

- Transparency to the citizens
- Information and accountability for the citizens as well as employees of the corporation
- Increase in revenue for the corporation

All this information is available on the website www.egovamc.com so that 24-hour remote access to AMC transactions and services are available.

E-Governance Project: e-Gram

The Gujarat Government implemented the e-government project named "e-Gram", with special concentration on the gram panchayats of villages of Gujarat. The aim of the project is to totally computerize the gram panchayats. This e-governance application entails computerization at the village level itself for instant processing of birth and death registrations and issuance agriculture, caste, income and electricity certificates, etc. The computerization also includes tax collection and issuance of certain forms.

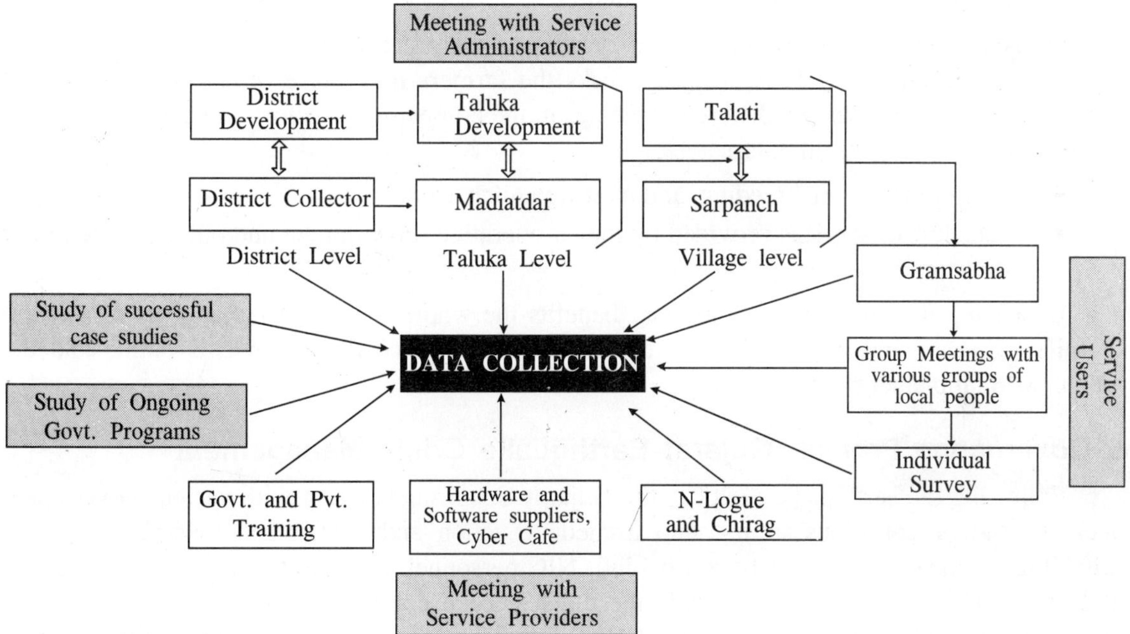

Fig. 11.1: ***Chart showing data collection from various primary sources***

Encouraged by the successful implementation of a pilot project in the Valukad village of Bhavnagar, the government has set a target of implementing this e-Gram concept across all villages of Gujarat. The Panchayat Department has planned to roll out e-Gram services in all villages of Gujarat State. The government aims to make these centres self sustainable and therefore it has been decided to provide technical and training support to these e-Gram computer centres.

E-Governance Project: Dairy Information Systems Kiosk (DISK)

The Government of Gujarat plans to serve milkmen with ICT to enhance milk production and breeds of cattle as well as to benefit the society of milkmen. DISK: Dairy Information Systems Kiosk is an initiative aimed at helping the dairy farmers with timely messages and educating them on the care for their milk cattle and enhancing the production of quality milk.

It also aims at assisting dairy unions in effectively scheduling and organizing veterinary, artificial insemination, cattle feed and other related services. The DISK project maintains a database including a complete history of all milk cattle owned by the farmers. The basic details maintained in the system are as follows:

- History of disease and breed
- Inoculations
- Artificial insemination
- Pregnancy details of breed
- Longitudinal data on milk production

Decision support systems have been developed to forecast milk collection, and provide feedback to the farmers. Through these kiosks the farmers may place orders for a variety of goods and services offered by different agencies in the co-operative sector, and seek information on a variety of subjects of interest like:

- Best practices in breeding and rearing milch cattle,
- Schedule of services provided by the co-operative, government and other private sector agencies

Enhancing the milkmen's community benefits the whole society of Gujarat, as production of milk increases and breeds also serve well. Milkmen place their problems online and the whole MIS implements this system.

E-Governance Project: Gujarat Earthquake Crisis Management

Following the earthquake in 2001, the Gujarat Government along with various government agencies and organizations sprang into immediate action and contributed towards relief and rehabilitation measures. Not to be left behind, NIC personnel in Gujarat and at the headquarters at Delhi worked relentlessly to provide the much needed communication support to the relief operations. Below we give an overview of NIC's contribution towards dealing with the calamity.

Video conferencing support

NIC Gujarat State Unit, set up a video-conferencing facility from Bhuj and Gandhinagar using portable SCPC VSATs. With the facility in place, it was possible to have a videoconference with Bhuj and Gandhinagar from any of the NIC video-conferencing studios operational in twenty- six cities of India. This communication facility helped the Gujarat State Government and the Government of India tremendously by ensuring better co-ordination of the massive relief work being undertaken in the quake-hit areas.

Natural disaster management control room

The Natural Disaster Management Division, Ministry of Agriculture, Government of India is the nodal agency for monitoring relief and rescue activities at a national level in the wake of a natural disaster. The NHMIS division of NIC provides valuable informatics support to this division.

PIB and web services support

Immediately following the earthquake, a special emergency feature was included in the Press Information Bureau's (PIB) website, to cover the same. As the PIB happens to be the official nodal agency to disseminate govt information to the print and electronic media, people relied heavily on the PIB website (http://pib.nic.in) to get the latest and up-to-date information about the earthquake crisis.

E-Governance Project: Mahiti Mitra

The Government of Gujarat's project, Mahiti Mitra was implemented in the year 2006, in the region of Kutch, targeting citizens of that region. This project started with the creation of ICT kiosks which enable gram panchayat bodies and gramsabhas to access various ICT technology applications. The kiosks provide information services in order to improve the citizen's abilities to set, govern and generate better development opportunities in 380 villages in the Kutch district of Gujarat State.

The objectives of the project are to satisfy and improve self governance under the panchayati raj system.

E-Governance Project: Mahiti Shakti

E-governance activities in Gujarat have been initiated by a number of government entities, at different levels such as departments, district offices, commissioners and also other state agencies. One such initiative has been taken in the Godhra district of Gujarat. This project is known as 'Mahiti Shakti' ("power of information").

The Mahiti Shakti project was started in 2001 and has facilitated information access for the rural citizens of the Panchmahal district. The target groups of the project and the primary foci are the tribal communities, populations living in backward areas and families living below the poverty line. The secondary focus is on the general citizens of Godhra district.

Goals of Mahiti Shakti

- Electronic/Online submission of forms, transactions and information exchange (e.g. citizen-government)
- Immediate access to information on government schemes and subsidies, etc.
- Online grievance redressal
- Enhanced and effective citizen-to government interaction
- Dissemination of useful citizen-centric information, transactions and services
- The broad goals of the project are:
  - Transparency: Periodic display of the progress/status of schemes and plans
  - Right to information: Empowering the consumers by giving information
  - Demystifying the office: Addressed with due support and access mechanisms

The project is implemented through about 80 information centres (Mahiti Shakti Kendras) through which citizens can access various types of information, Gujarat Geographic Information System (GGIS) maps, medical information, legal aid, online submission of applications, e-Darbar and opinion poll facilities, grievance redressal, Mahiti Mahisagar (an electronic newsletter), photo gallery, entertainment like music, magazines, other useful Internet sites, etc.

Services provided

- Over 200 forms have been made available for transactions between citizens and the government. These forms carry details of the documents to be attached with the main form at the time of submission.
- The forms and checklists have been made available as printouts at a prescribed fee at the MSKs.
- The web enabled version of the GGIS developed by the Gujarat Government agency, RESECO gives details of the resources available in every village of the district, which are available through a query-based system.
- An electronic newsletter called Mahiti Mahisagar featuring medical help, legal help, a science corner, a children's corner, etc., is published.
- There is also a grievance redressal forum for citizens to voice their specific complaints. Electronic submission of forms, for applications such as the National Old Age Pension Scheme (NOAPS), is available.
- For water-related grievances and ration card applications, the applicant fills out the form at the kiosk. The back-end process is carried out by the government staff and the final reply is sent to the applicant by e-mail and post.
- The portal also provides a chat session with the ministers and senior officers of the district. There is useful information on over 30 specific crops grown in Panchmahals, giving details of the seeds, fertilizers, insecticides, pesticides and organic manure, etc. exclusively prepared for the portal by the Gujarat State Fertilizer Corporation (GSFC) Foundation. Access to the electoral roll is also available.

Website: www.mahitishakti.net

GOVERNMENT OF HIMACHAL PRADESH

E-Governance Project: Pehal (e-initiative – The Citizens Service Centre)

The Himachal Pradesh Government implemented the project named "Pehal" (e-initiative – The Citizens Service Centre) for providing citizen centric services to their citizens. The project was implemented in the district of Kangra of Himachal Pradesh in 2002. With this project the Himachal Pradesh Government aimed to improve the quality of services of government departments by re-engineering the administrative processes in order for the convenience of users. The 'Pehal' e-governance centres offer many services to their citizens such as:

- Vehicle licensing
- Registration of vehicles
- Issue of records of rights related to property
- Passport applications
- Property registration
- Issuance of various certificates

The services are offered under one roof in a single window in a time bound manner using applications which are basically on-line transaction processing wherein the information is taken from the applicant on standard government prescribed formats/forms. In such cases applicants' photographs, digital signatures and finger print impressions are taken on the spot. Acceptance of online cash and services are provided almost immediately, which earlier used to take an unspecified time.

E-Governance Project: Integrated Community Service Centre (i-CoSC)

The Himachal Pradesh Government implemented the project with national and international agencies in 2005. The aim of the project is to empower the rural population by providing access to community-based information and communication resources and ICT-based applications. i-CoSC provides a one-stop shop information resource and service centre for the common man. The project focuses on the sectors covering:

- Health
- Education
- Agriculture resources
- Natural resources
- Rural enterprise development

Some of the services include the status of all applications and information pertaining to all departments (schemes etc.) through a web portal, touch screen kiosks and mobile phone.

E-Governance Project: Himachal Registration Information System (HIMRIS)

The Himachal Pradesh Government implemented the HIMRIS project in 2003. Himachal Registration Information System [HIMRIS] has been developed with the objective of providing:

- Single window services
- Timely registration
- Transparent and reliable transactions
- Monitoring of the revenue generated out of registration

The Himachal Registration Information System ensures a simple, uniform document registration process with a guarantee of returning the original document after registration and archival within same day with the implementation of ICT. The computerization process behaves in a workflow manner right from presentation of the deed, entry, checking by the sub registrar, marking for fees, deed number generation, endorsement, scanning, deed delivery etc. in a short period.

Besides, a standardized and systematic calculation of various duties and surcharges is ensured by the software. HIMRIS prevents frauds like impersonation, professional witnesses and ensures better monitoring of revenue collection and helps citizens to get hassle-free registration.

E-Governance Project: Him Bhoomi

The Himachal Pradesh Government implemented an e-government system for a transparent, effective and efficient land record delivery system: In the traditional system, records were not open for public scrutiny resulting in manipulation and favouritism. Bribes were extracted for issue of records.

Him Bhoomi (land records computerization) software for Himachal Pradesh is a work flow comprising many convoluted inherent linkages spanning various documents and computerizes not only the land records of rural and urban areas but also includes:

- Land reforms
- Irrigation census details
- Agriculture census statistics besides customary and forestry rights

E-Governance Project: e-Vikas

The G2C transition is a must for managing government in the IT age. The Himachal Pradesh Government implemented the e-Vikas project in the state with a vision to bring the entire spectrum of rural development programs and projects being implemented in the district under the common ambit of information technology based on the government to citizen (G2C) interface. e-Vikas is a state-of-the-art G2C interactive platform based on a touch screen, which gives information regarding various rural development schemes/programs being implemented by the district rural development agency. Citizens are able to access simple forms of information, while the government agencies present information through the information kiosks.

E-Governance Project: Department of Agriculture and Cooperation Network (DACNET)

The Himachal Pradesh Government planned the DACNET Project to facilitate agriculture-on-line by implementing the following aspects:

- Integrating government functions (G2G)
- Integrating agri-business partners (B2B)
- Connecting farmers (C2C)
- Empowering employees
- Enhancing government productivity
- Value and financial services

With the ICT implementation and technical help from government agencies, the DACNET platform facilitates e-governance and agricultural services like:

- Plant quarantine reports
- Weather watch
- State-wise prices for various agricultural products
- Market-wise prices for various agricultural products
- For planning and day-to-day operations by farmers

This project developed through adoption of various tools like

- XML
- SOAP
- UDDI
- Intranet to internet capability
- Mail/Messaging

All the services are available at the agriculture information centres (like Krishi Vikas Kendras) in each village. DACNET is implemented across the state with a central server. High configured network systems were also established to provide messaging and workflow solutions, portal services and decision support systems within the project. The website for DACNET is www.dacnet.nic.in

E-Governance Project: Lok-mitra

The Himachal Pradesh Government implemented the e-government project Lok-mitra in 2001, with an aim to provide the general public, especially those living in distant rural areas of Himachal Pradesh, the benefits of "using information technology (IT) in governance (e-governance)" at their doorstep.

Lok-mitra is a web-enabled G2C project of the government of Himachal Pradesh. For this project several citizen information centres (Lok-Mitra Soochna Kendra) have been set up at Hamidpur district in HP. Lok-Mitra Soochna Kendras are managed by the unemployed youth selected by the Lok-Mitra society on a self-sustaining basis. Various services are provided to the rural population at their doorstep as follows:

- Grievance redressal
- Queries
- Downloadable forms
- Details of development schemes
- How to avail of the benefits from various schemes
- Market rates
- Buying-selling
- Matrimonial
- Notices
- Tender
- Vacancy details

A nominal fee is charged from the users of this service.

E-Governance Project: Reference Monitoring System (REFNIC)

The Himachal Pradesh Government implemented REFNIC, an e-governance project in 2005, with the objective of eliminating use of paper in government offices by the eTracking system, so that citizen-centric services could be catered to more efficiently. Implemented across the Secretariat of Himachal Pradesh, The Reference Monitoring System (REFNIC) is software, which keeps track of the movement of files and letters and has features for e-Tracking any letter and file by searching for the same by subject, date, name or any keyword on the secretariat LAN as well as on the Internet. This project was developed by Government and State Agencies,

REFNIC generates the reminders automatically in printed form as well as by e-mail and pop-up message on the screen. It is standard software which can be replicated in all government offices as it is built around the current procedure of dealing papers, policies, letters, rules and files while introducing some systematic changes through process engineering. REFNIC is professional excellence and process of re-engineering.

GOVERNMENT OF JHARKHAND

E-Governance Project: Chalao Ho Gaon Mein

Jharkhand a newly formulated state has not lagged behind any other state in empowerment of their citizens. With the aim of empowerment and development of social communities, Jharkhand state government launched its Chalao Ho Gaon Mein project in 2001, a weekly evening programme broadcast over the local FM radio station dealing local issues like:

- Child marriage
- Dowry
- Superstitious beliefs
- Gender discrimination
- Village development
- Issues related to agriculture

The programme is aired in the local tribal language. The initiators of this project have provided technical support, to air a half-hour community broadcast on state-run radio. It also conducted a series of workshops to educate villagers on the benefit of community broadcasting.

Community radio has helped to connect 45 villages of Palamau. A recent internal impact study across 374 villages revealed that 98 per cent of the village folk listen to the programme regularly and have received benefits from this programme. For empowerment social awareness is must, as step of the process. The Jharkhand government initiated this project and the outcomes of this project go to the people of the state.

E-Governance Project: MAMTA

The Government of Jharkhand proposed a one of its kind of e-government project that focuses on "mother and child care", named "MAMTA". The "MAMTA" program caters to the health of pregnant women and newborns after birth. The nutritional aspects of women and the newborn are also taken care of under the program. The program will be a boon to the rural and tribal population of the state.

It is expected to considerably lower the infant as well as the maternal mortality rate. Jharkhand is determined to successfully implement this program. The state level agency developed software – MAMTA, which tracks both mother and child related care during pre- and post-natal phases. The special software will prove to be an effective tool for monitoring this very ambitious program.

GOVERNMENT OF KARNATAKA

E-Governance Project: e-Grama

The Karnataka Government initiated the project with the objective of not only helping to bridge the growing digital divide, but also to increase the computer literacy of those living in rural areas. It also aims at providing all e-governance facilities at the panchayat and village level.

The e-grama project makes e-grama centres available across the state. The target groups of the project are farmers and youths. The project provides all relevant information in the following areas:

- Agriculture
- Health
- Education
- Other areas concerning rural life

With the e-grama project, communication between the government and citizens increases and G2C transition allows the government to provide better service to citizens in service areas of the projects.

E-Governance Project: Bangalore One

The Government of Karnataka is keen to provide integrated services to citizens deploying the tools of Information and Communication Technology (ICT), with the objective of providing a 'one-stop-shop' facility for enhancing speed, convenience, certainty and accountability.

The Bangalore One project or B1 has been implemented in Karnataka. It seeks to redefine public service through its focus on the common man. The vision of the project is "to provide to the citizens of Karnataka, all G2C and G2B one-stop services and information of departments and agencies of central, state and local governments in an efficient, reliable, transparent and integrated manner on a sustained basis, with certainty, through easy access to a chain of computerized Integrated Citizen Service Centres (ICSC's) and through multiple delivery channels like electronic kiosks, mobile phones and the Internet".

The mission of the B1 project is "to be the one-stop-shop for all C2G interactions". It plans to cover more 100 G2B, G2C and B2C services in Banglore city. B1 aims to establish 15 service centres initially in different parts of the city and provide 24 basic services of 8 government departments participating initially in the B1 project. Each centre will be housed in 2,000 sq. ft. of air-conditioned office space.

The objectives of Bangalore One project

- To enhance the accountability, transparency and responsiveness to citizens' needs.
- To provide cost-effective methods of service provision to the departments and agencies.
- To provide efficient and real-time MIS and EIS to the departments.
- To ensure speed and certainty of providing the services through enforcement of a service level agreement with the selected partner.
- To enable the government departments and agencies to focus on their core functions and responsibilities by freeing them from routine operations like collection of revenues and accounting, issuing of certificates etc, and thereby enhance the overall productivity of the administrative machinery.

Services provided

- BWSSB & BESCOM: Bill payment, grievance redressal, application for new connections and statement of accounts.
- BCC: Property tax payment, issue of Khata certificate and extract, issue of copies of birth and death certificates, grievance redressal.
- RTO: Learner's license renewal, road tax payment, issue of B-extract for vehicles and payments against challan.
- Stamps and registration: Providing market value assistance.
- Passport: Sale of application forms and new passport application registration.
- CTO: Collection of KST/CST and entry tax.
- Police: Fine for traffic violations.
- Others: Booking of cinema tickets, payment of bills of all cell phone operators.

Expected outcomes of the B1 project

- The citizens should get the services of the government at any time, anywhere, without relation to the jurisdiction of a particular office of a particular department or agency.
- The quality of service should be comparable to the best service in the private sector.
- It should be possible to strictly enforce citizens' charters in respect of quality, efficiency and responsiveness in the provision of services.
- Citizens should be able to see the government as a single service provider, through one-stop facilities.
- Citizens should feel that government services are accessible equally to one and all, irrespective of one's social or economic status.
- The departments and agencies of the government should feel that they are service providers in letter and spirit but not rulers of citizens.

E-Governance Project: Bhoomi

The Karnataka state government implemented an e-governance project named "Bhoomi," which means land, in mid-1998 as a major initiative to computerize land records. The mission of the project is to ensure more secure title deeds and roll back the rampant cases of corruption. The existing registry of the Karnataka government crosses millions of land records of millions of land owners across the state. Karnataka has computerized these records and organized them into a central database.

The government intends to sustain Bhoomi and replicate it at many more delivery points at sub-district levels, by positioning the land records database, which will ensure kiosk operators a minimum income. Bhoomi is keen on private sector involvement and options are being explored for partnerships with the private sector for 'retailing'. The project works to formulate on G2C and G2G transaction processes.

E-Governance Project: Karnataka Valuation and e-Registration (KAVERI) Project

ICT is now used every where in government transactions. The Karnataka Government used ICT for the registration and stamps department, with the project KAVERI, which stands for Karnataka Valuation and e-Registration project. The aim of the KAVERI project is to automate and streamline the workflow of the registration and stamps department of Karnataka. The computerised network of KAVERI will enable the citizens of Karnataka to fulfil the registration process in a shorter turnaround time and give on demand access to valuation documents, encumbrance certificates and various other copies related to land records. The computerised process will ensure authenticity of transactions, safeguarding the citizens' interests against fraud.

All the transactions will be recorded in the centralized server, which can be accessed when necessary. All district registrar offices will be equipped with a server and an internal network that connects the computers and related accessories. Separate customer kiosks are placed at the centre.

E-Governance Project: Khajane: Online Treasury Computerisation

The Government of Karnataka's project "Khajane" is the first project of its kind in the country where the entire array of treasury activities has been computerised. This is the only project where from the time of approval of the state budget to the point of rendering accounts to the government the entire activity can be tracked in the system. Automating procedures and internal controls, has strengthened the financial controls and promoted accountability and resulted in huge expenditure and efficiency gains.

Objectives

- Network all the treasuries for easy access and better control
- Monitor all the transactions through the central server, online
- Eliminate all systemic deficiencies
- Introduce effective budget monitoring and ways and means to control through the system
- Automate generation of monthly accounts

- Set up a comprehensive Financial Management Information System (FMIS) for better management of state finances and contribute for meaningful review of progress of various schemes.

Project Khajane is a G2G project, implemented on a Public Private Partnership (PPP) model, aiming to improve the internal processes of the government treasury functions through online data capturing and central consolidation of the state's financial transactions by a networked system. It is implemented in various districts and talukas of the state. Some of the features of the project are as follows:

Payments

- Information on budget allocation, expenditure and allotment details
- Maintenance of bill process log for transactions
- Pay order generation

Receipts

- Online receipt details with updates of zilla and taluk panchayat balances
- Challan information linked with various modules (stamps, OAP, payments and deposits)
- Automatic generation of treasury transfer receipts

Deposits

- Easy tracking of account details, routed through agency bank or treasury
- Online information on account balances
- Calculation of interest and signature display online
- Lapsed deposits and their revival
- Maintenance of savings bank account details

Stamps

- Stamps inventory information maintained online
- Inter treasury unit transactions recorded
- Strong room details captured
- Information on stamp stocks, embossing of documents

Pension

- Maintenance of pension payment order details
- Automatic conversion of enhanced family pension to normal family pension
- Pensioner status information

E-Governance Project: Krishi Maratha Vahini (KMV)

The Karnataka Government implemented an e-government project to serve farmers in 2002, named Krishi Maratha Vahini (KVM). The aim of the project is to network agricultural produce markets for providing real time prices and other information on crop production, market prices of agri-products, and soil conditions to the farming community.

The project launched a website to provide reliable data on daily arrivals of agricultural commodities with minimum and maximum prices. In all there are over a hundred agricultural produce marketing centres in the state of which the majority are to be computerised. The website enables 24-hour automatic collection and dissemination of market information on around a hundred commodities. Information from other states on various commodities can also be obtained at the site and provision for a farmers' advisory service in local languages will be made in the second phase on the website. The Vahini website is linked to the Bhoomi program and will be linked to the existing Raita Mitra Kendras (RMK). The site will also provide information on various schemes proposed by government agencies working in the agricultural sector.

Website: www.agmarket.nic.in

E-Governance Project: Rural Digital Services

The Karnataka Government implemented an e-government project to maintain G2C transitions, named "Rural Digital Services", in 2003. With this project the government aims to provide services that are IT-enabled in a progressive manner. The project includes issuance of certificates relating to deaths, birth, caste, income, residence etc. The government also plans to issue orders with respect to social security schemes such as old age pensions, widow pensions.

These government services are delivered from more than twenty village Internet kiosks set up by private village entrepreneurs in the two talukas. In addition to providing government services from these kiosks, a pilot program for payment of electricity bills has been started from selected centres. The government will increase the variety of services in future with the rural digital services.

E-Governance Project: Yuva.com

Yuva.com is an IT training scheme conceived by the Department of Information Technology and the Department of Rural Development and Panchayat Raj as part of Mahiti – The Government of Karnataka's millennium IT policy, announced in 2000. It seeks to establish 225 computer training centres in all the assembly constituencies under the Yuva.com scheme for the purpose of training unemployed, educated youth in various IT skills.

Each Yuva.com centre will accommodate about 500 students per year. Special preference will be given to handicapped persons, women candidates, candidates from rural areas and those with an annual income below Rs. 24,000. The trainees will be charged a special fee, less than the normal fee otherwise charged by institutes like APTECH, KEONICS, NIIT, SSI and others.

In turn, the government will subsidize a part of this special fee. After training, the candidates will be able to set up their own ventures in the areas of job typing, desktop publishing etc. For regular employment with companies, placement assistance will be available at each centre.

GOVERNMENT OF KERALA

E-Governance Project: Rural Development Network (RD-net)

The Kerala Government launched an e-government project named "RD-net." The basic idea behind the project is to cover remote locations in the state. With this project the government is to take development information to the rural poor and empower them to become participants in village development activities.

The Rural Development Network (RD-net) provides Internet connectivity to the 152 development blocks in the Thiruvananthapuram district. The RD-net provides services such as:

- Email facilities,
- Data transfer,
- Data downloading,
- Application processing,
- Lodging and settling complaints through computers

The project, implemented with state and national governmental agencies, also provides instant details about poverty alleviation and rural schemes of the state and the central government to the villagers.

E-Governance Project: KISSAN Kerala

The Government of Kerala implemented an e-government project named "KISSAN Kerala", to serve farmers. The aim of the project is to cater to farmers of the entire state of Kerala with:

- The right information
- At the right time,
- In the right place
- In the right context

KISSAN-Kerala, is an ICT enabled project with an integrated and multi-modal delivery of agricultural information, aggregation and knowledge dissemination system created along with state government agencies. With this project the government is able to bring the knowledge and competencies of various agriculture related organisations and stakeholders to the community. It acts according to three basic criteria:

1. The advanced knowledge management portal of KISSAN Kerala, which provides comprehensive information on 55 major crops in Kerala:
   - o Daily agricultural market information system from major markets across the state
   - o Online query management system
   - o Expert system on fertiliser recommendation
   - o Online availability of planning material
   - o Fertilisers/Pesticides

2. An agriculture telephone call centre, with a toll-free number.
3. A popular weekly agriculture television program - Krishideepam, through Asianet, the leading commercial satellite channel in Kerala.

The website for this project is: www.kissankerala.net

E-Governance Project: Fast, Reliable, Instant, Efficient Network for the Disbursement of Services (FRIENDS)

The Kerala Government implemented an e-government project named "FRIENDS", standing for fast, reliable, instant, efficient network for the disbursement of services. This project is a one-stop-shop channel for the citizens of Kerala. The objective of the project is to extend the benefits of fully-fledged computerization of each and every department by offering a one-stop, front end, IT enabled payment counter facility to citizens to make all kinds of government payments.

The FRIENDS counters are equipped to handle more than a thousand types of payment bills (in various combinations) originating from various public sector departments/agencies.

The payments that citizens can make at the counters include:

- Utility payments for electricity
- Water bill payments
- Revenue taxes
- License fees
- Motor vehicle taxes
- University fees

The application has provisions for adding more modules and for rolling back incorrect entries without affecting the database even at the user level.

GOVERNMENT OF MADHYA PRADESH

E-Governance Project: Telebhugtan

The Madhya Pradesh Government planned an e-government project based on G2C relations as well on the citizen-centric-services system, named Telebhugtan. The project enables every citizen who has a telephone and bank account/credit card to pay his bills from anywhere. Telebhugtan is a simple utility bill payment system to pay electricity bills or BSNL telephone bills using any telephone. It eliminates the need to go to an office and stand in long queues, or to go to any ATM or other automatic machines.

This facility is open 24 hours, and can be simply used with a landline, any coin box phone or mobile phone. Anyone who has a bank account can sign up for Telebhugtan. Other utilities added are school fees, corporation taxes etc. The payee needs to personally contact the nearest Telebhugtan agent or the Telebhugtan office to fill up and sign the forms and declarations, only one time.

Once the registration process is completed the payees are given login and TelePIN password, and there is no need to come personally again. Telebhugtan has 3 different plans with different validity periods ranging from 6 months to 3 years. There are flat charges per transaction. The Telebhugtan system has been operative in MP from 2002 onwards without any errors in processing transactions, either from the customer side or the government side.

E-GOVERNANCE PROJECT: MADHYA PRADESH AGENCY FOR PROMOTION OF INFORMATION TECHNOLOGY (MAP_IT)

MAP_IT is an initiative of the Madhya Pradesh Government to serve Indian farmers, traders, and government agencies with appropriate, accurate and timely information for effective decision-making. MAP_IT works on sectoral and cross-sectoral promotion; it coordinates and networks with investors and industries, generates awareness amongst citizens, demystifying IT.

MAP_IT provides a comprehensive and cost effective means of disseminating information and supports infrastructure including telecom infrastructure. Through MAP_IT many other initiatives were taken like smart cards and online access to text and video information. An "e-agricultural marketing" system run by MAP_IT benefit the farmers and licensed traders in Madhya Pradesh.

E-Governance Project: Gyandoot

The Government of Madhya Pradesh has planned an e-government project named "Gyandoot." The aim of the project is to provide access to information and services offered by government to the rural population of Dhar, through a chain of computer kiosks.

Gyandoot is seen as a means to promote local self governance. This provides e-transparency-related information and services, that is:

- Land records
- Those living below the poverty line and other lists
- Grievance registration
- Market prices

Other services include:

- Rural e-mail facility
- A village auction site
- A matrimonial site
- An "ask the wiseman" service for children
- An "ask the expert" service for farmers
- A village newspaper
- An e-education site
- Employment news (aimed at semi-skilled workers)

The kiosks can be used free of charge by local government officials, e.g. for e-mail or to exchange health/education data with the district headquarters.

E-Governance Project: GyanSanchar

GyanSanchar, a project of the Madhya Pradesh Government, aims to develop a model for sustainable expansion of telecommunication services and ICT applications in rural India. It aims to bring affordable and cost effective services to rural India. Village Information Centres (VICs) are set up under the project to provide villagers with access to a broad range of applications based on:

- Telephony
- Internet-based government
- E-business services

It is a proven, sustainable business model for ICT in rural India that seeks to bring about socio-economic development and poverty reduction in villages, particularly for women and disadvantaged groups. Market development opportunities for small, medium, and large Indian businesses are also provided under the project.

Website:www.gyansanchar.net

E-Governance Project: Gram Sampark

'Gram sampark' is a flagship ICT product of the state of Madhya Pradesh. With this project the Madhya Pradesh Government aims to make the system more accountable to the people with the availability of information, basic amenities, beneficiaries of government programs and redressal of public grievances. They also want to bring about transparency in the work. A complete database of available resources, basic amenities, beneficiaries of government programs and public grievances in all the 51,000 villages of Madhya Pradesh can be obtained by accessing the website www.mp.nic.in/gramsampark/.

Gramsampark has three sections:

1. Gram Paridrashya (village scenario)
2. Samasya Nivaran (grievance redress)
3. Gram Prahari (village sentinel)

An eleven-point monitoring system has been put in place whereby programs are monitored village-wise every month. Four more programs are under the monitoring system, which includes eradication of untouchability, women's empowerment, water conservation and campaigns for sanitation.

E-governance Project: e-Gram Suvidha

The Madhya Pradesh Government inaugurated this project with the objective of creating awareness and demonstrating the benefits of geometrics-based systems in decentralized planning and decision making, and providing a user-friendly, low-cost geometrics-based decision support system. E-Gram Suvidha is a GIS based management information system that links the maps of village resolution with the associated data to generate thematic maps based on users' queries. It is easy to use software.

Implementation of the geometric system also enables the e-governance system to move into next generation service, and easily view and access information available at the state government's centre for e-Gram Suvidha.

E-Governance Project: Bhojpatra

The government of Madhya Pradesh implemented Project Bhojpatra an e-government initiative driven ICT with the objective of capacity building of public authorities for improving citizens' access to information for achieving transparency and accountability in the government at all levels, and strengthening the training of civil servants and sensitizing them about citizens' right to information.

The Bhojpatra project targets all the public of Madhya Pradesh and was implemented in 2006 to cover all people under an umbrella for availability of information to all. Bhojpatra, an outcome of mutual cooperation and involvement of various bodies/institutions has emerged as an effective instrument to deliver "improved access to information to citizens" with concomitant benefits of multifarious dimensions. The project is aimed at improving access to information for the citizens of Bhopal.

Website: www.bhojpatra.net

GOVERNMENT OF MAHARASHTRA

E-Governance Project: Warana Wired Villages Project

The Maharashtra Government planned an e-governance project focused on sugar cane co-operatives to enhance production of sugar cane. The Warana Wired Villages Project utilizes IT to increase the efficiency and productivity of the existing sugar cane cooperative enterprises by setting up a state-of-the-art computer communications network.

This project brings the benefits of Information and Communication Technology (ICT) to rural India. It provides links with the diverse business activities in the village and information to people through computerised kiosks.

The state-of-the-art computer communications network provides agricultural, medical, and educational information in the local language to villages around Warana in Maharashtra and neighbouring districts of Warana, in order to maintain long-term sustainability.

This project has been initiated to serve information to the farmers, right up to their village level, on various issues, such as:

- Different crop cultivation practices of major crops
- Sugar cane cultivation practices
- Pest and disease control
- Marketing information
- Dairy and sugarcane processing information

The project has resulted in a Web based information system on the agriculture produce market, agriculture schemes and crop technology, village information system, employment and self-employment schemes, educational and vocational guidance etc. It allows wired management of sugar cane cultivation and marketing over the Intranet. Land record documents will also be made available through the system.

E-Governance Project: Website of Mumbai Police

The Maharashtra Government planned a special project on the Mumbai police force, called Website of Mumbai Police. The aim of the project is to reach out to the citizens of Mumbai through the internet to make law enforcement easier. This project proposed a path towards citizen-centric-service by the Mumbai police department.

Recognizing the needs of citizens, the Mumbai police has now made it easier for citizens to lodge a FIR. They just have to log on to the website - www.mumbaipolice.org and register a non-cognizable offence. In case of a cognizable offence, a police officer from the area police station or the crime branch will immediately call the citizen and register an FIR.

A lot of other interactive and extremely useful features like a ready list of all police stations with their phone numbers, traffic updates, weather updates and advisories are made available. Photographs of missing persons and unidentified bodies are also flashed on the website, so that a larger number of citizens can help in identifying and reporting sightings of missing people. The service is available to citizens on 24×7 basis.

E-Governance Project: Integrated Citizen Facilitation Centres (SETU)

The Maharashtra Government implemented an e-governance initiative with NGOs for citizens who have to visit government offices. The project named "SETU", means a bridge, in fact the project is working to provide greater transparency, accessibility and efficiency to government procedures.

SETU was started in 2001 as a one-stop service centre for people who have to visit government offices for certificates, permits, authentication, affidavits and other services. The most important and frequently issued certificates are the ones related to domicile, nationality, caste, age verification, solvency, character verification, income and occupation. Service charges are liable to be refunded if the certificate is delayed. The centre works on holidays and after office hours on a two-shift basis. The government launched I-Setu kiosks, an electronic version of SETU, in the city of Mumbai from 2004.

E-Governance Project: Pravara Village IT Project (PRAGATI)

The Government of Maharashtra implemented an e-government project in Ahmednagar District in 1999, the aim of the project was to connect a hundred villages in Ahmednagar covering a population of more than 2.5 lakhs with a wireless MAN solution (WMAN). Its objective was to empower the rural population and improve their quality of life. It is a multi step program that helps the villages in establishing following facilities:

- Local IT centres
- Dissemination of information regarding government schemes

- Marketing of agricultural products
- Healthcare
- Education
- Agro processing
- Economic development

Farmers can communicate with the agricultural experts at the Krishi Vigyan Kendra and learn new farming techniques as well as better ways of storing and packing their products for marketing. Health care professionals at the villages can consult with specialists at the medical college and hospital thereby providing specialized treatment, especially during emergencies, at people's doorsteps.

The education sector will also be covered by linking all high schools in around 50 villages within a radius of 10 km. This allows teachers and staff to stay in touch, helping them introduce modern methods of teaching, including computer-based learning (virtual school) at convenient timings for children who have to work during the day.

E-Governance Project in Mumbai City: Online Complaint Monitoring System for Mumbai (OCMS)

The Brihan-Mumbai Municipal Corporation (BMC) planned the project OCMS (Online Complaint Monitoring System for Mumbai) in 2003. The project is the first of its kind anywhere in the world. The aim is to enable citizens of Mumbai, to register complaints and receive information on the complaint status quickly and easily.

The OCMS is a G2C transition based e-governance project, a cohesive system which files complaints from any source – the Internet, phone calls and letters to the BMC, and enters the data into the OCMS database. On submission of a form, a unique complaint tracking number is given, which helps to check the status of the complaint on the internet. OCMS also provides a number of reports regarding departments and the corporation as a whole that enable senior municipal corporation officials to monitor and improve the services.

The OCMS has many salient features, such as making it easier to respond, maintain, and evaluate a complaint. If the complaint is not heeded, it automatically goes to the higher official, bringing about transparency in governance. For the first time an NGO is partnering the government.

E-Governance Project: Digital Payment System

The objective of this project is to help poor farmers in using IT as a tool to help increase the productivity of their existing cooperatives. The vision is to provide comprehensive solutions to rural commerce to maintain day-to-day business processes, connect rural Indians and increase business transparency in rural commerce using information technology.

The DPS project has been designed keeping in view the larger sections of the population living in rural areas and their vast problems including their lack of access to the advancement of information technology.

The project focuses on improving the billing and collections for rural cooperatives through the provision of "SMART" cards, and timely disbursement of payments. Billing and payment collection is streamlined through creation of "smart cards" with electronic accounts of farmers' dues and revenues, which can be used to pay bills and purchase consumer products at cooperatives and other stores.

This will reduce the time required to obtain payments for milk, sugarcane and other products delivered by cooperative members.

GOVERNMENT OF NAGALAND

E-Governance Project: E-MODOP

The Government of Nagaland planned the project E-MODOP with the aim of redressing grievances of the people and keeping government officials informed of their problems. It is an endeavour of the Government of Nagaland to provide integrated services to all citizens, by utilizing the modern tools of information technology in order to ensure a reliable, efficient and transparent system of governance, through the project e-Modop, on the lines of similar projects implemented elsewhere in the country.

The vision of the e-Modop project is "to provide to the citizens of Nagaland all G2C services and information with regard to schemes and programs of departments and agencies of central, state and local governments in an efficient, reliable, transparent and integrated manner through easy access to integrated citizen service centres, kiosks, mobile phones and the internet". The mission statement of the e-Modop project is "to provide service to citizens that is reliable and always available". Such an ambitious project, which aims to redefine delivery of services of the government, will be implemented in a phased manner.

The pilot project is being implemented in Mokokchung district and delivery of services will be through CIC centres and Internet kiosks. E-Modop services are being offered through its website and also through a call centre where users can call anytime and register their public grievances. This facility is operational 24 hours a day and 7 days a week. In the next phase of the project, it will be rolled out to all the eleven districts and services will be available through mobile phones in addition to citizen service centres and kiosks. The number of services offered will be fifteen from seven government departments, in the first phase, which will gradually be increased to 20 basic services.

Website: http://www.emodop.com

GOVERNMENT OF ORISSA

E-Governance Project: e-Sahayata: A Citizen Information Centre

The Government of Orissa implemented an ICT enabled e-government project to create the right governance and institutional mechanism towards ensuring citizen-centricity by adopting suitable standards and best practices.

e-Sahayata is an integrated district level electronic information-cum service provider system, implemented under the National e-Governance Plan (NeGP), which will provide information and services pertaining to various departments of the government working in the district to the public in a friendly and efficient manner using information and communication technology (ICT).

e-Sahayata also aims to cater to the needs of the government machinery by handling office and inter-office automation needs with the kiosk. An e-Sahayata kiosk is an integrated e-platform through which the rural and urban population of the state can get desired information by means of touch screen kiosks suitably placed at state, district, sub-division, block and other locations. e-Sahayata information would also be made available on the Internet. The e-Sahayata service counter is a one-stop, citizen friendly computerised service delivery counter to provide a wide range of services under one roof.

E-Governance Project: Bhu Lekh

The Orissa government has planned this project with the aim of covering the whole state under an interaction channel. A G2C portal has been implemented by the Orissa government, called Bhu Lekh. The objective of the project is to make administration easy and reduce manual work and enable more transparency in the system. It also aims at centralized preservation and better access to land record data to all citizens.

Bhu-lekh is a G2C-R project in Orissa with a vision to deliver quality service to citizens in a timely and transparent manner and to ensure a transparent, user-friendly and efficient e-governance system through Citizen Service Centres (CSCs).

Services offered under the project at all Sampark Centres include issue of:

- RoR (Right of Record)
- Certificates like caste certificate
- Nativity certificate
- Residential certificate
- Income certificate
- Valuation certificate
- Legal heir certificate
- Online mutation of land

These services are available on a First in First Out (FIFO) basis.

Website: www.bhulekh.ori.nic.in

GOVERNMENT OF PUNJAB

E-Governance Project: Jagriti e-Sewa

The Punjab Government initiated the Jagriti e-Sewa project in 2003 with governmental agencies. The target group of the project is the rural population of Punjab. Jagriti is a platform for application of information technology for the rural masses. The Jagriti e-Sewa project was designed to bring development and technology together for the rural areas. The focus has been to develop low-cost (free/libre and open source) applications that are rural-centric and needed by the rural masses. The project aims at the deployment of IT enabled services for:

- Education
- Agricultural information
- Health, e-governance
- Other location-specific needs

The project involves setting up rural information kiosks, called Jagriti e-Sewa kendras, in nodal villages and other viable locations across Punjab. Each centre is franchised to educated youth or an ex-serviceman of the area.

The various services provided under the project include – Sending and receiving e-mails in Punjab, delivery of prepaid cards for cell phones, Virtual Calling Cards (VCC), Internet, internet phone, booking of seats - rail reservations, buses to Delhi airport - life insurance policies, vehicle financing, money transfers and precision agriculture, that includes input/produce linkages, contract, organic farming, soil testing and fertilizer dose guidance.

Website: www.jagriti.com

GOVERNMENT OF RAJASTHAN

E-Governance Project: Raj Nidhi

The Government of Rajasthan planned an e-governance project based on G2C, G2G transition named "Raj Nidhi". The aim of the project is to provide transparency in the functioning of the state administration and right to information to the general public. Raj Nidhi was planned with a clear vision to help people obtain information of a general nature related to various governmental departments providing public utility services with minimum effort and in a short time.

Raj Nidhi is a data warehouse system of all such information that is of interest to the general public and is not confidential. It is not openly accessible to the public but with appropriate requirements, citizens can obtain information on the requested subject. This is made available through ICT enabled information kiosks based on intranet technology. These kiosks are meant to provide the citizens access to information related to:

- Health
- Family planning
- Immunization schedules for children
- Employment
- Transportation
- Distance education
- Agriculture

- Water
- Electricity connection
- Birth registration
- Death registration
- Approved housing societies
- Rates of land and building taxes

Print outs of various forms that are required from time to time by the general public as well as government officers can also be obtained through "Raj Nidhi" on payment of nominal fees.

E-Governance Project: Grama Darpan

The Rajasthan Government implemented the project "Grama Darpan" in 2003 with the objectives of improving delivery of basic government services in rural areas and to improve internal efficiency of government departments dealing with the public. It aims at saving time, costs and resources, and enables easy and rapid access to information.

The project is based on the management information system to enable easy access to village level public utility services. Information gathered is complete, exact and up to date, on the basis of which remedial measures are taken by the concerned government department at the earliest.

E-Governance Project: Gramdoot

The Rajasthan Government plans to modernize and moderate the rural population, with the project "Gramdoot," which was implemented in 2002. This project is also in partnership with private companies. The aim of the project is to create a citizen friendly and smart government interface, and to promote entrepreneurship at the village level.

Gramdoot is a network of self employed entrepreneurs converging together to offer an improved delivery system aimed at total rural transformation at the village level with the help of an IT enabled platform. A network of Gramdoot sewa kendras have been set up at the district, tehsil and village level to complement each other in order to provide end-to-end business linkages.

E-Governance Project: Grameen Sanchar Sewak (GSS)

The Government of India company Bharat Sanchar Nigam Limited (BSNL), plans to make telephones accessible to the common man all over India. For this they planned the Grameen Sanchar Sewak. This project is also supported by the Department of Posts of the Government of India. Under the project, postmen in rural areas, who have been renamed Grameen Sanchar Sewaks (GSS), will carry handsets that operate on the Wireless in Local Loop (WLL) network when they go out for their normal routine of delivering letters and money orders. These phones will work on the BSNL network, and the project, initially in its pilot phase, will cover 8,000 villages in 21 telecom circles through 1,800 GSSs. The handsets are operable in an area of five km of the nearest tower. People will have to pay the call charges to the GSS. In this way people living in the remotest location, can easily communicate using a GSS's phone.

E-Governance Project: e-Mitra

The Rajasthan Government initiated an E-government project "e-Mitra", which is the first of its kind in the state, offering of electronic services. It aims to deploy information technology for the benefit of the masses. It offers one-stop, citizen friendly computerized centres. The project has provided relief to the common man as he receives efficient services through IT driven interfaces at a single window.

With a view to deploy IT for the benefit of citizens of the states, the Government of Rajasthan launched two citizen friendly projects in the year 2002, namely **Lok-Mitra** and **Jan-Mitra.**

Lok-Mitra

- An urban centric e-Governance project
- Was successfully operational in March 2002 in Jaipur
- Currently operational at Ajmer, Bikaner and Udaipur

Present status of automation

The services being offered by Lok-Mitra are as follows:

- Payment of electricity bills
- Payment of water bills of PHED
- Online bus ticketing of RSRTC
- Issuing birth and death certificates
- Payment of various dues/fee of the Jaipur municipal corporation
- Payment of various dues/fee of the Jaipur development authority
- Payment of various dues/fee of land and building tax department
- Payment of various dues/fee of the Rajasthan housing board
- Payment of land line and Cell One bills (BSNL)

Jan-Mitra

- A rural centric e-enabled service delivery system running successfully at Jhalawar and Jaipur.
- It provides a wide range of social services and information on relevant topics to citizens under one roof.
- It is a relevant case study of a successful public private partnership model.
- It has provided direct employment to about 350 rural youths and served around 4.5 citizens since its inception in March 2002.

The services being offered by Jan-Mitra are as follows:

- Public grievance redressal

- Online submission of application forms
- Access to land and revenue records (ROR)
- Access to government information
- Development schemes
- BPL list
- Immovable property rates (DLC)
- Agriculture information and mandi rates

E-Mitra integrated Lok-Mitra and Jan-Mitra

The E-Mitra Project integrates Lok-Mitra and Jan-Mitra to bring together all the departments under one single umbrella and give citizens of the state a multi-service single-window experience. The key objectives are to:

- Provide a hassle-free, one-stop solution to the citizens
- Provide a unified e-services platform to minimize multiple interaction points for the citizens and hence save time
- Combine the best features of the Lok-Mitra and Jan-Mitra models
- To provide an enhanced services basket to more departments including private sector services
- To provide uniform information interchange architecture
- Provide a public-private partnership model for front offices
- Have a back office owned by the government but operated by a technology partner
- Ultimately provide employment to over 2000 educated youths
- Use real time, Internet and batch processing modes
- Eventually cover the whole state in a phased manner

Functional features

There are two major components of the e-Mitra project. One is back office processing and the other is its service counters.

1. **Back office**
   - Includes computerization of participating departments and establishing an IT enabled hub in the form of a mini data centre at the district level.
   - The district level data centre (e-Mitra data centre) will be the platform on which customized software will run to ensure service access for citizens.
   - The e-Mitra data centre will be managed by a total solution provider (TSP) on behalf of the district e-Governance society (under the chairmanship of the district collector).
   - All the participating departments and service counters will hook on to the e-Mitra data centre to make the system work.
   - Financial resources for the purpose will have to be provided by the government.

2. **Service counters**
   - The counters to be set up in rural area will be known as Jan-Mitra kiosks and in the urban area as Lok-Mitra centres.
   - Citizens will be registered at the counter.
   - Citizens will be able to avail of services related to multiple departments/organizations at the same counter.
   - Right from deposition of applications to financial transactions to final deliverable collections, every activity will take place at these counters. Only in the case where there is some statutory requirement of personal verification, will the citizen be required to go to the concerned government functionary.
   - As many activities as possible in the complete cycle will be IT enabled but wherever there are legal limitations, the activities will be carried out manually. The main objective is to prevent the common man from having to run to multiple points in government offices to get his work done.
   - To make this contact point efficient, the interface will be through web or counters, which are managed by private partners (local service providers).

The service delivery will be on a charge basis so as to make the system self-sustaining. For services that any government department/organization wants to avail of, like bill/tax collection and awareness generation, the payment of service charges will be made by the concerned department. In the case of services which are rendered on citizens' demands, e.g. caste certificate, birth/death certificate etc. the payment will be made by the citizens themselves.

Website: http://www.emitra.gov.in/

GOVERNMENT OF TAMIL NADU

E-Governance Project: Tambaram Municipality

The Tamil Nadu Government's Tambaram municipality implemented an e-governance project with the vision to make the functioning of the municipality more accessible, accountable and transparent. The Tambaram municipality in its official website provides information on a variety of citizen centric services such as:

- Birth/Death certificates
- Water charges
- Property tax through an online database

It also has information on the rainwater harvesting structures in various locations like councillors' houses and government offices. The dynamically updated plan approvals on the website provide citizens with up-to-date status on their plan approvals. The 'submit your grievance' page provides users with a form wherein they can fill up their grievance and submit it online. The grievance is immediately recorded into the municipality database and an alert sent to the municipality administration. The site also features a comprehensive data-bank covering a wide variety of information on Tambaram, such as details of:

- Police stations
- Ambulance services
- First aid services
- Blood banks
- Electricity department
- Telegraph offices
- Banks
- Colleges
- Schools
- Hospitals
- Medical practitioners

This project implemented in a single municipal corporation is the best example of G2C based e-governance.

E-Governance Project: Tamil Nadu Info system on Land Administration and Management (Tamil NILAM)

The Tamil Nadu Government planned a specific system with ICT to computerize land record systems in the state. The e-governance project called "Tamil NILAM" stands for Tamil Nadu Info system on Land Administration and Management. The system aims at delivering all possible citizen-centric e-services.

The project handles all transactions relating to land records across the state. The various services provided are:

- Issue of chitta extract (record of right)
- A register extract
- Adangal extract to citizens
- Creation of a master database, plot wise
- Owner wise details of land-crop-revenue

Generation of periodic reports through the computerized system, improved service and made it more efficient. It enabled easy maintenance and updates of land records, transparent administration, made information available to the public through touch screen kiosks and allowed exchange of data with other departments such as the sub registrar office, agriculture department etc.

E-Governance Project: Simplified and Transparent Administration of Registration (STAR)

The Tamil Nadu Government implemented e-governance in each of their sectors. The state government implemented an ICT enabled project "STAR", which stands for Simplified and Transparent Administration of Registration. The aim of this project is to provide quick services to citizens and ensure transparency of the registration department by computerizing 560 sub registrar offices and 50 district registrar offices.

STAR is a software package developed to deliver quality services to the registrants. It is a G2C-U project with services offered to citizens and to government officials. Services offered to the public at a nominal cost are processing of land registration documents such as:

- Indexing of land registration records
- Land and building evaluation
- Scanning and storage of documents
- Marriage certificates
- Registration of societies and firms
- Birth and death certificates

Services offered to government officials are: Auto storage and archival of scanned documents, generation of reports at various levels etc. With computerization, the registration department has improved remarkably by reducing the processing time and error prone writing work.

E-Governance Project: Village Resource Centres (VRCs)

Village Resource Centres is an e-governance project implemented by the Tamil Nadu Government with the aim of providing multiple services to citizens. This project is developed in partnership by government agencies and private organizations. Services offered through a single window, include:

- Telemedicine
- Tele-education
- Remote sensing online decision support
- Interactive farmers' advisory services
- E-governance services
- Weather services
- Water management applications

This VRC project strives to promote a need based single window delivery system for providing services to villagers regarding all aspects, free of cost through the VSAT based network which has extended transponders. Users located at one node of this network can fully interact with others located at another node through video and audio links.

Each centre is provided with well equipped ICT infrastructure to enable voice communications and give information on education, health, nutrition, weather, environment, agriculture and jobs to the rural population to empower them to face challenges. It is planned to start more centres in other states of India.

E-Governance Project: Vidyal Information Service Provider (VISP)

The Tamil Nadu Government implemented an e-government project in 2003 with the aim of empowering the weaker sections of the rural community through the use of ICT and to create rural techno entrepreneurs through a network of private organisations. VISP centres provided many accessible services to villagers through the application of ICT. The services include:

- Prices of agricultural commodities
- Information on horoscopes
- Rural market places
- Matrimonial services
- Educational services
- Healthcare services
- Grievance redressals
- Provision of government forms

Users are also provided discount coupons for three private hospitals of Thiruchirapalli. Other services include net-to-phone and basic computer education. The society, Activists for Social Alternatives, is keen to extend the project to other villages, following the success of the first project.

E-Governance Project: Rural Access to Services through Internet - RASI MAIYAMS

The Government of Tamil Nadu proposed an e-government project in 2003 with the aim of providing a communication channel to the collectorate, including citizens' activities for grievances; providing information by linking panchayat offices; building a database of best practices like agriculture, commerce, trade and having an educational component.

RASI Maiyams are information centres set up for e-governance citizen centric activities. The various services offered are:

- Villages databases
- Networking with district/block level departments
- Online submission of petitions
- Progress of work at block level
- Buying/Selling databases
- Market prices
- Land records

Using a sustainable model of engaging the district administration, an NGO and entrepreneurs/self help groups from the district operate and maintain the RASI (Rural Access to Services through Internet) network. CDs on agricultural best practices, which will help local farmers, are also provided in these centres to increase the agricultural output of the state.

E-Governance Project: Chennai Kavigal

Each state of India has different local languages. Software is available in English, but it may be difficult for the common man to deal with, so although government agencies deal with English language based database software, information should be in local languages.

Towards this end, the Chennai Kavigal Kanini project launched a software named Chennai Kavigal, to create an array of software products in Tamil, which can be used and accessed by the masses, especially the rural populace. Chennai Kavigal provides software solutions and innovations to Indian language computing, like:

- **Padhami 2.0** - an advanced word processor
- **Shakthi** - a business suite
- **Vanigam** - an accounting and billing software

These products have been developed at Chennai Kavigal. 'Shakti', Chennai Kavigal's, product does the work of MS Office in Hindi-English and Tamil-English versions. Chennai Kavigal is working on other Indian languages such as Telugu, Marathi, Gujarati and Bengali.

Website: www.chennaikavigal.com

GOVERNMENT OF UTTARANCHAL

E-Governance Project: Suchana Kutir

The Uttaranchal Government implemented an e-government project named "Suchana Kutir", in partnership with national and international orgaisations. The aim of the project is to serve the youth community with ICT enabled channels of Suchana Kutirs. Suchana Kutir centres are well equipped centres spread across various panchyats of the state, which provide information to seekers on predefined subjects.

With this project the Uttarahchal Government initiated a G2C channel across the state and enabled e-governance services to the citizens at the panchayat level.

E-Governance Project: Kisan Soochana Kendra (KSK)

The Uttaranchal State Government implemented the KSK Project in 2005 along with national educational agencies, government agencies and international agencies. The Kisan Soochana Kendra project aims at providing various IT-enabled services to people from a single kiosk. The Kisan Soochana Kendras offer a variety of possibilities to the beneficiaries, especially to the youth of the state. Services available at KSK kiosks are:

- Governance information
- Online applications
- Forms
- Government schemes
- News
- Current affairs

- Eco and rural tourism
- E-medicine

The proposed expansion of this project will cover several services like, banks to be monitored online. Facilities at KSK create an environment which encourages industries to set up plants at remote locations.

GOVERNMENT OF UTTAR PRADESH

E-Governance Project: Lokvani

The Uttar Pradesh Government implemented "Lokvani" an e-government project in 2004, in the Sitapur district of UP. The project aims to eliminate digital divide and connect people to strategy/policy makers in a seamless manner. The main aim of the project is to help citizens to state their grievances related to government services in a simple manner and also to have their grievances redressed within a few days of filing a complaint through kiosk centres.

Lokvani is a unique G2C based program, which gives citizens an opportunity to interact with the government without physically visiting any government office and a majority of services are available at one window.

Some of the services offered are:

- Online submission
- Monitoring
- Public grievances
- Complaints
- Online land records
- Information about various government schemes
- Application forms
- Employment news

GOVERNMENT OF WEST BENGAL

E-Governance Project: West Bengal Citizen Portal

This is a project initiated by the West Bengal State Government for citizen centric services. This G2C-U project aims to facilitate an efficient interface between citizens and the administration of government services. The West Bengal Citizen Portal runs on a public private partnership and provides viewing and downloading of government tenders/tender notices and departmental forms, various examination results under educational bodies, value added e-mail services to establish direct communication with the government and general information and obtains agricultural related services directly from the agriculture department.

The project has resulted in various direct/indirect social as well as economic benefits to the masses such as bringing about transparency and better dissemination of government information resulting in better awareness about various government schemes. In future, emphasis will be given to e-education, health and other services that fulfil the basic needs of the population like poverty alleviation schemes, housing etc.

E-Governance Project: Sahaj Tathya Mitra: Common Service Centres

The West Bengal Government along with private organisation plans to spread e-governance enabling ICT with the project named "Sahaj Tathya Mitra". The WB Government aims to set up around five thousand Common Service Centres (CSC) with Internet kiosks, which will offer e-governance and commercial services to the rural populace. The Internet connectivity will offer e-governance services and other commercial services such as:

- Filling land returns
- Registering births and deaths
- Checking the weather pattern

The centres will also provide commercial and general information such as:

- Commodity prices
- Booking of railway tickets
- Agriculture
- Education
- Vocational training
- Health and hygiene related information

Women entrepreneurs and Self Help Groups are trained for this project.

List of Acronyms

APDIP	Asia Pacific Development Information Programme
APSWAN	Andhra Pradesh State Wide Area Network
BCC	Blind Carbon Copy
BESCOM	Bangalore Electricity Supply Company
BSNL	Bharat Sanchar Nigam Limited
BWSSB	Bangalore Water Supply and Sewerage Board
CBPS	Computerized Bus Pass System
CHiPS	Chhattisgarh InfoTech Promotion Society
CHOiCE	Chhattisgarh Online Information for Citizen Empowerment
CIC	Community Information Centres
CLR	Computerisation of Land Records
CMC Ltd	Computer-Mediated Communication
Coil-Net	Content Development and IT Localization Network
CRISP	Computerized Rural Information Systems Project
CSC	Citizen Service Centres
DEGIS	Delhi e-gov web based Information system
DRDA	District Rural Development Agencies
DTC	Delhi Transport Corporation
ECIL	Electronics Corporation of India Ltd.
G2B	Government to Business
G2C	Government to Citizens
G2E	Government to Employee
G2G	Government to Government

GIL	Gujarat Informatics Limited
GIS	Geographical Information Systems
GoI	Govt. of India
GPS	Global Positioning System
GSS	Grameen Sanchar Sewaks
HIMRIS	Himachal Registration Information System
ICT	Information and Communication Technology
IIT	Indian Institute of Technology
IVRS	Interactive Voice Response System
MAP-IT	Madhya Pradesh Agency for Promotion of Information Technology
MIS	Management Information System
NeGP	National e-Governance Plan
NFI	National Foundation for India
NGO	Non-Government Organization
NIC	National Informatics Centre
NISG	National Institute of Smart Governance
NNFI	National Network For India
PAOs	Pay and Account Offices
PIB	Press Information Bureau's
PPP	Public Private Partnership
RTO	Road and Transport Officer
SLA	Service Level Agreement
TEAM SANJOG	Solution Architect and Network Operation Group
UNDP	United Nations Development Program
UT	Union Territories
VDC	Village Development Committee
VOIP	Voice Over Internet Protocol
VSAT	Very Small Aperture Terminal
WAP	Wireless Application Protocol
WHO	World Health Organizations
WLL	Wireless Local Loop

Question Bank

1. (a) What do you understand by the term EDI? What role does EDI play in business?
   (b) Why is CRM an essential concept in today's business? What are the important ingredients in CRM that help a business in its growth?
   (c) What do you understand by the term logistics in supply chain management?
2. (a) Why is a virtual private network preferred over leased lines?
   (b) What do you understand by the term encryption? What are the various techniques by which encryption can be done?
3. (a) What are the different types of firewalls? What role is played by a firewall in transaction and network security?
   (b) What is client server technology? How does one handle the threats to a client server network?
   (c) What is WAP technology? What is M-Commerce?
4. (a) What do you understand by the term E-Commerce? What is the network infrastructure of E-Commerce?
   (b) What are the types of business carried out on the Internet?
   (c) What is the I-way? What are its components?
5. (a) How are electronic payments made on the Internet?
   (b) What is the role played by banks in electronic payments?
6. (a) What do you mean by term EDI? What role does EDI play in business?
   (b) Why is CRM an essential concept in today's business? What are the important ingredients in CRM that help a business in its growth?
   (c) What do you understand by the term logistics in supply chain management?
7. (a) What is E-Commerce? What are its objectives?
   (b) How is multimedia related to E-Commerce?
   (c) Explain the industry framework for E-Commerce.

(d) Name two E-Commerce applications currently used in organizations.

8. Describe the functioning of any two:

(a) (i) Supply chain management
(ii) Just-in-time manufacturing
(iii) Network access equipments

(b) What is the difference between cell relay and frame relay?

(c) What is meant by broadband telecommunication? What is its advantage over narrow band telecommunication?

9. (a) What is the objective of mobile commerce? What sort of switching and delivery technique has made M-commerce feasible?

(b) Name two mobile computing applications.

(c) What are digital signatures? Where are they used?

(d) How can one ensure data security in E-Commerce applications?

10. (a) Why are firewalls used? Explain the functioning of proxy application gateways as firewalls.

(b) Give three emerging client server security threats.

(c) How can client authentication be ensured in E-Commerce transactions?

11. (a) Explain how private key cryptography can ensure data security.

(b) What is the function of the security socket layer with respect to web security? How does it differ from S-HTTP?

(c) What are virtual private networks?

(d) How does data encryption standard work? Where it applicable?

12. (a) Briefly explain the implantation and management issues regarding encryption standards.

(b) What are public key certificates?

(c) What sort of security measures should be taken in WWW?

13. (a) What is the advantage of using a smart card over a credit card in e-Commerce transactions?

(b) What is home banking? How does it function?

(c) What sort of security measures do you think should be implemented for payment in e-commerce transactions?

14. (a) What is e-cash? How is it acquired over the Web?

(b) Explain the digital token based payment in e-commerce transactions.

(c) What are emerging financial instruments?

15. (a) Define EDI. How does EDI function?
    (b) Explain the layered architecture of EDI.
    (c) Name two applications of EDI in business.
    (d) What are MIME based protocols?
16. (a) What is the purpose of supply chain management? How is it related to E-commerce?
    (b) Briefly explain the functioning of customer relationship management.
    (c) What is the benefit of EDI in inter-organizational E-commerce?
17. (a) What do you mean by E-Commerce? Discuss the various types of E-commerce applications.
    (b) What do you mean by online education? Mention its advantages over the traditional approach.
18. Describe the architectural frame work for E-Commerce.
19. What is WAP technology? Give the layered architecture of a WAP stack.
20. (a) What are the emerging client-server security threats? How will you prevent them?
    (b) What is a firewall? Describe the working of an application gateway firewall.
21. How do SSL and secure HTTP provide data and transaction security on the internet? Compare these two methods.
22. What do you mean by digital signature? How can it be used for authentication?
23. How is e-cash different from paper cash? Discuss the security aspect of e-cash.
24. Discuss the working of an encrypted credit card based on the online payment system. How does this system prevent mistakes and fraud?
25. Define EDI. Discuss the applications of EDI in business.
26. (a) What do you mean by internal commerce? How does SCM help in customization of services?
    (b) Write short notes on –
        (i) JIT manufacturing
        (ii) Importance of CRM

FOURTH SEMESTER EXAMINATION, 2001 - 2002

FUNDAMENTALS OF E-COMMERCE

Time : Three hours Maximum Marks : 100

Note : Attempt ALL questions.

1. Answer any FOUR of the following:
   (a) What are the two pillars of e-commerce business? Describe in detail.
   (b) What are the main types of e-commerce? Explain.
   (c) Write short notes on: -
      (i) Just-in-time management
      (ii) Video on demand
      (iii) Quick response retailing
   (d) What is the difference between on-line & off-line transactions? How does e-commerce support the on-line transaction?
   (e) What are the major parts of I-way infrastructure?
   (f) What are the components and functions of NSFNET (National Science Foundation Network)?
2. Answer any FOUR of following:
   (a) Write short notes on any TWO of the following:
      (i) FDMA
      (ii) Mobile-commerce
      (iii) TDMA (Time division multiple access)
      (iv) CDMA (Code division multiple access)
   (b) What is WAP (Wireless Application Protocol)? How secure is WAP for commercial transaction?
   (c) Write short notes on the following: -
      (i) IP packet screening routers.
      (ii) Proxy application gateway.
   (d) What are the basic types of firewall? How will IPSEC make firewall obsolete?
   (e) Explain threats to security. What are the security problems in client server networks?
   (f) Explain the difference between a packet-filtering firewall and an application-level proxy server.
3. Answer any TWO of the following: -
   (a) Explain any Five of the following in brief: -
      (i) Digital signature
      (ii) Eaves dropping
      (iii) Spoofing

(iv) Authentication
(v) Non-repudiation
(vi) Kerberos

(b) Given the two prime numbers $p=19$ and $q=23$, try to find N, Kp and Ks. (*Hint*: Use RSA encryption method)

(c) Explain Virtual Private Networks. Give the implementations of VPN using IPSEC.

4. Answer any TWO of the following:

(a) Explain the meaning of the following terms:
(i) Cash is negotiable
(ii) Cash is legal tender
(iii) Cash is a bearer instrument
(iv) Protocol behind Blind Protocol

(b) Explain smart card as internet payment method. What are the components of smart card chip?

(c) What is home banking management? Explain basic services, intermediate services and advanced services.

5. Answer any TWO of the following:

(a) What do you understand by customer relationship management? What importance has customer relationship management got in E-commerce? How will you implement customer relationship management in your organization?

(b) Define SCM (Supply Chain Management). Give its characteristics. Explain push-based supply chain management vs pull-based supply chain. Also write primary elements of these models.

(c) Give the layered structure of EDI and compare EDI versus e-mail. Conceptualize EDI and describe its layered architecture. Discuss the legal issues related with e-commerce.

FOURTH SEMESTER EXAMINATION, 2002 - 2003

FUNDAMENTALS OF E-COMMERCE

Time : Three hours Maximum Marks : 100

Note : Attempt ALL questions.

1. Answer any FOUR of the following:
   (a) Explain the framework of electronic commerce and types of E-commerce.
   (b) What are the major technologies underpinning high speed Global Information Distribution Network.
   (c) Explain the various services and tools of Internet.
   (d) What are the various functions of National Science Foundation Network (NSFNET).
   (e) What is the role of Broad Band Technology in E-commerce?
   (f) Explain the various components of the I-way Infrastructure.
2. Answer any FOUR of the following:
   (a) Give the various types of Firewall. How does Firewall secure the Network?
   (b) What are the various client-server threats involved in E-commerce?
   (c) What do you mean by WAP (Wireless Application Protocol)? Also explain the working of WAP.
   (d) Define and differentiate TDMA (Time Division Multiple Access), FDMA (Frequency Division Multiple Access) and CDMA (Code Division Multiple Access).
   (e) What do you understand by Mobile Commerce? Explain the various components of mobile commerce.
   (f) Write short notes on: -
      (i) Biometric System
      (ii) Thrust based Security
3. Answer any TWO of the following:
   (a) What are Digital Signatures? Explain, with the general model of Digital Signature. How is the issue of confidentiality and Non-Repudiation of the document resolved?
   (b) Write short notes on any TWO of the following:
      (i) Public Key Cryptography
      (ii) Business Transactions
      (iii) Virtual Private Networks
   (c) Explain the Secret Key Encryption and Public Key Encryption. Giving examples, differentiate between the two.
4. Attempt any TWO of the following:
   (a) Explain the various issues involved in Electronic Payment System. Also give the various types of EPS.

(b) Explain with the help of suitable example, the ON-LINE Banking System. Make the difference table for ON-LINE Banking System and Home Banking System.

(c) Draw and discuss general models of Credit Card based Electronic Payment System. What are On-Line Credit Card processors? Discuss the flow of information which takes place amongst different components of Credit Card based Electronic Payments.

5. Answer any TWO parts of the following:

(a) What do you mean by Customer Relationship Management? What are the issues involved in e-CRM? List the advantages offered by e-CRM.

(b) What do you mean by Supply Chain? List your views on integration of Supply Chain Management to Electronic Commerce.

(c) Write short notes on the following: -

(i) EDI application in Business

(ii) Legal requirement in E-commerce

References

1. Ravi Kalakota, Andrew Winston, "*Frontiers of Electronic Commerce*", Addison Wesley.
2. Bajaj and Nag, "*E-Commerce—The Cutting Edge of Business*", TMH.
3. P. Loshin, John Vacca, "*Electronic Commerce*", Firewall Media, New Delhi.

Bibliography

1. Afuah, A., & Tucci, C. L., 2001. Internet Business Models and Strategies, Text and Cases. New York: McGraw-Hill. p.358
2. Amit, R., & Trott, C., 2001. Value Creation in E-Business. Strategic Management Journal, 22. pp. 493-520
3. Awad, E.M. 2002. Electronic Commerce: from vision to fulfillment. New Jersey: Prentice Hall. p. 497
4. MikroBitti (2002). Verkkokaupat eivät ole ihmisiä varten. No 2. p. 19
5. Rowley, J. 2002. E-business; principles & practice. New York: Palgrave. p.266
6. Tilastokeskus (2001). Internet ja sähköinen kauppa yrityksissä. Helsinki.
7. Tilastokeskus (2002a) in Hyytinen, T. (2002). Verkkokauppa kituuttaa, mutta kopiointi sujuu. Helsingin Sanomat. Nov. 17, p. A6.
8. Turban, E., & King, D., & Lee, J., & Warkentin, M., & Chung, H. M. 2002. Electronic Commerce A Managerial Perspective. New Jersey: Prentice Hall. p. 914

Internet Resources

9. Bazac, D. (2002). Why Dotcoms Fail – A Webmasters Perspective. Pandecta Magazine. [referred Nov 20, 2002]
10. <http://pandecta.com/dotcom.html>
11. Entrepreneur Resource Center. Start-up Facts and Figures. [referred Nov 24, 2002]
12. <http://www.ktec.com/erc/StartUp%20Facts%20Figures.htm>
13. BusinessWeek (2002). How Amazon Cleared the Profitability Hurdle. Feb 4. [referred Nov 20, 2002]
14. <http://www.businessweek.com/magazine/content/02_05/b3768079.htm>

15. Cronin, G. (2000). Surviving the B2C Shakeout. eAI Journal. October. pp. 106-107. [referred Nov 22, 2002]

16. <www.eaijournal.com/PDF/Shakeout%20-%20Cronin.pdf>

17. Daugherty, B. (2001). Why So Many Dotcoms Fail. [referred Nov 12, 2002]

18. <http://www.smithfam.com/news/jan01i.html>

19. Deluria, T. (2001) After the Bubble Bursts. Infotech. Mar 19. [referred Nov 20, 2002]

20. <http://www.inq7.net/inf/2001/mar/19/inf_webspeak-1.htm>

21. Fleming, D. P. (2002). The New Dotcom: Better, Stronger, and Faster. OTCBB News Network. Commentary, Feb 17. [referred Nov 22, 2002]

22. <http://www.otcbbnn.com/fpdb/active/html/newdotcom1.htm>

23. Forrester Research (2002). Online Sales Fall; Holiday Sales Will Inch Up. Techstrategy Brief. Oct 29. [referred Nov 18, 2002]

24. <http://www.forrester.com/ER/Research/Brief/0,1317,15857,00.html>

25. Fox, C. (2000). e-Commerce Business Models. IIR Best Strategy Practices Symposium. Nov 28. Johannesburg. [referred Nov 20, 2002]

26. <http://www.chrisfoxinc.com/eCommerceBusinessModels.doc>

27. Gambhir, A., Pawsey, C., Respini, I., Nichols, E., Garner, M. & Koshi, V. (2001) 3G Survival strategies: build, buy or share. Ovum Report. August 2001. [referred Nov 16, 2002]

28. <http://www.ovum.com/go/product/latestresearch/008308.htm>

29. GartnerG2 (2001). GartnerG2 Says by 2005 10 Percent of U.S. B2C E-Commerce will Be Done Without a PC. Press Release. Dec 5. [referred Nov 18, 2002]

30. <http://www.gartnerg2.com/pr/pr-2001-12-05.asp>

31. Greenspan, R. (2002).Good News for E-Biz. CyberAtlas. April 18. [referred Nov 20, 2002]

32. <http://cyberatlas.internet.com/markets/retailing/article/0,,6061_1011911,00.html>

33. Joyce, E. (2002). Paid Online Services a Tough Sell: Jupiter. Internetnews.com. [referred Nov 26, 2002]

34. <http://www.internetnews.com/ec-news/article.php/1142881>

35. Lang, P. (2002). Taking Care of the Pennies. Sell It! E-commerce Resource. Jan 16. [referred Nov 26, 2002]

36. <http://sellitontheweb.com/ezine/opinion091.shtml>

37. Nwachukwu, S.L.S. (2002). Analysis of the Failure of E-Commerce Businesses: A Strategic Management Perspective. ACME Conference, March 6-9, St.Louis, Missouri. [referred Nov 23, 2002]

38. <http://www.sbaer.uca.edu/Research/2002/ACME/Papers/02acme014.pdf>

39. Plant, D. (2001). Why Dotcoms Fail. [referred Nov 12, 2002]

40. <http://www.davidplant.net/B4UStart/dot_com_failures.htm>

41. POSMIS (2000). Electronic Commerce. Postech Strategic Management of Information Systems. [referred Nov 18, 2002]

42. <http://mis.postech.ac.kr/topic/ec_e.html>

43. Rappa, M. (2001). Managing the Digital Enterprise - Business Models on the Web. [referred Nov 10, 2002]

44. <http://digitalenterprise.org/models/models.html>

45. Silverstein, M., Abdelmessih, N. & Stanger, P. (2001). The Next Chapter in Business-to-Consumer E-Commerce: Advantage Incumbent. The Boston Consulting Group. [referred Nov 16, 2002]

46. <http://www.bcg.com/publications/files/Next_chapter_summary.pdf>

47. Starling, A. (2000). Dotcom Bubble – "The Emperor Has No Clothes!". Web Developers Journal. June 28. [referred Nov 16, 2002]

48. <http://www.webdevelopersjournal.com/columns/ajs_bubble.html>

49. Tehan, R. (2002). E-Commerce Statistics: Explanation and Sources. CRS Report for Congress. Congressional Research Service. [referred Nov 18, 2002]

50. <http://www.usembassy.de/usa/etexts/bus/crsstats.pdf>

51. Tilastokeskus (2002b). E-commerce. [referred Nov 18, 2002]

52. <http://www.stat.fi/tk/yr/tietoyhteiskunta/verkkokauppa_en.html>

53. Walters, J.S. (2002). Why Dotcoms failed (And What You Can Learn from Them). The CEO Refresher. Vol. 9, no 11.4. [referred Nov 16, 2002]

54. <http://www.refresher.com/!jswdotcom.html>